Legends *of* Winter Hill

Also by Jay Atkinson

NONFICTION
Ice Time: A Tale of Fathers, Sons, and Hometown Heroes

FICTION
Caveman Politics

Legends

of

Winter Hill

COPS, CON MEN,

AND JOE McCAIN,

THE LAST REAL DETECTIVE

Jay Atkinson

Crown Publishers / New York

The names of some of the subjects in this book have been changed.

Copyright © 2005 by Jay Atkinson

Published in the United States by Crown Publishers, an imprint of the Crown
Publishing Group, a division of Random House, Inc., New York.
www.crownpublishing.com

CROWN is a trademark and the Crown colophon is a registered trademark of
Random House, Inc.

Library of Congress Cataloging-in-Publication Data
Atkinson, Jay, 1957–
    Legends of Winter Hill: cops, con men, and Joe McCain, the last real
detective / Jay Atkinson.
    1. McCain, Joseph Elmer, d. 2001. 2. Police—Massachusetts—Somerville—
Biography. 3. Detectives—Massachusetts—Somerville—Biography. 4. Private
investigators—Massachusetts—Somerville—Biography. 5. Crime—
Massachusetts—Boston area. I. Title: Joe McCain, the last real detective.
II. Title.
    HV7911.A2M323 2005
    363.2'092—dc22   2004011605

ISBN 1-4000-5075-8

Printed in the United States of America

Design by Lenny Henderson

10 9 8 7 6 5 4 3

First Edition

For Harry Crews,
teacher and friend

CONTENTS

People sleep peaceably in their beds at night
only because rough men stand ready
to do violence on their behalf.
—GEORGE ORWELL

Legends *of* Winter Hill

"Somebody's Been Shot"

T HAT PARTICULAR MORNING Detective Joe McCain arrived late to the office of the MDC Special Investigations Unit, located on the sixth floor of the old Registry of Motor Vehicles building in Boston. A veteran cop with thirty years on the job, McCain, fifty-eight, was an imposing man, six foot three and every one of the three hundred and something pounds he admitted to, but solid, with fists like prize hams and forearms the circumference of a grown man's neck. He was whistling as he came into the Nashua Street office because during a recent physical the doctor had said he was in good shape—his heart was sound and his blood pressure was fine. He just needed to lose some weight, and there in the office Joseph E. McCain, Sr., announced that he was starting a new regimen that very day: January 29, 1988.

No more bloody steaks at the Parker House, or hot pastrami sandwiches from the North End. Big Joe was going on a diet.

His younger colleagues, Detectives Gene Kee and Al DiSalvo and Biff McLean, were eyeing each other over their desks and snickering like teenagers. "What a fat shit," Kee said under his breath.

"What'd you say?" asked McCain, looking over at them.

"He said you're a fat fuck," said DiSalvo, smiling over at Kee, who was trying to shush him.

McCain raised an eyebrow. "Well, I'd like you geniuses to know that I'm down to a svelte three twenty," he said, turning to profile.

"Fuck you, Joe, you're three forty-five, easy," Kee said, while the rest of them broke out laughing.

Gathered for a briefing on coke dealers in Hyde Park was a veritable all-star team of Metropolitan District Commission police detectives, or Mets, as they liked to be called. Their work was complicated and dangerous, and they were good at it. The leader of the unit, forty-one-year-old Sergeant Mark Cronin, a tall, quiet fellow, had served in Army Intelligence during the Vietnam War. Among such hard chargers, who drank and fought and crashed their share of police vehicles, Cronin was the most cerebral and straitlaced, and a meticulous planner and organizer. When Cronin walked into the office with a rookie detective named Dennis Febles and another man named Chris Brighton, who looked and acted like a drug dealer, the rest of the guys quit piling on Joe McCain and fell silent.

"Joe, what are you doing here?" asked Cronin.

"I'm working, Sarge, what the fuck does it look like?" McCain said, and the guys all laughed.

Sergeant Cronin was surprised to see McCain, who had requested the day off so he and his friend Jim O'Donovan and their wives could attend a dinner dance in Hingham. But when Joe McCain heard that "the kids," as he called his youthful counterparts, were going to sting the drug dealers today, he'd canceled his outing and driven to the office. And although the unit had made a large number of significant arrests in its short history and the other detectives were putting on a bold front, McCain detected a sense of gloom in the office that morning, an uneasiness that had never attached itself to their meetings in the past.

Wearing a scruffy beard for this operation, ex-Marine Christopher "Kegs" Brighton was the unit's undercover man, wiseass, and resident beer drinker. William "Battlin' Biff" McLean and thirty-five-year-old Gene Kee were adept at handling informants. "Fat Al" DiSalvo was the surveillance expert. In the unit for just two weeks, former New York

City gang member Dennis Febles spoke Spanish and had a hankering for some action.

Even among such a stellar cast of cops, Joe McCain stood out. Hailed on all sides as the genuine article, big Joe was punching out mobsters and solving murder cases when Gene Kee and Chris Brighton were in grade school. He was a Somerville guy, and lived with his wife, Helen, on a quiet street adjacent to the Tufts University campus. The McCains' only child, twenty-six-year-old Joe Jr., had just been discharged from the Marines and was planning on becoming a cop himself. But the figure of his old man was an imposing one. A large, white-haired, cigar-smoking fellow who resembled John Wayne in both physique and bearing, Joe McCain was a legend in law enforcement circles, and his file contained a sheaf of commendations over an inch thick.

On this case, thirty-nine-year-old Chris Brighton had spent weeks developing a relationship with a coke dealer named Melvin Lee, purchasing a half ounce here and an ounce there, building up the trust necessary for the sting to move ahead. Posing as a ski bum who drove down to Boston to score coke for the kids partying up at Cannon and Loon, Brighton had recently upped the ante with Melvin Lee. He told the dealer that he had $15,000 and wanted to buy a half kilo of cocaine. Subsequently, Mark Cronin had made the decision that they would arrest Lee today and perhaps get the dealer above him who could supply that much blow. When Joe McCain came into the office, Brighton and the rest of the guys were waiting for Lee to hit Brighton's beeper.

Finally the pager went off. Brighton saw Melvin Lee's phone number and went into an adjoining office to return the call. A few moments later, he emerged with a smile on his face. "It's on," he said.

One last time Mark Cronin went over each man's assignment. Also present that morning were two seasoned detectives from the Boston Police Department, Paul Hutchinson and Jack Honan. It was a practice of the Special Investigations Unit to work with other departments in the jurisdiction of a case, and men like Honan and Hutchinson would be helpful in the surveillance and arrest of Melvin Lee and his associates.

Jack Honan rode with Dennis Febles in an unmarked van driven by

Gene Kee. As part of the "takedown team," charged with taking the suspects into custody when the time came, all three detectives wore bullet-proof vests. Mark Cronin and Biff McLean were to park on the street behind Lee's house on Wood Avenue in Hyde Park, monitoring the whereabouts and conversations of Chris Brighton, who was wired with a hidden microphone. Al DiSalvo was on the far side of a park near Lee's residence, maintaining surveillance. And Joe McCain and Paul Hutchinson, both good-sized men, were squeezed like circus clowns into a tiny gray Toyota that had been seized in a different case. Their assignment was to stay close and watch the front door.

Following Brighton's vehicle at a safe distance, the teams moved to within a block of 276 Wood Avenue and took up their positions. Cronin and McLean found a secluded place behind the house and opened up the Kel, a briefcase-sized listening device that included a short antenna they attached to the roof of the car. The only two officers who could hear what Brighton was saying and what was being said to him, they relayed the necessary information to the other members of the unit. Inside the house, Lee told Brighton that the coke hadn't arrived yet and he should wait. Both men went into the kitchen and sat down.

Melvin Lee rose from his chair and paced back and forth, then returned to his seat opposite Brighton. A slightly built, forty-seven-year-old black man with close-cropped hair and a large, flat mustache, Lee was more nervous than he'd been on the other occasions when he and Brighton had done business.

"Miko checked you out, and he thinks you're a cop," said Lee, naming his supplier.

"I'm no cop," Brighton said. "I'm a businessman."

"If you're livin' in New Hampshire, skiing and shit, how come you got Mass. plates on that Camaro?"

"I rented it over at Logan. So it's got Mass. plates."

Lee hunched forward over the table. "You got a gun?" he asked.

"You carry money, you carry a gun," said Brighton with a shrug. He pointed to the right side of his sweater and put his hand on the butt of his revolver.

"You got handcuffs, too?" asked Lee.

Brighton laughed. "I'm not that kinky," he said.

The other man laughed with him. "Listen, we just gotta check things out," he said.

"Yeah. Right."

Brighton and Lee waited for several more minutes, but no one came to the house. "I'm gonna split," said Brighton, rising from the table. "If you wanna do it, call my pager number."

"Where you gonna be?"

"I'm gonna have a drink at the Marriott, and then I'm heading up north," said Brighton.

"I'll page you by three o'clock, three-thirty at the latest."

Brighton made for the door. "I'm not coming back here on some wild fuckin' goose chase," he said.

"You won't be," said Lee, and Brighton went out.

A short time after Chris Brighton emerged from the house, Sergeant Cronin announced to his teams that the deal was off, at least for now.

The detectives returned to their office around lunchtime and ordered submarine sandwiches. Joe McCain took a good deal of ribbing for the salad he ate, which would have filled a garbage can. It was Friday afternoon, and there was some talk of postponing the operation until the following week. McCain called Jim O'Donovan again to see if he and his wife had made other plans for the evening. It was looking like big Joe would be able to attend that dinner dance after all. But around three o'clock Chris Brighton was paged three times in succession, and he called the number and heard Melvin Lee's voice on the other end of the line.

"The stuff's here," said Lee.

"I'll be there in forty-five minutes," Brighton said.

McCain looked at his uneaten salad and pushed it away. "I feel like a fuckin' rabbit," he said.

Again the Special Investigations Unit hurried out to their vehicles and reestablished the surveillance. Wary of countersurveillance and the possibility of drug lookouts scattered through the neighborhood, Mark Cronin ordered the various teams to retreat one block from their previous locations. He didn't want to endanger his undercover man by getting "made."

The unit moved into place just after 4:00 P.M. In his leather jacket and jeans, with the fifteen grand locked in the trunk, Brighton pulled up in front of 276 Wood Avenue, a little dump of a house surrounded by a chain-link fence. It was growing dark by that hour, and a chill had descended onto the streets. As Chris passed through the front gate, Melvin Lee met him in the yard.

"The dude split," said Lee. "Said he was tired of waiting."

Brighton was irritated. "You know what, fuck you," he said, turning for his car. "The last coke you sold me, the guys at the ski lodge were giving me shit about it. It sucked."

"Hey, this is good blow," said Lee. "Come on in."

Brighton turned his head and spit onto the ground, extending his charade for another moment, then followed Lee up the stairs into the house. In the hallway he was introduced to a black male in jeans and a light-colored T-shirt by the name of Stoney. "Come back in half an hour," said Stoney. "The coke'll be here."

"I'll give you guys one more chance," said Brighton.

He returned to his car, gunned the engine, and drove off. The night was cold and clear, with very little snow on the ground and a waxing moon. For thirty minutes Brighton circled the neighborhood, and right at 4:45 he parked at the curb and went back inside, determined to make a deal. With Joe McCain behind the wheel, Paul Hutchinson beside him, and its headlights extinguished, the little Toyota came to a stop less than a hundred yards from 276 Wood Avenue.

Melvin Lee and Stoney herded Brighton into the kitchen. There was another man there, a white guy named Tommy, who was snorting lines of coke from a small pile on the table. Stoney told Lee to take Tommy upstairs so they could do business in private. Although the house was warm, Stoney wore a dark blue overcoat and a crumpled woolen hat.

"Take off your coat," said Stoney.

Brighton shook his head. "I'm not gonna be here long."

Stoney took a seat at the table and Brighton went around to the far end. "What do you do in Conway?" asked Stoney.

"Tend bar," said Brighton. "Ever been up there?"

"No," the other man said.

Stoney said that he was from New York and had been in jail. Talk at the table was strained, and after a short while Brighton asked, "Is he coming, or not?"

"Lemme see the money," said Stoney.

"Show me the product."

Just then Lee returned to the kitchen. "You gotta start trusting this dude," he told Stoney. "His money is good."

"You wanna see the money?" Brighton asked. "C'mon."

He got up and went outside, followed by Lee and Stoney. Lee waited on the porch, and Brighton and Stoney went down the front walk, through the gate, and around to the back of a bright red Camaro parked at the curb. Taking out his keys, Brighton unlocked the trunk and the interior light went on. Beside the spare tire were two stacks of hundred-dollar bills, fastened with rubber bands.

"Leave it there," Stoney said.

Brighton pocketed his keys, and he and Stoney went back into the house with Lee behind them. With his right hand deep in the pocket of his overcoat, Stoney led Brighton into the kitchen, and they returned to their previous spots at the table. It was five o'clock.

"Where is the stuff coming from—Bolivia?" Brighton asked.

Stoney rose from his seat and used his left hand to point at the clock. "If the shit ain't here by five-o-five, you can split," he said.

Since they had returned to the house, Stoney had not taken his right hand out of his pocket. Behind Chris to his right was a door into the bathroom, and without saying another word Stoney walked past the table and disappeared inside. There was no sound of water falling into the toilet, and after about twenty seconds Brighton heard a metallic click, then another. He began to turn around in his chair just as Stoney emerged from the bathroom with a sawed off shotgun.

"Gimme your fuckin' keys," Stoney said, pressing the barrel of the shotgun against Brighton's neck.

Parked on the street behind Lee's house, Mark Cronin feared that the operation had gone sour. "Gimme the coat," said Stoney's voice over the wire. "Strip."

Brighton stood up. "All right," he said.

He held out his keys and Stoney took them. While Brighton was shrugging out of his coat, Stoney circled the table, keeping the shotgun pointed at the detective's chest. "Hurry up," he said.

Brighton dropped his leather jacket on the floor.

"Take the sweater off," said Stoney.

Brighton's .38 service revolver was concealed beneath the waistband of his jeans, and as Stoney came up in front of him, he made a move toward Brighton like he meant to lift up his sweater. Lunging for the barrel of Stoney's shotgun, Brighton made a simultaneous grab for his own weapon, and he and the other man fell against the table and onto the floor, struggling for control of the two guns.

"I'm a cop," said Brighton.

"Motherfucker," said Stoney.

Wrenching the shotgun backward, Stoney created a gap between himself and Brighton and kicked the detective in the balls. Brighton fell hard onto his shoulder, and Stoney bolted from the kitchen. Scrambling around on his hands and knees, Brighton groped along the floor for his revolver but couldn't find it.

Hearing muffled curses and the thumping and banging that marked the onset of Brighton's fight, Cronin opened a channel to the other detectives in his unit and said, "He's in trouble. Get in there."

Gene Kee threw the van into drive and sped in the direction of the call; just as abruptly he jammed on his brakes and glanced left and right at the first intersection. The takedown team would have to cross two streets, one of them the main thoroughfare, before arriving at the house.

As soon as he gave the order, Cronin got out of his car and, followed by Biff McLean, the two detectives ran toward Lee's house, their shoes ringing against the pavement. In the rear of the dwelling was a run-down garage and, climbing the fence that protected it, Cronin went along the left side of the garage toward the house and McLean chose the right. A cement wall forced Cronin to double back, coming around the way his partner had gone.

The yard was empty. Approaching the house, Cronin heard several loud reports, like the sound of firecrackers going off, then watched as Chris Brighton dived out the back door and tumbled onto the ground. Brighton staggered to his feet, looking dazed and pale.

"Chris," said Cronin, his gun at the ready.

"I'm all right," said Brighton.

An impatient man by nature and an enterprising cop, Joe McCain had refused to sit still on the "peek" and happened to be cruising right by the house when Cronin gave his order. First on the scene, McCain and Hutchinson had jumped out of the Toyota and scrambled up the front walk with their guns drawn.

McCain reached the bottom of the stairs, with Hutchinson right behind him. As they hurried toward the doorway, a man rushed outside with a gun in each hand.

"Freeze—police officer," said Hutchinson, aiming his revolver.

Suddenly there was a loud explosion and two bright flashes from the hand of the unknown person. McCain and Hutchinson returned fire. Something struck the walkie-talkie in Hutchinson's left hand and then hit him in that shoulder, throwing him onto the ground.

The unidentified man ran toward McCain, shooting his weapon. Lumbering forward, McCain fired five shots, and in the cramped space of the yard the rounds flew back and forth. McCain felt a small sharp pain in his lower abdomen and reeled backward onto the stairs, and the suspect ran past him and down into the front yard.

Al DiSalvo raced his vehicle alongside the ballpark, turned right onto Wood Avenue, and skidded to a stop. He leaped from the car and went sprinting toward the front door. En route he heard six or eight gunshots and watched as an unidentified black male ran out the front door with the silhouette of a shotgun in his hand.

The suspect hurdled a chain-link fence surrounding the front yard, and at the same instant Al DiSalvo noticed Biff McLean coming around the side of the house. Just then someone called out, "I've been shot," from the vicinity of the front porch.

"I'm a police officer," shouted McLean to the suspect. "Stop."

A moment later McLean leveled his pistol and fired three shots at the suspect, who threw the shotgun aside and dashed into the street. As the man was sprinting away, McLean, an accomplished runner, decided to conserve his remaining two rounds and give chase.

Coming along the sidewalk, DiSalvo raised his weapon and was about to pull the trigger when the suspect lost all motor control and fell onto the pavement. Only then did DiSalvo notice Gene Kee and the other members of the takedown team coming from the van, which had just pulled up to the left of the house; they were directly in his line of fire. Kee looked at DiSalvo and made a grim little wave.

At the same instant Cronin opened the back door and went through the house. In the kitchen he saw an overturned chair and Brighton's crumpled jacket on the floor. The hallway was filled with smoke and the acrid smell of gunpowder. Out front Cronin heard officers yelling and the approach of sirens.

Detectives Kee, Honan, and McLean walked up to the fallen suspect with their guns drawn. The unidentified black male was bleeding from a wound in the center of his chest and lying facedown over the curb. Next to him on the ground lay a police revolver and Chris Brighton's car keys.

Jack Honan picked up the gun and the keys, and even though the suspect was unconscious, following procedure Honan applied the handcuffs while Kee and the others moved toward the house.

"We need an ambulance," Honan said over his radio. "Somebody's been shot."

Just then DiSalvo turned for the house and saw McCain stagger down from the porch, his revolver in one hand, the other clutching his midsection. He emptied his revolver onto the ground.

"I've been shot," said McCain. His voice was steady and calm, and he shook his head like he was disgusted with the fact. He walked a little ways toward the street, and DiSalvo grabbed for him just as McCain's knees buckled. "Al, I've been shot," he said. McCain lapsed into a sitting position on the front walk and then slumped over on his side, holding his abdomen. "Say an Act of Contrition with me," he said. DiSalvo took his hand, and the two detectives prayed together.

Hutchinson was still up on the porch, gun drawn, covering the front door. His walkie-talkie had been destroyed. "I've been hit, and Joe's hit," he called out.

"You all right?" asked McLean, returning to the yard.

"I'm okay. Joe's hurt pretty bad."

McLean ran up to McCain, bent over him, and placed a hand on the wounded man's shoulder. "Joe, it's me," he said.

McCain grimaced, looking up at him. "Helen is gonna kill me," he said. "This is a brand-new fuckin' coat."

When Cronin emerged from the house, McCain was lying on the front walk, attended by McLean and DiSalvo. Crouching beside McCain was Detective Brighton, eyes wide, his face red and marked by scratches. Hutchinson was nearby, holding his left shoulder, with Kee beside him. They looked all right.

Cronin approached McCain. "Joe—" he said, his eyes filling up.

Out on the sidewalk, Gene Kee gestured toward a black male lying in the street in a puddle of blood. "Joe got the shooter," he said. "He's dead."

McCain had gone very pale. His hand was pressed over his abdomen, and the other detectives looked on as water ran from the wound—he had been shot through the stomach. Holstering his gun, Cronin knelt on the ground beside him. "Joe," he said. He struggled to say more but couldn't, and dropped his head into his arms. The street was bright with headlights and keening with sirens.

An ambulance arrived, and Joe McCain was rushed the four and a half miles to Brigham and Women's Hospital. Although he didn't attend Mass very often, McCain considered himself a religious man. Keeping with his early training, he said three Hail Marys every day, and on those rare occasions when he did sneak into St. Clement's, he stood in the back of the church and put a couple bucks in the poor box, hedging his bets in the event that there was indeed a heaven. So Joe had to laugh to himself when he was wheeled into the emergency room and discovered that three priests had been summoned. A crowd was gathering, and they were all looking at him like he was the governor or something.

Extreme Unction was administered, and Joe McCain spent the entire night in surgery as the lower floor of the hospital filled up with colleagues, family members, and friends. Among them were Joe's old partners, Leo Papile and Jack Crowley; Deputy Superintendent Al Seghezzi; U.S. Secret Service Agent Stew Henry, a tough son of a gun from White Plains, New York, who had worked undercover for Joe and spent many a night drinking with him at the Parker House; Jim O'Donovan and one of his five boys, twenty-four-year-old Brian, noted street fighter and hell raiser from Ball Square, a kid who McCain saved from a jail cell more than once and who represented all those Somerville guys that turned to big Joe for advice and guidance. And barely noticed among the throng was a young medical student from Boston University whom Joe had befriended, a woman who had been beaten and sexually assaulted by a notorious serial rapist. Joe had spent a great deal of his scarce free time tracking the rapist and making a case against him, escorting the woman into the courtroom the day the scumbag was sentenced to fifteen years in prison. She had never forgotten that, and disguised in a hospital johnny to gain admittance to the ward, the young rape victim became one of the first people to see Joe in his room after the surgery.

At one point the doctor came out and told Helen McCain that he did not expect her husband to live through the night. But Joe hung on.

While members of the Special Investigations Unit waited for news about McCain, they learned that the shooter was a twenty-two-year-old from the South End whose real name was Vladimir Lafontant. Paul Hutchinson's radio had deflected one of Lafontant's bullets and saved his life. Melvin Lee had escaped the house but later turned himself in; he claimed not to know "Stoney" very well and said that he had no part in the shooting. Thomas E. "Tommy" Lofgren was discovered lying on the roof of 276 Wood Avenue and arrested.

Detective Hutchinson was treated for superficial wounds at Boston City Hospital, where Lafontant was also taken and pronounced dead. Joe McCain had fired five times at Lafontant; four rounds had struck the drug dealer, and one of them went straight through his heart. Fueled by adrenaline, Lafontant was, in effect, already dead when he ran down the stairs and into the street.

Gene Kee and his wife, Ellen, stayed at the hospital until 3:00 A.M., when Joe McCain's chances of survival were still very much in doubt. But the Kees had two young children at home, and on the drive back to Tewksbury, Gene, who considered McCain a second father, turned to his wife and said, "He's going to die."

"Gene, he's going to be all right," said Ellen. "Joe McCain is too stubborn to die."

McCain survived but lost a piece of his stomach, his gallbladder, spleen, and pancreas, becoming an instant diabetic. Ironically, the Mc-Cain family was haunted by diabetes, but during that physical examination just before the shooting Joe had been told that his blood sugar was normal, which had been a great comfort to him.

Joe stayed in the hospital for a month, gradually acquiring enough strength to be discharged, but he looked like hell when he got home. "He was such a strong guy, I used to wonder, is he going to be like this for the rest of his life?" Helen said. Joe didn't want to leave the police department, but he was such a brittle diabetic that there was talk of a forced retirement.

After just a few months, and while still wearing a corset to hold his long, jagged incision together, Joe started talking about getting back into the action. There was money to be made in the private detective business, he said, and a way to keep his hand in police work and stay in touch with his old friends. Helen didn't try very hard to talk him out of it. Joe was moody, getting under her skin at home and generally making a nuisance of himself. And she didn't think there was much danger in private investigations. As Joe himself had said, "Helen, what do you want me to do, sit in a chair and look out the window?"

For their actions on January 29, 1988, Joe McCain, Paul Hutchinson, and Christopher Brighton all received the George L. Hanna Medal of Honor, the highest honor awarded to police officers by the state of Massachusetts. Later that year, big Joe retired from the police department and founded McCain Investigations.

This is that story.

School of Hard Knocks

L AST WINTER I WAS COACHING youth hockey with a guy named Mark Donahue, who said he had a great idea for my next book. Upon hearing that phrase, I almost always change the subject, but Donahue is not the sort of person who usually suggests literary topics to me. With his square Irish face, jug ears and modified high-and-tight haircut, Mark Donahue's appearance belies his roots in the tenement district of Somerville, Mass., a hardscrabble town right outside of Boston. He's kind to children, solicitous to his wife, and cheerful enough with the other hockey coaches, but he's not a bookish fellow and has a real city kid's edge to the way he goes about things. Donahue and I both live in Methuen, a quiet place about twenty-five miles north of the city, on the New Hampshire border. (I often kid Donahue that, like everyone who grew up surrounded by pavement, a lot of Somerville guys moved here when they saw their first pine tree, thinking they had reached the White Mountains.)

In Methuen, the local grocery store puts out three copies of *The New York Times* every morning, and two of them are still there, unsold, when the store closes at nine o'clock. It's pretty much a blue-collar town, and most of the people I know are too busy roofing, paving, installing boilers, growing apples, or fighting fires to even consider what I might be interested in writing about. Even after I've published two books and seen my work appear in newspapers and magazines across the country, the first question I hear whenever I see someone I know is "You still writing?" like it's an affliction that I'm bound to get over. And if I'm ever approached with any enthusiasm, it usually means someone wants me to write about his impending divorce, or a piece for *The Eagle-Tribune* on his snow-plowing business.

So when Mark Donahue told me that he was a cop and a private detective, and that his mentor, the recently deceased Joe McCain, Sr., put all fictional detectives to shame, I became intrigued by the notion of working for McCain Investigations and writing such a book. Like all the kids in my neighborhood I grew up on detective stories, and when I was quite young thought that the English actor Basil Rathbone *was* Sherlock Holmes and that old black-and-white films like *The Hound of the Baskervilles* appearing on the Saturday matinee were some kind of primitive home movie. Sometimes I even crawled around with a magnifying glass, wearing two baseball caps back to front as I searched for clues to God-knows-what in the dusty reaches of my basement.

My favorite television show was *The Rockford Files*, and its star, James Garner, who lived in a beat-up house trailer in Malibu and kept his revolver in a cookie jar, was my idea of the ultimate detective. Forget Ironside and Cannon and Mannix, I was a dyed in the wool Rockford guy. Whether zooming up the coast in his gold Firebird or hurting his knuckles after punching a wiseguy, ex-con Jim Rockford was Everyman in a checked sport coat, a guy who, like me, enjoyed eating tacos and drinking beer and kept his accounts on the back of a wrinkled envelope. For nearly five years I was occupied on Friday nights, lost in the gritty details of Jim Rockford's caseload, and therefore predisposed when Mark Donahue uttered the words "private" and "detective" in the same sentence.

What Donahue was offering was a chance to go beyond the realm of television detectives, where the moral boundaries are black and white and even the most convoluted cases are wrapped up in under an hour. Roughly the same age, size, and complexion as Jim Rockford, Mark Donahue is an affable, gregarious man who dotes on his seven-year-old twin son and daughter. But on the street, he can change mien very quickly when challenged or threatened: his eyebrow arches up, his face darkens, and his voice drops into a guttural throb. Big Joe McCain and his operatives were all trained at the School of Hard Knocks, and almost all of the dudes opposite them—the junkies, bank frauds, and rogue cops—were a lot more experienced at the game than I was. At McCain Investigations, I'd be sent looking for people who didn't want to be found, following guys who didn't want to be followed, and entering neighborhoods in Somerville and Roxbury and Hyde Park where I was not at all welcome. It would be entertaining, no doubt, but there would be no commercials, no time-outs, and no "do-overs" if somebody got shot or stabbed or run over. These guys were playing for keeps.

Headquartered at 106 Fulton Street in Boston's North End, McCain Investigations has been in business for the past fifteen years, tackling everything from wife beatings and warehouse rip-offs to international smuggling and gangland murders. Staffed by tenacious, hard-nosed detectives with years of experience, the company specializes in covert video camera, environmental, and "general" investigations. Cases last from a few days to several months, and their client list includes jilted spouses, nervous business executives, endangered celebrities, wary corporations, and suspicious attorneys.

One area in which McCain Investigations has excelled is the recruitment and training of new investigators. Good thing, since other than an eye for detail, a good ear, and the ability, inherited from my late mother, to size people up upon meeting them, I have zero experience as a detective. Mark Donahue noted that it takes a solid year to break in a new investigator, as it takes that long to encounter the various types of cases. That was all the time any of us had.

Joe McCain, Jr., president of the company and its founder's namesake, is a police sergeant in Somerville, drummer in local bands, motorcycle enthusiast, and father to three rambunctious young sons. McCain's childhood pal Mark Donahue has recently been appointed to the police department in Salem, New Hampshire, has a young family of his own, and is working the graveyard shift in a cruiser. And Detective Kevin McKenna, a Boston Housing cop, has started working part-time for a P.I. firm closer to his home. In the months since big Joe's death, the three men have tackled enough cases to keep the doors open at Mc-Cain Investigations but have reached the sad conclusion that the business should be dissolved. At the end of the year, McCain Investigations is going to be sold to a guy interested in big Joe's client list and office space. By joining Mark and Joey and crazy Kevin McKenna for their last run, I'd have a once-in-a-lifetime opportunity to walk in the footsteps of Joe McCain, Sr., one of the most decorated cops in Boston history, and to steep myself in the history of a company and a profession whose core values are straight out of the Old School.

BENEATH THE LEGEND "WE NEVER SLEEP" and the world-famous logo of the unblinking eye, the former Scottish barrel maker Allan Pinkerton opened his Chicago private investigations firm in 1850. The Pinkerton National Detective Agency was the first of its kind in the United States, and Pinkerton and his sons, William and Robert, were involved in some of the most notorious cases of that century: the pursuit of Jesse and Frank James and shooting of the Younger brothers; the disruption of the "Wild Bunch," including George "Butch Cassidy" Parker and Harry "Sundance Kid" Longbaugh; the conviction and hanging of the Missouri Kid; and a foiled assassination attempt on Abraham Lincoln aboard a train to Baltimore in 1861.

In 1875 the undercover Pinkerton man James McFarland infiltrated a secret terrorist organization known as the "Molly Maguires," resulting in the execution of nearly two dozen of its members. And early in the 1900s, an ambitious young man from St. Mary's County, Maryland, named Samuel Dashiell Hammett worked a series of cases as a Pinkerton operative. His experiences formed the backbone of his indelible character Sam Spade and filled in the plots of *The Maltese Falcon* and *The Glass Key*, literary detective novels that are still being read the world over.

Even more than its most celebrated cases, however, the legacy of the Pinkerton Agency lies in the structure and intelligence of its investigative methods. Its Chicago headquarters became the original database of criminal activity, where meticulous files were kept on an ever-growing collection of wanted men and women, each of them adorned with another Pinkerton innovation—the "mug shot." And although Pinkerton himself was reported to have an outsize ego and botched some high-profile assignments, he was known as dogged, indefatigable, and incorruptible.

Despite all their state-of-the-art equipment and access to global information, the detectives at McCain Investigations are not that far removed from the golden age of sleuthing. Big, bluff Joe McCain, Sr., was, like Allan Pinkerton, a determined fellow who could handle himself and handle a gun, yet understood that his brain was a more potent weapon than his fists or what he wore on his hip. Both men knew their way around a courtroom and a barroom, and their daily lives brought them in contact with some of the most dangerous and influential figures of their time. When confronted with the facts of Joe McCain's life, few would disagree that he was what used to be referred to as "the genuine article." In a city where, for some inexplicable reason, chefs and restaurant owners are considered celebrities, and in a society that often confuses victims with heroes, Joe McCain is as close to the Greek ideal of the hero as an Irish kid from Somerville is ever going to get. His highlights are exemplary: taking a bullet while gunning down a homicidal drug dealer; going toe-to-toe with the ferocious mob hit man Joe "the Animal" Barboza; unraveling sophisticated criminal activities leading to hundreds of high-profile arrests and convictions; the list goes on.

But the true measure of Joe McCain's character lies not in the arrests he made or the lives he saved, but in the quiet moments he reveled in. How he loved his wife and son and friends and was more at home walking his dogs on Packard Avenue than at the testimonial dinners that marked his career. How for twenty-four years he dressed in a red suit and snowy beard—augmented by his own white hair—and as Santa Claus spent the entirety of Christmas Eve visiting his friends' and colleagues' and their neighbors' children, and homeless kids and kids with AIDS, sometimes arriving via State Police helicopter to meet all his appointments in one night; ending at home with his three beloved grandchildren, who lived upstairs and worshiped him. How he counseled the wildest lads from the old neighborhood and beyond, like Leo Martini, whose brother was a Met cop turned bad that ended up in jail and who became a cop himself and leaned on big Joe when the other side beckoned. And Timmy Doherty, who crossed the blue line and testified against a dirty cop, and guys like Brian O'Donovan, hailed as the "toughest guy in Somerville."

Not to mention the men and women big Joe put in jail and later befriended, and the victims of crimes he continued to advise and comfort and counsel long after he'd sent their tormentors to prison, and crooks turned informants he treated with genuine respect and meted out rewards and admonishments to with the forbearance of a kindly Dutch uncle. Joe McCain did all that, and still found time to assemble a pretty good golf game for a man over three hundred pounds with a couple of bullet holes in his stomach.

Although he was larger than life, in no single photograph does Joe McCain stand more than five inches tall. And I know him only via photographs, audiotapes, fleeting bits of old television interviews, and yellowed newspaper clippings; and through the tales and anecdotes of his former colleagues, neighbors, and friends. Certainly it would be easy to look at McCain's accomplishments and chalk them up to his Depression-era roots or membership in the "Greatest Generation." But it's a peculiarity of heroism, especially in the classical sense, that the hero strikes out alone—that he has the inner strength and absolute conviction in his own ideals and abilities to go against the grain of his fellow stalwarts. In an era when "reality" has become something we watch on television, the great pageant of Joe McCain's life is well worth examining. A genuine hero doesn't endure a single moment and then traffic in it. He or she doesn't take as the main goal parlaying the heroic experience into something else. As Winston Churchill demonstrated in World War II, being a hero is much less glamorous and more difficult than that. Simply put, a hero *lives* the truth.

It's difficult to tell a story about being a detective that isn't episodic and profane because that's the nature of the work; if you want politeness, continuity, and closure, go sell real estate. And certainly among cops in Boston and everywhere else, there's a fair amount of small-mindedness and bullying, and more than a few guys whose uniforms cover up their dearth of personality, but you only have to spend a night in a place like Somerville or Fall River or Lawrence to imagine what it would be like without them. So when a detective like Joe McCain, Sr., comes along, with his hard-knocks childhood and wartime naval service, with the street contacts and smarts, who can drink like a sailor and punch like a kangaroo and has the balls of an elephant, a guy who really enjoys the game and plays hard, you wind up with a collection of feats that, had they occurred in another age, would've been the sort of life the bards wrote songs about back in the old country, in Cork.

In *Legends of Winter Hill*, I'll serve the twin roles of "newsie" and gumshoe, creeping down alleys, interviewing witnesses, poring over files, and in the end, creating a portrait of a career and a calling that has intrigued us since the days of the original Pinkerton men.

ONE

Joey and the Angels

This is my son, mine own Telemachus
To whom I leave the sceptre and the isle.
—ALFRED, LORD TENNYSON

THE SOMERVILLE POLICE DEPARTMENT is a low concrete structure that looks like a small town library from the 1960s, with a fenced-in yard containing a fleet of half-serviceable patrol cars and a steep concrete ramp out front that leads to a walled parking lot. Right at noon, thirty-nine-year-old Joe McCain, Jr., pulls up and I climb in the passenger side of the sump-smelling cruiser and buckle myself in. Since we're working together and so much of the "cop job" spills over to the P.I. firm, McCain has suggested I ride along with him on his shift as a police sergeant and hear about a few past cases while getting familiar with the territory. He shakes my hand with a grip like a wrestler and pushes off beneath gloomy skies, past the convenience stores, pawnbrokers, and blocks of crowded tenements.

Two of the many truths contained in the hard-boiled detective oeuvre are that there's no money in it and a whole lot of sitting around. In Raymond Chandler's *The Big Sleep*, Philip Marlowe says, "I went back to the office and sat in my swivel chair and tried to catch up on my foot-dangling." As a working cop, Joe McCain has a distinct advantage over the classic gumshoe: instead of dangling his feet inside the Fulton Street office of McCain Investigations, four out of every six days he puts on a bulletproof vest, straps on his gun, and hits the pavement equipped with an up-to-the-minute criminal database and supported by 130 well-armed, well-trained partners. There's no down time on the streets of Somerville.

Just looking at him, Joey McCain is the kind of guy somebody would tire of knocking down long before he'd stop getting back up. He's a former U.S. Marine, a graduate of the University of Massachusetts–Boston, and possesses a master's degree in criminal justice. A compact, powerful man with a shaven head and neatly trimmed mustache, McCain is covered in tattoos, from his neck to his ankles. As he rides through Porter Square, he keeps up a running commentary on past investigations while peering into alleyways and sizing up the other drivers and their passengers.

Standing outside her Brazilian eatery, a tall, attractive female shopkeeper with a circle of bright lipstick whistles at McCain and waves. "What's up?" he asks through his open window. The woman smiles and blows him a kiss.

Not an especially large man, McCain is a presence nevertheless; he has the swagger of a city cop leavened with sympathy for those who are growing up on the same streets he did. He says he owes it all to his late father, who was his hero, mentor, and best friend. "He knew how to relate to people from all walks of life: doctors to dockworkers," says McCain. "That was his secret."

Very often, great dads are easier to lionize in death than they are to emulate in life. Being "Junior" is a hump some guys never get over, and they go running to another part of the country, a different sort of career, a new life. But Joe McCain, Jr., is not awed or intimidated by the legend of his father. Under the rough talk and the lurid swirl of tattoos, including a vengeful ex–undercover cop from Marvel Comics named "the Punisher" that fills his entire back, Joey's a character in his own right. He's also a guy who put on the uniform, staked out a piece of turf, and assumed the mantle of his old man out of respect, not as a way of keeping up. If you know Joey McCain, you can't imagine him doing anything but this: investigating crimes and putting away bad guys right where his father started, more than forty years ago.

Incorporated in 1842, Somerville is a city of four square miles and roughly 80,000 people, located along the northern edge of Boston. Once a stronghold of Irish and Italian immigrants, Somerville today is a mélange of over fifty nationalities, a diverse mix of students, shopkeepers, blue-collar and bohemian types, and a couple of posh, leafy neighborhoods bordering the campus of Tufts University. Guys like Joey McCain and his fellow P.I. Mark Donahue grew up playing baseball at Trum Field; went to Somerville High; swam at the Dilboy pool and learned to skate at the MDC rinks; drank beer in the McCain basement; and shot thousands of pucks off a sheet of plywood in the McCain driveway. Donahue eventually moved his family out, to suburban Methuen. But Joey McCain has always called Somerville home.

"I love the Somerville of today," says McCain. "The arts, the entertainment, the restaurants. You just gotta keep your eyes open."

In Teele Square, where several nondescript storefronts lie opposite a city firehouse, McCain tells me about the day in April 1999 that he was riding his bicycle on a community policing detail and came upon a joint called the Station Café. Piqued by something, he rode up to the entrance, dismounted his bike, and peered into the front window. The barroom was filled with Hells Angels and Outlaws, rival motorcycle gangs that were locked in a mortal struggle for the New England drug trade and that never, ever socialized together.

McCain has a long, bad history with the Hells Angels, who have at various times threatened him, his friends, and his wife and three children. Although he has dabbled in things such as scuba diving, marathon running, and playing drums in a jazz band, the one true passion of Joey McCain's adult life is motorcycling. He's been riding since he was nine years old, when his father bought him a used Yamaha 80. Today he own a KDX 200 Kawasaki dirt bike, a '92 K75S BMW street bike, and a '99 Electra Glide Standard Harley-Davidson. All three of his sons—Joseph, age eleven; Liam, nine; and Lucas, six—have their own motorcycles. And McCain is a card-carrying member of the Renegade Pigs, a national organization of police and firefighters that ride American-made motorcycles. The Renegade Pigs are composed of twenty-five chapters, including two in Massachusetts, and over five hundred members.

"Some people, even other police officers, categorize us as rogue cops, because we're heavily tattooed and wear leather vests," says McCain, cruising down Powderhouse Boulevard, alongside the flat, green planes of the Tufts athletic fields.

But the Renegade Pigs are nothing more than a group of law enforcement types who blow off steam by riding their Harleys, camping out, and drinking beer, McCain says. The enmity between Joe McCain, Jr., the Renegade Pigs, and the Hells Angels began in the mid-nineties, when McCain gave an interview to a New Hampshire newspaper that disparaged the Angels.

"I said that they were punks and drug dealers, and the funniest thing about it was, they didn't object to being called drug dealers, just punks," McCain tells me.

After the story was published, an accompanying photograph was passed around Angels' haunts, and word came down that Joe McCain should start watching his back. Friends said that his photo was hanging up in an Angels' clubhouse with a red line through it, that there was a bounty on him, and that Angels were competing to see who would strip the Renegade Pigs' insignia from Joey's leather jacket.

Estimates of the Hell Angels' involvement in the illegal methamphetamine trade nationwide are as high as 75 percent, McCain says, and they also traffic in cocaine, marijuana, prostitution, and the "chopping" and reselling of stolen motorcycles. Recent efforts to legitimize their existence by retailing club paraphernalia and portraying themselves as the last free Americans are nothing but a smoke screen for their true identity, according to McCain.

"They are the dregs of society," he says. "Stop me when I'm lying, is what I always say to them. They're nothing more than a fascist regime."

By the late 1990s, the Hells Angels were upset with the Renegade Pigs for a number of reasons, including the law enforcement group's habit of wearing their chapter name in semicircle formation on the back of their vests, an Angel practice that other clubs are "forbidden" to emulate. Then one night, just a few hours after someone in New York had affixed a Renegade Pigs sticker to a Hells Angels' motorcycle, a small group of the Pigs left the Red Rock bar in Manhattan's Meatpacking District. A dark blue SUV cruised up alongside them, the tinted windows came down, and someone inside the van opened fire.

"They shot a Washington, D.C. cop, in the ass, Dave Moseley, a buddy of mine," says McCain. No one was ever arrested for the shooting, but "it was definitely the Angels," he says.

It was against this backdrop that Joe McCain, Jr., rode up that night in April to the entrance of the Station Café. Seated at two tables pushed together in the rear of the saloon were approximately ten members of the Hells Angels and a dozen Outlaws, gangs that had been killing each other since the 1970s. Immediately, McCain radioed his division commander for backup units and asked that they keep out of sight.

Although the two gangs have always hated each other, their operations had been sufficiently undermined by law enforcement that they had convened to discuss a truce. As luck would have it, their sworn enemy, Joe McCain, Jr., working alone, had discovered the proceedings.

His heart hammering in his throat, McCain pushed open the door and went inside. "I felt like those guys in *Animal House*, when they walk into the bar and they're the only white guys," says McCain.

He passed through a small alcove, which was clad in dark 1970s paneling and badly lit; to his right was the long wooden bar and to the left a narrow room outfitted with benches and booths lined up along the wall. Every biker in the place turned and watched him come in, dressed in shorts and boots and wearing his badge and gun.

"Anyone with a brain in his head was finishing his drink and trying to leave as unnoticed as possible," says McCain.

As he neared the table, an Outlaw rose from his seat. A well-muscled, stocky man with thick shoulders and a military haircut, the gang member was a former corrections officer and Army Ranger whom McCain had been introduced to while hobnobbing at a local Harley shop.

"Hello, Joe," said the Outlaw, shaking McCain's hand. "There won't be any trouble here, and we'll be gone in half an hour."

McCain reinforced the notion that he didn't want any trouble, and that he wanted the gang members out of the neighborhood. Then he turned around and walked out.

This was unbelievable; the Angels and the Outlaws were having a summit in a public bar while offering peace terms to law enforcement. "I live near there, and I left my bike, went around the corner to my house and got my video camera, and went over to the firehouse across the street," says McCain. "I asked the guys there if I could get to the upper floor and hauled ass up the stairs. A little while later, the Angels and Outlaws started piling out of the bar, laughing like they're all great buddies now. You gotta see it."

We're approaching the end of McCain's shift, so we return to the station, park the cruiser in the lower lot, and enter through a reinforced door next to the mechanic's bay. As we pass through the dispatcher's area, where detailed maps of Somerville are pinned to the wall and a steady stream of radio traffic is heard, a tall, burly E-911 operator named Scott Lennon hails McCain. "You guys ready to eat?" he asks. "I'm starving. My stomach thinks my throat is cut."

McCain laughs. "Yeah. Let's get some chow."

In the division commander's office, Joey rigs up his video camera on the desk and rummages through a cardboard box for the Hells Angels tape. On top of a nearby file cabinet is a set of women's clothing in a stapled plastic bag, the evidence from a rape the night before. One of the dispatchers comes in and mentions that the rest of the rape kit is in the freezer down the hall. McCain continues searching until he finds the right tape, and then Lennon enters with the food: wire-handled containers of rice, mushy vegetables in sweet sauce, and candied pork and chicken from the Thai place across the street.

McCain finishes cueing up the tape, and we sit there with steaming plates of rice and chicken balanced on our knees. The Station Café is a long, yellow brick building with two picture windows fronting on Holland Street. The camera zooms in, panning across six husky figures in leather vests clustered around the bar. The "rockers" sewed onto their vests indicate that four of the men are Hells Angels and two are Outlaws. McCain's voice is heard on the tape, as well as that of a fireman who is standing beside him.

You don't usually see them together, the fireman says.

Never, McCain says. Something's up, for sure.

The camera settles on the Victorian-looking door, which contains a sheet of etched glass that doesn't allow a clear view into the bar. On tape, McCain says, C'mon, you guys. I want everybody to come out, so's I can . . .

In a moment the door opens and a huge, bald-headed Outlaw with a thick gold chain exits the bar, laughing with two Angels and an Angel prospect, identified as such because he lacks an upper rocker on his vest. As the gang members pass into the evening, McCain frames a nice, tight shot on each of their faces.

Outlaws and Angels smiling and joking, says McCain on tape. I love it.

Because of his own rightful distinction between motorcycling enthusiasts and what he calls "criminals disguised as bikers," McCain takes genuine pleasure in deflating the Angels. One after another they cross the threshold of the barroom like they're being introduced on a TV show, and Joey says, "Thank you, thank you, and *thank you*," as each man scowls into the camera.

Just then two Angels with long shaggy hair come outside. They are dressed in black jeans, black, long-sleeved T-shirts, and their vests, and are smoking cigarettes. One of them spots Joe's bicycle, which is still leaned up near the entrance, and he nudges the other gang member, exhales a plume of smoke, and says something. In a juvenile show of defiance, the Angel pantomimes getting on Joey's bicycle, and he and his crony roar with laughter.

"Tough guys. Except they're so fucking stupid they can't tell they're getting their pictures taken," McCain says to me.

While we're watching the tape, Joe McCain's phone rings; he picks it up, growls his name, and immediately drops into a more pleasant register. It's his mother calling. Helen McCain, sixty-six, a retired nurse and widowed for a year, is having a rough day. Today would have been Joe Sr. and Helen's forty-second wedding anniversary, and next week is the first anniversary of his death.

Joey speaks with his mother for a few minutes and promises to look in on her when his shift is over. Other than breaks for college and the Marine Corps, Joe McCain has lived in the house where he was born his entire life. The McCain residence is right off Powderhouse Boulevard in West Somerville, in a neighborhood bordering on the Tufts University campus and composed of half-million-dollar homes dating back to the Grover Cleveland administration.

"It used to be, in the thirties, forties, and fifties, that three generations would stay together as a single family unit," McCain tells me.

"That's the main reason we stayed in Somerville: I wanted to raise my kids in the same house as the greatest guy in the world, my father."

Just to give me an idea of the influence his dad had on him, as well as the impact of the old man's death on such a wide range of people, Joey McCain has shown me the notes he kept while sitting beside his father's bed in Mount Auburn Hospital last fall. The day before he died, Joe Sr. was lying on the ward listening to jazz music with his only son and telling stories about the old days. During the gangland murders back in the late fifties and early sixties in Somerville and Charlestown, Joe Sr. was a key witness for the prosecution. Joey writes:

> He had to testify before the grand jury against some heavy hitters and found out that my mother was getting [threatening] phone calls at the house. He found out who it was when he recognized the moron's voice one day. It was Rocco "Bobo" Petricone, later to land the role in the movie *The Godfather* as Moe Greene. The old man went to the club they were hanging out at on Winter Hill. He found the whole group of them sitting together inside the club. He went in and asked Bobo if he could talk with him privately outside. Bobo signaled his buddies that it was OK, figuring that the old man was going to tell him he was scared to death and was going to back off of the investigation. He figured wrong. The old man grabbed [Petricone] by the throat and slammed him into the plate glass picture window in the front of the establishment and told him that if his wife got one more phone call at the house he was going to come back here with a shotgun and take care of all of them, he said he didn't care that much about the job. The phone calls stopped. Dad testified, several of them went in the can. . . .
>
> Dad and me are listening to Chet Baker now. It's a recording made in West Germany two weeks before he died. He has the most beautiful tone. Dad just fell asleep listening to Chet blow 'My Funny Valentine.' I'm beginning to feel a strange sort of comfort when I am here; although it's hard to see him this way, I'm glad I'm here. Life is coming full circle. I was just

looking at him laying there. He looked uncomfortable. It made me think of a book I read some time ago about Christ; I thought about the suffering he went through before he died. I guess we all have to go through some type of suffering before we die. We all have a cross to bear, so to speak.

At the conclusion of his shift, Joe McCain takes me through the dispatcher's room, into a dingy hallway and out past the lockup. We pause at the head of the corridor that runs between the jail cells, empty but for a pair of boots and rumpled clothes set on the floor. They belong to the unit's sole prisoner.

"Hey, Richard," says McCain, hailing the guy in the cell. He's a regular tenant here, a fifty-year-old wheelchair-bound man who likes to get drunk and roll into traffic and has been in protective custody for forty-eight hours.

A man's voice echoes from the last cell. "What?"

"Where's your chair?" McCain asks.

"I don't know."

McCain stands there with his hands on hips, glancing into a nearby closet and down the adjoining hallway. "Well, we're gonna give you a fucking bicycle and you can pedal it with your hands," he says.

The prisoner laughs and swears at us and we duck out of the corridor and McCain presses a button on the wall and the heavy steel door of the mechanic's bay climbs up its track. We emerge onto the lot, and as we go across the wet pavement, my head is teeming with Angels and Outlaws and Rocco Petricone and big Joe McCain dying at Mount Auburn and Chet Baker at the end of his life playing "My Funny Valentine." Like it or not, realize it or not, life is about measuring up, finding out whether you can hang with the big boys. I wonder aloud what use I'm going to be at McCain Investigations. I have no law enforcement training and no real connections in the city, other than reporters at a couple of newspapers.

Joey McCain laughs and tells me not to worry about it. "Cops notoriously think they know everything," he says. "We'd rather have a college guy who doesn't know a thing, so we can teach him the job."

"When are we going to get a case?" I ask, getting into my car.

McCain grins at me. "Soon," he says.

As I weave my way through the jumble of old paved-over cart paths that form the nexus of downtown Somerville, past the muffler shops and taverns and the boarded up frontage of the Union Square Redemption Center, it occurs to me that I've got my first case: looking for Joe McCain, Sr.

On the night that his father died, Joe Jr., his fellow P.I. Mark Donahue, and another Somerville cop named Mike Mulcahy drove out to visit big Joe's old partner, Leo Papile. In Leo's reckoning there were two kinds of people in the world—cops and assholes. The seventy-seven-year-old retired detective lived alone in a modest, brick-faced Colonial just over the Neponset Bridge in Quincy. He and Joe Sr. had worked MDC cases together for over a decade, locking up shitbirds of every variety: bank robbers, murderers, drug dealers, pedophiles, even dirty cops. Leo was Joe McCain's comrade in arms, his best friend, and as young Joey knocked on the door, hauling along a bag full of imported beer, he swallowed hard and set his jaw.

Tall and slender, Leo had always been well-dressed and well-groomed, with the slicked down look of the old Vegas Rat Pack, clean shirt, nice tie, his hair shining and parted to one side. But when he opened the door on Joey and his friends, he was an old man in battered pants and a mothy brown cardigan, rheumy-eyed, his hands shaking. Nothing inside the house had changed since Leo's beloved wife, Susan, died of cancer in 1973. The kitchen floor was still covered in the original worn linoleum. Around the table were metal chairs with hard vinyl seats, and the wooden cabinets and simple black clock were right out of the mid-seventies; even the color scheme was from another era, everything in brown, light green, and yellow. It was like time had stopped.

The men all shook hands. The beer came out of the bag, and someone fumbled through the drawers for an opener. Leo was a good-hearted, friendly man but abrupt and rather gruff. At a banquet one time he found himself sitting beside the mother of Joey McCain's former girlfriend. "Do you know who I am?" he asked. "No," the woman said. "I'm afraid I don't." Leo glared across the table at the younger McCain. "Joey, who is this fucking broad?"

On this particular night, Leo is adamant about the ground rules for big Joe's funeral. "There'll be no crying," he says. "There's gonna be no bullshit."

Suddenly he rises from the kitchen table. "Let me show you guys something. Come here. Come in here," says Leo in his husky voice, leading his visitors into the next room. Spread over the dining room table are a raft of newspaper clippings, about his son Leo Jr., who is director of player personnel for the Boston Celtics, and stories about his grandchildren playing high school and college sports. When he wants to visit that part of his life, Leo explains, he goes into the dining room.

"Come over here," Leo says. He directs the three men back into the kitchen and opens up a cabinet just to the right of the sink. Taped on the back are three calendar pages, two of them yellowed and one from the current month. The first is from March 1973, with a date circled in red.

"See this right here?" Leo asks. "This is the day my wife died. And this other one, this is the day I retired from the cops—a job that I loved." The retired detective stabs his finger at the third calendar page, October 22, 2001. "And this is the day Joe McCain died. There are just three days. Guys, that's my life right there."

Four months later, Leo Papile himself would be dead.

There's steady drizzle over Somerville now, as I drive by the Boys & Girls Club and beneath the railroad underpass, a steady mist falling on heavily laden trees and the streets gleaming in the wet. Detectives are in the business of reconstruction, piecing together crime scenes, motives, patterns of behavior, even the trajectory of a life when the situation calls for it. But when I think of Leo Papile and his calendar pages, I can't help recalling something else that Joey had written about his father when he was laying up in that hospital bed at Mount Auburn.

We are all supposed to bury our parents; it's the way things should work. Still, it doesn't come easy. I just wish he could have stayed around a little longer so that my children could have really known their papa. Before my first son, Joseph, was born, Dad said to me, "Remember something, if you are not a success with your family, you are a success nowhere; measure your success by how much time you spend with your kids and your wife and how you treat them; because when all is said and done nothing else matters in this world."

I believe those words, and try like hell to live by them myself. And as I set out on my year at McCain Investigations, it occurs to me that my most difficult case will be reconstructing the life of Joe McCain, Sr., to conduct my own private investigation into the force of his personality and so come to know the man after he has gone.

TWO

The Wild, Wild East

A T T H E   S T A R T   O F   T H E   S E A S O N back in the 1950s and early
sixties, thirty Metropolitan District Commission policemen in
their dress blue uniforms, each over six feet tall, would march out of the
Revere Beach station two abreast. As families crowded the platform of
the gigantic Cyclone roller coaster and the kids all cheered, the Mets
would mount the steps in formation and take the first roller coaster ride
of the year. When they disembarked, the cops would say, "How you
doin', kids? Wanna take a ride?" while handing out fistfuls of tickets.
And a lot of the Mets kept a couple extra passes tucked in their wallets
so children with little or no money would be able to take a ride later in
the summer.

Joe McCain loved the action on Revere Beach and he loved the Met
uniform, which he first donned in 1959. Throughout his career, whenever he ran afoul of departmental politics and some vexed lieutenant
threatened to bust him out of plainclothes and back to uniform, shipping him to someplace like the Quabbin Reservoir, where he'd have to
patrol the old fire roads after midnight, McCain would laugh and say
"Go ahead," because his pride and joy was the double-breasted Met
tunic with the brass buttons. He intended to be buried in it.

The Metropolitan District Commission, originally known as the Parks Commission, was established by the Massachusetts state legislature in 1893, for the purpose of "suggesting a method of securing and holding a twelve mile area about Boston 'for open spaces for Exercises and Recreation.' " Initially composed of Boston and thirty-six surrounding cities and towns, the MDC grew to include fifty-three municipalities with a combined population of over two and a half million people. Administered by a commissioner and four associate commissioners, today the MDC presides over a vast array of passive and active recreation facilities that encompasses five major land reservations, seventeen artificial ice-skating rinks, two golf courses, seventeen major saltwater beaches and four freshwater beaches; a ski tow and slopes; two golf courses, dozens of playgrounds, tennis, handball, and basketball courts; foot trails and bridle paths; picnic areas, two urban zoos, a museum, the Hatch Memorial Shell on Boston's Esplanade, and a number of historical sites including the Bunker Hill Monument and Fort Warren on Georges Island in Boston Harbor. Assisted by local authorities, the MDC is responsible for operations in six major areas: parks, water, sewerage, engineering, construction, and in Joe McCain's heyday, municipal policing.

The Metropolitan District Commission police had a long and distinguished history when Joe McCain signed up to take the qualifying examination in 1956. The first officers were hired in 1894, and within two years, a sergeant, seven uniformed patrolmen, and four call men were given full police powers. The original Mets were also responsible for park maintenance and the supervision of laborers, an odd combination of law enforcement and municipal duties that survived until the modern era and fell under the purview of Met captains—a management two-for-one that represented an incredible bargain for the commonwealth. In the 1890s, a Metropolitan police officer's pay was $2.25 per day. However, a patrolman's uniform was $21.00, minus the cost of the brass buttons. In a typical bureaucratic irony, the commonwealth paid for the buttons while the officer was responsible for the uniform itself.

When Joe McCain applied to become a Met the force boasted 628 members and the salary was $48 per week, which was a considerable pay cut from the $150 he was earning as a roofer for the Hurley brothers, who ran a local construction company. In those days, the Chinese laundry would starch your shirts for ten cents apiece and bookies like Joe Rennaro walked up and down Marshall Street collecting the daily numbers from housewives in kerchiefs, teamsters on their way to work, and disabled soldiers and sailors. By law, women were not allowed to sit on barstools, and the horse-and-wagon junkman rattled up Winter Hill every morning at sunrise, calling to his team in Yiddish. Steel-wheeled trains ran from the car barns in Teele Square down the middle of Broadway, and young war vets like Joe McCain played hi-lo in Pop Travila's pool room and hung out at joints like the Capitol Café and the old 3-1-8 Club. Joe was making good money at Hurley Bros., with an extra fifty cents an hour for driving the truck.

But the romance of the cop job appealed to him, as well as the broad jurisdiction of the Mets. In the postwar era, business was booming in places like Somerville and Medford and Chelsea, and so was organized crime. Big Joe, his hands covered in tar from scratching out peastone roofs all day, spent his nights in the back row of Professor Bloomberg's law class at Suffolk University, prepping for the Met exam. Like many men of his generation, McCain possessed native intelligence and a great deal of common sense but never went to college; the police entrance test was the only blue book examination he ever took, earning a 100 percent on the law portion ("What is a crime? A crime is an act committed or omitted in violation of public law either forbidding it or commanding it to be done") but proving his city kid's weakness in geography. The one question that stumped him—what is the largest river flowing through Western Massachusetts?—had Joe McCain wondering, Jesus Christ, where the hell is Western Massachusetts? The correct answer was the Connecticut River, but Joe put down the Merrimack, which meanders through Lowell and Lawrence, 25 miles north of Boston.

McCain earned a 90 percent overall and went to third on the Met waiting list. Meanwhile, the Hurley brothers, two skinny, indefatigable men in their forties from Joe's old neighborhood on Winter Hill, kept their raw-boned young apprentice busy from sunrise to dusk, climbing up and down ladders and hauling buckets of tar. Joe also moonlighted for the teamsters hauling sides of beef, and while waiting for his appointment onto the police department, he surveyed his life and found it lacking in only one area. He needed a girl.

In the fall of 1957, twenty-year-old Helen Dunn was in her second year of nurse's training at Somerville Hospital when a middle-aged woman named Isabelle McCain was admitted to the floor to have her gallbladder removed. On the eve of the surgery, her three grown sons visited Mrs. McCain, and after they departed, with a sly glance Isabelle McCain asked the pretty young nursing student if she had liked any of them.

"Who's the tall one?" asked Helen Dunn. "He's handsome."

Isabelle McCain's tall, handsome son, the oldest of the three, was Joseph Elmer McCain, twenty-seven years old and a Navy war veteran. McCain was lean and brown from working all day in the sun and wore his dark hair in a crew cut. He had prominent ears, a sturdy jaw, and the long, bony face of a young Lee Marvin. That first evening he was dressed in khaki pants and an oxford shirt, the sleeves turned back to display the tattoo of a sailor wielding a mop on his right forearm. Helen learned that Joe had grown up on Marshall Street in the Winter Hill district of East Somerville, during the Depression. "If you came from there, you were either a criminal or a cop," she used to say.

The Dunns were "lace curtain Irish" from the west side of town, and Helen was a slim, lovely girl with auburn hair and blue eyes. The day after their meeting in the hospital, when Joe McCain returned to his mother's bedside alone, he asked young Helen if she would like a ride home after work.

Her heart fluttered; certainly, she would. But no sooner had Joe descended to the lobby to wait for her than Helen approached the female patient in the bed next to Isabelle McCain's. The young nurse explained that she was taking a ride home with Mrs. McCain's son, but that she really didn't know him. "If I don't come back tomorrow, call the police," she said to the startled woman.

Of course, Joe McCain was the perfect gentleman, a bit taciturn perhaps, but over the course of his mother's hospital stay, he told Helen a little about himself. He had attended St. Ann's grammer school and was an altar boy at the church. A natural lefty, Joe had had that hand tied behind his back by the nuns, who taught him the looping right-handed penmanship he was known for. In those days, Joe worked as a pinsetter in a bowling alley and a busboy in a downtown hotel and couldn't wait to get out of school. He enlisted in the Navy on his sixteenth birthday, April 20, 1945, intent on getting back at the Nazis after his father, a Navy veteran of World War I and also named Joseph, shipped out with the Merchant Marine and was torpedoed and wounded off Long Island. Joe grew six inches and put on forty pounds in the Navy, earning his high school equivalency before he was discharged.

Helen's mother loved Joe, who often joked upon his arrival at the Dunn residence that he was there to visit Mrs. Dunn, not her little girl. But Mr. Dunn, a cantankerous fellow, used to say, "What's he hanging around here for? He's too old for you." After Joe's father died of his war wounds in 1949, the family had lived for a few years in Miami, where Joe supported them by working as a steel erector. Mr. Dunn used the fact that Joe's car had Florida license plates as evidence that he was bound to take off at a moment's notice. But Joe McCain was home to stay.

After a year of dinners at the Venice Café, fancy dress balls, and long drives in Joe's old black Ford, which now had a set of Massachusetts tags, he proposed to Helen, and they were married at St. Clement's Church on October 12, 1959. Joe still hauled beef at night and worked every weekend for the Hurley brothers, but his new day job was the envy of other men who'd grown up on Winter Hill and dreamed of trading their labors for a real career. After two and a half years on the waiting list, Joe McCain was appointed to the Metropolitan Police shortly before his wedding day, and when the couple returned from their honeymoon journey through New Hampshire and Canada, he took up his duties patrolling on Revere Beach. Helen would stand at the door of their tiny apartment and watch him drive off in his uniform, the most handsome sight she had ever seen.

JOE MCCAIN WAS A SOFTY when it came to kids, dogs, and little old ladies, but early in his career he earned the reputation of a guy who could punch his way out of a tight corner. One night he and another cop named Tom O'Malley were injured when their cruiser rolled over during a chase. A large, fierce-tempered man with a round head and beetle brows, O'Malley had also grown up on Winter Hill and was known as a malingerer. After the accident, McCain stayed out a week; O'Malley remained on sick leave for a year. Shortly after Officer O'Malley returned to active duty, he ran into McCain inside the old Baltimore Post VFW, a small, ivy-covered brick building on the corner of Walnut Street and Broadway in Somerville.

"You went back to work just to embarrass me," said O'Malley, looming over Joe McCain, who was seated at the bar. "You should've stayed out as long as I did, and collected."

Joe remained on his barstool. "Well, Tommy, you're you and I'm me," he said.

"Fuck you, McCain," said O'Malley.

A crowd of teamsters and cops and their dates followed the two men out to the alley. Joe McCain removed his false tooth and bridge and placed it on the lip of a tractor trailer, then squared off with the much bigger man.

Three punches and O'Malley was on the ground. Eschewing the Marquis of Queensberry Rules, he tried to kick his opponent, and McCain leaped on him and administered a pretty good beating. "That's it," said O'Malley. "I had enough."

While McCain was retrieving his false tooth, he heard someone running over the gravel and turned to see the vanquished O'Malley charging at him. Stepping aside, McCain used the other guy's momentum to smash him into the solid steel hull of the tractor trailer. Again Joe pummeled him.

Back inside the Baltimore Post, McCain washed up in the men's room, tidying his nicks and bruises. Afterward he went to the bar and purchased two bottles of beer, carrying them across the room to O'Malley, who was alone and brooding at one of the tables.

"Hey, Tom, we're both cops," said Joe. "Have a beer on me."

"What're you, a fucking asshole?" asked O'Malley. He grabbed the beer bottle and cracked McCain across the forehead with it, then kicked him in the leg. The room erupted in pushing and shoving, and after McCain got a couple more punches in and the two were separated, he went home to discover that he had suffered a broken fibula in his right leg. He had accumulated very little sick time and dragged himself into work the next day barely able to stand up. After roll call, a grizzled lieutenant named Armitage told the young patrolman to see him in the office.

"Make yourself scarce, McCain," said Armitage, who had heard about the fight and, like everyone else, despised O'Malley. "Gimme a call in a couple of days."

McCain didn't say a word. Out the door he limped and climbed into his car and went home. Every other day McCain would call the station and tell Armitage that his leg was getting better but he still couldn't put any weight on it.

"When you can walk without a limp, come on back," the lieutenant said.

"Well, what about my—"

Armitage interrupted him. "Don't worry about it," he said.

After a week McCain returned, and nobody said a thing about his paid leave of absence. But he always worked like a bull when he was there, and McCain soon distinguished himself as a cop who could use either his fists or his noggin.

Sometimes patrolmen were assigned to a cruiser, but often they were on foot. As a "walking man," Joe McCain wore his dress blue uniform, a visored cap, and his traffic belt with a nightstick and his service revolver attached. There was no patrol car, no radio, and no partner out on the beat; if there was an emergency, Joe was supposed to find a call box and ring the station. On the boulevard one day, Officer McCain received a complaint that an intoxicated man was disturbing the peace. A short distance along Joe found a heavyset, forty-year-old guy with several drinks in him, bothering families and harassing members of the crowd that had gathered.

"Let's go," said McCain, taking the man's wrist. "You're under arrest."

The man tried to run away and McCain, still grasping him by the arm, ran alongside. Up and over a parked car the man went, with Joe right beside him. People in the crowd were encouraging him to pull out his nightstick and bash the guy's brains in, but Joe never used a baton in all his years on the job. He knew it was the quickest way to incite a riot. The two men ran, side by side the whole way, and as passersby stopped to watch, Joe McCain laughed to himself when the drunk began to tire and stopped in front of a hamburger stand, panting like a dog.

"Have you run out of gas yet?" asked McCain.

The man nodded, unable to speak. On the sidewalk half a dozen on-lookers were clapping, and one of them said, "Hey, that's pretty good, Officer."

Another time McCain was working the night shift when a caller to the station complained about a large group of men dressed as women making noise in front of a bar. The duty sergeant assembled a handful of patrolmen including Joe McCain and ordered them to round up the loiterers and bring them in. Most of the cross-dressers were performing at Mede's Log Cabin, a nightclub on Bennington Street that featured drag shows. (The proprietor, Eddie Mede, was a well-built fellow who possessed a black belt in karate and taught self-defense to the Revere Police.) Apparently one of the shows had spilled over to the street and was creating a nuisance.

Two dozen cross-dressers were arrested that day and shepherded into the paddy wagon. The Revere Beach station house contained a half dozen six-by-eight cells on the lower level, a padded cell, and three cells for women upstairs. While the prisoners were being booked, the ser-geant noticed something and hailed Joe McCain, who was escorting groups of two and three to the men's cellblock in the basement.

"Hey, Joe, we got a problem here," said the sergeant. "Some of these people we got downstairs are women."

McCain looked over at a pair of them who were being fingerprinted; they wore curly blond wigs and makeup, and were lacking in facial hair. They were almost pretty.

"What are you talking about, Sarge?" asked McCain.

"They don't have an Adam's apple," his boss said.

The sergeant was right. "What are we gonna do?" McCain asked.

The old desk sergeant looked at Joe McCain like he was about to as-sign the most important task in the history of police work. "Why don't you go downstairs and find out?" he said.

"Excuse me, Sarge, but how the fuck am I going to find out?"

"One by one," said the sergeant. "You know what I mean."

It dawned on McCain what was required of him, and taking another cop along, he trudged downstairs and had his partner open each of the cells in turn. "Come out here, you," said McCain, who reached down and felt each of the prisoners between his or her legs. "Upstairs," he said. "You stay here," he told another.

Half of the group was sent upstairs, and McCain called after them, "Hey, Sarge, how am I doing?"

"You're doing fuckin' wonders, kid," the sergeant said.

That sort of perseverance marked Joe McCain's early career and won him notice from his superiors. And he made some lasting friendships on Revere Beach, including Al Seghezzi, the son of a cement and terrazzo worker from Bergamo, Italy, who eventually rose to the position of deputy superintendent of the Mets, and the first and most legendary of Joe's detective partners, the colorful Leo Papile. But even a hero must have an idol, and when he was starting out Joe McCain found his in a cop named Bill Parsons. Shot by a Japanese sniper on Guadalcanal at age seventeen and drafted by the New York Giants, Parsons was a formidable presence on Revere Beach for nearly four decades. Despite his size—six foot five and 250 pounds—Parsons was known for his gentleness and the sympathetic way he dealt with a beat cop's problems. When he came across a seven- or eight-year-old who was crying because he'd lost at one of the carnival games—where the basketballs didn't quite fit through the hoops and the milk bottles were made of concrete and couldn't be knocked over—Parsons would fix the carny with a stare and say, "Give his money back," then carry the kid over to Khor's for an ice cream cone.

From Bill Parsons the young Joe McCain learned that a good cop remained in control of himself and the situation at all times. The little things were paramount: how you stood and how you conducted yourself and how you interacted with the "motoring public." One night in the Revere station, Parsons was having coffee with a patrolman named Moretti who had been his teammate on the only Revere High football team to go undefeated when an ill-tempered sergeant named Bob Smith walked in and said, "What the fuck are you guys doing here?"

Sitting in the corner was Joe McCain, new on the job and happy just listening to the old football buddies reminisce. Six years younger than Bill Parsons, Joe modeled himself on the ex-Marine and even wore his cap at the same angle. So he was surprised to hear another cop talk to Parsons that way, as the bald-headed titan was respected like no one else on the beachfront. Young Joe raised his eyes when the sergeant made his remark, and watched as Parsons came around the booking desk and stood in front of Smith.

"Watch what you say," said Parsons.

"Why, who's going to stop me?" asked the sergeant.

Parsons shot out a tremendous right hand—*bop*—and knocked Bobby Smith cold on the station house floor. Joe McCain leaped to his feet, wondering what to do, and Parsons grinned at him and said, "Relax, kid, you got thirty years. You're going to see it all, and it's going to be over before you know it."

Many a Saturday afternoon Joe McCain and Bill Parsons went to the practice range together, where both men were terrible shots with a handgun. They'd pull their targets up on the wire and look at the silhouettes and laugh, saying, "Good thing we never get in shoot-outs." But just a few years before Joe shot Vladimir Lafontant on Wood Avenue and won the Medal of Honor, Bill Parsons responded to a call with his partner Bill Delaney in the middle of the summer at the beach. Two stickup men from Dorchester had robbed a bank and were trying to go the wrong way down the boulevard. Parsons and Delaney stopped short in their cruiser and cut the bank robbers off. The two men jumped out with their guns ablaze; one of them shot Bill Delaney in the leg, and he went down.

The sidewalk was roiling with beachgoers, and women screamed at the noise of the gunfire. But carefully taking aim, Bill Parsons leveled his .38 on the roof of the patrol car and shot the bank robber through the head from forty feet away.

A bronze plaque commemorating Officer William Parsons's bravery is fixed to the wall just inside the door to the old Met station on Revere Beach, which is now manned by the State Police. When Parsons retired in 1985 after thirty-five years as a uniformed patrolman, he took a job in security at the Suffolk Downs racetrack, just a couple of miles from his old stomping grounds. But he wasn't happy there and could be found walking the beach at four and five o'clock in the morning, reliving the horror he'd witnessed as a young rifleman on Guadalcanal. Then one

May afternoon in 1986, Parsons walked into a men's room at the race-track, entered one of the stalls, sat down, and shot himself in the head.

Joe McCain managed the funeral, just as he'd handled the investigation on behalf of the department when Bill Parsons had killed the bank robber. There were rumors that Parsons, who still lifted weights and walked every day, had been diagnosed with the same form of cancer that had subjected his father-in-law to an excruciating death. But nobody knew for sure, and when the Marine Corps honor guard and the mounted policemen and all the young Mets he had tutored over the years were gathering for the funeral, Joe McCain walked up to the coffin, leaned over, and kissed Bill Parsons on his big, bald head.

"You asshole," said Joe. "Why didn't you call me?"

THREE

The Strange Case of Joe Jr. and Mr. Hyde

The wicked flee when no man pursueth:
but the righteous are as bold as a lion.
—PROVERBS 28:1

FOR MY FIRST CASE AT McCAIN INVESTIGATIONS, I expected to work the late night repo detail with Mark Donahue, retrieving cars from remote or inhospitable locales on behalf of an insurance company. If I was fortunate, I'd get to sit in the cab with the tow truck driver and tell him when to back up. But Joe McCain, Jr., called me late one Friday afternoon to say he needed my help with a counter-surveillance, right there at the McCain residence in Somerville. It seemed a neighbor had reported to Joe's wife that early on the previous Monday morning, after Maureen McCain had carried the family's trash out to the curbstone and gone back inside, a brown-haired stranger wearing a "carpenter's coat" had approached the McCains' house, grabbed the four bags of trash, pitched them into the trunk of his car, and driven away. The neighbor described the man's car as a plain, dark blue Crown Victoria—an undercover cop's car, Joe said.

Snatching a guy's trash is an old detective's trick, Joey told me, often used when trying to "do" somebody. Using the early morning darkness as cover, you tiptoe up to somebody's garbage, haul it away, and then pore over the receipts, phone bills, discarded bottles and wrappers, and any unusual or illicit paraphernalia that turns up. The goal is to deter-

44

mine what your subject is doing, buying, drinking, smoking, or snorting. What was unusual about this case was grabbing the trash at 7:00 A.M., after the light had come up; the dark blue Crown Vic, which indicated that the trashman was a fellow police officer; and the fact that the guy getting "done" was none other than Joe McCain, Jr.

Joe had a theory, too, about who it was. After his late father's high-profile career and his own propensity for grabbing headlines, Joey has his share of enemies both inside and outside the Somerville P.D. Working off the detail of the trash taker's "carpenter's coat," he surmised that his early morning visitor could have been a Somerville cop attached to the DEA named Jimmy Hyde.

A burly veteran cop, undercover operative, and martial arts expert in his mid-forties, Hyde often wears a scally cap and a lined, midlength canvas jacket like the one noted by the witness. An old enemy of Joe McCain, Sr., Jimmy Hyde is "no fucking good," according to Joe Jr. In 1999, two plaintiffs, Christopher Mittell and German Alfonso, brought a successful civil lawsuit against Jimmy Hyde, after alleging that he inflicted a beating on them and a handcuffed prisoner named Michael Henderson in 1994. The jury found that Hyde had used excessive force against Mittell. Both McCains went ballistic when they heard about that particular rights violation, but Joey says Hyde got off easy by intimidating the victim and his fellow police officers. Joey goes on to compare Hyde's use of force against Mittell with an episode his father was involved in several years earlier. On that occasion Joe Sr. got into a fistfight with another cop in the rear lot of the Revere police station because the guy had struck McCain's handcuffed suspect.

"Look. I've made three hundred arrests and pissed off about four of 'em," Joey says. "I treat 'em like human beings. I don't find it necessary to belittle people."

The day after the incident with Hyde and Mittell, Patrolman Timmy Doherty, who was an eyewitness, came to visit Joe Sr. and asked him what to do. Doherty was troubled by what he had seen happen to Michael Henderson that same night, but was reluctant to break the law enforcement code of silence. Nobody likes a rat.

"Tell the truth," said Joe Sr.

His young colleague wasn't so sure. But McCain Sr. repeated that

Doherty had to tell the truth—if only to avoid being named a cocon-spirator when the real story came out. When the case against Jimmy Hyde for violating Alfonso and Mittell's civil rights eventually went to federal court, Doherty testified that he had watched the beating of Henderson through a two-way mirror. Henderson had a couple of teeth knocked out, his eyes were swollen shut, and at one point an enraged Hyde had leaned over and bitten him on the chest, according to Do-herty. At trial, however, Michael Henderson contradicted Doherty's testimony by saying under oath that nothing had occurred, even though he had previously told news reporters that he had been bitten on the chest by Hyde. The police department never disciplined Jimmy Hyde, and a line was drawn between him and the McCains, who had sided with Doherty.

This is the sort of thing that Joey McCain fears the most. It's not difficult to damage someone—to ruin a career or a life, especially a cop's. With even the slightest taint to a good cop's reputation, he can be passed over for promotions, ostracized by his colleagues, and distrusted by his neighbors. McCain always believed that Henderson's waffling was a result of pressure from Hyde. Now he wondered if he was feeling some of that pressure himself.

Over the years, the McCains had accumulated a few enemies on the police force. An unscrupulous cop might be expected to rummage among Joey's trash for a few weeks, then produce some "evidence"—perhaps a tiny amount of planted cocaine, syringes, or a bogus record of drug transactions—showing enough to procure a search warrant. Dur-ing a subsequent tossing of the house, the dirty cop could slip a bag of coke into the McCains' bureau, let another cop find it, and *voilà*, the demise of Joey's career, as well as four decades' worth of a sterling fam-ily reputation.

It's not easy to get a search warrant, particularly for a cop's house. Joey was hoping that whoever it was (and wouldn't he like to know) would come back to gather more phony evidence, and he had arranged this countersurveillance to catch him in the act. The idea was, as Joe Sr. always said, to "think like the criminal" and thus head off his next move. If Joey could videotape the person who was grabbing his trash in the act of doing it again, I.D. the person, and then take the tape to the chief, he could make the argument that it was a setup. Then, later, when the guy went in to the chief and said, "Acting on a tip, I've been pulling Mc-Cain's trash for two months and found cocaine residue and syringes—I think we should get a warrant," the chief could turn around and say, "Yeah, Joe's been watching ya do it, and has a videotape, and this case you're trying to make is bullshit." The big question, then, is who's got the jump on whom right now?

It's 4:00 A.M. and as black as a dirty cop's soul when I get up and leave the house. As I go down the highway toward Somerville, it's thirteen degrees, the cold seeping in around my windshield and through the tiny spaces of the doorjambs. *These fucking guys, they can't pull Joey's trash in nicer weather?* No one is on the road at this hour, and the sleepy voices on the radio indicate that it's more last night than this morning. Rounding Stoneham, I enter the Central Artery and see the skyline of Boston spread out like a celestial city. The illuminated clock faces are shining atop the Schrafft building, and the dark spires of Boston Sand & Gravel show themselves black against the sky.

Mark Donahue has given me two conflicting pieces of advice. First, he said, whatever happens, don't get "made"—don't let this perp get a good look at me. I'm going to be helpful on this case only insofar as nobody on the other side knows who I am. But he also told me to do whatever I could to get the trash taker on videotape.

"It's gonna happen fast," he said. "If you think you might miss it for any reason, run right out there and put the camera on him." What if he sees me? I asked Donahue.

He shrugged. "Too bad for you," he said.

Situated toward the top of a quiet, crowded street near Tufts University, the McCain residence is a neat, clapboard structure three stories high. Joe and his family live on the upper floors; his mother lives downstairs. As I inch along, peering at the numbers in the dark, Joey materializes at his front door, standing beneath the giant American flag strung from his upstairs balcony. He's dressed in black jeans and a black sweatshirt, his shaven head gleaming in the dimness, and he points to a space farther up the road. I park my car and walk back to him, hands in my pockets, head bent against the cold. "Hey," he says, in a whisper. "What's up?"

We go inside, and Joey closes the door. "Most people don't live like this," he says. "They don't get up at four A.M. to set up a surveillance on their own house—just because they've been one of the good guys, like forever." With his father gone, Joe figures, Hyde is looking for some payback.

The key to a good surveillance is to keep from tipping off the suspect that you're watching for him. To that end, Joe plans to leave his car in the driveway and the house dark, since on his days off, like today, he'd be home sleeping. Maureen will put out the trash just after six-thirty, as always, and Joe and I will take up positions in his mother's living room on the first floor, armed with a video camera.

It's just after 5:00 A.M., and since I had to make sure to arrive before the trash puller, we have over an hour to kill before we set things up. Entering the hallway, we walk past the open door to his mother's house and tiptoe up the stairs. Inside the McCains' white pine kitchen, Joe switches on the tiny light above the stove and fills a kettle with water from the tap. "Want some tea?" he asks.

Tattooed arms bulging from his T-shirt, Joe puts a flame under the kettle and picks up a tiny dinosaur from underfoot, and places it on the kitchen table. A man is never so vulnerable as he is in the wee hours, his wife and children sleeping in adjacent rooms, his mother asleep downstairs. Even Joe McCain, Jr., professional hard guy, wears a troubled look as he pours the water for the tea and we stand in the half-lit kitchen, palming our mugs.

"What really sucks is, my wife and my mother, who's sixty-six and whose husband died last year, get pulled into this filthy little world," says Joe.

He moves aside a plastic rifle lying on the table; the McCain children are a well-armed bunch. There's an arsenal of toy weapons on the nearby counter and scattered over the furniture and floor: pistols and ray guns and a fake shotgun with a cork on a string. "My wife has to worry if her husband's gonna get framed and go to jail. What a great fucking place to work."

At my urging, Joe excavates his long, bad history with Jimmy Hyde. "The sad lesson learned in this case was that, in my opinion, the city's lawyers backed the cops who lied in open court, and the guy who was excoriated by cops and lawyers alike was Timmy Doherty, the one who got up there and told the truth," he says. "Timmy wasn't trying to fuck good cops, as was portrayed. It was the other way around."

Jimmy Hyde has gone around with Joe Jr. more than once. A few years ago, Denny "Rat" Shaughnessy, a friend of Joey's who owns a motorcycle shop, was being harassed by a merchant named Vincent Titone, whose tire shop was across the street. (Shaughnessy had begun living with Titone's ex-wife; aggravating perhaps, but not illegal.) One day Joe got a call from Shaughnessy, who said that Titone was pointing a silver handgun at him from across the street.

"If he does it again, call me back," Joe said.

A short while later Rat called again to say that Titone was now parked across from his store in a white pickup truck. "He's pointing it at me right now," Shaughnessy said.

Joe headed right down there with another Somerville cop named Jimmy McNally. They told Titone to get out of the truck, and McNally searched through the driver's side and Joe took the passenger side. Neither found anything; then they crossed over and switched. Joe stuck his hand way under the driver's seat, back where the wall of the truck bed comes down. Groping around, he felt a metal object inside the liner of a work glove that was pressed against the back of the cab. It was a silver-plated .38, with two loose rounds stuck in the fingers.

Titone was charged with assault and battery and possession of an unregistered handgun. The case was eventually dismissed because McCain and McNally had searched for the gun without a warrant. But later Joe Jr. heard rumors that Jimmy Hyde was behind a push with the district attorney to have him arrested for planting the gun in Titone's pickup. It went nowhere; Titone flunked a lie detector test.

"The only thing he got right was his name," says Joe.

"Maybe Hyde figures I don't have the juice anymore," says Joe Jr. "Look—there's only a couple people capable of 'doing' a cop. Is Hyde capable of doing this? Yes."

It's time to set up the surveillance. We pad down the staircase and into the front room of his mother's apartment. Against the windows, which let in some reflected light from the street, is a narrow table crowded with pictures of Helen McCain's three grandchildren and an old photograph of a youthful Joe Sr. in his double-breasted uniform with the pinched motorman's cap and glossy boots. In the photo, Joe and a grim-faced fireman are carrying a body up from the banks of the Mystic River. The figure on the stretcher is covered with a sodden blanket.

We each take up a position near one of the windows, and Joe Jr. gives me a quick lesson on how to operate the video camera. He points out where the Crown Vic was parked last week, and the approach its occupant took to the house.

"It sucks that it's right at eye level," he says. "So stay low, and I'll tape him until he gets to the sidewalk out front, then I'll hand you the camera and go outside and you follow me."

"You gonna confront him?" I ask.

"That's right. And I want you to tape the whole fucking thing. It ain't gonna last very long."

A faint odor of Murphy's Oil Soap inhabits the room, and not a speck of dust resides anywhere. Every Saturday morning Helen McCain blasts *The Irish Hour* on the radio and to the skirl of Gaelic music cleans her apartment from top to bottom. A ship's clock is ticking from the mantelpiece, and beside me on an end table is a propped open book of Psalms. I can't make out the entry in the dimness.

"You carrying a gun?" I ask Joe.

"Nah. These guys have balls, but they're not gonna draw down on me here. They wanna come back and take me out in handcuffs in front of my wife and kids."

I'm kneeling on the edge of the rug, which is patterned with a pink, aqua, and teal seascape. Three glass dolphins decorate the coffee table, and there are several vases filled with dried flowers scattered across the room. I drop my hand below the windowsill and press the little button that illuminates my wristwatch.

"What time is it?" Joey asks.

"Six-thirty."

There are several moments of quiet, just the ticking of the clock. "I'd be so psyched to see that car pull up," Joe says.

I tell him that I can't believe anyone would do it; that a snoop would just walk up to a man's house in daylight and grab his trash.

"I've done it a thousand times," Joe says. "You just act like it's the most normal thing in the world. No rush. Then you just walk away."

The floorboards creak overhead. We can hear the door tilt open, and Maureen comes down the stairs in her pajamas and Joe's leather jacket and goes out with the trash. She makes two trips to the curb, returns to the house, locks the front door, and goes back upstairs.

"If it's gonna happen, this is gonna be when," Joe says.

It's getting light. Neighbors begin to stir, heading off to work. "I gotta take a quick piss," says Joe, getting up. He hands me the video camera.

"Don't miss it," I say. Joe laughs and goes out.

I fiddle with the zoom for a couple of seconds, then pick my head up and stare out the window. Did I miss something? Somebody just walked by the end of the street. I shut my eyes for a nanosecond and study the image that's printed there: was it a guy in a brown coat?

You picture yourself in this situation like Sam Spade, cool, hatted, invisible, with a blackjack in your pocket and a snub nose in the waistband of your pants. But with Joe out of the room, I feel more like one of the extras in *Lancelot Link/Secret Chimp*, the old kids' show with live-action chimpanzees wearing trench coats and fedoras. Fumbling with the camera, I'm about as useful as a trained monkey, distinguished only by my clean-shaven face.

Joe returns from the bathroom and takes up the video camera. Full daylight has come up, and we crouch by the furniture to remain out of sight. "I'd love to get these bastards this morning," says Joe, peering out the window.

Suddenly there's a grinding noise at the end of the street, and Joe stands up. "Look at this," he says. Snorting plumes of exhaust, a garbage truck lurches around the corner and two men in reflective vests leap off the back and grab Joey's and his neighbor's trash. It's seven-thirty; the surveillance is over.

"Not this time," says McCain. "But they'll fuck up. You watch."

FOUR

Redbones

What can I say, except that the world
is no good anyway and we all know it.
—JACK KEROUAC

THREE DAYS LATER JOE McCAIN, JR., and I are having
lunch at Redbones, a funky little barbecue joint located just off
Davis Square in Somerville. The place features valet parking for bicycles and is redolent of Memphis pork ribs and fried Louisiana catfish.
Joey's in uniform, and a young guy with a towel over his arm tells us to
sit anywhere. Divided into a narrow bar on one side and a larger area
filled with picnic tables, Redbones has a boisterous noontime crowd of
mostly college kids, and we head over to an empty table near the
kitchen. Joe takes the gunfighter's seat, with his back against the wall so
he can see everyone coming and going.

I'm busy reading the menu, which is painted on the wall and illus-
trated with colorful drawings of sweet potato pie, et cetera, when Joey
says, "It's all about the red meat."

"It's all about the massive coronary," I say, shaking my head.

Over to the table comes a thin, dark woman with gray streaks in her
hair and a notch in her upper lip. I go for the pulled chicken sandwich
with black beans and Joe orders the Texas chili, and just seconds later,
the waitress delivers a bowl of the steaming meat stew piled high with
onions.

Joe takes a big bite and gasps, his blue eyes veined in red and bulging. "That's fucking hot," he says, reaching for his Coke.

Things are heating up around the Somerville Police Department, too. Advised by his lawyer, Joe Doyle, to inform his superiors about the trash pulling at his home, McCain wrote a letter to Chief George McLean and the mayor that has stirred up some old feuds in the department. Just as our waitress delivers his fried catfish sandwich and dirty rice, Joe pushes a copy of the letter across the table.

> This unknown white male then picked up the four green plastic trash bags that were on the sidewalk at the bottom of my front stairs. . . . He then proceeded back to his vehicle. . . . I am requesting that the Police Department and the City of Somerville treat this as a direct threat to me and my family; and immediately initiate an investigation into determining the identity of the person or persons that may be targeting myself and/or my family. I have informed my mother and my wife of this situation and as you can imagine they are frightened for their safety and the safety of my three young children.

After receiving the letter, the chief called Joe in for a meeting and asked him what could possibly be in his trash that anyone would want. "Beer bottles, tattoo magazines, and porn aren't illegal," Joe said to his boss. "It's not what they're going to find in my trash, it's what they're going to *put* in my trash."

While asserting that he believed the trash pulling was more likely connected with the P.I. business than with the police department, Chief McLean, who's known as a hard, fair guy, said he'd assign a detective to interview Joe's neighbors and launch an internal investigation. After his talk with the chief, Joe also learned that Jimmy Hyde had approached another sergeant in the department and asked, "What's up with McCain? He thinks the feds are looking at him?"

I let out a whistle. "The catfish is out of the bag now," I say.

During the meal, Joe's phone rings and it's Danny Rizzo, a friend who just got out of Walpole State Prison after serving three and a half years on a drug charge. Here in "Suma-vull," where everybody knows everyone else and there's a very thin margin separating the good guys from the bad—a dividing line that runs straight through some family living rooms—even a phone call out of the blue can be connected back to the Jimmy Hyde case.

According to Joey, Hyde arrested Rizzo on a motor vehicle charge a few years ago, and in exchange for leniency tried to coerce him into conducting a coke deal at Rat Shaughnessy's motorcycle shop while Joey was present. "If not to pinch me, to embarrass me," Joey says. An expert tile installer, Rizzo had been hired by Joe Sr., who didn't know he was doing drugs, to refurbish a bathroom at his house. When the cops and the DEA pinched him on the phony motor vehicle charge, they said they knew he'd been "frequenting" the McCain residence and wanted him to implicate Joe Jr. in drug trafficking and therefore disgrace his old man.

"Dad blew up," says Joey. "Not because they arrested Danny Rizzo, but because after all those years working with the DEA, nobody gave him a heads-up, nobody contacted him to say, 'We think that someone who's doing work at your house has a drug problem.' He was hurt."

I put my eyes on him across the table and say, "Maybe you should stay away from Rizzo for a while, until this thing blows over."

"My friends are my friends," says Joe. "You know what I got from my father? You learn nothing about human nature by hanging around only with guys in blue suits."

But Joe Sr. never encountered a vendetta quite like the one Joey is facing. Big Joe believed that a police officer should never work in his own community (as a Met detective, the elder McCain worked in several area towns at once, not just Somerville). The political and personal pressure is bound to haunt you. People who know you too well ask for favors that compromise your ability to conduct investigations or make a clean arrest. But Joey loves Somerville and often says that he'd never consider moving out of town.

We push our plates aside, and Joe takes out his wallet. But the waitress shakes her head. "You're all set," she says, cleaning up.

Joe leaves a wad of bills anyway. "She thinks we're both cops," he says.

"No, she's impressed that you're the only cop who drives around with his personal biographer," I tell him.

On the way out of Redbones, Joe gets a call from Timmy Doherty, the patrolman who witnessed the Henderson beating in '94 and testified against Jimmy Hyde in federal court. Now thirty-five years old, Doherty is still "on the job," assigned to the detective unit, where he specializes in gangs. He's in the neighborhood and wants to meet Joe and me for coffee. On the sidewalk in front of the restaurant, Joe whistles at an unmarked car and Doherty stops, idling in the street.

"What's up?" asks Joe, leaning in the window.

"Let's go over the hill," says Doherty, naming a coffee shop in Medford. He looks at me. "I learned the hard way to take it out of the city."

Joey and I climb into the baked stink of his patrol car, and two minutes later we arrive at a Dunkin' Donuts and Timmy Doherty pulls in beside us. He's a stout fellow in a gray scally cap and leather jacket. Married with three kids, he wears a gold claddagh ring on his left hand, with the heart turned inward, and his solid blue tie is fixed to his dark blue shirt with a gold harp pin.

"How was lunch?" he asks Joe.

Joe touches his sergeant's stripes. "She tried to put it on the sleeve," he says.

"The dark-haired one? She's Fleming's ex-wife," says Doherty, naming a fellow cop. "She gives it away to everyone, except Fleming. He has to pay."

Doherty and McCain laugh. An artificial Christmas tree stands inside the door, and we enter the cattle chute surrounded by the rich, earthy smell of brewing coffee. "Timmy, you still eatin' crullers the long way?" Joe asks.

"You just suck the cream out," says Doherty.

They laugh again, and we take the steaming drinks to a little Formica table in the corner, where both Doherty and McCain sit with their backs against the wall. Doherty has an impish, pie-shaped face, but when I am introduced and he shakes my hand, his palm dry and stiff like a board, his eyes harden into little black dots. It's the look of a skeptic.

In case I have doubts regarding Jimmy Hyde's ability to orchestrate a

conspiracy that includes cops lying on the witness stand, as well as per-
secuting the one guy who told the truth, Doherty has offered to tell his
story, as long as it's done outside of Somerville, away from those who
still have designs on him. Here in the coffee shop there's a rehearsed, almost metronomic quality to his utterances, which aren't responses to
my questions, because I'm not asking any. Rather, they are declarations
of what Timmy Doherty and his family have been through, delivered in
the flat and disinterested tone of someone with post-traumatic stress
disorder.

"The city chose to protect those guys over the truth, and the city is
gonna have to pay," he says. "Big."

Last February, after enduring more abuse from his fellow police
officers than he could stand, Doherty filed suit against the police department, the mayor's office, and the city of Somerville under the federal Whistleblower Protection Act. In his complaint Doherty itemizes
many of the indignities he has suffered, both on and off the job: repeated late night telephone threats to his home; posters on the wall in
the station featuring his likeness beside that of a rodent; the word "rat"
scrawled over his name on the daily roll. Right now he and his lawyer
are waiting for a judge's decision on the city's motion to dismiss. He's
optimistic that the judge won't allow it, and that the trial will begin
next year.

Doherty says he's put on fifty pounds because of the stress, and has
thoughts of suicide. Three years ago, shortly after he testified against
his fellow police officers, he nearly drank himself to death, and Joe Mc-
Cain, Jr., and another cop buddy carted him off to the Winchester Hospital. His blood alcohol content was 3.5, more than three times the legal
limit, and while Joey and the other cop sat outside the detox unit, Doherty kept returning to the tiny window to give them the finger.

"It'd be quiet for a while, and we figured he'd passed out," says Joey.
"Then he'd be back, telling us to go fuck ourselves."

Under whistle-blower's protection, Timmy Doherty says that he's
entitled to three times the amount of money asked for in the 1999 civil
rights trial where he testified against Jimmy Hyde and the others (the
two men arrested with Michael Henderson were asking for $1.5 mil-
lion), retraining in a new career ("I'm gonna tell 'em I want to go to

Tufts and be a fucking brain surgeon," Doherty says), and his full-time pay for the remainder of his life.

"There's two captains whose paychecks I want," says Doherty. "And I'll come in every Wednesday and pick them up. Fuck direct deposit."

Doherty figures it'll take four years for his litigation to wend its way through the federal court system. "Then my career's over," he says. "The big bucks."

And through the emotional accounting of someone who's been torched on the job, Doherty is familiar with all the recent instances of Massachusetts cops who have been left to swing in the wind by their fellow officers. Ironically, Doherty was a high school friend of Kenny Conley, a Boston cop who has fought a long and public battle over what occurred late one night in Mattapan.

On January 25, 1995, a black plainclothes cop named Michael A. Cox was mistaken for a suspect during a foot chase and suffered a terrible beating at the hands of his fellow police officers. Cox was out of work for six months with a severe concussion and other injuries; the initial police investigation blamed his "accident" on a patch of ice.

In a subsequent civil lawsuit, Cox named James J. Burgio, Ian A. Daley, and David C. Williams—all Boston cops—as his assailants. Boston Police Officer Kenneth Conley was reportedly the fourth cop on the scene. In his grand jury testimony, Conley denied ever seeing Michael Cox or witnessing the assault.

Conley, whose recollections were contradicted by Cox, one of the original suspects, and Police Officer Richard Walker, was found guilty of perjury and obstruction of justice and sentenced to thirty-four months in prison. The three assailants were found liable in civil court and lost their jobs. But not one of them ever faced criminal charges. The only cop on the scene that night who went to jail was Ken Conley—who never laid a finger on Michael Cox.

Over time public opinion has come down on the side of Conley; most people think he got railroaded for doing what a large number of police officers do every day—clam up to protect each other. Certainly, the "blue wall of silence" and petty-minded corruption are as old as law enforcement itself. Even the Praetorian Guard probably goofed off when Julius Caesar wasn't around. But as we exit Dunkin' Donuts, I recall that it was the black police officer, Michael Cox, who was beaten sense-less and wanted his fellow cops to own up to it, who had his tires slashed and received threatening phone calls for simply telling the truth. Maybe it's just a case of the Irish sticking up for the Irish, but it seems to me that Timmy Doherty's situation is closer to Cox's than to Conley's. However, Doherty never says a word about Michael Cox. That strikes me as odd, since Doherty and Cox both learned the same hard lesson, a lesson that was very familiar to a guy like Joe McCain, Sr.: You don't always get a medal for doing what's right.

FIVE

It All Comes Home to Papa

You don't hate him because you think he killed your brother.
You think he killed your brother because you hate him.
—DASHIELL HAMMETT

I N THE 1960S, WHEN A STRANGE CONFLUENCE OF SEX,
money, celebrity, and immense political power turned a brightly lit
honky-tonk in the Nevada desert into the biggest playground in America, a smaller, uglier version of that drama was unfolding on Revere
Beach. In Las Vegas, the mob boss Sam Giancana pimped for Jack
Kennedy while Sammy Davis, Jr., hoofed across the stage of the
Flamingo and Frank Sinatra pleaded with Ava Gardner to take him
back. At the Ebb Tide Lounge in Revere, the notorious hit man Joe
"the Animal" Barboza downed glasses of cheap Mr. Boston Scotch
poured out of a Chivas bottle as Fats Domino, pounding the keys of an
old Steinway and sweating under the lights, warbled through "Blueberry Hill." Girls from Charlestown and Medford shimmied in their
tight-fitting dresses while big touring cars filled the lot and the manager, Richie Castucci, parked his shiny new Cadillac out front, with
"E.T."—for "Ebb Tide"—monogrammed on the tail fin.

Less than a mile away, at the apex of the General Edwards Bridge,
separating Revere from Lynn, Joe McCain and Leo Papile stood outside their battered Crown Vic, jotting down license plates and swapping
jokes. The boulevard was illuminated from the Tiger's Tail to Kelly's

Roast Beef with the glittering hulk of the roller coaster in between and the wind steady from Nahant, carrying off snatches of music from the various barrooms and the heavy, sweet odor of fried food. A black Caddy with Rhode Island plates rolled up and over the General Edwards and Papile said something about imported dagos and McCain flicked his cigar over the rail and laughed, then the two detectives climbed into their car behind a thudding of doors and glided down toward the beach.

Long before he made it into plainclothes, McCain was aware of organized crime and how it was strangling the towns around Boston as well as the city itself. On a patrolman's salary, he always found it necessary to hold down a second job, roofing for the Hurley brothers, driving a cement truck for Boston Sand & Gravel, and unloading freight cars and lugging meat at the Stop & Shop warehouse in South Boston. Joe used to hook each two-hundred-pound hindquarter of beef, lean it on his shoulder, reach up with his left hand to twist it off the rack, and then stagger out with the meat slung over his back. After Stop & Shop conducted a time study indicating that it took a pair of experienced men three hours to unload each freight car, McCain and a club fighter from Southie by the name of Berry used Joe's technique to get it done in two. On a good night, they'd unload four cars in eight hours and get paid union wages for twelve, which no one else on the docks could match.

While Joe McCain was breaking his back on the freight platform, all the connected teamsters from Winter Hill were enjoying cushy jobs inside the warehouse. As soon as each hind was carried in, one of these wiseguys would rip out the fillet, stuff it in a bag, and later stow the bulging bag under his smock. They'd steal anything they could get their hands on: meat, produce, fish, even stacks of Campbell's soup cans. A lot of the truck drivers were in cahoots with them; and each warehouse for every company from Lynnfield to Quincy had at least one mob bookie, fence, and loan shark on the payroll. It was one-stop shopping for just about every type of criminal activity under the sun.

Each evening the bookie hands out the "armstrong," a list of horse and dog races being held around the country the next day, as well as the local daily number slip for what used to be called "the nigger pool." All the truck drivers and warehouse workers and even the guys in the office place their bets with the connected bookie, and eventually, inevitably, they lose. So the bookie says, "Hey, you're behind three hundred bucks here. You better go see Charlie for a loan." The next thing the poor working guy knows, the mob is into him for the loan and the weekly "vig," a form of interest that allows him to stay even. He falls further behind and tries to think of new ways to steal from the company to pay it off. If he refuses to settle up, the mob sends a leg breaker to extract payment, which inspires the rest of the delinquent borrowers to come up with the money. There's no end to it, and this cycle repeats itself in hundreds of union and nonunion shops every day.

There's a saying associated with this kind of activity: "It all comes home to Papa." That is, a piece of all the thousands of little pieces that get extorted from Mr. Average Citizen in a given territory always goes back to the top mob guys, and for many years in Boston, that meant the Angiulo brothers in the North End. In the sort of ruthless expansion that would've made the Borgias jealous, the Angiulos extended their gambling and loan sharking systems into the prisons and grabbed up most of the street action by using a simple ploy. Gangsters would visit every little dive and pizza joint on lower Broadway in Somerville to offer the owner an "insurance policy" for a thousand dollars a week. When they were refused, the mob would send a group of kids to block up the toilets or slash the leatherette in the booths. Then the gangsters would make another call: What about this insurance policy? Are you interested? And the bar owner would say, Please come back.

The Angiulos would replace the managers of these joints with their own people, and if a particular owner was easy to get along with, they'd consider making him an instant millionaire by giving him money to lend out. The newly appointed loan shark was given the money at 1 percent interest and told to put it on the street, anyplace he wanted, at 10 or 15 or 20 percent plus a weekly stay-even payment. If a guy borrowed $100 and couldn't pay it back at the end of the week, he had to pay a vig of $20. Each week the vig was due, and even if the guy was ready to settle the loan after a while, he still had to come up with $120 for the final payment. The loan shark could live pretty well on his end of the vig coming in every week. Multiply that by all the loan sharks operating under the Angiulos' control, and it was easy to see that big money was rolling in.

The Boston Mafia ran their operation like it was the home office. They granted dealerships to various handpicked associates, and those satellite offices were expected to funnel their profits back to the corporation. If anyone bucked the system, the North End would employ guys like Joe Barboza and Jimmy and Stevie Flemmi and the McLaughlin brothers as collectors and leg breakers. Sometimes they took a baseball bat to the delinquent borrower's head, or they shot him in the back and dumped his body in the Neponset River. At the start, the tough Irish guys from Somerville's Winter Hill were like pull toys for the Angiulos. But when the Irish gangsters decided to grab their own territory and the shooting started, big Joe was nearly caught in the crossfire.

The entire mess began at a party on September 2, 1961, in a cottage on Salisbury Beach, a run-down seaside resort twenty-five miles north of Boston. It was a hot day, and at a motley gathering of teamsters and longshoremen from Somerville and Charlestown, nearly all of them involved in the rackets, the beer was flowing when a Charlestown thug named George McLaughlin leaned over and groped the breasts of Margy Hickey. Her husband, Bill, was a Somerville teamster, and he and the teamster George Lloyd seized McLaughlin and beat him like a rented mule; his nose and jaw were broken, and he suffered a laceration of the right cheek, fractured left elbow, and a severe concussion. Afterward, Hickey and Lloyd and two other Somerville teamsters loaded the battered victim into a car and drove to Newburyport, where they dumped him at the entrance of Anna Jaques Hospital.

Joe McCain was not in attendance at this lighthearted shindig, but for the next thirty years he made his bones on what had occurred there. Of course, the three McLaughlin brothers and their Charlestown pals were not about to let George's beating go unpunished. They visited the leader of the Somerville gang, a rugged longshoreman named Buddy McLean, and asked him to give up Hickey and Lloyd. McLean told them to go screw; besides, the two assailants had already left town. Early the next morning Buddy McLean was awakened by the barking of his German shepherd and ran outside, carrying a .38 revolver. Three men were hovering around McLean's car, and as they ran off, McLean raised his pistol in the midst of the crowded neighborhood and emptied the clip at the fleeing men. Walking back, he noticed that several wires were hanging from the grille of his car. McLean dropped into a push-up position on the street and looked underneath: four sticks of dynamite were attached to the chassis.

Buddy McLean used his police contacts, especially the head of the Somerville detectives, a man named Gleason, to avoid gun charges and hush up his attempted murder. Suspecting, because of his Army training in explosives, that Bernie McLaughlin had wired the dynamite, McLean made it clear around town that Bernie was his principal target. Joe McCain was acquainted with all these guys, Buddy McLean and Bill Hickey and Georgie Lloyd; as kids they had played ball together in Foss Park and shot pool at Pop Travila's; most of them had joined the service together, gone off to catch the end of World War II or to fight in Korea, and returned home to join the teamsters. Even after becoming a cop, McCain drank with some of the guys at the Capitol Café and the old Baltimore Post, but he knew how to "divide the paper down the middle" and refused to take part in gambling or payoffs or anything else that stunk of the rackets.

Joe McCain probably could've avoided the McLean-McLaughlin feud altogether if he hadn't been driving up Winter Hill, on his way back from looking at a used De Soto with Met Sergeant Billy White, when a bulletin came over the car radio that Bernie McLaughlin had been shot dead in Charlestown's City Square. Three assailants, one of them wearing a "townie" football jacket, had fled the scene in a black Oldsmobile with its trunk open to hide the license plate.

As he and White ascended Broadway, McCain caught a glimpse of what he thought was Bobo Petricone's black Oldsmobile turning into a side street on Winter Hill. McCain had seen the car earlier when he was waiting for Billy White to pick him up: Buddy McLean, wearing a football jacket, sat beside Petricone up front, and the dirty Met cop Russ Nicholson was in the back. McCain told Billy White to turn right and go around the block, saying, "I'll bet we find Bobo's car, and I bet they did Bernie."

White ran back around and parked half a block from Dawn's Donut

shop. Walking up the alley, McCain found Petricone's black Oldsmobile pulled off the street, the engine still warm and its trunk lid in the
fully upright position, obscuring the license plate—all of which fit the
description from the bulletin Joe had heard. Immediately McCain telephoned one of the most honest cops he knew, a Boston Police detective
named Delbert Williams, who was looking into organized crime in
Somerville, and told him what he and White had observed. Minutes
later, Williams and his partner arrived, covered the front and rear doors
of the donut shop, and arrested McLean, Petricone, and Nicholson for
Bernie McLaughlin's murder.

Near eleven o'clock one night thereafter, McCain was working in the
rain on Revere Beach when the light atop the old brick station began to
flash and the foghorn sounded, instructing all walking men to go to the
nearest call box and "pull the hook." The desk sergeant told McCain to
come back in—the Boston police wanted to speak to him. Waiting for
him by the night man's desk was Captain Joe Fallon, an impressive,
silver-haired man with a deep baritone voice. Being pulled from your
shift to talk to the brass was rare enough; but seeing a captain from another department set Joe's heart to pounding. He knew Fallon had to be
there to ask about the McLaughlin killing; the first thing the captain
said was that Joe's information had made the probable cause hearing a
success. He went on to recite the facts of Joe's biography: his military
service, young family, and growing reputation as a police officer.

Then came the bad news. Captain Fallon knew that Joe came from
Winter Hill and would encounter tremendous difficulty if he testified
against his old buddies from the neighborhood. His family might be in
serious danger, too. Fallon said he'd tried to keep Joe out of it, but he
needed his testimony to make the case.

Big Joe stood there in his dripping mackinaw with his gaze locked on
Fallon. There was no bullshit in the captain's eyes; here was an honest
cop. "What more can I do?" McCain asked.

"I'd like to assign you to detectives," said Fallon. "You know as much
about these guys as anybody. And it's going to get worse."

Joe McCain had been on the Mets less than two years; even a hardworking, motivated cop might wait ten years to become a detective.
"Don't worry, Cap'n Fallon," he said, thrilled with his new assignment.

"If I walked away from this, I might as well take off the blue suit and become one of the rats myself."

The threats started right away. Helen got phone calls when Joe was on the beat in Revere, saying that if he testified they'd kill little Jocy and burn the house down. Because McCain and the Boston detectives feared a leak in the Somerville P.D., they decided not to file written reports on their investigation leading up to the grand jury hearing. Instead, they would meet in person for what they called "need to know" exchanges, trading bits of information on the gambling and loan sharking that had emboldened the two factions, and discussing what Joe knew about the Winter Hill gang. During one of these meetings, McCain learned that Bobo Petricone was the one making the calls to his house. In an episode he would relate on his deathbed, big Joe, after becoming fed up with the threats to his wife and infant son, went down to the Capitol Café by himself and knocked on the glass when he saw Petricone inside.

Leaning in at the door, in a soft voice McCain asked Bobo to come out. The lanky gangster, who later reinvented himself as an actor and played wiseguys in several Hollywood movies, winked at Buddy McLean and his associates and came sauntering out of the bar.

McCain maneuvered Petricone so he was in front of the plate-glass window, his back to his friends. Standing close, McCain stared into Petricone's blue eyes and said, "I know it's you that's making those phone calls. It stops today, right now, or I'm gonna come back here and shotgun every last one of you motherfuckers." Although McCain always believed Petricone was, at least, an accessory to Bernie McLaughlin's murder, the future actor was never charged.

The calls stopped, but the Winter Hill gang tried one more thing to deter McCain from testifying before the grand jury. Russ Nicholson, an old pal from Marshall Street who was present at Bernie McLaughlin's shooting, called McCain and asked to meet him at Dawn's Donut shop the following day. Without having to ask what it was about, McCain agreed to the rendezvous. Under suspension from the Metropolitan District Police for beating an employee of a Greek diner across from the Ford plant, "Nick" had served as an usher at Joe and Helen's wedding. A tall, blond-haired man with the good looks of a matinee idol,

Nicholson had received several commendations for bravery and done some excellent investigative work. But drinking and gambling had ruined his career, and he and the McCains didn't socialize anymore. Still, Joe figured that Buddy McLean was trying to use his old friendship with Nick to make him back off.

Arriving early, McCain sat in his car for ten minutes wondering where these events and his acquaintances were leading him. Right on time he saw Nicholson walking toward the donut shop and stepped out of the car. He glanced over his shoulder and realized for the first time in his life that he couldn't trust Nick.

The two men stopped just a few feet apart and regarded each other for several long moments.

Out on bail for his part in Bernie McLaughlin's murder, Russ Nicholson wouldn't be able to go back to his police job and would never testify against the ruthless McLean, which put him at the mercy of the McLaughlins. Eventually one of them, or one of their friends, would find him in a bar or a hotel room or train station somewhere and put an end to it. Nick had made a choice, and now there was no going back.

"You know I'm a dead man," said Nicholson.

"You're not a dead man if you weren't there," said McCain, offering a little hope.

Without saying another word Nicholson turned and walked away.

ON THE DAY THE GRAND JURY CONVENED, Joe McCain came through the front door of the district court, past a small army of reporters, cops, and more than a dozen men he recognized who held teamster or longshoreman union books. These men eyed him as he went by; one or two gave him a grudging nod or said hello. It was quite a thing to testify against three guys you had grown up with, played baseball with, gone to war with. It wasn't a popular decision but it was the right one, and that morning put all of Somerville on notice regarding Joe McCain and his integrity.

It was the sort of gumption that cops like Timmy Doherty and Michael Cox would exhibit in separate incidents more than thirty years later, a demonstration of guts and conviction that would turn around on them and nearly ruin their lives. But Joe McCain bore the weight of this very same burden lightly, easily; he even managed a wink to Captain Fallon as he strode into the courthouse.

Standing off to one side was Somerville Chief of Detectives Gleason, who had covered up the initial gun charges against Buddy McLean. Within earshot of the longshoremen and teamsters, Gleason asked, "What the fuck are you doing here, McCain?"

"Testifying against your friends," Joe said, looking him in the eye. "The three shooters."

OVER THE NEXT FEW YEARS the Somerville-Charlestown feud resulted in more than sixty gangland killings—George McLaughlin's appreciation of Mrs. Hickey's tits was the unlikely catalyst for a veritable bonanza at local funeral homes. Not long after Bernie McLaughlin was killed, Buddy McLean was shotgunned to death by McLaughlin associate Connie Hughes outside the 3–1–8 Club in Somerville. Hughes was later cut in half by machine gun fire, his brain knocked onto the floor of the car he was driving. "Punchy" McLaughlin was shot and killed at a West Roxbury bus stop. George McLaughlin gunned down a bank clerk and went to jail for murder. And Joe McCain, who often referred to himself as "an old street cop who wasn't in charge of anything," was right in the middle of it, developing informants, recognizing the predilections of his old acquaintances, making solid cases, and putting wiseguys in jail.

But of all the Somerville guys who went bad, Russ Nicholson affected big Joe the most. After their brief conversation in front of Dawn's Donut shop, the two men never spoke again. In fact, the next time Joe McCain saw his old friend was on a slab at the medical examiner's office when he went to identify the body. Nicholson had been shot twice in the back of the head.

SIX

The Seventh Basic Investigative Technique

If you want people to like you you have only to spend a little money.
— ERNEST HEMINGWAY

N EAR MIDNIGHT, WHEN JOE McCAIN and Leo Papile descended from the General Edwards Bridge, passed the open door of the Mickey Mouse Club, and hit the rotary that marked the edge of Revere Beach proper, they rolled down their windows and breathed in the scent of fried clams, roasted pavement, and spent gasoline, all of it underscored by the creeping marshy stench of low tide. In the four years since Bernie McLaughlin had been gunned down, McCain and Papile had moved up in the world; they were bona fide Met detectives, assigned to the beach. Patrons were lined up for a hundred yards in front of Kelly's Roast Beef, kids in hot rods gunned their engines, and a high, yodeling scream echoed along Ocean Avenue as the roller coaster plunged from its height.

McCain and Papile loved the action on Revere Beach. The carny games, the young families strolling the boulevard, and the giggling hordes of teenage girls outside the Rollaway rink, where Joe had once rescued the night watchman from a fire, brought back memories of their "walking man" days. Up and down they used to go in their heavy blue uniforms, equipped with three pair of handcuffs so if they pinched a drunk and received a more urgent call, they could cuff him to a pole and run off; and just the feeling they got when they passed among the summer crowds, all the kids smiling, wanting to be like them.

As detectives McCain and Papile wore narrow-lapeled jackets and skinny ties and worked at night. Wiseguys from East Boston and Winter Hill and the North End had adopted Revere Beach as their unofficial headquarters and playground; the mob boss Gennaro "Jerry" Angiulo owned two nightclubs on Revere Beach Boulevard, the Tiger's Tail and the Ebb Tide Lounge, which became havens for the likes of Stevie and Jimmy Flemmi, Jimmy Kearns, Joe Amico, Nicky Femia, John and Jimmy Martorano, and the three Frizzi brothers: Tony, Guy, and Conno. Capitalizing on the Somerville-Charlestown feud, Angiulo used the Flemmis, the Frizzis, the Martoranos, and the rest of his enforcers and leg breakers to consolidate the fractured gambling and loan sharking operations under his lieutenant Sal Sperlinga; he got Howie Winter and his Irish gang on Winter Hill to handle the truck hijackings, union extortion, and methamphetamine traffic, with a piece of everything, always, coming home to "Papa."

By the mid-1960s, Joe McCain had demonstrated his familiarity with the six basic investigative techniques used to solve crimes: the development of informants, employment of undercover agents, laboratory analysis of physical evidence, physical and electronic surveillance, interrogation, and where permitted by law, the use of wiretapping. In pursuit of the Angiulo brothers and their associates, McCain found that the seventh fundamental technique was one of the most useful: watch the money. A crime of passion aside, the principal motivation for racketeers involved in drug dealing, hijacking, fencing, shylocking, gambling, prostitution, and extortion is the desire for financial gain. You can always spot a big-time criminal when his reported income doesn't match his lifestyle.

Mob boss Jerry Angiulo and his brothers operated the Huntington Real Estate Company on Prince Street in the North End, a business endeavor that hardly explained his palatial oceanfront home in Nahant or the expensive pleasure boat docked out front. Measuring that discrepancy by poking around in his tax records and bank statements, Joe

McCain worked backward into the street, where the low-level mob enforcers and goons were harvesting all the cash and hauling it to their
boss, like an army of ants bringing crumbs to the colony.

During their free time the ants liked to drink, fight, and chase the
skirts down on Revere Beach. One rainy night Joe McCain and Leo Papile responded to a complaint about a brawl in Sammy's Patio Lounge
on the boulevard. When the two detectives burst through the door,
there was a melee in progress: bottles and glasses were flying, women
were screaming, and chairs and tables were being broken. The Frizzi
brothers had tripled up on some poor bastard from Dorchester, beating
the guy senseless amidst the hollering and shoving that occupied the
fringes. In those days Joe McCain was thirty-six years old, large and
solid at 250 pounds, with only a smattering of gray hair at the temples.
He ran over and grabbed Conno Frizzi, a stocky, flat-nosed man who
weighed close to 200 pounds, and used a headlock to drag him outside
to the paddy wagon.

As he hauled the biggest of the Frizzis over the threshold, McCain
felt a pinching sensation in his lower back but thought little of it. On his
way back inside, however, Leo Papile stopped him in the doorway.
"Hey, Joe," he said. "What the fuck is that?"

"What's what?"

Papile removed a jackknife that was hanging from the back of Mc-
Cain's raincoat. "This," he said, handing over the knife.

McCain reached around beneath his raincoat and shirt, and felt a
trickle of blood. Apparently, while he was on the way out the door, Tony
Frizzi, the youngest and lightest of the brothers, who preferred silk
shirts and combed his thick chestnut hair into a pompadour, had crept
up and stabbed McCain from behind. When Joe rushed across the bar
to thrash him, Tony cowered against the wall, putting out his wrists to
be handcuffed. Unfortunately, no one had seen Frizzi stab McCain.

After the prisoners had been driven to the station, fingerprinted, and
booked, McCain went downstairs and stood in front of Tony Frizzi's
cell. Making sure that everyone could hear him, he said, "You sneaky
fucking greaseball. I know you're the one that did it."

From that night forward, Tony Frizzi was persona non grata on the beach. All the cops knew he'd sneak-stabbed one of their own, so over the next several weeks Frizzi was arrested for disturbing the peace every time he set foot in one of the nightclubs on the boulevard. Eventually the young gangster got the message and stayed away.

But of all the vicious, unpredictable, and cowardly thugs who frequented the joints on Revere Beach, the worst was Joe "the Animal" Barboza, a thirty-four-year-old hired killer and loan collector who, when Joe McCain first saw him, had already served more than twelve years in Walpole State Prison for robbery, assault and battery with a dangerous weapon, and kidnapping. Barboza, alias Joe Baron, was a muscular, dark-haired thug who had once boxed professionally and had "Born to Lose" tattooed on his right arm. During the Charlestown-Somerville wars, Barboza had been aligned with Buddy McLean and later claimed responsibility for more than twenty-five murders, putting him in a class with the hit men Jimmy "the Bear" Flemmi and John "the Basin Street Butcher" Martorano.

Joe McCain was well acquainted with Joe Barboza and his Revere Beach haunts. The infamous Ebb Tide Lounge, managed by gin player and loan shark Richie Castucci, had a narrow, crooked entrance to prevent rival gangsters from storming the door. Inside, the bar ran along the right-hand wall with a stage opposite and several small, round tables in between. Although the Ebb Tide often featured colorful, relatively harmless mob types like the gambler and fence Eddie Miami, and Castucci's ability to trim performers like Fats Domino at gin attracted top-notch entertainment and a good-sized crowd, the dank little nightclub was like a second home to Barboza and his gang of enforcers and strong arms, including Nicky Femia, Joe "Chico" Amico, and Guy Frizzi. Two months earlier, Joe McCain had arrested Barboza after the killer had brained a twenty-two-year-old patron with an ashtray, ditched a knife beneath a parked car, and threatened to put a bullet in the kid's head if he testified. On that occasion, when McCain was locking Barboza up, the former boxer accused McCain of hiding behind his badge, baton, and gun—that he wouldn't be so tough if he didn't have guys like Billy Parsons and a dozen other cops to back him up.

McCain sent Parsons and the other cops upstairs. While Barboza looked on, he unbuckled his utility belt, put aside his nightstick, and entered the cell.

"Go ahead," said McCain. "Take a shot."

Barboza stared at him. Then he backed away.

"I thought so," McCain said.

On that Friday night in the summer of 1965, standing on the General Edwards Bridge, Joe McCain and Leo Papile spotted a Rhode Island license plate—OP880—that belonged to the mob boss Henry Tameleo. Later, as McCain and Papile came up Revere Beach Boulevard, they saw Tameleo's Cadillac parked outside the Ebb Tide Lounge and pulled to the curb. Above the entrance the marquee read, "Fats Domino—Two Weeks," and before McCain could set the hand brake the crowd massing on the sidewalk parted and Joe Barboza walked up, sneering, with Conno Frizzi, Nicky Femia, Jimmy Kearns, and Joe Amico following behind him like jackals.

Barboza took off his coat and handed it to Femia. Making straight for McCain's car, Barboza flexed his hands and loosened his shirt collar. "Look who's here," said the killer, blocking McCain's exit from the vehicle by standing against the door.

Not long before this, Joe McCain's younger brother Eddie, a former paratrooper, had done a short stint in Walpole for robbery. The McCains weren't the only family on Winter Hill that had one boy on the P.D. and another in the can, but Joe didn't talk about Eddie much. Knowing this was a sore spot, Barboza leaned into the Crown Vic and said, "If I ever do time again, I'll take out on your brother what I shoulda taken out on you, you motherfucker."

In the same instant McCain kicked his door open, knocking Barboza aside. Before the gangster could steady himself, McCain was right there—bang, boom—a left hand and a straight right, and Barboza was on the ground, kicking at McCain with his ripple-soled shoes and frothing at the mouth. They rolled off the sidewalk into the gutter, and Barboza caught McCain in the right temple with his heel.

With Barboza kicking and swearing, McCain wrestled on top of him and pulled out his service revolver. The gun came up, knocking against Barboza's teeth, and went straight into his mouth. The killer went limp.

Surrounded by a couple of hundred onlookers, McCain stood up, rolled Barboza onto his stomach, and applied the handcuffs.

Standing back a little ways, Nicky Femia tried to hand Barboza's coat off to Amico, and a .38 pistol fell onto the sidewalk. "Fuck," he said.

"What do we have here?" asked Papile, shooing the crowd away from Barboza's gun. "This is turning into a good fucking night, Joe."

Billy Parsons arrived with the paddy wagon and hauled Barboza away. Later, during the routine inspection of the wagon, the Met cops found five .38 shells hidden behind a heating unit bolted to the floor. When Barboza had been transported to the station, he was rehandcuffed in front instead of behind his back, which allowed him to ditch the cartridges before he was thoroughly searched.

Barboza's gun, which turned out to be unregistered, proved that the gangster had malice aforethought; McCain had relied on his street instincts to move quickly and get in the first whack. But back at the police station, Joe McCain learned that Barboza was planning to charge him with assault and battery, and excessive force. While he and Leo Papile sat in the detectives' room, pondering this turn of events, Joe noted that he hadn't received a scratch in his tussle with the mobster. On the other hand, Barboza looked like he'd been run over.

"Hey, Joe," said Papile, standing on his partner's blind side.

McCain swiveled around and—*wham*—Papile bashed him in the forehead with the telephone. "Jesus Christ," said Joe, clutching his head. "What the fuck are you doing?"

Papile admired the lump that had already risen on his partner's forehead. "Now you look like you been in a fight," he said.

Five months later, half of Revere Beach turned out to watch the state try their case against Barboza for the unregistered handgun; for assault—barring a motorist's exit from his vehicle—and for battery with a dangerous weapon, his shod foot, on Metropolitan Police Officer Joseph E. McCain. Representing Barboza was the criminal defense attorney F. Lee Bailey, who later assisted in O. J. Simpson's murder trial. To intimidate the jury in the Barboza case, Bailey instructed Joe Barboza's gang to sit in the front row of the spectators' gallery. There they were every day, the Frizzis and Nicky Femia and Jimmy Kearns and Joe Amico, dressed in their tight black chesterfield coats with the velvet collars, homburg hats canted over their knees, looking like what they were: members of La Cosa Nostra.

During a recess on the first day of the trial, McCain sent Papile to the Steaming Kettle across the street from the courthouse to buy coffee and pastries. Out in the corridor a few minutes later, McCain approached a bench that was laden with Danish and styrofoam cups of coffee, taking one in each hand. As McCain leaned against the wall relishing his snack, Bailey and Barboza and his gangland associates emerged from the courtroom and stood a short distance away.

After a moment Bailey came over. "Hey, Joe, that's our stuff," he said.

"What the fuck are you talking about?" asked McCain, keeping his voice low.

"You're drinking our coffee," Bailey said.

McCain snorted at him. "Fuck you. I sent people out to get this," he said, pointing at the bench. "That's *my* fucking pastry, Lee, and don't you forget it."

At that moment the elevator doors opened, revealing Leo Papile with a smile on his face, holding a large cardboard tray of coffee and pastry.

"Well, here," said McCain, rubbing his half-eaten pastry over Barboza's order of Danish and replacing the cup of coffee after he'd practically spit into it. "No hard feelings."

Because F. Lee Bailey had a measure of success convincing the jury that McCain and Papile were harassing Barboza, the wiseguy was convicted on the lesser charge of disturbing the peace and received only a year in Walpole. But within a few years he would be arrested for another illegal handgun and held on a million dollars bail. Eventually, Barboza became a key witness for the government against the mob bosses Raymond Patriarca and Jerry Angiulo, and was one of the first career criminals admitted to the federal witness protection program.

This sort of dubious bargaining drove Joe McCain nuts. One of his favorite sayings was "You can trust a thief once in a while, but never trust a liar." When he heard that Barboza had negotiated a plea agreement and entered witness protection, McCain remarked, "Would a murderer lie? Hell, you've got the big score already. You've got Mr. Shooter. Put him in the electric chair. Get rid of him. You're gonna make a deal with this guy? For what? There's no redeeming value to him."

And he was right. Just a few years later, Joe Barboza, while still under witness protection, killed a man named Ricky Clay Wilson out West over $300,000 in stolen securities.

But McCain was comforted by the fact that he and Papile had taken Joe Barboza off the street twice, saving untold lives in the process. And it took ten years, but Barboza finally got his, out in San Francisco in 1976. A vengeful Jerry Angiulo dispatched one of East Boston's alleged assassins, Joseph "J. R." Russo, a starch-shirted, silver-haired dandy. Russo caught up with Barboza shortly after he was paroled for Ricky Clay Wilson's murder and shot him dead, at close range.

IN THE MINDS OF THE GENERAL PUBLIC, organized crime has become, in recent years, a charming anachronism: cable television's motley assembly of middle-aged Italian men adorned with colorful nicknames and loud sport clothes. But twenty years after Joe Barboza was killed, with Jerry Angiulo in prison and the old Winter Hill gang on the run, Joe McCain appeared on a Boston TV talk show called *Adler on Line*. The host was Charles Adler, a bearded, bespectacled populist with a red sweater vest and a game show host's blow-dried hair. Across from him sat big Joe, dressed in a neat blue suit, blue-and-red patterned tie, and gold-rimmed eyeglasses.

Joe was debating a criminal justice professor from Framingham State College on the topic of organized crime and the strength of its grip on the city of Boston. "Maybe these wiseguys put money in the poor box and are good to their mothers and grandmothers, but they're killers," McCain said. "And I don't like them."

Chafing under the lights, Joe McCain listened as the professor explained that law enforcement had broken the back of organized crime and anyone who felt differently ought to go play for the Red Sox because he was "out in left field."

Big Joe couldn't contain himself. "I think you're talking through your hat," he said.

The professor was taken aback, but Adler turned to McCain and asked, "What do you mean by that?"

Beyond the camera and banks of light the director nodded his head, pointing at McCain. "With all due respect to the professor here, that's not quite true," said Joe. "The gangsters might be in jail, but the millions and millions of dollars they've made over the last forty years is out on the street. When you have that much money, you have power; when you have power, you have people who'll do anything for money who'll go out and do your bidding. And if you think they're still not controlling their empire, you're dead wrong."

Joseph E. McCain had made a career out of watching that money, watching it come in through the bookie joints and massage parlors and dimly lit nightclubs by the barrelful, watching it corrupt good men and destroy their families and send one generation after the next to Walpole and Concord and Framingham MCI. That money was still out there, still circulating from Winter Hill to Uphams Corner and through Charlestown's City Square and in and out of the joints on Revere Beach, just as it always had. And no egghead was going to convince Joe McCain otherwise.

SEVEN

God Rest Ye Merry, Gentlemen

Many an exuberant voice and lively countenance
I could revive from that vanished cavalcade.
— SIEGFRIED SASSOON

A S FAR AS OUR FAMILIES ARE CONCERNED, Mark Donahue and I are going to the Somerville Police Department's annual holiday party to wish Joe McCain, Jr., a merry little Christmas. But as I drive south on Route 93, Mark is fidgeting in the passenger seat, worrying about his old buddy and his troubles with Jimmy Hyde. New developments have Joey in a "world of shit," stressed out and raging over what he believes Hyde is trying to do to him. A friend of Joe's whom I'll call Vinnie Carbone, a motorcycle enthusiast and a former corrections officer, just yesterday reported that another cop friend of his overheard some DEA guys talking about Joey McCain. Vinnie's buddy was standing nearby and began to listen only when he heard Carbone's name mentioned.

One of the DEA guys said that Vinnie Carbone, Joe McCain, Jr., and another Somerville cop, a good friend of Joey's named Johnny Barnhardt, are the subjects of a DEA surveillance aimed at cracking the three cops' purported drug ring. Vinnie's brother is a convicted dealer of steroids and last June, when they raided the Carbones' house in Saugus, where both Vinnie and his brother live with their parents, they found Vinnie's gun in the wall safe along with his brother's stuff. On the day Vinnie was fired from the sheriff's department for his possible role in the steroid business, Joey says that Jimmy Hyde and another agent followed him after he left the office.

As Mark Donahue has explained to me, when someone involved in a conspiracy is popped for it, often the first place he goes is to his coconspirator, partner, or boss to warn that person about the heat. Vinnie Carbone went straight to Fulton Street in Boston's North End, to the offices of McCain Investigations. Thus, the notion of a drug link between McCain and the Carbones was born in the minds of the DEA.

What Jimmy Hyde and his cohorts perhaps didn't realize was that Carbone was already working part-time on cases at the P.I. firm. Now out of the sheriff's job, he was looking to replace his lost income by putting in more hours at his friend's company. But Hyde didn't consider that, or the possibility that a family might have one honest guy in the sheriff's department and another who sold drugs.

"Small minds don't think big," said Donahue.

Mark figures that Jimmy Hyde has a "hard-on" for Joe McCain, and the Carbone connection is the key to igniting the same ardor in his associates. Carbone's source said that the DEA guys are right now watching McCain, Carbone, and Barnhardt, looking for evidence. Joey is afraid he might be set up.

Mark says that Joey is supposed to call the number-two man in DEA operations, Billy Simpkins, who is an old friend of Joe Sr.'s and in a position to help him. In fact, Joey is angling for permission to sting whoever might be trying to get him. Should anyone apply for a search warrant for Joe's house, the idea is to have officers complicit in the sting accompany this person to McCain's and, before they can get inside, arrest the person who applied for the warrant. If there are any drugs concealed on that person, it will be clear that the whole thing is a setup. It's risky, but with Hyde's move gathering strength and speed, Joe has to make a bold counter or he might be the guy who goes down in flames.

The lights on the dash throw a weird tint over the inside of the car, and the moon, high and white, shines down on the highway like a beacon. I ask Mark why Hyde would move against Joe through the DEA when the McCains are good friends with Billy Simpkins. He says that

Hyde doesn't know Simpkins came to big Joe's funeral and repeats his line about small minds. I mention that the ideal scenario would be that Hyde gets caught in the act and Joey and the other good guys ride off into the sunset.

"That'll be great, if it ends up happening that way," Mark says, although more and more that appears to be a long shot.

We arrive in Davis Square and hunt around for a parking space. The night is cold and black, and late shoppers crisscross the street, rushing past the lighted windows of the stores. The heavy thrum of an electric bass marks the site of the party, and Mark and I nod to the doorman and go inside. The bar is one of those two-level, brass rail and cell phone joints, with piped-in ambient music and sloe-eyed, racially ambiguous waitresses in snug black clothing. Up on a raised platform at the front of the room, two dozen cops are drinking beer in pint glasses and gnawing on chicken wings.

Joe McCain, Jr., is there, with an arm around his wife, Maureen, talking and laughing with a bald, jug-eared man with a chest like a piano.

The jug-eared cop is forty-eight-year-old Leo Martini, one of the toughest guys in Somerville. His legendary grip, applied between neck and shoulders, can take even a big guy like Mark Donahue to his knees. When I'm introduced and shake Martini's hand, it's like trying to squeeze an oak tree. The son of a union boss who ran with the Howie Winter gang and brother to a dirty Met cop who did time in prison, Martini is a complicated guy. Mark and Joey have said that he's like the Lone Ranger, still going out on patrol, still doing things his own way. Popular with kids throughout the city, Martini is a former boxer and star athlete who ran the Somerville recreation program for many years. He has also tangled with Jimmy Hyde.

Although not a close friend of Timmy Doherty, Martini supported the young cop in his battles with Hyde and his cronies. I've also heard that, a year or so later, Jimmy Hyde attempted to frame Martini for the same sort of thing Hyde allegedly had done to Michael Henderson. From across the room, I can feel Martini staring at the back of my head, sizing me up. I plan on talking to him but can sense that it's not going to be tonight. Around here, these things take time.

Joey introduces me around the party, indicating a young kid who was paralyzed in a motorcycle accident and has worked at the P.D. answering the 911 line. "See the guy in the wheelchair?" he asks.

Maureen McCain darts over and sticks her head between us. "He can't walk," she says.

Joe grabs his wife's chin and moves her aside. "Wiseass," he says.

As soon as he can, Mark Donahue sidles up to McCain, puts a big paw on his friend's shoulder, and leans down to Joe's ear. "You call Simpkins yet?" he asks.

Joe grimaces. "No. I will. Tomorrow."

Donahue edges in closer, dropping his voice. "These guys are trying to fuck you, Joey. Call Billy Simpkins before it's too late."

"I'll call him tomorrow," says Joe. He looks at me. "You want another beer?"

Mark relaxes a little. This is the message that he's come to deliver, and now it's up to Joe to follow through. When they were kids, Mark and Joey accompanied Joe Sr. to Billy Simpkins's rented beach house in Plymouth, where the young DEA agent would wrestle with Joey on the living room rug.

"He used to beat the crap out of him," Mark says. "But in a good way."

Billy Simpkins is the only guy who has enough juice to extricate Joey from the mess he's in. But as Joe buys another tray full of beers and pounds Leo Martini on the back, he doesn't look worried at all—which troubles me a great deal.

Around 10:00 P.M. the party begins to break up, and Joe hatches a plan to move across town to an Irish pub called the Tir na nOg. Joey occasionally sits in on drums with the Ronan Quinn Band and they're playing at the nOg tonight. The cops and their wives drift off in various directions and a small group of us spill onto the sidewalk in front of the bar. Suddenly a city bus arrives farther up the block and because they've been drinking and wish to abandon their cars, Joe and Maureen and a few others run for the bus, grabbing at their hats like the Keystone Kops.

"We'll see you there," says Donahue, laughing, and we head down an alley to where my car is parked. On the way to the nOg, Mark says,

"Ever since he was a kid, Joey's wanted to be a history teacher and a musician. He became a cop when his father got shot, which opened up a spot on the list. Big Joe wanted him to do it."

"Do you think that, deep down, Joe thinks this trash-pulling thing is a way out?" I ask. "That an investigation and countersuit and all that will let Joe quit his job and then he can get his Ph.D. and play drums four nights a week?"

"I told Joey, Hyde isn't just trying to get you fired," Mark says. "He wants to handcuff you in front of the kids and put you in jail."

We arrive at the Tir na nOg, a green, trolley-shaped pub tucked against a larger building in Somerville's Union Square. Joe McCain is already out front, talking on his cell phone, and as we pull up, four members of the band emerge from the pub, troop across the alley like they're the Beatles, and go into the apartment house next door.

"Hmm. I wonder where they're going," says Joe, snapping his phone shut. "They must be checking the air pressure on their tires."

Inside the nOg, Eartha Kitt is singing "Santa Baby" from hidden speakers. It's a crowded warren of a place, narrow and deep, with bicycle wheels and miniature canoes and heavy gilt-edged mirrors hanging from the walls. There are about a hundred people in a space for fifty, dressed in old woolen coats and ski hats, piled against the bar. In the back, near the tiny stage, Joe McCain introduces me to one of his non-cop friends, a guy named Moose Analetto. Beneath his floppy cowboy hat, Moose has a jowled face and thick black beard, and is decked out in a leather vest and black T-shirt. Joe says that Moose once made a cross-country pilgrimage to Merle Haggard's house in Bakersfield, California.

"He wasn't home," says Moose, who, upon finding the country legend absent, turned around and came back.

Although he has no formal training, Moose Analetto is a musical savant who reveres American outlaw singers and can imitate them to a T. Back in high school, when Moose was a quiet kid with very few friends, he arrived on Senior Day in a limousine, dressed as Elvis Presley and giving the hang loose sign out the sunroof.

"We thought he was a retard," says Donahue. "We were the fucking retards. Moose was so far ahead of us, it wasn't funny."

Joey and Moose go pretty far back. When Joey first became a cop, he responded to a 911 call and found Moose's father stricken with a heart attack. First on the scene, Joe applied CPR and although Mr. Analetto ended up dying, Moose always believed Joe gave his father a shot.

The guys in the band return from next door and squeeze past the bar and take the stage. Ronan Quinn, the bearded, rugby-shirt-wearing lead singer, hails the crowd in his Irish brogue and then launches into Joe Strummer's version of a Pogues tune, "Once upon a Time."

Joey studies the band like a medical student watching open-heart surgery. The music pounds out from the four musicians, driving us all back against the wall. Beneath the mismatched faux Tiffany lamps and tin suitcases hanging from the ceiling, Joe McCain, Jr., is in his element.

When the number concludes, Quinn announces that a friend of the band will come up and sing a song. He smiles at Moose, and the big fellow lumbers up to the microphone while the drummer relinquishes his kit to Joe McCain. Amidst the closed-in, stale beer and cigarette smell, Joe marks off four beats on the rim of the snare, and Moose throws out his hands, launching into an old Johnny Cash number. It's like the Man in Black has materialized in the Tir na nOg.

Far from Folsom Prison
That's where I want to stay

The room is hazed over with smoke and the crowd presses in on all sides. In her newspaper boy's cap and skintight jeans, Maureen McCain undulates in front of the stage, her eyes closed. On the drum kit, Joe keeps a hard, steady beat, mouthing the words of the next verse, and when he looks toward us, he smiles like a little kid. The cop job is a million miles away.

The music rattles the bric-a-brac strung from the walls and ceiling, and the drinkers packed against the bar sway against one another as Moose digs deep for the final chorus. It's not far removed from the days of big Joe and Stew Henry and Chris Brighton at the Parker House, telling stories and singing along with the band. This is a Somerville Christmas: Moose Analetto crooning about that train rollin' round the bend, and about hard guys doing hard time and making no bones about it.

EIGHT

The Halls of Montezuma

I thought of Beowulf lying wrapped in a blanket
among his platoon of drunken thanes in the Gothland billet.
— ROBERT GRAVES

E VERY YEAR AT THE McCAIN INVESTIGATIONS'S Christmas party, held right there in the office on Fulton Street, big Joe and the fellows pushed the desks against the wall, laid out an array of catered food on garnished silver trays, and hired a bartender for the night. Meanwhile, Lori Hays, pretty much the agency's most vital employee, and Joe's niece Lynn Harrington, a crackerjack undercover investigator, shopped for $700 or $800 in gifts, wrapped them at Lori's desk, and then big Joe, dressed as Santa Claus, delivered them to children with AIDS at the local homeless shelter. Returning to Fulton Street, he'd pose for photographs with the early arrivals and then change back into his shirt and tie and the annual Yuletide festivities would commence.

If Charles Dickens had grown up in Somerville, this was the sort of gathering the old scribbler would've reveled in: cops and ex-cops and feds and bail bondsmen in green jackets and red silk ties, their wives dressed in gaudy Christmas sweaters. Defense lawyers in Santa Claus hats, parolees, pizza shop owners, former pugilists, and white-haired judges accompanied by their Ivy League wives. Helen McCain and Al and Mary Seghezzi and professional snitches with three pagers clipped to their belts, gabbling in an undifferentiated mass and eating little meatballs speared on toothpicks. Mark Donahue and his wife, Maureen, talking to Joe Jr. and *his* wife, Maureen, the younger McCain wearing his trademark black T-shirt accessorized by a leather Renegade Pigs vest for such an auspicious occasion. Laughing and beaming and palming his glass of Chivas, big Joe presided over them all, his arm around Helen and his eyes watching the door for the arrival of his favorite guest.

Leo Papile always made a grand entrance, often accompanied by a retired pal or two from Quincy, who acted as his comic foils, as gofer and chauffeur. Upon sighting his old partner, Joe McCain raised his glass and called out, but Leo needed to make his rounds first, kissing all the wives and girlfriends, flattering them, whispering that he was available if their plans for the evening didn't work out. Leo inevitably made a scene when he stopped at the bar, complaining that Joe was too fucking cheap to stock this or that, whereupon he settled for the usual: a whiskey and soda.

Approaching his host, Leo would say something like "Where'd you get that tie, Joe—off a corpse?"

"Yeah," said Joe. "And that sweater matches those pants like nobody's fucking business."

In his trademark hoarse voice, Leo would turn to his buddies from Quincy and say, "How many times I saved this guy's ass and now he's insulting me? Merry Christmas, everybody. Hey, fuck you."

It would go on like this for a few minutes, and then Joe Doyle would announce that he was leaving, or the firm's landlord and principal client, Mike Kettenbach, would come through the door and Joe Mc-Cain would be called away. But he always felt better when Leo was there, flirting with the ladies and belittling the men, forever the star of his own traveling show.

Joe McCain had a number of partners over the years, and he got a kick out of each and every one of them: the hefty and soft-spoken Dick Horrigan, looking like some 1970 Telly Savalas sidekick cop; Jack Crowley, bearish and jovial, with a quip for every occasion; and the "kids" from Special Investigations, Gene Kee and Dennis Febles and Mark Lemieux, each a fixture at the annual holiday gathering and indelible in his own right. But Leo Papile was Ward Bond to McCain's

John Wayne; he was Buzz Aldrin to Joe's Neil Armstrong. Second banana, perhaps, but first in his colleague's heart and beloved despite his quick temper and blunt manner of speaking. When they worked together all those years in Revere, clearing out the bars, Leo talked a lot and threatened to use his fists or the stick; Joe said very little and meted out punches like an accountant doling out pennies: why use two if one is enough?

In the most typical scenario, some beady-eyed wiseguy at Hurley's Palm Gardens or the Ebb Tide would cross the line, pushing and shoving or uttering a threat. Then Leo would rush forward, barking obscenities, his raincoat bunched around his shoulders and the veins popping in his neck. In the end, either Joe held Leo back, or Leo held Joe's coat.

After his wife died Leo got a little wild, drinking in the joints down on the beach. Whenever possible, Joe would go keep an eye on him. One time a club owner offered Leo "a little pipe job" from a showgirl and some of Boston's best chicken cacciatore.

"Well . . . ," said Leo.

Big Joe grabbed his partner and shoved him toward the door. "Are you out of your fucking mind?" he asked. "They'll have you on video, and then they'll put Ex-Lax in the cacciatore."

Despite the trouble Leo could get them into, he was loyal, and Joe McCain prized loyalty above all else. And when they were busy putting away heavies like Joe Barboza, Nick Angiulo, and the Bear, one of the nastiest criminals they encountered was a shooter and home invader named Richard Smith, who was once accused of cutting off a woman's finger to get her diamond ring. Smith was chummy with eighteen-year-old Myles Connor, later to become a shifty art thief and mastermind but in those days the front man for a rock 'n' roll band that played the clubs on Revere Beach. Looking for Smith on a home invasion warrant and expecting him to show up, McCain and Papile staked out a joint called the Beach Ball, and sure enough, near midnight Richard Smith appeared in a stolen car and the two Mets gave chase but he escaped down Ocean Avenue.

Joe and Leo returned to a side street near the club. "I'll bet you he comes back on the train," said Joe.

Leo laughed. "Nobody's that fuckin' stupid," he said.

The detectives walked over to the Beachmont Station and melted into the shadows. When the last train rolled in, Smith sauntered over the platform with a rolled up paper bag under his arm, and Joe and Leo approached him as he crossed the street.

"Hey, Smith," said McCain, and the bad guy wheeled around.

Joe grabbed Smith, and the two men fell to the pavement, wrestling over the paper bag. It got tossed aside, and a number of guns clattered over the asphalt. Leo picked them all up, and by the time help arrived, Joe had the bad guy trussed up in a pair of handcuffs and Leo gripped Smith by the back of his neck and the seat of his pants.

By now a crowd had gathered, and rushing Smith toward the open doors of the paddy wagon, Leo said, "In you go, scumbag," and propelled the crook over the threshold with a swift boot in the ass.

Richard Smith was indicted in Suffolk District Court and tried on several counts of home invasion, as well as possession of unlicensed firearms. A large gallery observed the opening of the trial, where Smith was expected to plead guilty but instead received a continuance. In the hallway afterward he emerged with his lawyer, Al DeFelice, and stood waiting among a large group of people for one of the two elevators.

Spotting Leo Papile nearby, Smith smirked as the first elevator arrived. "Hey, there's Mr. Kick," he said, nudging his attorney.

McCain and Papile were dressed in suits and ties, and very few people in the corridor knew they were police officers. "You fucking asshole," Leo said, lunging toward Smith.

Just then the door of the second car opened, and Joe, wary of Leo's temper, pretended they were strangers. "Hey you, cut that out," he said, shoving Leo into the vacant elevator. "Behave yourself."

At the annual McCain Investigations's Christmas party, Leo "behaved" by quarreling with Joe, spilling the requisite number of drinks, and perhaps even saying something indelicate to somebody's wife. Then, at what he deemed the appropriate hour, he would drag a chair into the middle of the room, stand on it, and wave his arms. "I need everyone's attention. Listen up. Hey, fuck nuts, listen to me," said Papile, frowning at Mark Donahue or one of the other young investigators. "Many years ago, I served in the United States Marine Corps, which were the proudest years of my life. My good friend Joe was in the Navy, and that's very good, but fuck him and fuck the Navy."

In the midst of Joe's laughter, Leo would take off his shirt and stand there in the middle of the crowded room, bare-chested and smiling at the judges' wives. "I am now going to sing the Marine Corps Hymn. Most of you do not know the words," said the old jarhead. "Do not try to sing. I will sing the song."

After two verses and a cacophony of jeers and applause, Leo buttoned his shirt and put on his coat, engaged in some final repartee with big Joe, then gathered up his pals from Quincy and hustled out. North End bookies could've set the line at 2 to 1 that Leo would arrive late at the annual shindig and leave early; his personality required an audience, and he didn't like to drive at night. But the pulse of the gathering always fell after Leo's departure, and soon the washed up boxers and rival P.I.'s and tipsy DEA agents were looking at their watches and calling for taxis.

Seated in a chair somewhere, his tie loosened and an empty glass in his hand, Joe McCain would nod and smile and take part in abstracted conversation, but his face bore a wistful expression and his gaze kept wandering to the door where Leo had gone out. This went on for over a decade, until Joe got sick and died, and then Leo passed away and the office parties at McCain Investigations came to an end.

HELEN MCCAIN WAS WORKING A THREE to eleven shift on the floor at Somerville Hospital on the cold, gray afternoon of January 29, 1988. Around five-thirty Helen's supervisor approached with a worried look in her eyes and asked for a quick status report on each of Helen's patients. Immediately after fulfilling this strange request, Helen spotted Leo Papile coming toward her in the hallway.

"Leo, what are you doing here?" she asked.

Leo put his hand on her shoulder. "There's been an accident," he said.

"Was it a car accident?"

"No," said Leo.

"Is he dead?"

"No."

Leo drove Helen straight to Brigham and Women's Hospital in his detective's car. Joey, then twenty-six years old and recently discharged from the Marines, entered the hospital lobby at the same time, and mother and son looked at each other and began to cry.

Every hour through the night a surgical nurse would come out and tell Joey and Helen that Joe was still on the table and holding his own. At 5:30 A.M. the surgeon, Dr. Theodore Pappas, came down to the family room.

"We do not expect him to survive," he said.

After a couple of hours at home, Helen returned to Brigham and Women's. Police Commissioner Mickey Roache sought her out in the family room and asked if he could do anything to help. She had one very important request. "I want Leo Papile to be my chauffeur," said Helen. And Roache saw to it.

In their heyday, Joe and Leo encountered situations that ranged from the tragic to the comic, and even a few cases that encompassed both. During the gangland wars, after the murder of Bernie McLaughlin and when their partnership was fairly new, big Joe and Leo were investigating the star-crossed Joynt brothers from Union Square. "Ox" Joynt was a friend of McLaughlin's and a heavy drinker, and one night in the Capitol Café the bartender told him not to sit in a particular seat, which belonged to McLaughlin's purported assassin, Buddy McLean.

"Fuck him," said Ox Joynt. "He ain't gonna be around much longer, the lousy fuckin' killer."

The story Joe McCain heard was that McLean and his henchmen waited until later that night, when Ox Joynt was good and drunk, and rousted him up and led him staggering from the Capitol. They drove him to a swampy location in Wellington Circle and made Ox dig his own grave, whereupon they shot him and buried him there. Within a short time the word was passed down that Ox's brother Bobby, a bricklayer and tough kid, was going around town with a stolen gun looking for Buddy McLean. In a place like Somerville, Joe McCain knew that he wouldn't have to wait long or work hard to find Bobby Joynt.

Driving along the McGrath Highway, Joe and Leo received a general radio call about a stolen car, and sure enough, a while later they spotted

Bobby Joynt in a vehicle that fit the description, taking a left-hand turn onto lower Broadway. Joe threw the bubble light on the dashboard, and Leo jammed the accelerator to the floorboards and they gave chase. The two cars flew up and over Winter Hill past Paul Revere Park, and on the downslope Bobby Joynt stuck a gun out the window and fired a couple of shots in the direction of his pursuers.

When they made a right onto Main Street down near Cousin's Gym, Joynt skidded wide on the turn and Leo broadsided him, knocking the stolen car into a house and tearing off the front porch. Dazed and trapped in the wreckage, Joynt put his hands up and surrendered to the Mets, admitting that he was trying to find Buddy McLean. McCain actually felt sorry for him, realizing that Bobby Joynt's anguish over his brother and his penchant for booze had compelled him to do it.

At the police station Joynt said the gun, which was a police revolver, had been stolen from a Boston cop and given to a young prostitute named Mary Anne for safekeeping; Joynt wouldn't say how he'd ended up with it. Acquiring a search warrant, Joe and Leo headed for Brookline to interview Mary Anne at her apartment.

Mary Anne lived in a well-kept, three-story brick building in a quiet, leafy neighborhood. Unsure what they would find, Joe and Leo crept up the staircase accompanied by two Brookline cops.

The apartment had two doors leading into the hallway, and Joe and the Brookline captain of detectives lined up in front of one entrance while Leo and the uniformed sergeant positioned themselves near the other. On the count of three, they charged across the hallway, and the force of big Joe and the hefty Brookline detective knocked the door right off its hinges. It flew into the room and landed on the bed, just missing the most beautiful young woman Joe McCain had ever seen and coming to rest beside her trick, a tall, gangling MIT professor clad only in a pair of red bikini underpants. On a tripod beside the bed was an elaborate camera system, on which the randy professor had been documenting his adventures.

Curled up like a kitten and registering only mild surprise, seventeen-year-old Mary Anne was a buxom, green-eyed lass with tawny skin and long, golden brown hair streaked by the sun. Leo and the other cop had knocked in the main door, and even with four strange men gaping at her, Mary Anne didn't blush or blink an eye but remained naked on the bed, smiling at her antagonists.

"Let's go, you two," said Joe, trying not to stare. "Into the other room."

"Whatever you say, Officer," said Mary Anne.

Rising from the bed, the lovely young prostitute waltzed into the living room and sat naked on the couch with her long legs crossed at the knees. Light streaming in the picture window accented the contours of her body, the freckled shoulders, perfect upright breasts, and trim little hips.

"Is this the best you can do?" she asked Joe, keeping her eyes on his. "Aren't there any other criminals out there? The gangsters who shoot people."

"Actually, we're here to talk to you about a gun," Joe said. "Who gave—"

Just then the intercom buzzed, and Joe asked Mary Anne if she was expecting anyone. "Yes, a guy by the name of Gallo," said Mary Anne.

"Gallo? Not the deputy chief?" asked Joe.

Mary Anne smirked. "No," she said. "His brother."

Joe and Leo glanced at each other and shrugged their shoulders. "Are you sure?" asked Joe. The intercom buzzed again, and he motioned for the young prostitute to remain quiet.

"Yeah, what is it?" asked McCain, pressing the button on the speaker.

A man's voice broke over the intercom. "What's going on?" he asked.

"Come on up," Joe said. "I'm just leaving."

Joe went into the hallway and started down the stairs. Making a turn onto the first landing, he encountered a short, broad-shouldered man dressed like a Quincy Market fruit peddler: a long, grayish white jacket with a round brown collar and khaki pants. Gallo looked at McCain, arching his eyebrows, and big Joe smiled, raised his thumb, and jerked it over his shoulder without saying anything.

The peddler mastered the last flight of stairs, turned into the hallway, and stood dumbfounded at the entrance to the apartment. The front door was gone. He looked in, and there was Mary Anne naked on the couch, waving to him. Meanwhile, big Joe had followed Gallo up the carpeted stairs and was standing a foot behind him.

The fruit peddler glanced over his shoulder at McCain and looked back at Mary Anne, who was now accompanied by Leo Papile, and his shoulders fell. "Step inside," said Joe, and Gallo trudged over the threshold.

The Brookline detective patted Gallo down and took his ID and motioned for him to sit down. "Oh, shit," said the fruit peddler, dropping his head into his hands. "I was just up here to deliver—"

"Deliver what?" asked Joe, indicating that Gallo was empty-handed by thrusting his own palms outward and upward.

Leo laughed at the downcast fruit peddler. "Don't lie. You're up here to get laid," he said. "She's only a teenager, you fucking degenerate."

"Officer, I am—"

Leo cut him off. "A horny fucking fruit peddler. Who are you kidding? Cut a hole in one of your watermelons and fuck it next time, if they serve watermelons up at Walpole."

Gallo took the abuse without another word. When Leo was finished, and the other cops had nearly choked on their laughter, he threw the man's wallet back at him and made a gesture that included the MIT professor, who had put his clothes back on.

"Get lost," said Leo.

The fruit peddler gulped twice. "Am-m I al-lll right?" he asked.

"Get the fuck out of here," Leo said.

The professor stopped near the gaping doorway, clutching his tripod and camera. "Can I have my pictures back?" he asked.

"Sure," said Leo. He took the handful of photographs and tore them into small pieces, and flung the chemical-covered bits in the direction of the hallway, where they fluttered to the carpet. "Is there anything else we can do for you?"

The professor bit his lip and followed Gallo down the stairs. Joe and Leo began their questioning.

It turned out that a shady customer named Goldstein had given Mary Anne the .38 for protection. Another trick stole the gun from the young whore and passed it along to Bobby Joynt, who meant to kill McLean with it.

Leo and Joe saved Buddy McLean from Bobby Joynt, but they were only a couple of cops, not his guardian angels. One night just a few months later McLean was with "Suitcase" Fiddler's wife, Helen, and Tony "Blue" Agostino, coming out of Pal Joey's on Winter Hill, and Connie and Stevie Hughes jumped out of an alley between the nightclub and the Capitol Theatre. McLean bolted into the street, but they gunned him down, right there, in the middle of Broadway.

OFTEN, JOE McCAIN AND LEO PAPILE'S hard work and timeliness prevented such bloodshed. It was simple: people knew they could be trusted and would tell them things they might not tell other cops. An old neighbor of Joe's from Marshall Street, Peggy O'Malley, was never the prettiest girl on Winter Hill, but she was one of the nicest. Part of a hardworking, respectable family that lived on the top floor of a triple decker, O'Malley was rarely on the street after dark and limited her conversations with the young Joe McCain to what was polite and proper. But after having fallen out of touch for several years, McCain recognized the voice and the name when O'Malley telephoned him one night, stammering that her husband was in trouble.

She was married to an Armenian named Nazelian, a bailiff in the Essex County Courthouse, and the couple had two teenage sons. Apparently Nazelian had accepted $18,000 from a man seeking a court officer's job. The sum, which represented a year's pay for an officer of the court, was a "fixer's fee." In exchange, Nazelian promised to grease the man's application, a common practice in those days.

Nazelian kept the money but failed to deliver on his promise. The aspiring court officer took his complaint to mob kingpin Jerry Angiulo, the man he probably should've turned to in the first place. Angiulo said he would get the money back for a 50 percent fee and assigned the collection to his principal leg breaker and enforcer, a thug named Richard "the Pig" DeVincent. Six foot four and heavyset, DeVincent was a known shooter and intimidator, complete with the typical black, velvet-collared overcoat, homburg hat, and a big, smoldering cigar.

When the Pig appeared on the Nazelians' stoop demanding the $18,000, Peggy O'Malley's husband went rigid with fear. In a shaky voice Nazelian replied that he didn't have the money right then but would get it by the next day. DeVincent flung his cigar away and said he'd be back.

The phone calls started that night, hang-ups mostly, and a few that threatened to burn the house down and made pointed reference to O'Malley's children. Before the appointed hour, Nazelian ran off without saying where he was headed or when he would return. Peggy O'Malley was left to face DeVincent alone and when the Pig discovered that the money wasn't there, he flew into a rage.

"I'm coming back tonight and if it ain't here, I'm gonna stick dynamite up your ass," said the enforcer, gesturing to indicate the two teenagers, "and the kids' asses, and blow this fucking place up."

When Joe and Leo heard all this, they told O'Malley to tell DeVincent that her husband would meet him that night at the Red Coach Grille on the Lynn Fells Parkway at nine o'clock and that he'd have the money. With other cops watching the restaurant, DeVincent appeared but left immediately after figuring out that Nazelian wasn't there. He drove to a phone booth and called O'Malley, while Joe McCain listened on the extension. It was a brief conversation.

"Who the fuck do you think you are?" asked the Pig. "When I get my hands on you, I'll fucking kill you."

McCain had coached his old neighbor to insist it was a mix-up, and to tell DeVincent to come to the house: the money was all there, in an envelope, waiting for him. An hour later, when the Pig arrived, the Nazelians' lights were off and the shades were drawn. The street was empty and quiet, and emerging from his car, DeVincent strode up the front walk and pulled at the bell.

O'Malley answered the door. "Come in," she said. "I have the money."

"You better fucking have it," he said, brushing past her.

"It's right in there," O'Malley said.

Off the main foyer a single lamp illuminated the dining room, and there on the polished oak table was an envelope filled with hundred-dollar bills. Spotting the cash, DeVincent crossed the hall and as prearranged, O'Malley went straight through the house and out the back door.

There were two entrances to the dining room; Joe was hidden behind one door and Leo the other. The Pig walked into the room without so much as a glance to either side and as he reached for the envelope, Joe stepped out from behind him, cocked his pistol and rested the muzzle against the back of DeVincent's head.

"So long, Richie," he said.

Suddenly, there was a hissing sound, and the powerful stench of urine filled the room: DeVincent had pissed himself. Leo came out from behind the other door, his gun raised, laughing. "You're not such a big shot now, are you?" asked Papile, bending the mobster's arms behind his back to apply the handcuffs. "The big o.c. guy. A fucking pussy."

The Pig wasn't carrying a gun, but he had a small, incriminating slip of paper that represented the marker for the debt. While patting him down, Leo also discovered a leather cigar pouch in DeVincent's coat pocket. Inside the pouch were two giant Cubans, and Leo held them up where Joe could see them.

"Joe, what does Red Auerbach do when the Celtics win a big game?" asked Papile.

McCain shrugged his shoulders. "Has a cigar?"

"Here, Joe," said Leo, handing him one of the Cubans. "Light up a victory cigar. The best fuckin' pinch we ever made."

Richard DeVincent was convicted of extortion and received eight to twelve years in prison. Up on Winter Hill several years later, in front of a used car lot owned by two disgraced MDC cops, Joe McCain was driving the cement mixer for Boston Sand & Gravel when he spotted Richie the Pig on the sidewalk. Barreling toward him, McCain inched the great heavy bulk of the mixer over to that side of the road. Closer and closer to DeVincent, looming high above the street, Joe down-shifted and laughed to himself. At the last instant he nudged the massive tonnage of the cement mixer, its tires as high as a man's head, to where a slice of cheese wouldn't have fit between his bumper and the back of DeVincent's shoes.

Watching in his mirrors and snickering, Joe saw DeVincent throw his arms up like a bullfighter and then sprawl forward, onto the hood of his car. Joe kept going up and over Winter Hill, feeling justified that, for all the harm DeVincent had caused Peggy O'Malley's two sons by barging into their home, he could've dragged the Pig's body halfway to Lechmere Station.

That wasn't the last time Joe saw Richie the Pig. While in private practice, McCain investigated a homosexual murder in Everett, and the information he gathered was useful in clearing DeVincent's son in the crime. (The younger DeVincent later died of AIDS.) In 1990 Joe attended the wake of a heroin-addled young woman, the daughter of a former Met cop. Passing through the funeral home, McCain encountered several ex-cops, and out of respect for the deceased, he made small talk with his former colleagues, then turned to leave.

"Hey, Joe," called a man's voice. McCain looked back as he went out the door: it was Richard DeVincent.

Joe stuck his hands in his pockets; he didn't have a gun. His and Leo's testimony against DeVincent more than fifteen years earlier had been brutal, and from what he'd heard, the Pig had returned to his old ways since getting out of Walpole. Lines of sweat began running down Joe's back as he stood on the green-carpeted stairs, and the Pig descended toward him. It was dark on the street and the two men were alone.

By now DeVincent was right on top of him, and Joe squared his shoulders. "What do you want?" he asked.

DeVincent extended his hand. "I want to thank you for helping out my son," he said, shaking Joe's hand.

"Your son?"

DeVincent nodded, looking at the ground. "Over in Everett . . ."

"Oh yeah, right," said Joe.

Extricating himself from the handshake, Joe made another vacant remark and walked away under the giant elm trees that overhung the sidewalk, relieved that DeVincent had nothing more in mind.

A short while later Richie the Pig was murdered, and they draped his body over a little granite monument in Medford Square; he died the way he had lived. But that night, as he'd groped in his pockets watching Richie come toward him in the dark, Joe McCain realized it wasn't his gun he was missing the most. It was Leo.

For despite his reputation as a guy who got things done, in his own way, on his own terms, Joe McCain knew he was only as good as the people he surrounded himself with.

And some of these people were a little shady.

NINE

Slow Walking

A MAN'S REPUTATION IS A FUNNY THING, built out of the little things like a house is made brick by brick as much as by the cornerstone. Over time, a name and a face get associated with words and actions until, in the end, the very idea of that man's life is surrounded by an imposing edifice, good, bad, or indifferent, that can never be altered. Right now the uproar surrounding Joe McCain, Jr., and his suspension from the Somerville P.D. and the trash-pulling incident and all of Joey's idiosyncrasies and peccadilloes are coming together to determine his image and how he'll be remembered.

Not so his father. Because of his handy fists and kind heart, not to mention the sheer number of big cases he tackled and solved, Joe Sr.'s reputation is already tinted with the sorts of hues attached to icons like Santa Claus and John Wayne, figures he was often compared to. And this spring, when Joe McCain's name goes on the memorial to slain police officers in Washington, D.C., the true depth, breadth, and color of his life will be established once and for all.

But the most definitive way to gauge big Joe's reputation is not through the testimonials of other cops or district attorneys or through the recollections of family and friends. To really understand the measure of his influence, you have to hear from the guys on the other side of the street. The hustlers, gangsters, check kiters, con men, and thieves who dealt with Joe McCain every day knew just what kind of man he was.

Now in his early sixties, Black Jimmy is the sort of anonymous fellow you might see hanging around the pari-mutuel window at the dog track. Average height, slender of build, dressed in jeans, sneakers, and sweat-shirts, Black Jimmy, a Lebanese Catholic who grew up poor in Boston's South End, is so called because of his olive complexion and his dark hair, which is salted with gray. Known for his fast, nervous patter, Black Jimmy always has an angle, is always edging closer to the score that's going to get him off the treadmill of busted trifectas and petty cons. And you probably will see him at the track, since in his declining years the harmless-looking handicapper makes his living there, following the 'hounds from Massachusetts to Florida to Colorado and back again.

Black Jimmy goes all the way back to the start of Joe McCain's career as a Met detective. He covered the spectrum of being an informant, doing all he could to keep himself out of jail by dropping a dime on somebody else. And he had balls, since more than one of the guys Black Jimmy put the finger on were mobsters who knew the dope on them was coming from somewhere and would just start killing off the likely suspects until they got the right one. So on a rainy night just after Christmas 1969, it was with considerable trepidation that Black Jimmy donned his favorite sport coat and headed out to meet James Vincent "the Bear" Flemmi at a Jamaica Plain nightspot called the Pond Café.

At that time, the shifting roster of the Winter Hill gang was comprised of the Bear, his brother Stephen "the Rifleman" Flemmi, Howie Winter, James "Whitey" Bulger, and Joseph "the Animal" Barboza, along with the usual motley assortment of strong arms and collectors. Loosely organized and reckless even for mobsters, they were all "graduates" of Walpole State Prison, where most of them had served time in the early sixties. By the decade's midpoint, the Winter Hill gang had a piece of the loan sharking, gambling, prostitution, drug trade, and truck hijacking from Somerville to Mattapan, but the North End Mafiosi Jerry and Donato Angiulo had a lot more, and the Flemmis coveted it.

Jimmy "the Bear" Flemmi was flamboyant, outgoing, and crazy; even the Angiulos, who employed a string of contract killers themselves, were scared to death of him. Law enforcement officials, including Joe McCain, estimated that the Bear had committed as many as thirty murders, often brutalizing the corpses beyond recognition. In one case that bore Flemmi's imprint, McCain and Leo Papile helped to fish a body out of the Muddy River near the *Boston Globe* offices on Morrissey Boulevard. The corpse, which had been deposited in the ocean, eventually floated down through Quincy and lodged itself in a narrow canal. The killer, or killers, had shot the man in the chest, obscuring his identity by cutting off the victim's head and arms, and burying a hatchet in his torso to hide the bullet wound.

It was well known that the Bear liked to chop 'em up, that he loved guns and knives and hatchets. At one time he had owned a butcher shop on Dudley Street.

Black Jimmy had done four and a half years in Walpole State Prison while James Flemmi was serving a much longer sentence for aggravated assault. They were both local guys, and to a degree, the young con artist had a rapport with Flemmi. But the Bear, a stocky, balding man who weighed over two hundred pounds, was the type that could smile at you one minute and stab you the next. One day in prison Black Jimmy was talking to another inmate named Jimmy O'Toole, a tough son of a bitch who had shot and wounded Flemmi on the outside, and the Bear followed Black Jimmy to his cell. "If you ever talk to that motherfucker again I'll kill you," Flemmi said. Then he asked Black Jimmy if he knew a fellow named John Murray. Jimmy did; he and Murray were friends. "I killed John Murray," said the Bear, with a smirk. "And then I cut his fuckin' head off."

When Black Jimmy got out of Walpole and was assembling his crew and working out a new con, the Bear allowed him to do business, for old times' sake. The con was running like a dream, and Black Jimmy was cruising around town in a brand-new Buick convertible, brown with a cream leather interior, the same car driven by one of the leading wiseguys in the Winter Hill mob. But Jimmy's new Electra raised suspicions; what exactly was he doing to be doing well enough to afford such a sweet ride? The Winter Hill gang was roaming all over in those days, extracting penalties from crooks of every description as a form of tribute. Whatever Black Jimmy's game was, the Bear wanted a percentage.

Jimmy's game, which he had just about perfected, was called slow walking. It was the culmination of several lesser schemes: a sleight-of-hand activity known as shortchanging, a vacuum cleaner scam, and a two-man operation called the wedding ring con. To make the game work, Black Jimmy had pieced together a reliable crew of actors that included his childhood pal from the South End, Billy Dennett; Al Forzese, who sang in a rock band that played the Combat Zone; a degenerate gambler known as the Cowboy, who Black Jimmy met in a Denver card game; and a light-complected Irishman from West Roxbury, James O'Grady, who was referred to as White Jimmy.

White Jimmy taught his counterparts how to 'loid a door, using the thin edge of a plastic card to pry open a lock—his favorite tool was a prayer card from the Mission Church imprinted with the slogan "Never Give Up." He also said that, if the boys were casing for jewels and there were four mailboxes, Shaughnessy, Shapiro, Goldman, and Sullivan, "go for the Jews, 'cause the Irishman, he's got nothin'."

As their cons grew more elaborate, demanding a larger ensemble, Black Jimmy occasionally invited a jewel thief named Richie Carney to participate. A charming, handsome fellow, Carney talked like a Harvard grad and was the son of the Massachusetts Port Authority director. But one day on Storrow Drive he surprised Black Jimmy when he was unable to read a street sign. Although possessing a genius IQ and as well-dressed as a Back Bay stockbroker, Richie Carney was illiterate.

In the classic version of the slow walk game, the actors would rent a room and install a pair of telephones—one for incoming calls and one for outgoing. Using the yellow pages, Black Jimmy would call up a string of bars, identifying himself as "Al, the UPS guy," and when he got the owner or manager on the line, he'd say, "You still interested in that TV?"

"Huh? What TV is that?"

Parlaying the bar owner's initial confusion ("Is this Joe? Oh, I'm sorry, I thought it was Joe. We talked about this last week") into an offer to buy televisions far below cost, Black Jimmy would suggest that he drop by with more information. A short while later he'd show up, dressed in the brown shirt and trousers of a UPS driver, equipped with a full-color brochure from Sears.

"Check these model numbers out," Black Jimmy would say, explaining that Sears had received an overshipment and he knew someone inside who would sell the TVs straight from the loading dock, complete with store receipt and warranties. "The guy wants five hundred apiece for these eighteen-hundred-dollar models."

As the sucker perused the brochure, Jimmy would add, "Grab seven or eight and we'll give you one for nothing. You can sell 'em to your friends for eight hundred, make yourself a little profit."

The game preyed on the sucker's greed. As soon as a guy said "No shit?" and began scheming out loud to sell himself ten or twelve or sixteen televisions, Black Jimmy knew he had one on the line. All the bar owner had to do was consolidate a few orders, Jimmy said, and he stood to make well over a thousand dollars.

Once the sucker was hooked, Black Jimmy would make arrangements to meet him in a Sears parking lot. Deals were cash only, he'd say, and the selected mall would usually require a drive of twenty or thirty miles, to ensure the sucker's commitment. The sucker was instructed to tell no one: Al the UPS guy and his buddy at Sears would lose their jobs if anyone found out.

In the Sears parking lot, the sucker would meet Billy Dennett, a chubby, jocular man who told dirty jokes and was an expert at closing the deal. It was a psychological game, what Black Jimmy referred to as "dress up," wigs and horn-rimmed spectacles with ordinary glass in them and a prop as basic as a shipper's vest. All Billy Dennett had to do was slip on that flimsy gray vest with "Sears" embroidered on it, stick a pencil behind his ear and a clipboard under his arm, and he became the Shipper, master of the loading dock.

White Jimmy, a trim, narrow-shouldered fellow who dressed like Johnny Carson, usually played the part of the store manager. One time he went into a bar at the North Shore Mall to get the cash from a couple of suckers, and an hour and a half later he hadn't returned, which worried the other guys. So Black Jimmy crept into the mall and up to the bar entrance just in time to see a table loaded with five suckers, all of them drunk, regaling White Jimmy with "For He's a Jolly Good Fellow." When O'Grady came out, the two Jimmies rode off with an extra eighteen hundred dollars.

When Black Jimmy brought Dennett and White Jimmy in, he revealed the secret to making the game work: go for the kill right away, before the sucker could change his mind. In the mall parking lot, Billy Dennett would hand over an invoice for the TVs, take the envelope filled with cash, and tell the sucker to meet him around back. Dennett promised to stamp the invoice paid when the man picked up his TVs on the loading dock, just like a regular transaction.

The sucker got in his car or pickup truck, eager to see his new televisions. And Black Jimmy and Billy Dennett walked off in different directions; moments later, they reunited in a far corner of the lot, jumped in a beautiful brand-new convertible with cream leather interior, and zoomed away, counting the sucker's money.

Dennett coined the term slow walking after an old con where he followed half a block behind the mailman, clipping the welfare checks. The idea was to avoid rushing the play by talking or walking too fast, keeping it cool and natural to put the sucker at ease. One time Dennett and Black Jimmy sent a rookie, a twenty-year-old kid who wasn't too bright, to collect the envelope. From a parked car they watched the kid approach the sucker with a flurry of nervous tics. When the envelope came out, the kid grabbed it and sprinted across the parking lot and down the main road.

Dennett and Jimmy caught up to him and opened the door so the kid could jump in. "I got the money," he said, flourishing the envelope, his eyes glazed with adrenaline.

"What the fuck are you running for?" asked Dennett. "The name of the game is slow walking."

In the crudest form of the game, Black Jimmy might get away with a few grand. But what had attracted the Winter Hill gang's attention was the size and frequency of the hits Jimmy was making. Adding the Cowboy to the crew brought a whole new dimension to the con. He was a big man, six foot three and 230 pounds, with a size fourteen shoe. (Black Jimmy used to tell the Cowboy to tiptoe up on the suckers; his flapping feet would scare them away.) In the latest permutation of the slow walk, the Cowboy, dressed in suit and tie, would go into the electronics department at Sears and ask to see the manager. Hale and hearty, he would slap the man on the back and say that he represented the Ramada Inn and that it was the manager's lucky day: the chain wanted to buy fifty entertainment units for one of its hotels.

That's just great, the manager would say.

"Listen, I gotta couple of my people coming in this afternoon to finalize things," the Cowboy would say. "Let me borrow your office for a half hour." He'd explain that he needed a quiet place to fill out the paperwork.

Later that day, the Cowboy would lead a sucker into the mall. Somewhere along the way a bartender who had been slipped a hundred bucks would call out, "Hey, Bob, how's things over at Sears?" Farther along, the Cowboy would stop outside a boutique and tell the sucker, "Wait here a second. See that girl in there? I like her sister." Then, out of the sucker's earshot, he'd go inside the store, smile at the girl, say something funny, and ask her where Sears was. The salesgirl would laugh and point and the sucker would think that she and "Bob" were discussing her sister.

On a big hit, Al Forzese would be hanging around the men's wear department, dressed in a nice shirt and slacks and wearing a phony I.D. badge. He'd wink at the Cowboy and mention that he loved his new TV and wanted another one. See me later, the Cowboy would say.

The Cowboy and the sucker would walk into the manager's office, and there would be White Jimmy, who had slipped inside at the last moment. Posing as the manager in his well-tailored suit, White Jimmy would tell the sucker that he had some excess inventory and would be willing to make a nice side deal—he'd even throw in the warranties. Then White Jimmy would call Black Jimmy at a pay phone and pretend he was talking to the warehouse, and a few seconds later Billy Dennett would appear in his floppy gray shipper's vest and it would be all over. The sucker would hand over an envelope filled with ten, fifteen, twenty thousand dollars, and White Jimmy would tell him to drive around back and he'd get his television sets.

As soon as the sucker left, the crew would split up, head for the exits, and disappear. On a good day, they'd work a couple of hours and net up to five thousand dollars apiece. Everyone would go away happy, except the sucker. And he had very little recourse: he couldn't go to the police and say, "I was going to buy some stolen TVs that didn't exist and I got ripped off."

Black Jimmy was a student of human behavior, a genius really, and in a short time he and his crew were beating suckers for even larger amounts of money. One of their best scores came on the vacuum cleaner scam. White Jimmy, posing as a district manager for the Howard Johnson restaurant and hotel chain, approached the Kirby Vacuum Cleaner Company and said that HoJo's wanted to change their entire system over to Kirby's. In advance of this, White Jimmy had visited the coffee shop at the local HoJo's, got friendly with the waitresses, spread a little money around on tips, and told the staff that his name was Mr. Parker. When he returned to HoJo's with the Kirby salesman in tow, everyone knew and liked him, and the sucker had no trouble believing he was the manager.

Mr. Parker told the Kirby salesman that if his initial order panned out, he'd go through this dealership for a nationwide buy. To fill HoJo's order, which was a rush, the Kirby salesman collected fifty units and drove them over to Howard Johnson's in a company truck. Clad in overalls, Black Jimmy and the Cowboy unloaded the vacuums while White Jimmy took the salesman into the coffee shop. There "Mr. Parker" was greeted by name and treated to a bevy of smiles.

The two men sat down in a booth near the exit, and Mr. Parker asked one of the waitresses, a girl named Tammy, which items on the menu looked good that day. "Get whatever you want," said Mr. Parker to the salesman. "I'll take care of it."

So the Kirby salesman ordered a BLT with French fries and a chocolate frappe and Mr. Parker told him that he was a very smart man indeed as the HoJo frappes were excellent. Meanwhile, Black Jimmy and the Cowboy had finished loading the vacuums into their own truck and, by a prearranged signal, called White Jimmy in the coffee shop and had him paged.

"Mr. Parker, your office is on the line," said Tammy. "They want you to run up there."

Telling the Kirby salesman that he'd return in a minute, bringing the thirty-day purchase order with him, White Jimmy strode out of the restaurant. Shortly thereafter he and Black Jimmy and the Cowboy were on their way down the road with fifty vacuum cleaners. Later they heard that the sucker waited for a half hour before approaching the front desk to inquire about Mr. Parker.

"Who?" asked the clerk. "There's no Mr. Parker here."

The Kirby salesman began to cry, and the desk clerk phoned the Boston Police. When the cops arrived, one of them said, "You gave him a truckload of vacuums, wholesale value $450 apiece, and what'd he give you? Nothing." The cops thought it was hilarious.

As Black Jimmy expanded his group of cons, he realized that more players in the game meant more risks: Richie Carney had been drinking at a bar called the Forum in Kenmore Square, bragging about a score he had made, when the Bear caught wind of it. Flemmi wasn't sure how the con worked, but he knew Black Jimmy was running it. And there were rumors that Jimmy and Billy Dennett were giving information to the cops on the Flemmis and their associates to keep the heat off themselves.

The rumors about ratting on the Bear were true. The complicated rules that Black Jimmy lived by allowed him to ring up a score in one arena while informing on the dirty players in another. Meanwhile, Joe McCain, with his active stable of informants, pending arrests, grand jury testimonies, and Herculean caseload, was like the nous of Greek cosmology; he saw most of what Black Jimmy and his associates were doing but intervened only when necessary. Big Joe was willing to ignore the shady activities of bookmakers and con men if they helped him to pinch a violent criminal. His Marshall Street upbringing made him a realist: there were lesser evils and greater evils in the world, and greater and lesser goods. In police work, the greatest good was getting a shooter off the street. Therefore, turning someone like Barboza into an informant made no sense, as the best you could hope for was to trade a stone killer for another killer. On the other hand, Black Jimmy never hurt anyone and was often the source of up-to-the-minute information on the most dangerous crooks.

Black Jimmy and Joe McCain struck their first bargain when the thirty-year-old flimflam man, straight out of Walpole and still on probation, got in a beef over the wedding ring con. In that game, an actor would walk into a nice middle-class joint, hail the bartender, and say that his wife had lost a diamond ring there the night before. Again preying on the bartender's greed, the actor would offer a five-hundred-dollar reward for the safe return of the diamond, saying he'd come back the next day to see if anything had turned up.

A couple of hours later, the second actor would turn up with a paste diamond that looked like the real thing. Claiming he'd found the ring beneath one of the tables, the actor would feign surprise when he heard that there was a reward being offered. "Gee whiz, I could really use five hundred bucks, but I can't stick around," he'd say. "Tell you what, I'll split it with you. Give me two-fifty from the till, and when the reward comes in, you can keep it."

At $250 a whack, it was a pretty short con, but Black Jimmy got pinched on it anyway. Billy Dennett, who was already an informant, introduced him to McCain, and Joe fixed it: restitution of $250, charges dismissed, in exchange for Jimmy's promise to let Joe know if anything big was about to go down on Winter Hill. It was the beginning of a beautiful friendship.

THE NIGHT JAMES "THE BEAR" FLEMMI summoned him to the Pond Café, Black Jimmy had the feeling that something was going to go down, all right: him. Still, he kept his nerve and, with Richie Carney along for moral support, drove across town to erase Flemmi's concern that he might be an informant. It was raining hard, a fine, cold sleet that hung like wires in the sky above Jamaica Plain, when he parked the Buick across the street from the bar and he and Carney sprinted over with yesterday's racing form covering their heads. They stamped their feet on the mat and burst into the crowded, smoky club, shaking off their overcoats and scanning the room for the Bear.

Black Jimmy cursed himself for not bringing a gun—*ehh, not even the Bear would shoot someone in front of so many people.* But he felt his luck returning when another wiseguy said that Flemmi hadn't been there all night, and Jimmy signaled to Carney, who was up at the bar ordering a drink: let's go.

As soon as Black Jimmy and Carney stepped outside, Flemmi

appeared in front of them, dripping with rain. "Hey, where're you guys going?" he asked.

"Nowhere," said Jimmy.

"Gimme a ride to the Forum," the Bear said.

Black Jimmy didn't want to do it, but he had very little choice. If he wasn't talking to the cops—and he certainly wanted Flemmi to believe that—then there was no reason to carry a gun or refuse the Bear a lift. Playing suckers had taught him to maintain an easy, open demeanor, and never to tip his hand. But James "the Bear" Flemmi was no sucker.

Black Jimmy tossed his keys to Carney and got in the passenger side; if the shit went down, he figured he'd jump out of the car. The Bear ducked into the backseat and moved over directly behind Jimmy. Carney started the engine with a roar, and they drove off.

In the backseat Flemmi was uncharacteristically silent. But as Jimmy wondered what to do next, he heard two metallic clicks. Glancing back, he saw that the Bear held a silver-plated .32 down by his ankles and had drawn the extractor back, chambering a round. Jimmy leaped over the seat, clamping both hands over Flemmi's as they wrestled for the gun. Driving along May Street at thirty miles an hour, Richie Carney looked over his shoulder at the two combatants, unlatched the driver's side door, and jumped into the street and tumbled away.

The Buick careered along the shiny thoroughfare with no one at the wheel. Snarling and pumping his elbows, Black Jimmy braced his feet against the door and tried to wrest the pistol from Flemmi's grasp; the Bear leaned down and bit Jimmy's finger to the knuckle, and at that instant, the gun fired twice. One round lodged itself in Flemmi's right shoulder and the second bullet creased the top of his head and passed through the rear window. Then the Buick struck a parked car, jumped the curb, and piled into an oak tree, springing open the passenger side door.

Dazed, Black Jimmy climbed out of the backseat into the pouring rain. Flemmi groaned from inside the Electra, crawling over the floorboards as he searched for the gun. Taking a last look at his beautiful new car, its fender crumpled and steam whistling through the grille, Jimmy shed his tattered sport coat.

And he ran.

TEN

The Confidence Man

RAIN FELL FROM THE DARKENED SKY in a great pixilated mass. Dashing between two houses, Black Jimmy lost his right shoe, tripped, lurched like a drunken man, and kept on running; climbing over an alley fence, he tore his pant leg, jumped onto the cinders, and went limping in the direction of Hyde Park. He imagined that Jimmy Flemmi, bleeding from his wounds, was chasing him armed with guns, knives, and a hatchet. Stumbling along, he pictured the Bear driving his battered convertible, its headlights broken, searching for him block by block.

The streets were empty in the rain. Finally Black Jimmy turned into a more cramped neighborhood and ran into a tenement and began pounding on doors. "Help, I've been robbed," he said.

On the third floor a man wearing an undershirt opened his apartment door. Inside the man's wife and two young children were sitting in the shifting light of a television.

Gasping for air, Jimmy asked to use the telephone, and the man pointed to the kitchen. Black Jimmy pulled out a slip of paper and dialed the number that was printed on it and Joe McCain answered.

"Joe, someone's trying to kill me," Jimmy said. "Can you come and get me?" He covered the phone and asked the man's address. "I'm at eleven Paul Gore Street in Hyde Park."

McCain wanted to know what had happened, and who Black Jimmy had been with. "I can't talk on the phone," said Jimmy. "I don't want to scare these people."

Twenty minutes later, Joe McCain arrived at the tenement and then drove his passenger to the Holiday Inn across from Mass General. On the way Black Jimmy told McCain about his fight with the Bear and how Flemmi suspected that he was cooperating with the police.

"Why the hell did you go there?" McCain asked.

"I didn't want a guy like the Bear to think I was talking to the cops," said Black Jimmy.

McCain and a Secret Service agent named Dave Lee, who was investigating Flemmi on a counterfeiting charge, questioned Black Jimmy for over an hour. The con man had two options: either go into protective custody and testify against the Bear on attempted murder charges, or handle everything on his own.

Dry and warm and bolstered by a couple shots of whiskey, Black Jimmy began to speculate about going home; perhaps he could talk his way out of this and wouldn't need Joe McCain's help after all. He wondered aloud if Flemmi really had tried to kill him, or whether he had overreacted at the sight of a gun.

"I think I can square this away," said Jimmy. "Me and the Bear go way back."

Just to be sure, Joe McCain had four uniformed cops meet them outside the hotel, and accompanied by this escort, he and Dave Lee drove Black Jimmy to a phone booth near the Somerville incinerator. It was well after midnight when McCain put a "zinger" on the telephone and Jimmy called the Bear's number and asked whoever answered to have Flemmi call him back as soon as possible.

McCain and Black Jimmy waited on the corner of Joy Street in the rain. Twenty minutes later, the phone rang and Jimmy picked it up.

"You stupid motherfucker," said the Bear. "I'll cut your fuckin' head off."

Jimmy hung up, his face gone pale. McCain, who had been listening through a tiny earpiece, acted like nothing unusual had occurred. "Do you still think you can resolve this, Jimmy?" he asked.

Black Jimmy was ready to faint. "I'll testify," he said.

McCain winked at Dave Lee. "Are you sure, Jimmy? Because we'll drop you off, if you want."

"Stop fucking around, Joe," said Jimmy.

They stashed Jimmy in the hospital ward at the Charles Street jail, and then McCain and Lee arrested James Flemmi for attempted murder.

Three months later, Flemmi went to trial. Assistant District Attorney Jack Zalkind represented the government and Joe Balliro was Flemmi's defense lawyer. Balliro's strategy was to parade every known criminal to the stand, each of them swearing that he knew Black Jimmy and that Jimmy had been threatening to kill the Bear. At the very worst, Balliro argued, the incident in Jamaica Plain was a couple of tough guys who were trying to kill each other. In fact, James Flemmi had suffered the only real injuries in their fight—the bullet wound to the shoulder and a cut on his head. Balliro also noted that Black Jimmy had a criminal record, and that several "reliable" witnesses had stated Jimmy was going around that night with a gun in his belt saying, "Where's the Bear?" (This was so improbable that Balliro's comment drew snickers from the gallery, which contained a large number of mob types.) According to Balliro, James Vincent Flemmi was the victim here, not the perpetrator.

Zalkind argued that if Black Jimmy had been out Bear hunting as the defense had argued, he would have taken a bear gun, not a little bitty .32. Additionally, investigators had learned that Flemmi had gone to a man named Dr. Chin and had the bullet removed in exchange for a bundle of cash, the typical practice of North End wiseguys and not the action of an innocent victim. But in the end, it was Black Jimmy's testimony and dumb-as-a-fox Joe McCain who turned the tide for the prosecution. In reconstructing the struggle for the gun, big Joe reasoned that Black Jimmy's hand was on the outside—otherwise, Flemmi couldn't have bitten his finger, which would've been protected by the trigger guard. Therefore, it was Flemmi who had brandished the .32. With that, the government rested its case.

During a recess, Joe McCain and Dave Lee and Leo Papile and a bunch of other cops were milling about in the hallway. Across from them were Joe Balliro and Flemmi, who was out on bail throughout the trial. Glowering at McCain, the Bear said, "Oh yeah. Six-three-five-nine-three-nine-nine," reciting the McCains' home number. Joe went right after him. Havoc broke loose, as Papile grabbed McCain by the throat and two other cops helped pull him away from Flemmi. "Don't fuck with me," said McCain, pointing at the Bear.

The jury began deliberating that night, with a verdict expected in the morning. Black Jimmy remained locked up in protective custody. Throughout the trial, his wife had received telephone threats. That night Black Jimmy thought he saw the mobster Frank "Cadillac" Salemme outside the jail and refused to go near any windows, thinking Salemme was there to kill him. When Joe McCain heard about it, he visited Jimmy's wife to reassure her that she and Jimmy were receiving police protection and would continue to do so. Then McCain went over to the Charles Street jail, bringing sandwiches and coffee, and he and Jimmy sat and talked for hours.

During this conversation McCain learned that Black Jimmy had been on his own since the age of fifteen, just trying to get something going and starving half the time. The South End was like Skid Row in that era, not the tony enclave it is nowadays. Jimmy's father, who was a toy maker, died of tuberculosis when he was very young, and his mother was an alcoholic, shuttling in and out of psychiatric hospitals. Although he was shattered by his father's death, Jimmy's loyalty to his mother and retarded sister, Evelyn, kept him hustling for a couple of bucks to take home. On the street he made friends with a kid named Billy Dennett, whose father was a wino and who was even poorer than Jimmy. And he made the acquaintance of a Canadian heroin addict named Maxie, a kind of surrogate father who taught him how to shortchange.

Shortchanging is a small-time hustle that combines sleight of hand with a bit of mental confusion. In its simplest form, the hustler sandwiches a five-dollar bill in the middle of four ones. Approaching the sucker, he says that he needs a five-dollar bill to enclose in a birthday card for a little kid and hands over his money. The sucker hands back a five, then discovers that he's been given a five himself: he's now holding nine dollars and the hustler has his five. Gimme back the five, I got another dollar, says the hustler.

The hustler sends the sucker "back to school" by starting him off in a false count ("your four and my six is ten; gimme ten") and in the wink of an eye has handed all the money to the sucker and then taken it all back, for a net gain of five dollars. End of transaction.

Jimmy and Billy Dennett would start each morning by shortchanging the milkman, going on from there to hustle the grocers and butchers and florists when their shops opened up. For protection, they joined a local gang and ended up clashing with the blacks who were crossing over Mass. Ave. into the South End. The gangs fought with knives and garrison belts, and although Jimmy was only "the third or fourth toughest" in his outfit, he "could talk a little bit," and black activist Mel King recruited him in an attempt to make peace between the two races. On the stoop in the fifties, the higher up you were, the more seniority you had. The kid sitting on the top step was "the judge," and Jimmy was respected enough on both sides of Mass. Ave. that he was allowed to climb up to the black judge and shoot the shit for a few minutes.

Years later, Mel King's strength as a community leader and colorful bow ties would propel an unsuccessful but groundbreaking campaign for mayor of Boston. In the late fifties King was director of a neighborhood drop-in center called the South End House on Rutland Street. He coached the local baseball team, which included fifteen-year-old Black Jimmy at catcher, and the two met often to discuss what was going on in the neighborhood. A giant of a man who tilted his little car to one side when he drove along, King was "on the square," always true to his word, and would loan Black Jimmy small amounts of money. On occasion, Jimmy would shortchange King a few bucks, just to stay sharp.

But not even Mel King could keep Jimmy out of juvenile detention. He and Dennett went to jail for stealing cars, and for fighting. While they were locked up, they got stabbed a couple times and stabbed other kids. Out on probation that first time, Black Jimmy got his one and only legitimate job, working for a shoe manufacturer at seventy-five cents an hour. The crowded, smelly factory and low pay taught him a valuable lesson: only suckers work for a living. Soon he was shortchanging again, making a couple hundred bucks in just a few hours, out in the sunshine, talking to girls. "Everybody was a thief in them days," according to Black Jimmy. At least, everybody that he knew.

WHILE THE JURY PONDERED THE FATE of James Vincent Flemmi, Joe McCain sat in Black Jimmy's cell at the Charles Street jail, and the two men cemented a bond that would last for thirty years. It was a classic illustration of McCain's most valuable trait, the asset that more than anything else made him a cop's cop: his ability to empathize with people from all walks of life. Even the crooks loved him for it.

When the trial resumed the next day, James "the Bear" Flemmi was nowhere to be found. After several minutes of hubbub, his attorney informed the judge that his client had not appeared. Still, the jury was brought in and Flemmi was convicted in absentia of assault with intent to murder.

Joe McCain and the D.A. were elated; Black Jimmy was wary. With Flemmi on the loose, Black Jimmy was in serious danger, and McCain took Jimmy back to his house to strategize on their next move. Helen made corned beef sandwiches and coffee, and the two men sat in the kitchen all night talking about the case. To soothe Jimmy's fears, McCain recounted a conversation he had engaged in with his captain and the D.A., who were concerned about the expenses associated with protecting Joe's informant.

"We have a guy who testified against the commonwealth's biggest killer," said McCain. "Do you want me to abandon him, or would you always want me to be at his beck and call?"

And Joe McCain always was. The next morning, he rented a truck in his second cousin's name and loaded Black Jimmy and his wife and baby into the U-Haul, and followed them up Route 2 in his own car. He had arranged new identities for Jimmy and his wife: driver's licenses, social security numbers, a little bit of cash. And in the middle of the Concord rotary Joe McCain pretended to have engine trouble and stopped his car, backing up traffic while Black Jimmy drove off to start his new life.

ELEVEN

The Chief Gets His Hair Cut

A WEEK AFTER THEIR CHRISTMAS PARTY, I walk into the
Somerville police station and meet Timmy Doherty walking out.
It's payday and he's trussed into a camel-hair topcoat like the ones my
father wore when he sold insurance, and Doherty's tie and shirt collar
are pin-neat and he's had a fresh shave and shoeshine. His gaze veers
over to mine and there's a moment of recognition, and I stop and shake
his hand.

"Hi, Timmy. I—"

He smiles at me but his face is grim. "Not here," he says.

I glance around the empty concrete hall, adorned with the mayor's
portrait, an American flag, and the blue-and-white flag of the commonwealth. The only other person in sight is the woman in the reception
area, and she's behind several inches of bulletproof glass. Timmy Doherty's eyes are small and hard, steady on mine. "Never in here," he
says. From what I've heard, Doherty's harassment at work continues,
and he prefers to keep even the minutiae of his life private.

"I just want to wish you happy holidays."

"Yeah. Merry Christmas," says Doherty and goes out.

The woman behind the glass says that Joe McCain is expecting me and unlatches the door. "You know where to go," she says.

I cross behind the dispatch area and knock on the door to the division commander's office. As usual, Joe McCain sits in the near dark, his bald head shining like a mushroom. There's a big, heavy-faced cop with red hands opposite, and he gives a start when I come through the door.

"Jesus, I thought it was Caliguri," the cop says.

Apparently I bear a resemblance to Donald Caliguri, the ex-chief, a lean, stone-faced lawyer who was named in Doherty's whistle-blower's lawsuit and who, like me, favors a wardrobe of nylon wind pants and fleece sweatshirts. "You got the same old-fashioned haircut, too," says McCain.

"I prefer the term 'classic,' " I tell him.

"If you just walk around, ignoring anyone that says hello and treating them like pieces of shit, they'll all wonder why the old chief is here," says the other cop, laughing. He stands up, and he's about six and a half feet tall, with gold hash marks up the sleeve of his leather jacket. "All right, I better get back to traffic duty," he says. "High-level stuff."

Joey laughs and walks over to the door with him and asks E-911 operator Scott Lennon to order us some red chicken sandwiches from Lacascia's Bakery in Medford.

"I'm like your bitch," says Lennon, a self-professed music-and-movie freak. He and McCain are good friends and are looking forward to attending the Henry Rollins spoken word show next month at Avalon. The tall, amiable Lennon lives with his brother in his grandmother's old house and spends every cent he has adding to his collection of three thousands CDs and over four hundred DVDs. He's always reminding Joe McCain that without the "nonsense" in life we'd all go crazy.

During lunch we shut ourselves into the office. Joe plays a little Miles Davis on his MP3 player to muffle our conversation and with the lights down low, it's more like a cocktail lounge than the police station. When he first came on the job in 1988, Joe was assigned to a patrol car with a veteran cop who carried a list of things to do on a clipboard with the number "3,232" written on the bottom. The list varied every day and contained items like "pick up dry cleaning" and "return videos" and the number kept being reduced by one.

Joe asked his partner about it, and the man explained that any police officer worth a shit took care of his errands while on duty. "The chief never gets a haircut on his day off," said Joe's mentor, adding that the number on the bottom of the clipboard represented the number of days before he could retire.

Joey keeps his own retirement number in the back of his head somewhere. As much as he enjoys being a cop, in just a few years he'll have served his twenty. He'll buy a little place up north with a pool for the kids and teach history at a regional high school and play his drums every night. Nobody within two hundred miles will realize he was a cop or have the slightest interest in the contents of his trash.

In the bar the other night I didn't get the whole story on Vinnie Carbone and Johnny Barnhardt and the DEA surveillance, and today we're supposed to hash this over and come up with a little strategy to counter. Here's what happened: Vinnie Carbone got a call from a Nahant cop who overheard "four task force guys" talking in a hallway at the Lynn District Courthouse. "We like this Somerville cop as being a coke dealer, this Johnny Barnhardt," one of them said.

The task force guy also said that Barnhardt was a friend of a sergeant in Somerville named McCain. In turn, McCain was seen hanging around the North End with Vinnie Carbone, a former corrections officer who was arrested for steroids last June.

"That's their drug ring?" I ask Joe.

Joey nods, smoothing the edges of his mustache. "Look, this narcotics work ain't rocket science. You get some real morons in there," he says. "Let me tell you this: Johnny Barnhardt is getting divorced. If he's a drug dealer, he's the worst drug dealer in history. Drives an old shit-box. Can't keep his phone turned on."

I want to know how the DEA connected Joe and Carbone to Johnny Barnhardt, besides the fact that McCain and Barnhardt work together in Somerville.

Joey says the vendetta against Johnny Barnhardt arose out of an incident between Barnhardt and Jimmy Hyde's old partner, a cop named Richter. Last summer at a pool party where a bunch of cops drank beer and their families played in the water, Barnhardt scolded one of Richter's kids when a fracas broke out. Richter took offense at

Barnhardt singling out his kid, and angry words were exchanged. As Joe describes it, Richter took a swing at Barnhardt, a much younger man, and the ex-Marine punched Richter out.

"Made him look like a fool," says Joey. "For these idiots, that's enough."

In the dimness I notice a weird little object on Joe's desk. It looks like one of those hairy plastic trolls we used to collect as kids. But it's the disembodied head of a Barbie doll, complete with long, wavy yellow hair. Joe says that his wife made a joke about how stressed out he was and threw the doll into his cruiser just before he went out on patrol.

"Whenever you get upset, you can think about a little head," said Maureen.

Scott Lennon arrives with the sandwiches: broiled chicken coated in Ah-So sauce on warm, crusty Italian bread. Nobody eats like the cops.

"How is it?" asks Joey.

"It's great," I tell him. "Chicken basted in carcinogens."

Joe laughs. "Something's gotta kill you."

Joe McCain makes and takes phone calls with the frenetic industry of an AT&T operator. His eleven-year-old, Joseph, calls to finalize their last-minute Christmas shopping plans, and Joe confirms that right after work he and his three boys will ride the T into Harvard Square so they can pick up something for their mother and grandmother. A moment later Maureen calls, fretting over what to buy her mother-in-law, who lives downstairs and has everything she needs.

Joe is soothing. "Look at it like this: my father is easy to buy for this year. He's dead."

While Joe is talking to his wife, Mark Donahue's voice breaks in, using the intercom feature on his cell phone. "Hey, fuck nuts," he says. "Pick up."

Joe hangs up with Maureen and answers the intercom. "What do you want?" he asks.

Donahue is working a police detail up at Rockingham Mall in Salem, New Hampshire, part of the twenty-four hours he's worked in the last thirty, including two midnight-to-eight shifts in the cruiser. He's working another graveyard shift when the detail ends, taking him through to Christmas Eve day.

"Fucking new guy," says Joe. "I hope you get a sudden at seven-ten tomorrow morning and have to work all day."

"What's a 'sudden'?" I ask.

Donahue's voice crackles over the intercom: "A sudden death."

"Just as long as it isn't your sudden death, who gives a fuck," says Joey.

Donahue wants to know if Joe has gotten in touch with Billy Simpkins at the DEA. "That's a roger," Joey says.

Joe reached Simpkins, who is the number-two operations guy in the DEA, at Baltimore/Washington International Airport the morning after the Somerville P.D. Christmas party. Of Billy Simpkins, who acted as a pallbearer at Joe Sr.'s funeral, Joey says: "He's a tough, grizzled prick, and he cried like a baby. He loved my father."

Back in the 1980s, when Billy Simpkins was an up-and-coming DEA agent, he and big Joe worked on a number of big cases together. During one memorable escapade, they chased a Harvard-educated drug runner around Miami Beach in a taxicab, with Simpkins pretending to be the driver and McCain his fare. In front of the coke dealer's hotel, Simpkins made the cab overheat so big Joe could take some photographs without being noticed. The guy got away but crash-landed his plane at sea and died of an overdose when he tried to offload the coke and absorbed too much of it through his skin.

In their recent phone conversation, Joey impressed upon Simpkins that the Boston DEA guys think Jimmy Hyde "walks between the raindrops—that he can do no wrong."

"Hyde has all kinds of juice with these local feds," Joe said to Simpkins.

"Joe, he doesn't have any juice with me," Simpkins said.

Billy Simpkins proposed a meeting with the head of the Boston DEA office so McCain and his lawyer could go in and put their cards on the table. "They're a thousand miles off base," says Joe. In the meantime, he's been trying to find out if Jimmy Hyde has put in an overtime slip for the Lynn District Courthouse over the last couple of weeks. That would confirm his suspicion that Hyde was one of the "task force guys" Carbone's friend overheard talking about him.

"I may ride a fucking motorcycle and drink too much, but I'm the antithesis of a dope dealer," says Joe, recalling one of his father's favorite sayings, "I might be fat and my mother dresses me funny, but I'm not stupid."

Joe calls his lawyer Joe Doyle next, to discuss their meeting with the DEA. Playing devil's advocate, Doyle suggests that meeting with members of the task force might be like walking into a hornets' nest. For instance, what if Jimmy Hyde is there, saying that McCain is a scumbag? Doyle asks. The Boston DEA agent in charge works under Billy Simpkins but has, presumably, a close relationship with Hyde, who is attached to his office. What if it's all a setup? What if they've already briefed Simpkins and convinced him there's something there?

Joey holds the tiny cell phone in two fingers, but the veins in his forearm are popping out. His eyebrow flutters, and the muscles in his jaw are delineated into two vertical strips on each side.

"Bad guys knew which side my father was on, and they know which side I'm on," he says. "Does it mean that if Danny Rizzo went away for three and a half years, I can't go to the Ocean Reef and eat fish with him? Do I have to look over my shoulder every time I go to lunch? Does it mean that every time I see a bad guy on the street, I'm involved in bad things? I say prove it, or shut the fuck up."

TWELVE

Cold, Cold Heart

IGHT A.M. ON THE LAST DAY OF A PRETTY TOUGH YEAR, and Maureen McCain goes downstairs in the cold to answer the bell. Stomping his feet on the front porch is her husband's colleague Lieutenant Jimmy Paulito, dressed in uniform with his car running at the curb.

"Is he home?" asks Paulito.

Joe McCain has been out sick for five days with a miserable combination of the flu, chronic allergies, and a bout with his asthma. During a recent appointment Dr. Joel Blier of Medford told him, "You are allergic to everything inside the house and everything outside. You'd have to live in a bubble not to have problems."

"You want me to get him?" Maureen asks Paulito.

"No, just give him this," the lieutenant says. He hands Maureen an envelope printed with the city seal and beats it back to his car.

Amidst the post-Christmas clutter of toys, games, and frazzled decorations, the three McCain children are up, playing and fighting, as boys will do. Roused by the commotion, Joe lurches into the kitchen, hacking and coughing. Maureen puts on the kettle for tea, and her husband spies the envelope on the counter and tears it open.

SERGEANT MCCAIN:

Pursuant to M.G.L. c. 31, sections 41–45, you are hereby notified that you are suspended from the Somerville Police Department for a period of three (3) days, without pay. Your suspension shall occur on January 3, 4, and 5.

This suspension is a result of your conduct on December 18th, while out of work allegedly due to illness, you were at a liquor establishment (Tir na nOg) shortly after midnight and were observed by Captain John O'Connor drinking an alcoholic beverage (Guinness Stout). The following morning you remained out of work, again allegedly due to illness.

The letter cites Joey under Departmental Rules and Regulations Section G, Rule 8: "feigning an illness or injury." Captain John T. O'Connor has signed it.

Seeing the look on Joey's face, Maureen shepherds the kids into the other room to play with their new Xbox. Joe picks up the phone and calls his good friend Somerville Patrolman Mike Kennelly. "This is great, Joe," says Kennelly, who is known for his sense of irony. "You get the whole weekend off." In Kennelly's opinion, the suspension and the letter will help Joe build a case that certain elements in the department are arrayed against him. "Before it just looked like you were paranoid," he says. "Now everyone can see they *are* out to get you."

Joe McCain isn't surprised by this latest development. In a letter he wrote to Chief George McLean sent just before Christmas, he recounted being called into Captain O'Connor's office regarding his midnight appearance at the nOg a week earlier. In his explanation to O'Connor and subsequent letter to the chief, McCain stated that the bar staff at the pub was not answering the phone that night and he had driven there to ask "fellow musician Mr. Ronin Quinn" if they'd be playing a gig together the following Sunday. The restorative powers of Guinness notwithstanding, after a brief conversation with Quinn, Sergeant McCain reported back home, where his dutiful wife tucked him into bed.

John O'Connor happened to be the watch commander the night Jimmy Hyde reportedly beat up a handcuffed Michael Henderson inside the police station. In his whistle-blower's lawsuit, Timmy Doherty noted that O'Connor was the one person who could've prevented or stopped the beating, yet he did nothing and later ignored the harassment Doherty continues to endure. Of course, the McCains were on Doherty's side in that matter, and now O'Connor just happens to be snooping around the Tir na nOg after midnight and writes up Joe Jr. for having a glass of stout. This strange coincidence fails to make it into Joey's letter to the chief, as there is no official policy relative to "ball busting."

Joey notes in his letter that the department is filled with "the sick, the lame and the lazy"—officers who falsify illnesses and stay out for years at a time. Before this bout with asthma, Joe McCain had taken fewer than ten days of sick time in three years, according to departmental records. Clearly, he does not fall into the lazy category.

Joey does have three written reprimands in his jacket, all related to a single incident. A letter dated November 16, 1998, from then–Night Commander Captain George McLean details a "snake incident" that occurred while Joe was on patrol. A citizen who reported that his pet boa constrictor was on the loose had called an officer to a downtown residence. The patrolman summoned the animal control officer, and while he was waiting made sarcastic comments about the snake and its owner over the radio.

Back at the police station, Lieutenant Dave Damron came over the radio and ordered the patrolman to "lift the hook"—stop transmitting over the radio and call the station on the telephone. At that moment, Sergeant Joe McCain, who was also out in a patrol car, called over his radio, "189 to 184. Yeah, just let the commander know, we can go back to shoot the snake, if he would like that."

In a triumph of administrative hairsplitting, Joe was cited as being negligent for not admonishing the other officer, which was his duty as street supervisor that night, and for his wisecrack. In fact, his bosses found three separate rules violations in Joe's brief radio call. Over fifteen years of street-level police work, these are the only written reprimands on McCain's record—far below the average for such a proactive cop.

On the other hand, his jacket contains eleven letters of commendation, from his superiors in the department, other city employees, and citizens—for helping to free hostages, for recovering stolen property, and for speaking to youth groups on his days off, among other things.

An hour after receiving O'Connor's letter, Joey is ensconced in his personal command center and music studio in his basement. Two worn leather sofas face each other, connected by a wall filled with old vinyl albums and CDs, the top portion of which is adorned with black-and-white photographs of Joe Sr. in his double-breasted Met uniform. Beside those is a portrait of Joe Jr., bare-chested and holding his then-infant son Joseph, who is swaddled in an American flag. Tattooed across Joey's upper chest is the Gaelic phrase *An te is laidre*, "Stronger Than All."

Joey crumples up O'Connor's letter and tosses it on the floor. "My dad would say, 'You're not a police officer until you've been suspended,'" he says. "If you're a do-nothing, you never get in any trouble."

Vocalist Norah Jones is crooning one of her ballads from the stereo when Joe's mother comes laboring down the stairs. Helen McCain is dressed in blue jeans and a nautical-looking striped sweater, her ash-blond hair done up in a careful, swirling permanent. The retired nurse, sixty-six, moves slowly, but her advice to her only child is swift and pointed: "Don't be an instigator," she says. "You're out three days' pay."

Joe nods. "They hit me in the pocket," he says.

After stooping to pick up a guitar magazine that has fallen on the floor, Helen grasps her lower back when she straightens up. "I'll be happy when you can retire," she says.

"That's why I'm going back to school," says Joe, who'll be taking two graduate courses in history at UMass Boston. "Five more years and I can retire."

The basement is a zigzagging warren filled with Joe's computer, two drum kits, extra cymbals, a keyboard, guitars and guitar cases, and a clutter of cables, microphones, amps, and speakers—all of it presided over by a picture of John Coltrane. The night before, Joe had jammed on his trumpet for two hours, accompanied by his eight-year-old son, Liam, on bass guitar and eleven-year-old Joseph on drums. Helen McCain lives directly above this makeshift recording studio, equipped, no doubt, with the forbearance of a saint.

"I never say anything I don't want repeated," she says, starting back up the stairs. "That's what I get for living with a detective all those years."

When his mother closes the door to her apartment, Joey sits on the sofa with his head tilted back, listening to Jones's cover of Hank Williams's "Cold, Cold Heart." He smiles at the observation that a lot more effort has gone into drafting his suspension letter than the chief's "investigation" into the trash-pulling incident.

"I pushed, so the dark side pushed back," says Joe. "This is just the beginning."

Norah Jones is singing in a pure, sweet, mellow tone, her voice flowing along like one of the instruments in the ensemble. Joey mentions that Jones's father is the sitar master and Beatles collaborator Ravi Shankar. The story goes that the lovely, dark-haired Jones was "discovered" waitressing in New York, where she occasionally sang with the house band. McCain says that Jones changed her name so that she could make it on her own.

But escaping a famous father is not so easy, as Joe Jr. well knows. In his initial discussion with superior officers over the Guinness-at-midnight incident, Joey says, Captain O'Connor accused him of being one of those "unaccountable and protected" members of the department that Joey disdains. O'Connor went on to accuse McCain of disappearing for hours at a time while on duty as street supervisor. When Joe pressed him on the source of this information, O'Connor said, "This is the rumor" and "It's what people in the department tell me." O'Connor also stated that up until now McCain has gotten away with such behavior because of his "reputation"—a veiled reference to Joe Sr.

Seen in a certain grim light, Joe's three-day suspension for such a minor offense could be a signal that big Joe's reach does not extend beyond the grave.

"What would your father think of all this, if he was alive?" I ask.

"If my father was alive, none of this would've happened," says Joe. "They wouldn't have the balls." He erupts in a deep, rattling cough, which he muffles with his sleeve. "They're gonna try and fire me. They build up suspensions and reprimands, and then they fire you and make you fight to get your job back."

THIRTEEN

We Don't Need No Stinkin' Badges

M ARK DONAHUE AND I ARE DRIVING through the snow-crowded streets of downtown Lawrence, a gritty old mill town adjacent to the New Hampshire border, past La Vecina Meat Market and Tienda Elegante and Loan USA. It's fifteen degrees, typical for January, and plumes of exhaust are curling up from the cars inching along Common Street, while the low arc of the sun illuminates the empty dooryards and alleyways. Leaning over the street is the brick edifice of the old district courthouse, its central entrance up a steep flight of stairs flanked by street-level doors on the left and right. We're headed for the Essex County Sheriff's Office.

When I first met Donahue we were coaching youth hockey and his stories about detective work were filled with cocksure wiseguys and their jailhouse revelations, with high-stakes defense lawyers sweating out strategy, and complicated pretexts that often transformed McCain operatives into latter-day Marlon Brandos with their Stanislavskian posing. It was exciting stuff, Donahue told me, and I'd be getting in on the ground floor, "delving into things" like Joe McCain himself. They always had a bunch of great cases.

When mobster Johnny Peru was up on two counts of first-degree murder, his lawyer hired McCain Investigations, and Joe Sr. sent Donahue to Peru's "office" to interview his associates about any other recent troubles they might've had with the law. Mark was excited; it was his first mob case.

Peru's office was a little pizza joint in Medford, decorated in old wood paneling with pictures of Frank Sinatra and Tony Bennett on the wall. Inside, Donahue sat at a table with three young criminals, including a slick-haired tough named Bobby "Wannabe Gotti" Santasky.

As soon as they were settled, Santasky opened a menu, shot a look around the table, and asked, "Whattaya want? Whattaya gonna eat?" and immediately the other two soldiers looked at each other and at Donahue and repeated, "Whattaya gonna eat? Whattaya want?"

All other parties took up their menus, and Santasky said, "Whattaya want, Mark? You wanna square?"

The other two wiseguys nudged each other and asked, "You wanna square? You gonna have a square?"

An Irish kid from Somerville, Mark was dumbfounded. "What's a 'square'?"

"What's a square?" asked Santasky, incredulous. He looked around the table. "What's a square, he wants to know."

"What's a square?" repeated the other two wiseguys.

The answer to the riddle hung in the garlic-scented air for a moment, and Santasky said, "It's a fuckin' pizza."

"Yeah, I'll have a square," Donahue said.

"Whattaya want, a salad with that? You wanna salad? A salad. Whattaya gonna have to drink? A Coke? Gonna have a Coke?"

Their lunch order finally resolved, Donahue asked Santasky to sketch out his background, including any past or pending legal action that might come up at Johnny Peru's trial and affect Santasky's credibility. The aspiring mobster explained that he had a job setting up events at the Fleet Center and was doing good. Pressed on that subject, he admitted, "Well, I'm kinda fired right now, I'm not working."

"Why?" asked Donahue.

"I stabbed a guy," said Santasky, his face tightening like a fist. "But he fucking deserved it."

"I'm thinking to myself, Oh, that's all right, then. No problem. He deserved it," recalled Donahue.

A few months later Johnny Peru was found guilty of murder, sentenced to life in prison without parole, and Mark Donahue ran into Bobby Santasky on the street in Medford. The young mobster was walking his pit bull and, spotting him from a distance, Mark caught Bobby's eye and they acknowledged each other. Then Bobby screwed up his face and shrugged his shoulders in that universal expression of "What happened?" and Mark did the same. A second later, Santasky twisted his mouth in the other direction and held out his hands, palms up, as if to say "Whattaya gonna do?" and Mark reciprocated in pantomime. Then both men continued on their way.

A year later Bobby Santasky was dead, shot in the head at close range by an unknown assailant.

My initiation into the detective business is not quite so dramatic. Stuffed between the front seats of Mark Donahue's car are thirteen active case files, including the names, addresses, occupations, and credit reports for what might be termed "voluntarily missing persons." In each of the folders is an "interlocutory orders on injunction for return of vehicle," stripping the delinquent car loan recipient of his ownership and assigning it to a fair-sized local bank. Today, Mark and I are working for the bank. We're repo men.

We're out looking for twenty-nine-year-old Denny Dexteris of Rowley, who borrowed the money for a $30,000 truck, made half a dozen payments, then dropped out of sight. The address on Dexteris's loan application turned out to be false, his most recent employer and girlfriend haven't seen him in weeks, and his only known family member is an uncooperative stepfather whom Donahue has visited twice.

On the second visit to the stepfather's auto body shop, Mark had informed him that the sheriffs were going to get involved soon and would begin haunting his business. "Hold on a minute," said the man, reaching for his wallet. He opened it up, revealing a small tin badge issued to him as the local harbormaster. "I'm in law enforcement, just so you know. I know all about the law."

Donahue won that skirmish by producing his policeman's shield. "Good, I am, too. Now we're both on the same page," he said. "Where's your stepson? If he doesn't turn up soon, he's going to have warrants on him."

Trying a new tack, the stepfather insisted that Dexteris was out to sea, working on a tugboat.

"He doesn't need a truck in the ocean," Mark says to me as we walk toward the courthouse. As a last resort, we're here to turn over the order repossessing Dexteris's welding truck to the county sheriff. "He's at the end of the line," Mark says.

Mark Donahue is a pretty big guy and his black fleece sweatshirt, embroidered with "Salem Police" in silver letters, has a visible effect on just about everyone we meet. Two youths in tight ski caps and bulky jackets are smoking cigarettes outside, leaning on a door that says "Probation Department." They move aside and we go up the gritty steps, down a windowless hallway, and knock on a frosted glass door. From inside we hear a voice, and a tall, hulking, gray-haired man with a thick gray mustache emerges and invites us into his office. The chief deputy wears a shirt and tie, and his walls are covered in photographs taken with the sheriff, the governor, and former Boston Celtics great Larry Bird.

Mark hands the deputy his business card and explains who we're working for and summarizes the predicament of Denny Dexteris. "The bank figures if we find him, we find the truck," says Mark. "We just can't find him." Dexteris is a welder, and the truck is an F-450 with the toolboxes on the back. "He needs it for work," Mark says.

Looking over the paperwork, the chief deputy recalls that there's a Bobby Dexteris from Rowley who works as a plumber for the sheriff's department. "Gotta be a relation," he says.

"Small world," says Donahue. He winks at me.

We all stand up and shake hands. "We'll hit Bobby Dexteris, see if we can turn him that way," the chief deputy says.

A couple minutes later, we're driving through downtown Lawrence, over the ice-clogged Merrimack River, up the long, curving ramp by the gasworks and north on Route 495. We're headed up the coast to Newburyport, with an injunction for a dark blue Dodge four-by-four. This time there's a fixed address, and an out-of-work carpenter who hangs up every time the bank calls him on the phone.

Newburyport is half an hour away and to pass the time, Mark tells me about his early days at McCain Investigations. He was attending UMass Boston after getting out of the Coast Guard in 1987 and was trying to make ends meet by working as a bouncer at a Faneuil Hall nightclub and living in Lynn, Mass., with his girlfriend, Maureen, who he would marry a couple of years later. A close childhood friend of Joey McCain's and surrogate son to big Joe, Mark had always known that Joe wanted to open a P.I. firm when he retired. In the fall of 1988, just months after he'd been gunned down in Hyde Park, Joe told Mark to come work for him. "He said there was a ton of money to be made," Mark says. "Joe was still ripped open when he started the business. He wore a girdle to hold his guts in. He couldn't even stay in the office a full day."

Mark started out part-time, investigating fraudulent workmen's compensation claims, "bottom of the barrel, shit work." By January he was full-time, at the less than gaudy annual salary of $19,900. After a few months of steady improvement, he was given his first big assignment, a police brutality case being handled by the longtime McCain family retainer, Attorney Joe Doyle.

"The first case I ever fucked up," Mark says.

The facts indicated that Doyle's client, a young car thief, had snapped a brand-new Z28 from the Car-A-Torium in Billerica, Mass. Spotted within a mile of the dealership, the thief led a parade of cops from Tewksbury, Lowell, Wilmington, Billerica, and the Andover State Police barracks on a high-speed midnight chase that attracted a dozen cruisers and covered over ten miles. At the conclusion of this adventure, the Z28 jumped the curb, went airborne, and landed on a stone wall. The kid pushed open the door and tried to flee, but the cops ran him down.

The thief ended up with nine broken bones in his face, including his nose, jaw, and both cheekbones. The cops said he injured his face on the windshield during the crash. The kid said the cops beat him up. "They beat the living fuck out of him," says Mark. "Even a car thief didn't deserve that."

Witnesses stated that there was no damage to the Z28's windshield—

indicating the thief did not break his own nose. The trouble was, after just one day in the tow yard, the car disappeared. Detectives from Mc-Cain Investigations were sent to look for it.

As we approach Newburyport, Mark pauses in his tale. The Chain Bridge is closed for winter repairs, and we must detour through the lower end of Salisbury Beach, past the tidal flats and the small, brightly painted stores, their signs mounted on two-wheelers proclaiming "Totally Nude Dancing" and "We Have Seaworms." Over the Route I bridge we descend the ramp into Newburyport, a posh little town composed of old sea captains' homes and various boutiques and restaurants arranged along State Street. We are armed with a book of New England street maps, and I plot a course through the tangled downtown streets while Mark drives. Two blocks, and we enter a working-class neighborhood of two- and three-family homes clustered on a narrow street overlooking the old port and the delta of the Merrimack. Because of their proximity to the ocean, even these rickety saltboxes are worth a pretty penny.

Mark slows down, peering at the house numbers and the various trucks parked along the street. "There it is," he says, pulling in behind a new-looking Dodge four-by-four. The bed is piled high with snow.

This is my first "door knock," and I'm a little queasy when we step out of the car. Mark is six foot three and he's a cop, but I don't have a badge or a gun or a court order; I'm hiding behind my sunglasses. As we approach the house, Mark imparts a little wisdom acquired from Joe McCain, advice that has stood him in good stead over the fifteen years he's been rapping on doors.

"It's all about your demeanor," he says. "The guy might have a machete, or it might be a Ph.D. with a pipe. You read your situation and you react to it. Grovel. Play dumb. Be forceful. Whatever it is."

"How do you know?" I ask.

"You have to think on your feet," he says. "Peek inside. Does he have a picture of Bobby Orr on the wall, or JFK? Connect with that. Joe always broke the ice with his grandchildren, to get the guy talking. 'I'm everybody's grampa,' he used to say."

We turn in at the gate and go up the walk, and I feel totally unequipped for the task at hand. It's a funny feeling, like being twelve years old again and out in the woods with seventh-grade beauty Cheryl LaPlante and afraid to kiss her.

We're looking for a guy named Paul Browning, who has taken a very hard line with the bank's collection officer, yelling about his lawyer on those rare occasions that he's remained on the phone long enough to utter an intelligible remark. Glancing at the weather-beaten clapboards and the dead, snow-strangled geraniums in the window boxes, I'm expecting a large, raving, whiskey-soaked lunatic with forearms the size of championship salmon.

Mark rings the bell. A moment later the door opens to reveal a small, chunky man in stained gray sweats. He has a sallow, indoor complexion and lank brown hair, and is wearing an old pair of socks with a hole in the big toe of his right foot. Behind him in the entranceway is a lopsided piano, the keyboard deep in unopened mail, all of it bills.

"Paul Browning?" asks Mark, handing the man his business card. Browning nods, blinking in the sunlight.

Inside the house is dark, smelling of mothballs and paint thinner. "What do you want?" Browning asks, his gaze shifting from Mark to me and then back again. I feel ridiculous.

"You're in default on your car loan," Mark says. "Three months in arrears."

Browning insists that his check for two of those three payments cleared the day before, and that the third payment is now only twenty-four hours late. "The bank has been royal ball-busters about this," he says. "I'm seriously thinking about suing them. They're discussing my credit with third parties, and that's clearly illegal."

He says that his carpentry business is foundering, and his only income at present is the rent he collects from the other half of his two-family. Mark is diplomatic, commiserating about the lousy economy. While we stand on the front stoop, he produces his cell phone and speed-dials Ray, the collections officer at the bank. Browning recoils like he's a vampire and Donahue has just produced a crucifix.

"I'm just trying to work things out," Mark says.

Crossing his arms over his chest, Browning says, "I refuse to talk to anyone from the bank."

Donahue acts as go-between, relaying information from the bank to the offending creditor. Once he fell three months behind, Mark explains to Browning, the double payment was inadequate to remove the flag on his loan. Now Browning is on the hook for the full amount and has to pay it all right away, even if the truck is repossessed and sold at auction. It's a discomfiting aspect of contracts law that the bank could win a judgment for, say, $12,000, and Browning would be deprived of the truck yet required to pay back the entire amount or never get another car loan.

"Oh," he says, eyes downcast.

When Mark tries once more to get him on the phone with the bank, or give us a postdated check for his late payment, Browning retreats behind his threat of a lawsuit, and the glum admission that he does not have the money.

Mark wishes him luck, and we head off down the walkway. Arriving at the car, he says, "Deadbeat. We'll be back with the tow truck."

We're going to Taunton next, an hour and a half to the south. This is the grunt work at a P.I. firm, the stuff that keeps the lights turned on and the office heated. Out on 495, huge embankments of snow are folded back from the shoulder, the woods and fields stretching away to the horizon on either side. The highway is flecked with bits of sand and salt, metallic blue in the sunlight, and as we cruise along in the center lane, Mark resumes his story of the car thief and police brutality case. In the course of their investigation, he and Joe McCain learned from Attorney Doyle that the Car-A-Torium in Billerica had suffered a large number of car thefts, all of them Z28s and Camaros. It had gotten so bad that the dealer had created a separate fenced-in area for his "muscle cars," but the larceny continued.

With Joe Doyle's help, McCain Investigations was able to determine that an employee of the dealership was having new keys made and leaving the doors unlocked and extra ignition keys beneath the floor mats of the designated cars. That employee's identity became crucial to the police brutality case.

McCain instructed Donahue to set up an appointment with the auto dealer's head of security. Donahue was told to offer the dealer a trade: produce the Z28 from the police chase, which they'd heard via the rumor mill had been sent from the tow yard to the dealership for repairs, and McCain Investigations would tell the head of security who the inside guy was.

"We'll all get what we need," said Donahue.

The head of security was a muscular, dark-haired fellow named Chuck Rossevetti, and the meeting was held in an airless little room overlooking the sales yard. Outside, row after row of new cars were lined up, their gleaming snouts pointed toward the street. After hearing the offer, Rossevetti left the office for a few minutes. "I can't find it," he said, when he got back.

"Who has it?" Donahue asked.

"We don't know where it is. It got picked up."

Donahue returned the next day to try again and Rossevetti asked why he wanted to see that particular Z28. "Look, give us the Z and we'll tell you how they're stealing the cars," he said.

"I already have that," said Rossevetti.

Donahue felt he was bluffing. "I have the person's name, the scam, their chop shop," he said. "You'll look like a fucking hero."

"I have to go talk to corporate legal," said Rossevetti and left the office again. A few minutes later, he came back and said, "Legal says they can't find the car right now, but if you want to tell us who the inside person is, that would be great."

"Let me tell you something," said Donahue, taking a gamble. "The car is part of a police brutality case. The cops beat up the kid pretty bad and we want to inspect the interior to check out their story that he was hurt in the wreck."

Rossevetti stood up. "I was a cop for six years. I would never 'do' a fellow cop that way," he said. "Get out."

Suddenly, Rossevetti's intransigence and unpleasantness made a lot more sense: he knew the cops had beat up the car thief and, as an ex-cop, was helping them hide the Z28 with the undamaged windshield.

"It was all my fault—I told him the truth," Mark recalls.

"I don't need an ambulance-chasing, lowlife P.I. coming in here to tell me who's stealing cars off my lot," Rossevetti said.

Holding onto the negotiation by a very slender thread, Donahue let it go. "Talk about lowlife, you work in a fucking car dealership," he said.

"Get the fuck out of here," said Rossevetti.

Driving away from the Car-A-Torium, Donahue called Joe McCain to give him the news. McCain dialed in Joe Doyle the lawyer and Donahue explained what had happened.

"You sent this rookie, and he fucked up my case," said Doyle, blowing a fuse. "You better get to the bottom of this, McCain, and call me back."

Doyle hung up. In the years since the shooting, Joe McCain's hypoglycemia had grown worse, and so had his mood swings. Mark expected a barrage of insults from his boss and mentor, but there was only silence on the line.

"Hello?" said Mark.

"Yeah, I'm here," said McCain in a quiet voice. "Just come back in and we'll talk about it."

Mark chuckles at the recollection. "I thought Joe was gonna kill me," he says. "But he knew it was his mistake in sending me there."

Back at the office, Mark explained to Joe that he thought the dealership would want to nab the car thief and find out the truth. "You thought what you thought," said McCain. "You gotta do what you're told, and you weren't told to say a goddamned thing about police brutality." When Mark mentioned Rossevetti's six-year career in law enforcement, Joe let out a snort. "He didn't last very long," said McCain. "He couldn't have been much of a cop."

Arriving in Taunton, Mark and I use the street map to locate the residence of Eugene F. Rearborne, who has defaulted on his loan for an Isuzu Trooper. The Rearborne home is a modest, brown-shingled ranch on a quiet street. American flags line the walk, fluttering in the breeze, and Mark and I pass two small concrete angels when we go up and knock on the door. There's a dusting of snow on the driveway marked by tire tracks running down from the garage and the house is dark. No one answers the door.

"Let's try where he works," says Mark.

Back on the highway to Weymouth, and a small industrial park beside the Expressway. On the drive Mark uses his cell phone to call Rearborne's employer and when the receptionist pages him over the intercom, Donahue hangs up.

"Okay, he's there," Mark says.

In the case file is a description of the vehicle—a new gray, four-door Isuzu Trooper—and a blurry, third-generation photocopy of Eugene Rearborne's driver's license. It's barely a smudge, like looking at a Rorschach, but I see his squat, oval head, the shape of a compressed bowling ball, and the staring skull holes of his eyes. Then Donahue tells me that I'm going to work this one. I gaze out the window at the industrial wreckage that lines the southern approach to Boston and wonder just what I'll say to Eugene Rearborne.

Rearborne's occupation is "shipping and receiving," and as we cruise through the lot of the small manufacturing company where he works, Donahue spots a gray SUV parked on the slanted drive in front of the loading dock. "Bingo," he says.

Mark drives around to the side of the building and parks in the deep well of shade, out of sight. The company is housed in a boxlike, corrugated metal shed, and this part of the building is windowless. Mark speed-dials Ray, the bank collections officer, and reaches across and opens my door.

"Go get the VIN [the vehicle identification number]," he says. "Make sure we've got the right car."

I get out and stand by the car. "Where should I look?"

Donahue points to a little metal strip on the driver's side dash. "Right here," he says. "All I need are the last five numbers. One-oh-nine-seven-seven."

I shut the car door, and the concussion booms across the empty lot. Apparently most of the workers are at lunch. As I cross the snowy strip of lawn, there's a moment when I'm conscious of the absolute nullity of my experience as a detective. My heart starts to beat more rapidly.

The front of the building is deserted. I walk around the hood of the car and lean over the appropriate spot in the windshield, trying to look casual. My eyes scan back and forth, up and down. The only printed material is a little plastic strip that says "air bag."

It feels like I've been standing there for an hour. Without anything to report, I retrace my footprints to where Mark is waiting, a huge grin on his face. He rolls down his window and gives me a thumbs-up, and I decant my own thumb downward.

"What happened?" he asks.

"I can't find it."

Donahue laughs. He reaches outside the car and runs his fingers up and down the vertical edge of the driver's side windshield. "Sometimes it's etched on a little plate right along here," he says.

"Okay." I linger by the car for a moment. "What do I say if he comes out?"

"Have a pretext," says Mark, rolling up his window against the cold.

On the way to the truck I realize that I've forgotten the sequence of numbers but decide not to go back and get them. I figure on seeing what's there and sneaking a look at the file upon my return, so Mark doesn't know how stupid I am. The pretext is another concern. What am I going to say? *Nice truck, how much are you asking? My sister has the same thing. How do you like it? I work around the corner and was walking by and thought, What a great-looking truck. . . .*

If Eugene Rearborne comes out, it's going to take all my resolve not to just shriek and run away. What do I care if he owes the bank money? In the time before caller I.D., when they used to hound me about my student loan, I would lie and say I wasn't home. Everybody does it.

The truck is still there, like an insult. Again I study the edge of the windshield all around, feeling very conspicuous, then move along the driver's side window. Suddenly a critical piece of evidence presents itself, and I retreat over the battered lawn.

"It's a Mitsubishi," I tell Donahue.

"Wrong car," he says, with a shrug. "It happens. How'd that feel?"

I climb in, exhaling a long breath. "Like I was about to receive the opening kickoff in the Super Bowl. The pretext had me all screwed up. I was gonna ask him how much he paid for it, and then realized that wasn't such a good idea."

"He's probably at lunch. Let's go get something to eat," says Mark. "Then we'll come back."

As I've seen time and again, nobody eats lunch like cops from Somerville. Within minutes I'm enjoying a piece of haddock at a faux country tavern a short distance from the industrial park. Mark feels sorry for me and picks up the check.

When we return to the manufacturing company, there are several more cars in the lot but no Isuzu Trooper. Figuring that Rearborne's wife drives the Trooper and he's got some old beater for commuting to Weymouth, Mark decides to visit the front desk and have Mr. Rearborne paged. Because, in the end, the bank doesn't want the car, they want the money.

The "lobby" is just a space containing a worn sofa and coffee table scattered with old magazines, located at the foot of a very steep staircase. The receptionist peers over the railing from above and asks our business, and Mark climbs partway up the stairs and extends his arm, handing the woman a business card printed only with his name and a cell phone number.

"We'd like to speak to Eugene Rearborne, please," he says.

The woman tells us to have a seat and a moment later pages Rearborne over the intercom. Based on the indistinct license photo, I am expecting some kind of war criminal, but in reality Eugene F. Rearborne is a small, porcine fellow in his late fifties, with gray bristles atop his head and the gray, sagging skin of a heavy smoker. He descends the stairs, looks Mark up and down, and glances over at me.

"What's this about?" asks Rearborne.

The receptionist is staring at us from above. "Let's go outside," says Mark.

The temperature is dropping, and our conversation makes little white clouds that stream away from us on the wintry air. Donahue explains that we represent the bank and have an order to repossess Rearborne's car. We've come to talk it over with him to save the indignity of having the vehicle towed away in front of his co-workers or neighbors.

"I'm seeing my lawyer at three o'clock," says Rearborne. "The dealership forged my signature on some papers and that's illegal. My beef is with the dealership."

But his loan is with the bank, Donahue reminds him. Basically, Rearborne has two choices: give up the vehicle or pay off his arrears. His dispute with the car dealership is a separate, civil matter. "I want to talk to you about the repossession order," Mark says. "You're going to fuck up your credit."

He goes on to tell Rearborne that he could still win a judgment from the dealership in the amount of the loan that he could keep, after the payments are made or the vehicle is turned over to the bank.

Mr. Rearborne is not hostile or angry. Mostly he's just embarrassed, and I am embarrassed for him. Private detectives are rarely, if ever, called in when someone is having a run of good luck.

"I'm not giving anybody a hard time," says Rearborne. "If my lawyer tells me to give up the car when I meet with him today, I'll leave it in my driveway for you."

Mark is satisfied with that. He shakes Rearborne's hand, and then I shake the guy's hand and he goes back to work and we head for our car, stamping our feet against the paving stones and flapping our arms to stay warm.

"I feel bad for the guy," I tell Mark as we're driving away.

"That's why I took him outside," says Donahue. "He's a nine-to-fiver. He's got a house, a family. He's not like that bullshitter on the tugboat."

I shake my head. "Everybody's got a lawyer these days. Everybody's suing somebody."

Mark holds the car at the intersection, watching the traffic roll past. "Yeah, it's all fuckin' lawyers," he says.

FOURTEEN

The Gentleman from Milton

The law is whatever is plausibly asserted and vigorously maintained.
— MONTAIGNE

SOMERVILLE CITY HALL IS A THREE-STORY Georgian brick building perched atop the apex of Highland Avenue. Its windows are framed in peeling white woodwork and two huge Doric columns flank the entrance. Packed into his uniform, bald head sporting a fresh shave, Joe McCain, Jr., occupies a good bit of the lobby, cracking his knuckles and occasionally reaching up to snip at a cuticle with his sharp white teeth. In a room on the second floor, McCain's longtime attorney, Joe Doyle, is about to sit down with an impartial hearing officer, police union representatives, the chief, Captain O'Connor, and the mayor for a hearing on Joey's three-day suspension.

Doyle and McCain are asserting that the discipline far exceeds the seriousness of the offense—being seen briefly at the Tir na nOg on a night that Joe had called in sick—and are asking that his lost wages be restored and the infraction expunged from his record.

"Disappear for a while," McCain says to me. "We'll meet you outside in thirty minutes."

An hour and a half later, McCain and his lawyer emerge from city hall. Joe Doyle is a bantamweight Teddy Roosevelt of a man, with little round glasses and a head of curly brown hair tinged with gray. He's dressed in polished black wingtips and a blue oxford shirt with a striped tie and a khaki L.L. Bean jacket. The wind is coming off Boston Harbor and, finding an aperture between city hall and the high school, chilling every passerby to the bone. Immediately upon coming outside, Doyle and McCain are joined on the frozen stone of the parking lot by another man in a pinstriped suit, who turns up the collar of his overcoat. Union rep Charlie Femino is a lawyer and police officer, yet he and Joe McCain do little more than smile as Doyle summarizes what just occurred.

"When we left the room and all four of the remaining participants stayed inside—the mayor, the chief, O'Connor, and the 'impartial hearing officer'—the city was meeting ex parte," says Doyle. "That's bullshit."

Doyle explains that a judicial proceeding is ex parte when it is held at the instance of, or for the benefit of, one party only and without notice to, or contested by, any person adversely affected.

"It's a fucking kangaroo court," says McCain, nodding his head.

The union attorney is busy scribbling everything Joe Doyle says on a yellow legal pad. "This is great stuff," he says. "Thanks, Joe."

Doyle's inference is that the city is concerned far less with their sick time policy than with applying it selectively to punish someone who, for whatever reason, has fallen out of favor. At one time Joe McCain, Jr., acted as personal security and driver for the mayor; today he's in the parking lot with two lawyers while illegal meetings are being held to figure out how to screw him.

In a two-year-old management study of the Somerville Police Department conducted by MMA Consulting Group, Inc., of Boston, the first page of the executive summary includes the following sentences: "There are many statements and presentations of details which may be viewed as uncomplimentary." Elaborating on the reasons for that, the report goes on, "The Somerville Police Department does not make the best use of available resources, resulting in the under-utilization of personnel, poor or limited supervision, lack of management controls, and decreased operational efficiency." In light of the charge against

Joe Jr., the most surprising fact in the management study is that, although abuse of the department's liberal sick time policy is widespread, "we are aware of only one member of the department who has been penalized, or even charged, with improper use of sick time in recent memory."

It's a short march from these facts to Attorney Doyle's assertion that the city is attempting to keelhaul Joe Jr. for the questionable offense of drinking a pint of Guinness.

Like many of big Joe's old cronies, here in the courthouse parking lot Doyle begins our acquaintance with the spontaneous rendering of a vintage McCain story. It seems that one night Joe Sr., his longtime Met partner Jack Crowley, and Doyle were drinking at the Parker House while a live band was crashing away beside the dance floor. The downstairs lounge was packed and big Joe, wearing an old raincoat with cigar burns on the collar, was drinking Scotch and leaning over the raw bar to maintain his conversation with the bartender. Crowley and Doyle, fueled by ample drafts of liquor, began stealing clams from the bar and surreptitiously pitching them into the crowd. The shells were bouncing off tables and onto various patrons, creating quite a ruckus.

Unconscious of all this, McCain was busy chattering away when Doyle and Crowley struck upon the notion of loading additional raw clams into the pockets of Joe's coat. They were in the process of doing so when a little redheaded fellow wearing a business suit approached, his face tight with anger.

"Are you throwing those fuckin' clams?" the guy asked Joe. The top of his head didn't reach McCain's shoulder, and Joe had to look for him when he turned around.

"What?" asked McCain.

The man held up the smooth gray shell of a cherrystone. "Are you the one throwing the clams?" he asked.

McCain put his hand on top of the guy's head and shoved him away from the bar. "What are you talking about?" he asked. "Get out of here."

The night raged to its drunken conclusion and Joe went home and hung up his raincoat and forgot about it. The weather grew sunny and warm and several days later, when the stench of the tidal flats had crept into her well-maintained home, Helen McCain paced from room to room saying, "*Joe*, what is that smell?"

Doyle howls in the retelling, one hand on my forearm, the other on Joe Jr.'s shoulder, his head thrown back and all his teeth displayed. A graduate of Thayer Academy, Holy Cross, and the Cornell University Law School, the fifty-three-year-old Doyle and his eighty-year-old father and namesake share a private practice with eight other lawyers in Quincy, Mass. But his relationship with big Joe stretches back to 1976, when as a young assistant district attorney Joe Doyle was assigned to the Suffolk County Investigation and Prosecution Project, or SCIPP, as it was known. SCIPP was a federally funded group that combined state prosecutors, police officers, and investigators focused on rooting out organized crime and public corruption.

"We were supposed to initiate cases," says Doyle, who in his first weeks at SCIPP met a large, imposing man with an abundance of good street information—a fellow nicknamed "the Silver Fox" because of his thick white hair.

Twenty-six-year-old Joe Doyle was fresh out of law school and in those days a lot of veteran investigators considered their dealings with young, inexperienced D.A.s to be an inconvenience at best and, more often, a real pain in the ass. But Joe McCain had a deep admiration for book learning and respected the young lawyers, going so far as to reveal the identities of his informants to them.

"If Joe trusted you, he'd tell you who they were—so you wouldn't think he was just making the stuff up," says Doyle.

And it didn't take long for the trust between Joe McCain and the young, green D.A. to pay off in a big case. Through his longtime informant Black Jimmy, McCain learned that a nineteen-year-old secretary named Deborah Brody, who worked at New England Universal Life Insurance Company, had taken up with a lowlife named Michael Spinelli. In her position at the insurance company, Miss Brody had access to the facsimile signature machine and stole a batch of checks at the urging of her boyfriend, who had a criminal record and was married and lived in Revere with his wife and children. Spinelli's accomplice,

Richard Knight, was an experienced fence who knew the ins and outs of getting the checks cashed—he sold them to other criminals for a percentage of their face value.

Black Jimmy told Joe McCain that $40,000 found among contraband in the possession of career criminal Ernie Field had come from a stolen New England Universal Life check. This information was so fresh that the investigators at SCIPP were on to the scam before the insurance company had discovered it, and they decided to catch the perpetrators in the act of stealing checks. Big Joe always made it a point to ingratiate himself with people he arrested—out of his natural sense of empathy and with an eye toward having them provide information. Years earlier he had done it with Black Jimmy, and upon the arrest of Deborah Brody, Joe persuaded the slender young blonde to cooperate in the investigation and testify against her Svengali of a boyfriend, Spinelli, and his accomplice. Brody agreed to make a monitored telephone call asking Spinelli to meet her at a particular place and time. When he appeared, the police arrested him. At the same time Knight was apprehended at a house in Medford, whereupon the police obtained a search warrant for the premises and discovered the remaining stolen checks.

Knight and Spinelli were indicted, and Joe Doyle was chosen as prosecutor, with the Honorable Superior Court Justice Roger Donahue presiding. As the government's key witness, Deborah Brody was granted immunity, situated in a hotel under an assumed name, and placed under round-the-clock police guard. Meanwhile, the two crooks retained two old-time Boston defense lawyers, Al DeFelice and Ron Rosenthal. An elderly man with dyed black hair, DeFelice never entered a courtroom without his Marine Corps tie clip, making it a point to tell jurors that he'd fought at Iwo Jima. Rosenthal, also in his late sixties, wanted the jury to believe that he was a helpless old guy down to his last nickel and so would appear in court rumpled and unshaven and dressed like a hobo. His favorite accessory was a hospital bracelet, worn to garner sympathy over his "condition," which forever remained a mystery.

The case was tried in the old Suffolk Superior Courthouse in Boston's Pemberton Square, a boxy, high-ceilinged room accoutered with mahogany wainscoting and a tall, paneled judge's bench straight out of the previous century. From this aerie, Judge Donahue looked down upon the stenographer and a pair of court officers. Directly back of that was the prosecutor's table, staffed by Assistant District Attorney Joseph Doyle and his lead investigator, Joe McCain.

Behind them and exactly parallel was the defense table, close enough for Al DeFelice to whisper things like "We're gonna wipe the floor with you" to the inexperienced Doyle. And at the rear of the courtroom, separated by the bar from the spectators' area, was the defendants' dock—a waist-high wooden box where Spinelli and Knight were required to sit. The jury occupied a box to Judge Donahue's right.

Before Deborah Brody's appearance on the stand, Joe McCain noticed that the defense had moved their table closer to the jury box, and every so often DeFelice would turn and mouth "What a liar" to the jurors. Joe Doyle was busy trying to watch Rosenthal's cross-examination of the police officer who had arrested Michael Spinelli. The cop was fumbling through his testimony and Doyle became irritated with McCain, who was elbowing him and whispering something about DeFelice.

"Look what they're doing back there," said McCain. "Jack Gaffney would never let them get away with that. What kind of lawyer are you?"

"Shut the fuck up, Joe," Doyle said. "Leave me alone."

Finally McCain alerted the court officers to Rosenthal and DeFelice's gambit, and they picked up the defense table and moved it back again.

Deborah Brody took the stand and shortly thereafter court was adjourned, with her direct testimony to continue the next day. Sometime during the night, Brody slipped her police guard and disappeared. Very early the next morning she telephoned McCain to confess that she'd spent the night in a Revere hotel room with Spinelli, where they'd had sex and he had tried to convince her that he'd had nothing to do with the check kiting scheme—it was all Richard Knight's idea.

McCain was dumbfounded. Brody added that she intended to tell the truth in court that day, and that she'd informed Spinelli of that fact. She also confided the reason Spinelli had been able to sneak away to spend the night with her. Armed with that surprising bit of information, McCain hung up and drove to the office to break the news to Joe Doyle.

Just before 10:00 A.M., the judge left his chambers to retrieve a law book and was astonished to find the two elderly defense lawyers again trying to edge their heavy wooden table closer to the jury box. Roger Donahue had a reputation as a stern, competent jurist, with little tolerance for courtroom high jinks or melodrama. Upon spotting DeFelice and Rosenthal, he called over to his team of court officers and barked, "Make sure those two guys move that table back. And if they try it again, I'm going to lock them both up."

At the same time Joe Doyle took Rosenthal and DeFelice aside to tell them what had occurred the night before—the skip out, the sex, everything. Although the news was disastrous to their case, the wily old litigators walked away without uttering a word.

When testimony resumed, Brody admitted to Doyle that she had met Spinelli on the previous evening, that they'd had intercourse, and that he had attempted to persuade her to lie about his role in the case. She said she'd refused to lie, and when Doyle asked her how the defendant, who was free on bail, was able to get away from his family, the young blonde replied that Spinelli's wife was in the hospital giving birth to their child. A female juror gasped out loud, and Doyle stated that he had no more questions.

Just the fact that Deborah Brody needed police protection indicated to the jury that Knight and Spinelli were dangerous men. Additionally, Brody's testimony proved Spinelli was a man totally devoid of character. But Rosenthal and DeFelice, with their Marine Corps tie clips and hospital bracelets and strategically placed bandages, still had a few hoary old tricks up their wrinkled shirtsleeves.

Among the evidence against their clients was a handwritten list of the stolen checks, including the amounts tendered, who was going to fence them, and where they were going to be cashed. To prove that the handwriting on this ledger belonged to Michael Spinelli, the D.A.'s office engaged Elizabeth McCarthy, the dean of New England handwriting experts but by this time quite advanced in years and, because of a recent hip operation, hobbling around with a cane. McCarthy had concluded that the handwriting on the ledger was in fact Spinelli's, and to demonstrate this fact the prosecution had created two large easels in sight of the jury box, one displaying the "unknown" handwriting and the other containing the sample Judge Donahue had ordered Spinelli to give.

In an attempt to try Elizabeth McCarthy's patience, Al DeFelice kept asking her to go over from the stand to the writing samples to justify how she could have mistaken some loop or slant in the unknown handwriting for Michael Spinelli's distinct cursive. The witness box was elevated by two stairs and no sooner had the elderly woman climbed up to her seat when the heartless old defense lawyer would require her to go stumping back to the easels. The tactic backfired: McCarthy's patience remained intact, but the jurors were aghast at DeFelice's cavalier treatment of the white-haired old woman.

As the trial stretched into its third day, Joe Doyle grew apprehensive about one of the very few weak spots in his case. Somewhere in Joe McCain's affidavit that had led to the search warrant was a misstatement of fact, and Doyle knew Rosenthal and DeFelice were going to harp on that error. He spent several hours with Joe McCain preparing for his testimony, and when they reached that particular detail the young D.A. advised big Joe to admit he'd made a mistake. Cops in that era would go to great lengths to avoid such an admission, because it made them look inferior to the lawyers on both sides and because they reasoned that such foibles might undermine an otherwise solid case. And here the twenty-six-year-old Joe Doyle, with a sum total of two cases under his belt, was instructing a prestigious veteran investigator on what to say in court. McCain had an abundance of pride in his reputation and his skills, and Doyle knew it was going to be very difficult for him to admit that he'd screwed up. So when he left the D.A.'s office late that night, there was still some question in Joe Doyle's mind about what was going to happen in court the next day.

When testimony resumed, Doyle watched as Joe McCain was called to the stand. In his affidavit McCain had provided the wrong date for an observation he had made that was probable cause for the search warrants in the case. McCain said that Spinelli and Knight had moved certain items from one place to another on April 11, when the events had actually occurred on April 2. In addition to the affidavit, DeFelice had Joe McCain's police report for April 11, and there was no mention of the observation noted in it; the account was recorded in McCain's April

2 report instead. The implication was that McCain had made it all up to acquire the warrant and perhaps even plant the stolen checks. In essence, DeFelice was going to argue that Joe McCain was a liar.

Doyle could sense DeFelice building up to that crucial section of the affidavit. "Now, Mr. McCain, please turn your attention to paragraph fifteen of your affidavit," said the defense lawyer.

"You mean where I made a mistake?" McCain asked. "The mistake I made was that in the affidavit I said that I observed these things on April eleventh and I observed them on April second."

Joe McCain's answer—honest and unexpected—was in keeping with the directness of his personality and his ulterior motive as a detective. "Joe was never bigger than the case," said Doyle. "That was the beauty of the guy."

Al DeFelice stumbled along with a few more questions, but the trial was over. In the end, the jury found Michael Spinelli and Richard Knight guilty of bank fraud, and Judge Donahue gave them the maximum sentence of eight to ten years in the state penitentiary.

Joe McCain and Joe Doyle remained good friends long after the SCIPP unit was history. Their mutual respect grew out of experiences like the Brody case, and twenty-seven years later that respect continues to inform Joe Doyle's relationship with the McCain family and tints the advice he gives Joe Jr. with a paternal forbearance. There are ten thousand Irish lawyers in the Boston phone book, but whenever Joe McCain, Jr., is in a pinch, like he is now, he calls on Joe Doyle.

"He's not like these guys coming out of Suffolk, or New England School of Law. He's Cornell. Joe's a smart fucking guy," says McCain, as Doyle climbs into his eight-year-old Mercedes and takes off down Highland Avenue.

Joey and I get in the front seat of his cruiser, and he starts the engine up with a roar. Doyle's "got a lot of street attitude and street influence, and I'd bet he'd say he got a lot of that from my father," says McCain.

Joey and I are listening to Charlie Parker on National Public Radio, and here at noon, the sun is low and bright, tracking its arc across the Boston skyline. Driving alongside the raised Expressway, we cross the Charles River and enter a tiny parking area behind the Museum of Science that says "Police Vehicles Only." As we turn in, smokestacks on the far bank of the river send up plumes of exhaust and cars whiz past us on Storrow Drive.

The Lower Basin is tucked in a small, dirty space beneath the old T bridge and a concrete abutment engraved with "1910." Beside the short driveway there's an incongruous pair of tennis courts, but those belong to the public park next door. I start to open my door, but Joe Jr. thrusts his arm across my chest. "Wait here," he says.

An American flag, a Massachusetts state flag, and a black POW flag are flying above the barred windows of the station's lower half. Gray-and-blue State Police cruisers, grimed with salt from the highway, are nosed right up to the building where a bright yellow candy machine and two juice dispensers flank the heavy steel entrance door. A young trooper in his jodhpurs and glossy boots emerges from the door and glances over at me without expression, leans into his car for a packet of papers, and returns inside. There's no sign marking this place, no plant-strewn lobby for visitors. And inside, fifty-four-year-old State Trooper Christopher Brighton remains anonymous himself.

I've heard rumors that Brighton doesn't want to talk about the night Joe McCain got shot. When I covered that subject with Gene Kee, the affable State Police lieutenant retreated across the kitchen without even realizing it, until he was narrating the outcome of that particular sur-veillance from his dining room. While Mark Cronin, who had given the order to move in on the house, was describing it, his scalp became flushed and he dropped his head in his hand and was silent for several moments. With his angular limbs and long, bony hands, Cronin re-minded me of the statue of Laocoön, who warned against the Trojan Horse and was killed, along with his two sons, by serpents.

Although it happened fifteen years ago, there was the clear sense that their champion had fallen, and each man still struggled with that, second-guessing his own actions and turning over the what-ifs? Gene Kee and Mark Cronin were at least somewhat removed from the events that led to Joe McCain exchanging gunfire with Vladimir Lafontant. Chris Brighton had been just a few feet away, and Joe was shot with his gun.

After a long while Joey comes out and gets back behind the wheel of his cruiser. "Is he here?" I ask.

"Yeah, he's there."

"Let's go back in, and I can meet him."

Joe Jr. puts the cruiser in gear and backs out of the parking space. "He's kinda busy," says McCain. "But clear your schedule for Monday. Monday at noon."

FIFTEEN

You Never Come Around Much Anymore

*Well, go ahead, investigate something for us—anything—just
to show us how it's done.*
—DASHIELL HAMMETT

J OE McCAIN, JR., AND I MEET FOR LUNCH that next Monday at a little place in Teele Square called the Soleil Café. Once
again, Chris Brighton has canceled at the last minute. It's a brilliant day
in February and the restaurant is deserted except for a scruffy fellow in
a denim jacket scribbling on a legal pad and our waitress, a young
woman with a milky complexion and short, dark hair, like a girl in a
verse by Ezra Pound. Amidst the odors of baking bread and roasted
herbs, Joey and I order Cuban sandwiches, and the girl smiles with her
eyes and fades away while some kind of marimba jazz plays from the
kitchen.

"Wanna hear a funny story? A good cop story?" asks Joey, trying to
cheer me up. "New guy on the job—I was just telling Mark this story—
his name is John Bogle. He comes on, and his lieutenant is Richie Heyward, who's been on about thirty years. Richie used to be a fighter,
boxer, Somerville guy, drinks all the time, a tough, tough guy but not a
bad— Never hurt ya, you know? Always stays in shape, but, uh, so
Richie's really gruff, smokes cigarettes, he's got a uniform, no patches
and no badge, nothing that says he's a lieutenant; nothing, 'cause he
could give a shit's worth—he couldn't care less. He's thrown the

149

captains out of his office—'Jimmy, get the fuck out of my office. Get out of here.' 'Richie, you can't talk to me like that.' So he says to John Bogle, they're coming down from roll call, now he's got the sheet filled out with where everybody's working, they just did roll call. So Heyward says to him, 'Hey, uh, you, make me a photocopy of that, will ya?' So Bogle—'Okay, lieutenant'—so Bogle goes over, now he walks over— he's not an 'inside guy'—he walks over to what he thinks is the copier machine. It's the fucking shredder. He walks over, and he goes like this, Jay, it goes *zi-iii-ip*, and then he stands there like this—he talks with a kind of lisp and he says, 'Where's the, um, where's the copy come out?' and a guy says, 'You just shredded the fucking roll, you jerk.' Fuckin', you could see Heyward looking out of his office, he sits like this in his chair in the office, smoking like this—you just cost him probably an hour's worth of work, to redo the whole fucking thing. But Bogle's a good guy. Plays the trumpet. He comes over sometimes and sits on my porch."

Things have quieted down at work for Joey. The mayor's office has postponed his suspension on appeal after downgrading it from three days to one, and Joe Doyle is busy trying to get that reduced to a written reprimand. In the meantime, an opening in the Somerville P.D. detective unit arose near the end of January, and Joey put in a bid for it. Based on his rank and seniority, he's just been named to detectives. His trash hasn't been disturbed in several weeks, and most of his detective shifts on the "first half," 4:00 P.M. to midnight, have been uneventful, a pleasing routine of minor investigations and calm, clear nights. Since the new year began, Joe has been taking graduate courses at UMass Boston and has announced that when he retires from the police department, he'll pursue his dream of becoming a history teacher.

Being a teacher was not something that he talked about much when his father was around. Big Joe was proud of his son, tolerant to the point of spoiling him, and never would've expressed displeasure at anything that Joey wanted to do. But the old Met was pleased that his son had followed him into police work, and had taken on the Hells Angels and broken down doors and thrown punks in jail. He was also proud that young Joey knew when to give a guy a break, when to just smile and spit on the ground and walk away. Joe Sr. considered his son a real cop.

Our sandwiches arrive, the blunt, aromatic bread sliced into triangles, and Joey notes that a recent shake-up in the detective bureau has forced Jimmy Hyde out of his privileged assignment with the DEA and back into regular shifts. In a letter from Police Chief George McLean, Hyde has been reminded that his paychecks come from the city of Somerville, not the federal government, and as an employee of the city he's subject to the will of the chief and under supervision from the chain of command, the same as any other police officer. Hyde was also told that he must report to the P.D. at the beginning of his shift, like everyone else, and that his movements and whereabouts are not to be kept secret. The message is clear: Jimmy Hyde is a member of the Somerville Police Department, not a vigilante or self-styled lone wolf.

As far as Joey is concerned, his trouble with Hyde is over. But since we never got him on videotape, and the possibility remains that he might try to do Joey, I'm curious about Jimmy Hyde and his motives. I've heard rumors that Hyde despised big Joe and is taking shots at Joey because his father is no longer around to advise and protect him. What happened to Timmy Doherty after he witnessed Hyde using excessive force against a prisoner leads me to believe that Jimmy Hyde is dangerous—that he's capable of going on what big Joe would've described as "a frolic of his own." So he still bears looking into.

After we pay our tab and Joey heads into work, I go poking around Somerville for a couple of hours. For some reason, I need to get to the bottom of this Jimmy Hyde thing. Nor do I think I'll ever get a handle on big Joe and what made him tick until I hear the story from each of the young Mets who were there when he got shot. So far, Chris Brighton has been like the will-o'-the-wisp. I haven't taken it personally; his old partners, Gene Kee and Al DiSalvo and Biff McLean, have trouble getting in touch with him. Although Brighton had already proven his mettle in Vietnam and took most of the risks that night in Hyde Park, I'm told he still feels guilty about Joe's injuries and blames himself.

But Brighton hasn't been the only guy who's hard to track down. I've been trying to get hold of Leo Martini since the Somerville P.D. Christmas party. We were introduced, and after Leo almost broke my hand by shaking it, Mark Donahue said that big Joe had once intervened on

Martini's behalf when he got in a jam at work, and that Jimmy Hyde was involved. By this time we were across the room from Martini, who was fixing me with a hard-eyed squint, and I nodded at him and decided to broach the subject another time.

As a kid, Leo Martini captained the football and baseball teams at Matignon High and in '72 was headed to UMass on an athletic scholarship when the last in a series of concussions ended his football career. One of seven children, he grew up tough in a tough part of Somerville. His old man was a teamster, Local 25, the same union Joe McCain, Sr., had belonged to. The Martini household was often a gathering place for Winter Hill criminals, and Leo's older brother, who got on the Mets through his father's union ties, was later indicted on criminal charges and fired.

Despite his family history, Leo Martini's in a category all his own. A legendary street cop with muscles on top of his muscles, Martini has been a fixture in Somerville for more than thirty years: walking the beat; riding a bicycle; coaching kids in basketball, football, and baseball; and cracking a few heads, if the situation warrants it. But I'm not from Somerville, and he's been difficult to pin down.

Coming up Broadway at dusk, I spot Martini working a detail in front of a housing project and use the bus turnaround to change direction. He looks like a prison guard in a sitcom: thick forearms over his bulkhead of a chest, no neck, a slick bald head and cauliflower ears supporting a pair of very dark sunglasses. Cars slow down, and scary looking kids in baggy jackets and do-rags avert their eyes when they see the cop on the corner. Nobody messes with Leo Martini.

I park my car and hail Martini from a distance and he comes walking over. On the way he recognizes me, and his stone face cracks into a smile and he grabs my hand and squeezes it in a death grip. Mark Donahue has told me that I'll be all right with Leo if he starts punching me on the arm and twisting my shoulder. Martini calls me "kid," and after about three minutes my biceps feels like it's been tenderized by a sledgehammer and the cap of my shoulder is throbbing at the pressure points.

Leo Martini is forty-nine years old and a solid 235 pounds. He never touched a weight until his late thirties; his father used to train boxers, and as a teenager and young man Leo gained his core strength and thickness from sparring thousands of rounds, often with heavier, older professional fighters. He and his brothers scrapped with each other and endured hundreds of street fights. It got so bad that when he was twenty-three or twenty-four years old, out on a date somewhere with the lovely girl he's now married to, Martini would be approached by all the local hard guys.

"Are you Martini?" his antagonist would say. "I heard you're pretty tough."

Leo would look the kid in the eye and say, "You wanna fight, meet me here tomorrow night at nine o'clock. Otherwise, leave me the fuck alone."

Telling his stories, Martini throws a punch I can't even see, bringing it up from his hip and stopping a quarter inch from my right eye—his fist hovers there for an instant, like the moon—and taking it away in a blur. He's still pretty fast.

All this is pertinent to understanding Leo Martini and what he was accused of. Shortly before Thanksgiving 1995, Martini responded to a call for backup outside a group of tenements in East Somerville. Upon arrival, he learned that another cop had arrested a crack dealer named Martin Mickle. Martini has worked uniformed patrol on rotating nights over his entire seventeen-year career. He knows a lot of people on the street. Also, Leo grew up in what he calls a "crossroads" household, where gangsters like Sal Sperlinga and Howie Winter and Whitey Bulger often congregated. So he hears things. One of the things he'd heard was that a shitbird named Mickle was throwing his name around East Somerville.

"Which one of you is Leo Martini?" asked Mickle when one of the cops mentioned the name.

"Funny you don't know who I am, when you can't stop fuckin' talking about me," said Martini.

Leo had a few more things to say that you wouldn't hear in church, and then the wagon arrived and he pitched Mickle into the back. That would have been the end of it, except that within a few days the crack dealer was saying Leo Martini had dragged him fifty yards over the pavement, struck him in the face several times, and even pulled out his service revolver and threatened him with it. The slightly built Mickle filed assault charges against Martini and the police department, and soon the FBI, Mass. State Police, and the Somerville internal affairs unit were investigating.

It turned out that Mickle was a snitch, according to Martini, working for the feds and Jimmy Hyde in spite of his significant crack cocaine habit. When Hyde had been accused of beating Michael Henderson while he was handcuffed two years earlier, Leo Martini had supported Timmy Doherty's version of what happened. He and Doherty were not close friends; they rarely socialized and had never been to each other's homes or met each other's wives. Martini had been away on vacation when Henderson was allegedly beaten in the police station. But he believed Doherty was telling the truth and made his opinion known. Martini thought Jimmy Hyde was looking for some payback.

When Martini found out he was being investigated he unearthed the photographs of Michael Henderson and Martin Mickle, taken shortly after the respective incidents had occurred, and brought them up to Chief Robert Carroll. Henderson was a mass of lumps and bruises; he looked like the Elephant Man. Mickle didn't have a mark on him.

"Look at these," said Martini. "Who's telling the fucking truth—me or Jimmy Hyde?"

On Christmas Eve 1995, Leo Martini was at home with his wife and baby and nine-year-old son when Somerville police knocked on the door. They arrested him and told his wife that there was a cash bail of $15,000. "Where am I gonna get that kind of money on Christmas Eve?" asked Martini. "And where am I gonna go? I've lived in Somerville my whole life."

The patrolmen's union bailed him out, and Martini entered a whirlwind of police interviews, grand jury appearances, and an indictment. He was suspended without pay and watched his life and career go into the sewer on the testimony of a junkie. Besides hiring a lawyer, there was little Martini could do about it until he decided to pay a visit to Joe McCain's P.I. office in the North End.

It was an interesting situation for both men. They had only a nodding acquaintance and were aware of each other's reputation. But Leo Martini had a less sanitized view of Joe McCain than most people did.

His father's pals had always insisted that big Joe had shaken them down in his Revere Beach days. McCain was quick to use his fists or the stick, they would say, and he knew how to accept an envelope. Leo Martini had heard all the stories but decided to make his own judgment.

For his part, McCain was acquainted with Martini's father and didn't think much of the old man's choice in friends. He considered Leo's brother a rogue cop and a thug and had no use for him whatsoever. But McCain, unlike folks in other parts of the country, had never used a man's family as a line of demarcation. In Somerville, and certainly on Winter Hill, a single family might include a "good" cop, a bad cop, a priest, and a wiseguy—with a lot of gray area even between them. Leo Martini is his own man, and the McCains never held what his father or brother did against him.

When Leo Martini came to the office, big Joe asked him to describe that night with Mickle and to outline the charges that were being made. When Martini finished telling his story, the old Met detective was gazing straight into his face. "I know you," said McCain, citing the work Leo had done with kids in the city. "I know you wouldn't do something like this."

Big Joe sent a couple of his operatives to interview the various parties to the incident and find out who had seen what. It didn't take them long to whittle down the prosecutor's list of witnesses: most of them hadn't seen a thing. One of Joe's guys found an elderly neighbor who signed an affidavit stating that Leo Martini had used a lot of profane language but had barely touched Martin Mickle.

Soon the case began to disappear. The FBI dropped out, then the State Police, and finally the Somerville cops. By May 1996, Leo Martini was reinstated with full back pay. No disciplinary action was ever brought against Jimmy Hyde, who, according to Leo Martini, had led the witch hunt against him.

While Martini and I are standing there, he gets hailed from passing cars and talks to half a dozen passersby. A wiry man in his sixties with a dyed pompadour stops to chat for a minute. Martini calls him Rock and promises to talk to a guy he knows about a bartending job.

"A man with a head of hair like yours ought to be working," says Leo, running a hand over the smooth dome of his own head.

Rock laughs and saunters down Broadway. A woman of a certain age stops her gleaming sedan and gets out to ask Officer Martini for directions. She is wearing an expensive overcoat over a brown-and-yellow flowered dress and high heels, and smells of lilacs. Saying that she's late for a wedding in Medford, the woman flutters her eyelashes when Martini points her in the right direction and walks into the middle of Broadway to direct her back into traffic.

"You are *so* nice," she says, blushing.

A pudgy young school committeeman with his eye on an alderman's seat arrives a few minutes later. He's wearing a tired gray trench coat and has an armload of campaign brochures and before Leo can introduce us, he hands me one.

"Where're you going?" asks Martini.

The school committeeman jabs his chin toward the housing project.

"Nobody votes in there," Martini says. He's a public servant himself, serving as a volunteer commissioner on the Somerville Recreation Commission.

The young politician stifles a yawn. One at a time, he removes his shoes despite the cold and massages his tired dogs. "It's a free meal," he says. "You should come over."

"What're they having?" Martini asks.

"Chinese."

Leo makes a face. "I don't eat that stuff," he says.

After shaking our hands once more, the school committeeman walks away, heading for his egg roll and wonton soup. Horns are honking in the street and a guy leans out from a passing SUV and says "Mar-ti-ni" and the big bald cop waves to him.

"See that kid? He went to school with Jimmy Hyde. They were best friends," Leo says. "In seventh grade, Hyde came up to him and said that he'd decided to become a cop and the two of them couldn't be friends anymore. That he was 'going in a different direction.' Who says that to his best friend? What a piece of shit."

Behind the three towers of the housing project, the sky is darkening and there's a pronounced chill in the air. For the first time, Leo Martini removes his sunglasses. His small blue eyes are lined with crow's-feet, more kind and humane than I'd expected. When I ask why he and Joey and Timmy Doherty have persevered over Jimmy Hyde and his crew, Martini laughs.

"Because we're telling the truth," he says. "Listen, kid. It's easy to tell the truth cuz you don't have to remember nothing. If you're gonna lie, you gotta have everyone lie with you."

SIXTEEN

Cyrano de McCainiac

L EO MARTINI AND TIMMY DOHERTY weren't the only cops that Joe McCain helped out. Big Joe always taught his guys that it's never about who gets the glory, what matters most is playing hard and fair and enjoying the rough-and-tumble of the game. One time Joe had a line on a wiseguy who was flying out of Logan Airport, headed for Switzerland with a load of stolen jewelry and bearer bonds. It was Friday evening, and McCain was alone in the D.A.'s office at 73 Tremont Street in Boston, without the authority to stop the plane and looking for help.

After making a few phone calls, McCain was getting irritated because no one would listen to him. Finally he reached a guy he knew in the Boston FBI office named Eddie Quinn and said, "Look, Eddie, I got a flight going out about eleven o'clock tonight with some stolen goods on it."

"What's this all about, Joe?" the FBI agent asked.

"Bonds—bearer bonds going to Bern, Switzerland. I got the flight number and everything else."

"How'd you get it?" asked Quinn.

McCain was growing a little impatient. "I'm in the office right now," he said.

"Ehh, let's wait till Monday," Quinn said.

"*Monday?* For crissakes, this guy's gonna be long gone by then."

"Joe, we have an office over in Europe, but we couldn't get anybody now. With the time changes, it's the middle of the night over there."

McCain was furious but reined in his anger, speaking in a clipped tone that piqued his friend's interest. "Hey, Eddie, I'll take care of it," he said.

"Joe, how you gonna do it?" Quinn asked.

"Why should I tell you?" asked McCain, and then he hung up.

Sitting in the deserted office, Joe McCain was far from certain about what he was going to do next. After a few minutes spent pulling on his earlobe, Joe picked up the phone and dialed the overseas operator. "Bern, Switzerland," he said. "The police department."

A short while later the call broke through to a secondary line and there was a distant ringing noise that lasted quite a while and a series of clicking sounds and finally, after several minutes, a policeman on the far side of the Atlantic Ocean reached up and lifted the hook.

"Do you speak English?" asked McCain.

For all he knew, the guy on the other end of the line was Hans Christian Andersen, but McCain figured it had to be somebody like him, a regular cop, interested only in doing his job.

"Listen, take a pencil out. This is Detective Joe McCain, uh, District Attorney's Office, Suffolk County, Boston, Massachusetts, USA."

McCain went on to describe the case and who was headed to Switzerland and what he was carrying, and pretty soon the officer in Bern had a supervisor listening in and the two Swiss cops were bombarding McCain with questions. "The flight is just about to leave Boston and will be there in five or six hours," Joe said. "All I want you to do is meet this plane and get this guy, because he's coming over with all these stolen goods."

"Okay, we'll see what we can do," said the Swiss cop.

Joe McCain hung up and put on his coat and left the office. It was close to midnight, and riding the elevator down to the Fatted Calf for a drink he laughed at his own earnestness. He made a bet with himself that nothing was going to happen and that he'd never hear another word about the case. Then he had his Scotch and drove home and went to bed.

The telephone in the McCain bedroom rang at four o'clock in the morning. "What is it?" asked Joe, his voice thick with sleep.

"You fucking McCain," said a man's voice. "You got us to do it by them calling Washington. Washington—"

"Who is this?" Joe asked. "What are you talking about?"

"It's me, Eddie. Eddie Quinn. You know how it works, Joe? You call Bern and they call Washington and then Washington calls the Boston office and gets the fucking agent in charge out of bed. And that's me, for fuck's sake. That's me."

Tangled in his bedclothes, McCain started laughing. "You're kidding."

"Do I sound like I'm kidding? You know what they said? Who is this fucking cop in Boston, this detective, Joe McCain, that's calling Bern, Switzerland?"

"Did you get him, Eddie?"

Quinn was calm now, almost laughing along with McCain. "Did we get who?"

"My guy at Logan."

"Yeah, we pinched him."

"Good night, Eddie," said McCain, rolling over to go back to sleep.

In a pattern that he would follow his entire career, Joe ducked credit for solving the case while taking some heat from the D.A.'s bookkeeper for his overseas phone call. In a profession where who gets the credit, deservedly or not, and who gets the newspaper coverage often plays a huge role in whose career takes off and who ends up in a cruiser patrolling the Blue Hills, Joe McCain's indifference toward his own reputation was an anomaly. When he and his partner Jack Crowley and assistant D.A.s like Joe Doyle, Roger Emanuelson and Tom Peisch were working together in the Suffolk County Investigation and Prosecution Project, the old SCIPP unit, the man in charge was eighty-year-old district attorney Garrett Byrne. And if photographers from the *Boston Herald* and *Boston Globe* and news crews from Channels 4, 5, and 7 were coming to Tremont Street to take pictures of a table loaded with counterfeit money or a valuable painting or statue they had recovered, Joe McCain would tell Crowley to go fetch Gary Byrne. After all, he was the boss.

"For Christ's sake, why do I always have to wake Gary up?" asked Crowley, tongue in cheek.

A few minutes later, Crowley would return and Doyle or Emanuelson would ask if the boss was on his way. Crowley was a great practical joker and impressionist, and he'd drop right into his Igor routine, hunched over, squinting, one arm thrust out, and dragging his right leg behind him.

In a perfect Bela Lugosi imitation, Crowley would say, "Yes, master, I went down to the morgue and I put thirteen pints in him and he's ready to run for another term."

Everybody would laugh and Byrne would show up for the photo session in his tinted glasses and they'd all go downstairs to the Fatted Calf for a couple of drinks. But Joe McCain's good-natured largesse reached its apotheosis with a Somerville cop named Billy White. Both Local 25 teamsters and native sons from Winter Hill, McCain and White became friends as teenagers and were together the day McCain spotted Bobo Petricone's Oldsmobile and got involved in the Bernie McLaughlin murder investigation. A former Marine, Billy White was honest, hardworking, and a devout Catholic; he and his wife and three daughters attended Mass at St. Clement's every week without fail. (He also had a brother "Red" White, with a bad hand, whom everyone called Lobster.)

Billy White was always grinding out a buck. Long before discount warehouses were in vogue, White used to buy tuna fish and Campbell's soup by the case in an effort to save money, and he and his family were just getting by. In the mid-1960s he and Joe McCain and another Met cop named Frank Donovan, a former World War II POW and inveterate gambler, got in the orange juice business. For an original investment of five hundred dollars apiece, White and his new partners bought an orange juice recipe and a vat for crushing the fruit, and rented a little storefront down near Union Square in Somerville. White made the juice, McCain loaded the gallons and quarts into the back of his pink

Cadillac convertible and delivered to the bars in Lynn, Revere, and Peabody, and Donovan handled local deliveries and went around collecting the money.

There weren't any huge profits in this seat-of-the-pants operation, but things went reasonably well until White and McCain figured out that, as quickly as Donovan was collecting the money, he was taking it to Suffolk Downs and losing it on the horses. During this period Billy White was studying for the sergeant's exam, and before their fortunes took a downturn, he'd promised to donate five hundred dollars to St. Clement's Church if he was successful in acquiring the rank. White topped the list and made sergeant; the same day, he picked up Joe McCain, drove over to the bank and took out a loan for five hundred dollars, and delivered it to the priest at St. Clement's.

Billy White worked just as hard on the cop job as he did moonlighting and ran off a long string of gambling arrests, locking up several prominent Somerville bookies. In those days bookmaking and Somerville politics went hand in hand, and as a dubious reward for all the pinches he was making, White got transferred to a walking beat, midnight to 8:00 A.M., down around the Swift meatpacking plant beyond Union Square, a stinking, desolate end of town where he couldn't even buy a cup of coffee. Sergeant White was in exile.

The long-standing enmity between certain factions of the Somerville P.D. and the McCain family, which has reemerged over Joe Jr.'s suspension and the trash-pulling incident, goes all the way back to the midsixties and big Joe's early career as a detective. The sort of treatment White was getting aggravated Joe McCain and he swore that he was going to help Billy out. On his job, McCain acquired a list of six "wanted" men who had jumped their parole and were hiding in Billy White's jurisdiction. (A cop who was injured on the job recognized one of the parolees in his neighborhood and called Joe.) McCain gave the list to Billy White and he and Leo Papile accompanied Sergeant White and a handful of Somerville cops, all armed with shotguns, as they surrounded a house on Flint Street early one morning.

"You and me are gonna go through the front door," said White to Joe McCain. "Just like the old days."

McCain shook his head. "No Mets," he said. "It's your pinch. Leo and I'll just wait out here and help you I.D. them."

The Somerville cops raided the house, and as McCain and Papile squatted half a block away, laughing to themselves, they were startled by the noise of a shotgun blast. They ran up Flint Street as Billy and his men reemerged, leading six grimy and unshaven parolees out the door in handcuffs.

"What the hell happened?" asked McCain.

Billy White jerked his head toward one of the patrolmen, who was standing there with a sheepish look on his face. "Accidental discharge," he said. "Right through the ceiling, upstairs, and through the roof. Lucky we didn't kill somebody."

It was a great pinch, diminished by the fact that one of the shotguns had been fired. Dogged cop that he was, Billy White responded by training every man under his command in the shotgun; on their off hours, they were required to practice down by the Mystic River, since the range couldn't accommodate all that firepower. And Joe McCain, with his unparalleled street sources, determined to restore the luster to his friend's career, kept hunting for another good case.

A short while later McCain heard about a shipment of pistols, shotguns, and machine guns stolen from a local dealer and began keeping an eye on a bar near the junction of Highland Avenue and the McGrath Highway. Across from the bar was a firehouse, and McCain and White decided to use the top of the tower to look down into the joint and take pictures of the gang that had stolen the guns. Eventually they hit a house on Walnut Street and arrested the thieves and recovered all the guns. Although they worked the case together, McCain threw all the credit to White, who drove the Somerville police crazy. Chief Thomas O'Brien was in tight with the bookies, and White kept getting his picture in the newspaper for busting up the neighborhood. O'Brien couldn't decide if he was more upset over his friends getting arrested or Billy White becoming famous.

Because of his disdain for law enforcement politics and the silly jurisdictional battle that was undermining Billy White's reputation, Joe McCain worked overtime developing a case large and dramatic enough to resurrect his old pal once and for all. From a biker named Dougherty he knew from Revere Beach, McCain learned of a cache of imported food and wine worth over $300,000 that had been hijacked from the docks. At the corner of Summer and Center Streets was an auto body shop with a false wall made of cinder blocks, and neatly stacked in the cavity behind it were the odd-shaped bottles of olive oil, wheels of cheese, and gallon after gallon of expensive Italian and French wines.

Joe called Billy White and asked, "Do you want it?"

"You're kidding me," said White. "Who stole it?"

"Well, shit, if you don't want it . . ."

White cut him off. "I want it, Joe," he said. "But I gotta really know it's there."

"Whaddaya need?" McCain asked. "A block of cheese or something?"

"Jesus, Joe, I'm in deep shit with the chief for this stuff," said White. "I just gotta know."

So one night around 2:00 A.M. McCain parked his car halfway down the block and tiptoed up to the auto body shop, climbed through a window, discovered a ladder in the corner, and leaned it against a freshly mortared wall at the far end of the garage. The cinder blocks stopped a couple of feet from the ceiling, and McCain climbed up and thrust his head over the top of the wall and shined his flashlight. There in the crawl space was the entire shipment: the netted bottles of Merlot and Cabernet, the great chunks of Brie, everything. Chuckling to himself, McCain replaced the ladder and went back out through the window.

Going straight to a pay phone, Joe called Billy White and woke him up. "Billy, get dressed. Get a warrant. And go get it," he said. "It's all there."

By 6:00 A.M. Billy White arrived at the auto body shop with a phalanx of police officers, a search warrant, and every city truck that he could scare up. All the uniformed cops were excited to be part of something this big, and as the sun rose over Somerville, they gathered in front of the auto body shop with their pickaxes and shotguns, the trucks lined up along the sidewalk like floats in a parade. Once again, Joe McCain and Leo Papile were hiding up the street, and as Billy White, resplendent in his dress blue uniform, was about to give the order, Chief O'Brien rode past on his way to work and almost had an infarction.

The cops broke the wall down and began unloading the stolen goods, and as the work went on, television crews showed up and filmed the operation for the evening news. Billy White's picture appeared on the front page of the *Somerville Journal,* and within a few months he had passed the detective lieutenant's exam and moved over to the State Police. Finally, he was safe from his enemies in the Somerville P.D.

But a day after the big bust, he and Joe McCain were having a drink over in Cambridge, and big Joe raised his glass and said, "You're really making a name for yourself, Billy. You're gonna work your way right out of there."

White laughed. "I'm working myself into goddamn heart failure, you son of a bitch. Don't give me any more of these."

McCain was always quick to lend a hand. But it was his old pal on the Mets, Billy Parsons, who arranged Joe's most eventful moonlighting experience. The former Marine's cousin John Thistle owned a rigging company and in the mid-eighties Thistle hired Parsons and McCain to haul the contents of a downtown bank to a new location in Worcester, Mass. The two behemoths were part of the crew that moved the thirty-ton vault doors by means of cold-rolled steel bars, along with safe deposit boxes that had been sealed by a notary public and were transported to Worcester in a convoy of trucks guarded by policemen with machine guns.

It was backbreaking, technical work. The safe deposit boxes, which were filled with valuables, could be jacked up to only a certain height and then carried out in blocks of twenty through a hole that had been blasted in the sidewalk. The process took a couple of weeks and while they were at it, the steelworkers and riggers stayed at a beautiful new hotel in downtown Worcester. Every night up on the twenty-second floor, they were treated to a fantastic spread of lobster, shrimp cocktail, and porterhouse steaks, augmented by the finest wines and whiskeys and a keg of ice cold beer.

On their last evening, at the height of the conviviality, Chief Rigger John Thistle, who like his brothers was missing part of a finger here and a toe there, climbed out the window of the hospitality room onto the narrow granite ledge. With the ease of a man walking along a sidewalk, Thistle sauntered around the corner of the building while Joe McCain leaned out the window, gaping at him. "You crazy bastard," said McCain.

A few moments later, Thistle returned. "C'mere, Joe," he said.

Big Joe mustered himself and crawled onto the ledge. It was a cold winter night, the stars glittering above the hotel and a steady wind from the north. More than two hundred feet below, the empty swimming pool was the size of a dinner plate and tiny cars moved up and down the streets. Slowly McCain stood up and followed Thistle around the corner of the hotel on the twelve-inch ledge.

Most of the other rooms were dark at that hour, but once they turned the corner Thistle paused near a glowing window, motioning for McCain to come and take a look. "They should charge admission," said Thistle.

As gusts of wind drove the two men against the building, McCain couldn't begin to imagine what was so mesmerizing. But he crept forward, inching right up to the heels of Thistle's shoes and peering around him into the room. What McCain saw would fuel his barroom conversations for the next six months.

A middle-aged man and his chubby wife were naked on the bed, in flagrante delicto. As they grappled and sawed at each other, a little gray poodle scampered around them in a frenzy, licking at their dangling appendages and barking in a hoarse voice.

The two men stared at these bizarre antics and then at each other. "Sweet mother of God," said Thistle.

"Okay, John," said McCain, making a quick U-turn. "I've seen enough."

It's the same sense of camaraderie that has Joe McCain, Jr., his music pal Moose Analetto, and 911 operator Scott Lennon sitting at the McCain kitchen table, the kids and the wife out shopping, the counter dotted with wire-handled containers of pork strips with lobster sauce, fried rice, and chicken fingers. Joey has dropped his appeal, and the boys are "celebrating" his twenty-four-hour suspension, which takes place today, drinking beers and collectively not giving a hoot about the politics of the Somerville P.D.

Joe Jr. and his friends are goofing on the unlikely television detectives of the 1970s, Banacek and Barnaby Jones and Cannon, old and fat and lame yet somehow expert at disabling their opponents with a single karate chop, delivered to a precise spot between neck and shoulder. The stars of those far-fetched TV shows were so aged and arthritic they couldn't have opened an envelope, let alone knocked anyone out.

They're all laughing like maniacs and Joey snorts into his food when Lennon brings up *Star Trek* and says, "Like Captain Kirk battling a Gorn whose skeletal structure isn't even close to a human's and he throws a chop at what passes for the alien's shoulder and the thing goes down in a blob."

SEVENTEEN

Incident in Fall River

Has not a man hard service upon the earth,
And are not his days like the days of a hireling?
—Job 7:1

MARK DONAHUE AND I ARE GOING NORTH on the Expressway, past the colorful gas tanks that feature the profile of Ho Chi Minh etched into the artless-looking blue swath. Maps and files and court orders are scattered all over the inside of my car, along with orange peels, banana peels, apple cores, and old, sopping tea bags. It's Presidents' Day weekend and for the past month, this has been our rolling office. Buried in the back somewhere is my hockey equipment.

"*Whew.* That's what I smell," says Donahue. "Your fucking hockey stuff."

I laugh and roll down the window. "That smell is music to my ears, Coach," I say.

Salt has turned the highway white, and near Melnea Cass Boulevard we turn off the highway and pass beneath a huge crane looming above the Boston Medical Center. "We're going to Roxbury," says Donahue. He indicates the black pouch he wears on his belt. "I got my gun."

"I don't have mine," I say, "cuz I don't own one."

Colorful panels mount the facade of a brand-new school on the edge of the Orchard Park Projects, the site protected by a ten-foot construction fence. We negotiate the odd-shaped intersection, studying the map and the overhead signs for a tiny one-way called Ambrose Street. Temperatures are in the single digits and a nasty wind is blowing up the sidewalk, creating little tornadoes of paper, cigarette ends and grit. Two young men in large black-and-white leather jackets with pink-and-orange sleeves are standing on the corner, blowing on their hands and stamping their feet, and a short ways along a woman smokes a cigarette at the bus stop. There's a dearth of white people around here and I don't have a problem with that. But we're conspicuous.

Behind the Dearborn School are three or four short streets into the project and we spot the one we think is Ambrose and have to drive around again since it's all one-way. On the second pass the corner and bus stop are deserted.

"The white man never brings good news around here," says Donahue.

We turn into Ambrose Street, just an alley between the clapboard row houses, all of it newly paved and burgeoning to a double row of parking spaces on either side. The vehicle in question is a seven-year-old Ford Explorer, green on black, registered to a Clemzie Rostock. Halfway down the first row is a green truck with black interior and a vanity plate that reads "Clemzie." Dust on the windshield and little mounds of plowed snow in front of the tires indicate it hasn't moved in a while.

"Think that's it?" I ask Mark, who is studying the cars on the other side and has missed it.

"Very funny, Coach," he says, backing into the space beside the Explorer. "Get out and check the VIN."

I glance over my shoulder, peering toward the windows of the nearest apartment. "The tag says 'Clemzie.' How many can there be?"

"Sometimes a car gets wrecked or stolen and a guy'll buy the same model, different year, and put the old plate on," says Donahue. "You come around, snap the car and boom—wrongful repossession. They win a judgment against the bank, and against us." He screws his head around; the sidewalk is empty. "Jump out and check the VIN," he says. "Ten seconds."

I look in the file for the last five digits. Easing out of the car, I take one step and lean over the Explorer, cupping my hand against the glass to shield the sun. Again I find the "air bag" label and search up and down the dash but can't find the VIN. A couple of years ago, I detached the retina in my left eye while playing rugby and the operation to fix it was less than a complete success.

I get back in the car. "You're not gonna believe this," I say.

"Jesus Christ," says Donahue. He bursts from the driver's side with the file clutched in his hand, takes four giant steps around the hood of the car, whips open the manila folder, stabs his finger at the number, and raises his sunglasses to his forehead and leans over the dash. Unhurried, he returns to the car.

"Your eyes are going, Coach," says Donahue.

Mark calls the wrecker on his cell phone and schedules the pickup for later that day. "The car looks good, but it hasn't been driven lately," he tells the driver. "Clemzie's probably in the joint."

Twenty minutes later, Donahue and I arrive in Winthrop, a small, neatly arranged town on a peninsula just north of Boston. Riding around the town's perimeter on Winthrop Shore Drive, we're afforded a great view of the ocean, the sky above dotted with gulls. Out beyond the jetty, the waves look like mountains viewed from a distance.

"It's rough out there," says Donahue, the one-time harbormaster.

And it's rough in here. We turn onto Wave Way, dirty sections of old newspaper flapping ahead of us. Close on either side are three-families with their vinyl siding half stripped off, fronted by broken railings and jumbled up patio furniture. We're looking for Marco Zapato, and in front of the appropriate house Mark stops the car and I run out to check the mailboxes. One unit has six names on little plastic labels but no Zapato, and I take a quick look through the utility bills and missing children flyers stuffed into each of the rusted boxes. Mark gets out and we ring the doorbell to the apartments but nobody's home. The car we're looking for is a Honda Accord and that's not here either.

"Let's go to the father's house," says Mark, and we climb back in the car and head north on the shore road, armies of gulls soaring ahead of us over the empty beach.

Zapato's father lives in "Severe," which is what Donahue calls Revere, part of a lexicon that includes "Slum-erville," "Poor-chester" (Dorchester), and "Murder-pan" (Mattapan). In front of a three-story brick building on a narrow, dingy street Donahue stops the car and skims over the Zapato file. The information is sketchy. Either Zapato's father lives in this building or he used to, and now a friend of Zapato's named Alberto Flores lives here. Flores is listed as a reference on Marco Zapato's loan application.

Inside the tiny foyer we study the various combinations of names listed over the security buzzers. Donahue presses one of them and asks the woman who answers if she knows anyone named Zapato or Flores.

"No," she says, terminating the conversation.

While we're standing there, a man in a black ski hat enters the cramped foyer. He's wearing a perforated black face mask against the cold, with only his eyes showing. They are wide and blue, with exclamatory black dots in the center.

Donahue turns to him. "Does Marco Zapato or Alberto Flores live here?"

"Who are you?" the man asks.

Looming over him, Donahue asks, "Who are *you*?"

I can't see Mark's face from this angle but I have a fair idea of what it looks like. Most of the time he's a gregarious, easygoing family man, and I often leave him in charge of my son, who is eight years old and whom Mark treats like his own child. But under fight or flight conditions, Mark stretches himself to his full six feet three, his ears turn red and his jaw drops and he maintains a petulant Irish squint that usually backs the other fellow up.

The man unhooks his mask; he is in his late fifties, with a narrow, lined face and humanitarian eyes. "This is my building," he says, with touches of Central America in his accent.

"I'm from the bank," Mark says, handing him a business card. "We're looking for Alberto Flores or Marco Zapato."

The super unlocks the inner door and waves us inside. Going up the stairs, he says something to Donahue that I can't make out and upon the first landing he gestures toward the door opposite and then unlocks his own unit and disappears inside without another word.

Mark knocks on the door to Number 4. There's the sound of a television from inside, a couple of loud bumps against the wall, and muffled voices. After a long interval the chain is removed and the latch unbolted and the door opens. Standing there is a chubby, preadolescent boy in a pajama top and sweatpants with bare feet although it is approaching noon on a school day. The apartment is dark behind him, except for the play of light from the television, and from the look of a sleeping bag on the floor, which still bears his impression, the boy has been lying around in that dank, stuffy room all morning.

"Does Marco Zapato live here?" asks Donahue.

The boy is staring up at Mark. His straight black hair droops over his forehead and his body is soft all over, like it's never been used for anything. "No," he says.

"What about Alberto Flores?"

"I don't know," says the boy.

"You don't know if he lives here?" asks Mark.

"I don't know."

Suddenly a dark-haired woman in a bathrobe appears and puts her arms around the boy's shoulders like she's protecting him. "What do you want?" she asks.

"We're from the bank and we're looking for Marco Zapato," says Mark. "Does Alberto Flores live here?"

"No," the woman says.

"You don't know Marco Zapato?"

The woman eases the boy out of the way and closes the door. "No," she says, as the door clicks shut.

Back on the road Donahue expresses surprise over the building superintendent's cooperation. "What an idiot," he says. "All I showed him was a little piece of cardboard. He never should have let us in."

"Every man for himself," I say.

After he calls Ray at the bank to fill him in, Mark asks, "What's your instinct?"

"I think the woman sent the kid to the door, which is disgusting. I think Zapato doesn't live there and the kid doesn't know him. But I bet Alberto Flores lives there."

Mark nods his head. "The kid knows Flores. He was lying through his skull."

It's a long drive from Revere to Fall River, and to break up the monotony we're treated to a phone call from Joe McCain. "Ass bag," says Donahue, greeting his old friend. "Whatcha doin'?"

Detectives in Somerville have their own separate locked area and a degree of autonomy not enjoyed by the patrol division. Joe's plan for his space includes a Persian rug (which for some reason Donahue advises him to buy at Home Depot) and a beaded curtain instead of a door. Above his desk he's going to hang a portrait of his late father.

"Real cops on this side, fake cops on the other," he says.

Donahue is amused by his buddy's antics and after I shout over that I'll help Joey get a couple of file cabinets from the office on Fulton Street, they hang up. Joe is in a hurry to have lunch.

"He'll probably call Mike Kennelly to ask him where he should eat," I say. "He always tells me that Kennelly is a genius. His lunch guru."

Mark and Joey "Elbows" McCain have been friends since they played peewee hockey together in Somerville. From those days up through their stint on the Winnissimett Chiefs when they were fifteen all the way to the high school varsity, the two played street hockey in Foss Park, sat in class together, and drank beer and listened to music in the McCain basement. In the early years, big Joe drove a cement truck for Boston Sand & Gravel while also working as a cop, and Mark rarely saw him, although the reputation of the elder McCain was well established. He was a real-life detective, a large, impressive man who drove around in jazzy sports cars, in sleek black undercover cars, and in race cars that had been seized from drug lords and kingpins.

Joe Sr. often drove the two boys to hockey practice, roaring up Route 93 at 120 miles an hour, with Joey laughing like hell up front and Donahue terrified in the backseat. "Don't worry, boys, I'm a *professional*," said Joe, who once covered the ten miles from the McCain residence to the Stoneham rink in just six minutes.

While we putter toward Fall River at seventy, Mark receives a flurry of telephone calls on his two cell phones. One of the calls is from Kevin McKenna, a veteran McCain operative who's busy with several workmen's comp cases, and the next one is from Eugene Rearborne of Taunton, the factory worker we visited last week who said that he would turn over his Isuzu Trooper later that day after consulting with his lawyer. In the meantime, Rearborne's father-in-law has grown ill and died, his lawyer has gone out of town, and the car has disappeared again. Rearborne himself has been incommunicado for a while but is now responding to messages left with his employer.

"You're fucking up my job," he says. "Don't call me at work."

"I'm not fucking up your job, you are," says Mark. "If the sheriffs show up with an injunction that's really gonna fuck things up. I didn't default on the bank loan—you did. I'm just trying to schedule the car for pickup."

Rearborne hangs up, and Donahue pitches the tiny plastic phone into the file folders, banana peels, and court orders piled around my ankles. "His main objective every day is to hide that car," says Mark.

The phone rings again and I go rummaging for it, look at the caller's name on the tiny screen and hand the phone to Mark: "Rearborne again."

Calmer this time, Eugene Rearborne admits that he removed the battery and hid the car behind his house to "protect it." Apparently his lawyer has abandoned the case and he wants to give the car up now. "Please don't let it go to the sheriff," he says.

Mark tells Rearborne to put the battery back in the car, get it started, and drive it two blocks to the parking lot at Stop & Shop and he'll send the wrecker for it. "The neighbors won't have to see," he says.

A couple of minutes later, Ray calls from the bank to tell us that Essex County sheriffs found Denny Dexteris's welding truck hidden in a grove of trees behind his uncle's house in Rowley, Mass. When Mark had visited Dexteris's stepfather the first time, the Rowley harbormaster said that his twenty-nine-year-old stepson had gone to sea in a tugboat, and not to venture into those particular woods because of the dogs. Mark didn't go there but in the end, the sheriff did and found some Doberman pinschers and the truck.

Soon we are passing over the expanse of Battleship Cove into north Fall River. Once filled with more than one hundred textile mills employing thirty thousand immigrants from around the world, "the Spindle City" never really crawled out of the Great Depression back in the twenties and thirties. Earthmovers and cranes are pushing great mounds of frozen dirt beneath the pilings of the bridge and puffs of steam are floating into the vast blue sky above the city. The traffic lights run in our favor and we glide past the tiny used car lots, tenements, and beauty shops, the B's Nest Liquor Store and several Portuguese markets. But dominating every aspect of the landscape from this vantage point is the battleship *Massachusetts*, tied up at the bridge, painted with "53" in large white numerals and bristling with guns.

Nicknamed Big Mamie, the *Massachusetts* was launched in 1941 just up the coast in Quincy, Mass., the heaviest ship ever built in the yard. She participated in the invasion of the Marshall Islands in '44 and helped bombard Iwo Jima and Okinawa. The *Massachusetts* fired the last sixteen-inch projectile of World War II, and in the early sixties was saved from the scrap yard by its remaining crew members. It has been a historic landmark since 1965. But seeing it docked by the highway— large, gray, and incongruous—gives me a strange feeling in the pit of my stomach.

Against this backdrop, we're searching for a woman named Martha Pacquin and her Kia Spectra, no color or year listed on the application. She lives at 593 Sunrise Hill, and an obliging postman directs us past Coney Island Hot Dogs to the grim-looking row houses of the Sunrise Hill projects. Each section is a squat brick building resembling a military barracks, the complex arranged over the expanse of a bald ridge overlooking the river and a large, foul-smelling industrial plant on the other bank. Standing on an empty stretch of lowland, the factory is medieval and sinister, throwing huge plumes of smoke into the air.

Donahue parks the car just as Ray calls again from the bank and I get out and go looking for Number 593. There's very little snow here and the bare earth is strewn with condom wrappers and lumps of frozen dog shit. A clothesline rattles in the wind and a young man with buzzed hair and a dozen piercings in his face walks past on the sidewalk. Unit 593 is located beside a Fall River police outstation, and I whistle to Mark and raise my arm. The car we're looking for is nowhere in sight.

At first the noise of the wind blocks out everything else, but as I wait for Donahue to catch up, I tune in the various sounds coming from the apartments. A loud television dominates in many of them, but I can also make out a man and a woman arguing in Number 592 and a drunken voice singing in Spanish in the apartment next door. Right in front of me, I can hear a woman talking to herself or to someone on the phone.

Mark knocks on the door to Number 593 and the woman answers the door. "Are you Martha Pacquin?" he asks.

The occupant of Number 593 is a rail-thin female of indeterminate age, with a tattered mop of long brown hair. A pointy nose and dark circles under her eyes give her the look of an anemic raccoon. "I'm Martha's roommate, Sandra Dionne," the woman says. She's lost in the beer company sweatshirt she's wearing and carries a small, hairy dog under her right arm. "What's this about?"

"Where's Martha?"

"Martha ain't here," says Dionne with her small, ugly, mobile mouth. "She's at work."

Donahue raises himself to the top step. "Where does Martha work?"

"Over in New Bedford," says Dionne. "She's a metal finisher."

"Really? What's the name of the place?"

"I don't know," Dionne says. "So, what's this about?"

Donahue explains the terms and conditions of Martha Pacquin's bank loan. Sandy Dionne replies that Martha gives her cash and she deposits it in her account and mails a check for $224.92 to the bank every month. "I just faxed everything over to them, every check, every stub, everything about the car," says Dionne, pronouncing it "cawh," a New Yorker. "Just yesterday I faxed it all over. I got it all upstairs. Everything. You wanna see it?"

The apartment is poorly lit and smells of dog. When Dionne, despite Mark's remonstrance, slips away to produce some document or other, there's just the shaggy-haired mutt pressing his nose against the screen. But Mark keeps his foot against the bottom of the door so the mutt can't escape.

"It's just a little Pekingese or something," I tell him.

"There's another one in there," says Mark.

Dionne reappears with a small white envelope in her hand. "Oh, I got a Rottweiler—she's trained," she says, turning to flip the envelope onto the counter. "If you live down here, you gotta have a Rott or a gun."

"What kind of gun you have?" asks Donahue, joking with her.

"I ain't got no gun. I got my baby here," Dionne says, laughing. She bends to scratch the ears of the Rottweiler, who's an indistinct shape from where I'm standing. "Right, baby? You protect us."

There's a certain ragged charm to Sandy Dionne's monologue as she runs out the length and breadth of the effort that she has expended to keep Martha Pacquin rolling down the road to her job in New Bedford. "I got the checks, the money order stubs, the stamped envelopes, and the files," she says. "The files I have, you wouldn't believe."

Mark speed-dials Ray at the bank and explains the situation. Ray wants to talk to Sandra and Mark hands over the phone. "That's impossible. That's bullshit," says Dionne. "I paid it and I got the stub to prove it . . . last week. . . . I make out all the envelopes. . . . I already faxed it to you, all of it. . . . Don't I fuckin' know it. . . . You wanna hear a secret? Listen."

She hangs up on Ray. "That's what I call it—a secret," she says with a nasty laugh. "I don't have to listen to *that* bullshit for another minute."

The long-suffering Ray calls back and Donahue answers and takes a little walk into the quad, picking his way around the frozen turds and flat, yellowish disks of used condoms. Dionne hoists up her own cell phone and dials Martha Pacquin at work and gets her voice mail. "She don't turn on her phone when she's working," Dionne says to me. "Martha, this is Sandy. There's two gentlemen here wanna tawk to you about your cawh. Call me back."

Sandy clicks the phone shut and gropes around on the counter behind her and produces the envelope, which she presses against the screen. "Lookit. I got one right here," she says, beckoning me up to the top step. It's a self-addressed envelope, made out to the bank in shaky blue script. "I send the checks in these every month."

The envelope doesn't even have a stamp, but it makes for good theater. Mark walks back over and gives me the eye; we're leaving.

"Tell Martha that the bank wants the car," he says. "Forget about the money—she's nine hundred sixty-eight dollars in arrears."

Dionne shakes her head. "I'll tell her."

We move off down the sidewalk, and I turn back for a moment. "Martha's car, is it the green one?" I ask Dionne.

"It's cranberry," she says. "I ain't gonna lie to you."

We're about twenty feet apart, looking at each other through the screen. "You from Staten Island?" I ask. "You sound like you're from New York."

"Manhattan, born and bred," says Sandra. She throws out her arms. "And now I'm living here."

We get in the car and drive up the hill. Offstage throughout this dark little comedy is Martha Pacquin, who's just the sort of person Joe Mc-Cain would have taken pity on. She's at some metal-finishing plant over in New Bedford, struggling for her wages. At the end of each day she comes home to the stench of dogs and the blare of a television and with Sandra Dionne concocts whatever schemes are necessary to make it through the week. No doubt her days are swifter than a weaver's shuttle, and will come to their end without hope.

"Ray says he got their fax, all right," Mark tells me. "All the checks—but just the fronts. Know why? The backs are stamped 'insufficient funds.' "

Donahue turns left onto South Main Street. "You're learning, Coach," he says. "You got the color of the vehicle out of her. But you didn't see the knife, did you?"

"What knife?"

We pass the oxidized spires of St. Anne's Church, and then the square, brick buildings occupied by the Dominican Sisters of Hope. "She had a paring knife in her left hand the entire time," Mark says. "With about a three-inch blade. Always watch the hands, Coach. The bad guys are gonna hurt you with their hands."

When I think of being called to the top step to look at that envelope I get that same queasy feeling I had when I saw the battleship *Massachusetts*. My midsection was right against the screen and if she had felt like it, Sandra Dionne could have stabbed me through the liver.

"What do you think?" Mark asks. "Will she leave the car out?"

I make no reply, but my guess is that the malevolent forces arrayed against Martha Pacquin will grind her down to some tortured end and she'll finish up on top of the hill at St. Anne's Church. Under the best of circumstances she'll be wearing a clean set of clothes amidst the incense and gladiolus, and a nice woman from the choir will sing "Ave Maria," with burial to follow in Notre Dame Cemetery.

EIGHTEEN

The Return of Billy Dennett

A ROUND THE TIME THAT JOE BARBOZA was using Revere Beach as his headquarters, and Black Jimmy nearly got killed by James "the Bear" Flemmi, Jimmy's old shortchanging buddy from the South End, Billy Dennett was implicated in the disappearance and murder of a small-time hoodlum named Tony Veranis. Veranis was last seen above a bar called Walter's Lounge on Dudley Street, playing poker with Dennett, the Bear, and several other known criminals. Rumors circulated that Veranis was beaten and killed after he insulted someone in the game—and there were a number of suspects, as many of the cardplayers were known to have short fuses. The murder was said to have occurred a short while after Veranis was shoved into the passenger seat of Dennett's '66 Thunderbird and driven away from Walter's Lounge.

All this came as a surprise to Joe McCain, who considered Billy Dennett one in a troupe of happy-go-lucky con artists, not violent men at all and certainly not a bunch of shooters. But acting on a tip, McCain found Veranis's body in a remote section of the Blue Hills, left in a kneeling position with bruises on his face and neck and two entry wounds in his head. The practical-joke-loving Dennett was long gone, heading west, McCain heard, in the company of someone else who had been at the card game, a vicious thug named William Geraway.

At the autopsy, the medical examiner waved Joe McCain closer so he could take a look at Tony Veranis's brain. An ex-boxer, Veranis was a tough, well-built, but not very bright twenty-eight-year-old kid from Dorchester. He had been badly beaten and shot twice in the head at close range, and the M.E. had laid open the skull, halving it like a cantaloupe. Taking up a stainless steel probe, McCain measured the depth of the wounds.

"Joe, have you ever seen a skull that fucking thick?" asked the M.E. McCain noted that the bone wasn't thick enough to stop a .38.

At first there were very few leads in the case. But as McCain was to find out later, Billy Dennett had stolen identification from the president of Gulf Oil, forged a driver's license to match, and he and Geraway were passing checks at a string of banks in Michigan. They had over $100,000 in the trunk of the T-bird, and with Dennett at the wheel and Geraway passed out beside him, the fugitives ran a stoplight and were pulled over by a black policeman.

Wearing a suit and tie, Dennett was polite and cheerful to the Michigan cop, handing over his license with a smile. "I'm very sorry, Officer," he said. "Where I'm from, the lights are on the corners and I drove right under that one and never saw it."

The cop was about to let Dennett go when Geraway began to stir. Scratching at himself, he looked over at Billy Dennett and then past him to the cop, who was leaning in the window. "C'mon," Geraway said. "Give the nigger a sawbuck and let's go."

The patrolman arrested Dennett and Geraway on the spot, and they ended up two cells apart in the local jail. Unaware at this point that Geraway had murdered Tony Veranis, Dennett couldn't believe the sudden downturn in his fortunes. "You couldn't keep your fucking mouth shut," he shouted at Geraway.

"You're lucky I wasn't sober," said Geraway. "I was gonna fuckin' kill you. You were never going back to Boston with me."

Startled by this, Dennett used his phone call to reach Joe McCain back in Somerville. Meanwhile, Geraway was indicted on a previous check scam and sent to the federal penitentiary in Terre Haute, Indiana.

Dennett was on his way to Marquette Penitentiary on the check charge, a remote maximum-security facility on the Upper Peninsula in Michigan, where it snows from September to early May and where patches of the white stuff can be found in the woods as late as July.

"Get me out of here, Joe," said Dennett.

"What're you gonna give me?" McCain asked.

"Geraway. He did Veranis."

McCain had already seized Billy Dennett's car and had it shipped back to Boston. Then McCain and Leo Papile bought a brand-new vacuum cleaner to avoid any contamination of the evidence. They vacuumed up fibers from the Thunderbird, including some that matched those on Veranis's clothing, as well as traces of the dead fighter's blood. Right now Billy Dennett looked good for Veranis's murder, but Joe McCain was listening.

"Okay, Billy," he said. "But the trip out there better be worth it."

"I'll give you everything," said Dennett. "Just get me out of this fucking place."

McCain and a detective from the Boston P.D. flew out to Chicago's O'Hare Airport. From there they took a small prop-engine plane to Green Bay, Wisconsin, and then a little puddle jumper over Iron Mountain to Marquette. It was snowing when they flew into Michigan, the pilot somehow finding the runway in the midst of an encompassing whiteness; and it continued to snow that night and all the next day. Triple-bladed plows were everywhere and there on the spit between Lake Superior and Lake Michigan most of the locals walked around in snowshoes.

An imposing brick edifice constructed on the shores of Lake Superior in 1889, Marquette Prison is a tough joint. It's surrounded by a concrete wall, razor-ribbon wire, and electronic detection systems and overseen by eight gun towers. Six thousand prisoners were housed there when Dennett arrived, almost all of them from Detroit and very few of them white; Billy Dennett was petrified.

Taking along his arrest warrant and Dennett's rendition papers, McCain and the Boston detective arrived at the gates of the prison. The warden, a tall, gaunt fellow who escorted Joe and his partner inside the walls, explained that no one had ever escaped from Marquette. To keep this record intact, the warden said, they had developed certain security procedures that even other law enforcement personnel were required to follow.

The warden and his guests entered a room, where the two visiting cops turned over their weapons and handcuffs for safekeeping. From there, still accompanied by the warden, they proceeded into "the trap," a small concrete chamber with iron grates in place of the ceiling and floor.

"We're going to strip down, gentlemen," said the warden, unbuckling his belt.

McCain laughed. "Pardon me?" he asked.

"It's one of my rules—take all your clothes off," the warden said.

McCain looked at his partner and shrugged. A few moments later, the three men stood naked in the cold, empty room, shivering as they waited for the guards to open the door in front of them. "You go in with nothing," said the warden, as the bolt shot back. "I'll give you pencil and paper if you like, and you can talk to the prisoner in a conference room I have inside the jail. Take it or leave it."

"You're the boss," McCain said.

In the next chamber, McCain, his partner, and the warden endured a thorough strip search; they were told to bend over and spread their cheeks, and the guards looked in their mouths, ears, and hair. Then they were allowed to put their clothes, which had also been searched, back on and were treated to sandwiches and coffee.

A few minutes later, Billy Dennett was led into the windowless conference room, dressed in prison overalls and wearing shackles. He had lost a little weight, and his present circumstances had robbed him of his usual ebullience, but Dennett still managed a grin when he saw his old friend.

"Hey, Joe," he said. "How's tricks?"

"Do you want to go back?" McCain asked.

"Yeah. Can you arrange it?"

McCain nodded. "I'll just call back there and say you're coming, and we'll have to get the tickets."

"What tickets?" Dennett asked.

"The plane tickets."

Billy Dennett looked at McCain in surprise. "Oh, no," he said. "I don't fly."

"Whattaya mean, you don't fly?" asked McCain.

"I'm not gonna fly back."

"The fuck you ain't," McCain said. "I'm not spending a week trying to drive out of these mountains."

Two days later Billy Dennett was remanded into Joe McCain's custody, and handcuffed together, they departed Marquette's snowy little airport for O'Hare. And the Michigan authorities were happy to get rid of him—it was one less body the state would have to feed. Onboard the plane, Dennett was fidgeting in his seat, pawing the floor, and twisting his wrist in the shackle.

"For crissakes, sit still," said McCain.

Billy Dennett looked like he was going to cry. "Can I get a drink, Joe?" he asked.

McCain glanced at his partner and the other detective made a palms-up gesture. "You can have a couple pops," Joe said.

After three whiskeys they landed in Chicago, and Dennett became his old fun-loving self. During the layover, the two police officers and the convict were walking through the terminal when Dennett said he was hungry. He convinced McCain to stop into a nearby pancake house for breakfast. While the busboy and waitress looked on, Joe's partner unlocked the handcuffs and all three men took up their menus.

"Behave yourself," Dennett said to McCain, wagging his finger. "Otherwise, I'll put the cuffs right back on you."

The waitress delivered their menus and retreated to the kitchen, staring at Joe McCain like he was an escaped ax murderer. Billy Dennett had a good laugh and when they arrived in Massachusetts, he said that he'd testify in front of the Suffolk grand jury that it was William T. Geraway who had killed Anthony Veranis.

In Joe's mind, Billy Dennett was still the most likely suspect. Known as a dissembler and opportunist and never adept at choosing his companions, Dennett had been running with a murderous crowd at the time and his car had been loaded with material evidence. But in his conversations with McCain, the affable con man insisted that he and Geraway had been in cahoots while passing bad checks and that they'd paid cash for the Thunderbird after a big score. Although the car was registered in Dennett's name, Geraway believed he had a claim on the T-bird and would borrow it whenever he felt like it.

The night Veranis was murdered, according to Billy Dennett, Geraway took the T-bird from outside Walter's Lounge after the card game. A few weeks earlier, Geraway had mouthed off to Veranis and the former welterweight had dropped him with a quick right hand. Geraway hadn't forgotten that embarrassment, but Veranis, who was punchy from his years in the ring, apparently had; when Geraway asked him to take a ride that night so they could force open a safe he had hidden on Castle Island, the slow-thinking pug agreed to go along.

Dennett said that Geraway, who had related this sordid tale during a whiskey binge, drove Veranis to the remote South Boston park, lured him out of the car, and produced the murder weapon. He tied Veranis's hands behind his back, pistol-whipped him for the punch he had thrown, and then, in a fit of rage, shot Veranis twice in the head. He stuffed the dead man back into the Thunderbird, drove up to the Blue Hills and dumped the body at the foot of an embankment, returning the car to Billy Dennett.

The story was, at least, plausible. And Dennett had one other thing going for him as far as Joe McCain was concerned: he had no history of violent crime. On the other hand, Geraway did; he was a suspect in the murder of David Sidlaukas, who had been found dead on Moon Island Road in Quincy a year earlier; Sidlaukas had also been shot twice in the head. Geraway was also believed to have some connection to the 1965 murder of Edward "Teddy" Deegan, a muddy event that would turn into one of the most notorious cases of wrongful imprisonment in Boston history and would involve Joe McCain at the height of his abilities.

There was just enough doubt nagging at McCain about the Veranis killing that he decided to check out Dennett's story. Working with Billy's scenario and poking around on his days off, McCain began spending time at Castle Island, talking to the dog walkers and other habitués. One afternoon he found a young woman, a nurse from Mass General, who remembered seeing a brand-new Thunderbird parked in the lot. She said there were two men in the car, and when Joe showed her a picture of Tony Veranis, she recognized him. Back at the D.A.'s office, McCain asked the young nurse to look through a collection of photographs that included Billy Dennett and William Geraway.

Without hesitation, she drew one out of the pile and said, "That's him—that's the one I saw on Castle Island." It was Geraway.

Still in handcuffs, Billy Dennett testified in front of the grand jury that William Geraway had murdered Tony Veranis. Bolstered by the nurse's testimony, the D.A. won a conviction and Geraway received a life sentence in Walpole State Prison. But the case would have another surprising twist. A few years into his sentence, Geraway told authorities that a convict who was in an adjacent cell for a few months in 1970 before being released admitted that he'd killed a man named Wilson in California. This jailhouse confession was noteworthy because Geraway's neighbor had been in the federal witness protection program when he'd committed the murder. In a successful attempt to reduce his own sentence to time served, Geraway testified against his fellow jailbird, which resulted in the man's return to Folsom Prison in California. Geraway's neighbor in Walpole was Joe Barboza.

Avoiding the murder charge, Billy Dennett did time in Walpole for passing checks. As soon as he got out, he reunited with Black Jimmy in Boston. There was too much heat on slow walking, and the art of short-changing, which might bring in a couple of hundred bucks in an afternoon, seemed too much like work. In the nick of time Jimmy and Billy learned that a wiseguy had slipped Los Angeles Lakers basketball star Wilt Chamberlain some bad crabmeat at the Sheraton the night before L.A. was supposed to play against the Celtics. Chamberlain was weakened by ptomaine poisoning but hardly anyone knew about it, and Jimmy and Billy pooled the last of their cash and called a bookie they knew in Chelsea to place a thousand-dollar bet on the Celts. Since they'd never bet more than a hundred dollars at a time, the bookie made them come in and pay the grand in advance, which they did.

An hour later, Billy and Jimmy were just settling into their seats at the Boston Garden when they noticed the bookmaker sitting right behind the Lakers bench. Then the teams came out for the warm-up, and Wilt the Stilt was not among them.

"Billy, Chamberlain ain't playing," Black Jimmy said. "We got a fuckin' lock here."

Just then the bookie turned around and glared at Jimmy. "You dirty motherfucker," he said.

At halftime Jimmy ran into the bookmaker under the stands. "Why the fuck didn't you tell me Chamberlain was out?" he said.

"How the fuck did I know?" asked Jimmy.

The bookie walked away, fuming. The Celtics won, and the next day Black Jimmy phoned in to collect on the bet and was told to drop by at 6:30 P.M. "But you close at six," said Jimmy.

"Yeah, well, come at six-thirty," the bookmaker said.

Black Jimmy called Dennett and relayed the bookie's instructions. "Bring your gun," he said. "Something's wrong."

On the drive over, Jimmy said to Billy, "Stand against the door. If the shooting starts, it's better we're split up." Black Jimmy had a .357 in his coat pocket. "I don't know what they're comin' out with, but I ain't goin' down without a fight."

Jimmy and Billy arrived at the bookie's storefront office right at 6:30. When they walked in, John "the Basin Street Butcher" Martorano was sitting in the corner. (A notorious mob enforcer, Martorano later admitted to more than twenty murders and cut a deal that amounted to eight years in prison.)

"Why didn't you tell me Chamberlain was gonna be out?" asked the bookmaker.

"Look, if I knew Chamberlain was out, I woulda come to you and said, 'Bet a hundred thousand—Chamberlain ain't playin'. But I want in for ten thousand,' and you woulda went for it in a minute," Jimmy said. "We bet a lousy five hundred apiece, and you're gonna hassle us for that?"

Martorano nodded to the bookie and said, "Pay 'em."

Within a few days, the Basin Street Butcher had conducted a little criminal investigation of his own, and the three wiseguys who had fixed the Celtics game turned up in Boston Harbor with the backs of their heads blown off. Happy to be alive, Billy and Jimmy went off looking for an easier way to make their living.

When times were bad, the two con men usually sought out White Jimmy. Unlike some of his companions, James O'Grady had once worked a straight job, pounding the asphalt as a mailman for a couple of years. During that time O'Grady made the acquaintance of the North End P.O. manager, Pasquale Luzzo, who for several years was running a sweet little game nobody else had tried. Luzzo and a group of confederates were responsible for collecting the enormous volume of mail that was dumped into relay boxes around the city. If anything looked interesting, they'd cull it out of the pile and forward it to Luzzo, who would steam open the envelopes and peek inside. One day Luzzo found a sheaf of certificates that turned out to contain $300 million in bearer bonds from the state of Maine. The difficulty lay in trying to cash or fence the bonds, and seeking help, Luzzo reached out to James O'Grady. In turn, O'Grady consulted with Black Jimmy and Billy Dennett.

The trio was sitting on a gold mine. Clearing just 10 percent on the face value of the certificates meant they would be set for life, and one afternoon in Billy Settipane's bar, they racked their brains on how to proceed. Black Jimmy said he knew a banker in Denver named Myron Levertov who had enough capital to offer thirty or forty points on the bonds. His partners decided it was worth a shot.

Carrying half the bonds in a valise and leaving half behind for safekeeping, Jimmy flew into Stapleton airport late one night and grabbed a room in the best hotel on Colfax Ave. His accommodations were pricey, but soon he'd be off the carousel of petty cons and living the high life. Arriving in his suite, he admired the gilt-edged curtains and drapery, and with its tight, expensive linens, the bed was like a vellum envelope.

The next morning he arranged to meet Levertov in his office at the bank, his heart racing at the possibility of such a big score. But Levertov took one look at the certificates, pronounced them too hot to handle, and Black Jimmy returned to his hotel room with $150 million and no way to spend it.

Jimmy called O'Grady back in Boston. "Fuckin' guy wouldn't touch 'em with a ten-foot pole," he said.

The two grifters mulled over their options. The longer they held on to the bonds, the greater the chance they'd be pinched for the theft. And $300 million was hard to keep secret; pretty soon every wiseguy from Braintree to Lynn was going to be looking for a piece of the action.

"Let's give 'em back," said Black Jimmy.

"To who?" asked O'Grady. "Maine?"

"No, asshole. To Luzzo. And then we'll throw it to McCain. I owe him one, anyway."

After more discussion, White Jimmy agreed that turning the case over to Joe McCain was their best bet. Maybe there was a reward for the bonds, or Joe might convince the D.A. to pay them a fee if they helped set up Luzzo. In any event, they wouldn't be going to prison again.

"Sayonara, three hundred million," said O'Grady as he signed off.

At 73 Tremont Street the next day, Joe McCain cataloged 164 Maine municipal bonds in the E, F, G, and H series, instructing James O'Grady to return them to Pasquale Luzzo. In the meantime, White Jimmy had learned that the slippery postal clerk had also stolen twenty-five Avco commercial notes worth a total of $6 million and a number of securities marked "African Gold Mining." Luzzo stored all these notes and securities in a Filene's gift box, which he kept hidden behind the sofa in his home on Newman Street in Revere.

While McCain's partner Jack Crowley and another detective tailed Luzzo, McCain accompanied Joe Doyle to the home of Chelsea Court Clerk Fred Gillis in Winthrop, where the curly-haired assistant D.A. produced the documentation necessary for Gillis to issue a search warrant for Luzzo's home.

Shortly thereafter, Crowley radioed McCain to tell him that Luzzo was at his residence, with his wife and two young children. Spreading a cordon of plainclothes Mets and postal inspectors around the home, a two-story wooden Colonial with a red brick front, Joe McCain walked up to the front stoop and knocked. He heard someone descend the interior staircase, and then Luzzo's wife, Delores, opened the door.

"Can I help you?" she asked.

"I need to speak to your husband," McCain said.

A man's voice called from upstairs. "Who is it?" he asked.

"You better come down here," said his wife.

McCain passed over the threshold, and Luzzo met him in the foyer. "What's the problem?" he asked.

"Step out here for a minute," said McCain. They went onto the stoop, and McCain handed over a copy of the search warrant. "I'm a Metropolitan police officer," he said. "I got an army of people here, and we're going to search your entire house."

Luzzo glanced at his wife, and she shook her head. On the way back inside, Pasquale read the warrant, and upon reaching the kitchen, he dropped the paper on the floor and began massaging his forehead.

"Have your wife take the kids next door—less embarrassing that way," said McCain. "We're looking for some papers. If you want to give this stuff up, we'll sit down right here, we'll talk, and everything will be okay."

Luzzo nodded. "I'll give you what you're looking for," he said.

They went into the living room, and Luzzo moved the sofa away from the wall to retrieve the Filene's box. "A guy dropped this off and asked me to hold on to it," he said. "I don't know what's in it."

McCain opened the box and found the $6 million in Avco commercial notes and the mining certificates but not the bearer bonds. "Is that it?" he asked.

"That's all I got," Luzzo said.

For the next two hours McCain and his team searched every room and the attic and basement without finding a thing. The Luzzo home was decorated in heavy, dark furniture, mirrored walls, and shag carpeting, the living room hung with paintings of sad-faced clowns and the ruins of the Colosseum. After they were ready to concede that the bonds were someplace else, big Joe was standing in front of a brick fireplace that occupied half the room. Though it was late spring and the nights had been warm, a pile of birch logs was stacked across the andirons.

Bending down for a closer inspection, McCain noticed a paper bag hidden beneath the logs. He pulled it out and looked inside: all 164 Maine municipal bonds, ready for burning if Luzzo had been given the chance. Instead, he was arrested and held on $50,000 bail.

For their trouble, Black Jimmy and James O'Grady earned a couple hundred dollars from the district attorney's office and a ton of Joe

McCain's goodwill. And when they made Joe happy, he'd ignore most of their shenanigans—as long as they kept providing him with information. Working with the two Jimmies, McCain and Jack Crowley also broke the Veterans' Services case, in which a group of crooks, including the veterans' investigators Eddie and Robert Reardon, enlisted scores of men to falsify military records, file them with the veterans' services offices in their respective towns, and receive monthly checks. Typically, the phony veterans would cash the checks and turn over half the money to the Reardons and their partners.

The scam had been going on for years, involving hundreds of non-veterans in Massachusetts and beyond, and defrauding the U.S. government out of millions of dollars. Late one night McCain and Crowley posted guards all around Boston City Hall, and went into the veterans' services office and examined the rolls. Within minutes they discovered the files of several known criminals from Charlestown and Somerville who had never served in the military and yet had DD-214 discharge papers and other bogus records. Firemen and police officers and city workers and teamsters from all over the city were involved, and before long a virtual army of lawyers and their clients were parading into the district attorney's office looking to plead out. The commissioner of veterans' services for the city of Boston, a fellow named Mullen, went to state prison along with the Reardons and several other plotters; their homes in Falmouth and boats and fancy cars were seized, and the entire system of veterans' payments was thrown into an uproar.

The case generated mountains of paperwork, and one day Joe McCain was in his office on Tremont Street, his desk and the floor surrounding it buried in manila folders. Black Jimmy and Billy Dennett arrived intending to have lunch at the Fatted Calf and were surprised to find McCain, after his latest triumph, wearing such a glum look.

"What's the matter, Joe?" asked Black Jimmy.

McCain tossed a folder onto the pile. "I'm gonna be doing fucking reports on this for the rest of my life," he said.

Nearby, Billy Dennett was perusing the files and he reached down and held one aloft. "This is Ronnie Zagini's," he said. "Shit, Joe, you're not gonna press charges against Ronnie, are you?"

"Yeah, Ronnie Zagini's a great guy," said Jimmy. "Don't do it, Joe."

McCain stood up, knee deep in file folders. "He's a fuckin' thief," he said.

Black Jimmy and Billy Dennett looked at each other like *So what?* Putting on his sport coat, McCain asked, "You're saying he's a good guy?"

"The best, Joe," said Dennett. "Ronnie's aces."

McCain took Zagini's file and opened it and looked inside. "Ehh," he said, pitching it into the wastebasket. "One less fuckin' headache."

BILLY DENNETT LOVED THE RACETRACK and the whores, but it was the booze that finally caught up with him. In Florida he fell ill but, wary of a shortchanging beef in Tampa, was reluctant to check himself into the hospital. Nor did he have the money to pay for his care until Black Jimmy, busy handicapping the dogs over in Sarasota, gave Billy five hundred dollars and convinced him to enter a Bradenton hospital under his brother's name and social security number.

At least he had a clean, quiet place to rest, because not long after occupying the room Billy lapsed into a diabetic coma. Listed on his record as next of kin, Black Jimmy got the call after a losing day at the track that his friend's luck was running out.

Jimmy opened the door to Billy's room and padded in, clutching the racing form and some trinkets from the gift shop. A nurse in orthopedic stockings was looking at Billy's chart, and glancing up, she smiled for a moment but shook her head. Billy was lying in a heap with an oxygen mask over his nose and mouth, breathing in a shallow rhythm. Taking a chair beside him, Jimmy put the newspaper and plastic hula girl aside and sat gazing at the wallpaper.

"Talk to him," the nurse said.

"Can he hear me?"

"I don't know," said the nurse. "I think so."

After she went out, Black Jimmy spoke in a confidential tone for quite a while, telling Billy about which dogs were going well at Sarasota and rhapsodizing over all the lovely young girls working the concession stands. If anyone had passed by the room just then, he or she would've thought that its occupant was a psych case, in there whispering to himself, his soliloquy punctuated now and then by a low, raspy chuckle.

Billy Dennett made no response. After falling silent for a minute or so, Black Jimmy glanced around the room and heaved his shoulders. Then he got to his feet, looking past his old friend and out the window at the deepening twilight.

"I'm wasting my fucking breath," he said, heading for the door. "I'm talking to a dead man here."

NINETEEN

Appointment with Dr. Sommerov

I'M WORKING WITH KEVIN McKENNA TODAY, and I've heard he likes to break balls. We've never met, but over the telephone he gives me an address down in Burlington and a description of the subject in a workmen's compensation case, a dark-haired, middle-aged man named Christmas Langlois who has been collecting eight hundred dollars a week in disability payments. Suffering from a back injury, Langlois has been out a year and is not able to drive a car or walk without a cane. Despite these infirmities, his employer, a large commercial transportation company, has heard rumors that Langlois is cruising around in his new Ford Explorer and doing work as a landscaper. The subject and his family live at 26 Temple Street in Burlington, which is a left off of Plummer Avenue.

"He's one of the reasons our insurance premiums are so high," McKenna says. He's coming up from the South Shore, and I tell him what I'm driving and the color shirt I'm wearing and ask how I'll be able to spot him. "That's your fucking problem," says McKenna, and he hangs up.

A forty-five-year-old Boston Housing cop, Kevin McKenna has a wife and three kids and has been moonlighting as a P.I. for several years, working for the McCains as well as SOS, which stands for "Surveillance Our Specialty," an adroit little firm out of Kingston, Mass. He's made over four thousand arrests as a police officer in the housing developments scattered throughout the city, part of a thirty-five-man force charged with serving sixty thousand residents in an environment where organized crime, drug trafficking, and gangs are rampant. As a result, McKenna is said to be crazier than a shithouse rat but a great detective, with the mind of a logician and the nose of a bloodhound.

It's a little after 7:00 A.M. on Sunday when I exit off Route 93 and go rolling into Burlington, a quiet residential town twenty miles north of Boston. Early in March the snow is gone, and a hint of spring is wafting in beneath the chill. I don't have a map book and go creeping down Main Street, peering up at the street signs. Less than a mile from the highway I get lucky when Plummer Ave. pops up on my right. Temple Street appears on my left a few seconds later, and I drive along past immaculate, low-slung homes equipped with two- or three-stall garages and fronted by expanses of manicured lawn.

A blue-and-gold tricycle sits abandoned on the sidewalk, and the roadway is devoid of parked cars or pedestrians. Halfway down Temple Street I realize it's a cul-de-sac, and then I spot the subject's house, Number 26, a two-story brown Colonial with a replica of an old New England barn for a mailbox. Early morning light reflects off the windows, and there's an aroma of cut grass and honeysuckle. The house and property are well-maintained and the brand-new Ford Explorer, shining with a fresh coat of wax, is parked in the driveway.

At the end of the street I turn around and drive by 26 Temple again. No one is stirring. Unfortunately, there's nowhere to park that isn't conspicuous and no place to sit on the house without tipping the neighbors. But there's no other way off Temple Street for the subject, either. Convinced that Langlois is at home, I turn left onto Plummer Ave. and soon discover that it's a dead end, too. The natural surveillance point, therefore, is back on Main Street. The subject can't leave the area without using that route.

Emerging onto Main, I spot two possible surveillance locations: the head of an unmarked gravel road opposite Plummer Ave. and, a little farther along, the parking lot of a business named Kitchen World.

It's only then that I notice McKenna. There's a dark blue van with tinted windows parked in front of the kitchenette store, with the driver's seat all the way back and a man with a baseball cap pulled low on his forehead. I cross over Main Street in very light traffic and pull in beside the van.

McKenna rolls down his window. "Took you long enough," he says.

"Did you see me go by?" I ask, climbing into the passenger seat.

"I saw you," he says, reaching out to shake my hand. "You figured it out, though. There's no place closer to sit on the house without being made."

McKenna reminds me of Dashiell Hammett's famous detective the Continental Op. He's a short, stocky fellow dressed in khaki shorts, a rumpled polo shirt, and sneakers. His calves are the size of two cantaloupes and he wears a scruffy beard and his hair is graying at the temples. His hand, gripping mine, is stubby and broad, and he squeezes me like a vise.

"What did you notice about the guy's house?" asks McKenna.

I run off the details I picked up, which are scant in number and colorless. In the same ten-second drive-by, McKenna has memorized the license plate of the subject's car and noted the locations of the picnic table and toolshed, backyard swimming pool and various toys. He also declares that two cops live on Temple Street and at least one of them may be friendly with the subject.

"How do you know that?"

"Wiffle ball bat and hockey net in the subject's yard. Soccer ball and Big Wheel in the cop's yard," says McKenna. "They both have kids about the same age."

"But what makes you think he's a cop?"

The whole time McKenna is staring at the top of Plummer Ave.; he never even looks at me. "Did you notice my front license plate?" he asks.

Come to think of it, I did. The plate features a little starburst design and the initials M.P.A. I don't know what they mean.

"Mass. Police Association," McKenna says. "Just about every cop has an M.P.A. sticker on his car, and Langlois's neighbor has one. And a cop is gonna notice a strange vehicle parked on his street. And that cop is probably a friend of Langlois's. So we're gonna stay here."

But allowing that Langlois probably has another car inside his garage and could get by us without being recognized, McKenna takes a chance on getting "made" and drives past the house. On workmen's comp cases our job is to find out if the subject is defying his medical order, video-tape the activity if possible, and write a report about it. Even on a week-end, Langlois might be pulling stumps in his backyard or building the kids a swing set, and if he is, we're supposed to document these feats on tape.

We cruise along Plummer Ave. in McKenna's van and take a left. Temple Street is deserted, but McKenna points to a For Sale sign on the lawn of a home two doors away from the Langloises'. "There's our pre-text," he says, turning the van around. "We're looking at houses."

As I go rubbernecking out my window, McKenna studies the Lan-gloises' house on the way past. Mark Donahue has told me that Kevin McKenna is the undisputed pretext champion of the world. On a do-mestic case last March, he was following a divorced woman who had just been awarded custody of her two children but ordered by the court not to drink alcohol. One Saturday afternoon the woman left the house all dolled up and by herself, with McKenna tailing in the van. A stun-ning brunette with a gorgeous body, she drove to a wedding in Ply-mouth, Mass., and on to the reception at the White Cliffs Country Club. Watching the front door of the club, McKenna was possessed by an idea, broke off his surveillance and raced home.

It was St. Patrick's Day weekend and McKenna returned to the coun-try club fresh-shaven and dressed in a well-tailored green suit, with a camcorder on a strap around his neck. At the registration table he grabbed a place card with the name of someone who hadn't shown up and proceeded into the reception, where the party was in full swing. If anyone bothered to ask—and very few people did—McKenna said that he was the bride's cousin's date and helped himself to the filet mignon and open bar.

After dinner he made the rounds, pointing his camcorder at various tables and asking people to say a few words. Only he didn't bother to press the Record button until he reached the subject's table. The woman was pounding shots of Sambuca and when asked to address the bride, she raised her glass and said, "Don't fucking do it. Marriage sucks."

She thought McKenna was funny, and soon they were cutting up the dance floor—with the video camera perched on a corner of the bar, recording their moves. The woman drank like a sailor, bumping and grinding to the wedding singer's rendition of "Get Down Tonight." It was a great time, McKenna said, and the best thing was that McCain Investigations's client, the divorced dad, got his kids back.

"The woman was a lot of fun but a complete alcoholic," says McKenna. "She was soused, driving around with the kids in the car seats."

In front of Kitchen World, McKenna and I watch Burlington come to life as people head out for their morning coffee and a string of joggers go tramping along the sidewalk in either direction. Once every hour until noon we ride past the Langloises', but the Explorer hasn't moved and all the doors and windows in the house remain closed. McKenna says that the biggest part of surveillance is the waiting; usually nothing happens. On our fourth pass, a woman who lives across from the Langloises stares as we go by and McKenna decides to break it off.

"If he's working, we'll catch him," says the pudgy detective. "And if he isn't, they're all billable hours."

Among the chewed up dog pillows, baseball gloves, and dusty jars of "food thickener" in the back of the van is an old briefcase that looks like a cardboard accordion. McKenna shuffles around in there for a moment and pulls out three case files and looks them over. "Y'like clams?" he asks. When I reply that I do, McKenna says, "Good, cuz we're going to the beach."

Twenty minutes later we arrive at Houghs Neck in Quincy, a spit of land that curves off the southern end of Wollaston Beach. The neck contains a single main artery, Sea Street, which is peppered with little shops and a gas station or two. Branching off to either side is a network of small, crooked lanes with panoramic views of the Boston skyline, the harbor, and several outlying islands.

After a drive past three houses on three different streets, McKenna parks the van on a little hill behind an apartment building. From here, we can see through a hole in the fence and over an empty swimming pool to the only real intersection in Houghs Neck. McKenna says we'll be keeping tabs on three subjects at once, all employees of the same transportation company: a woman with an ankle injury who drives an airport shuttle van; a rarely seen auto mechanic with pork chop sideburns and a bad back; and the most difficult case, a truck driver named Billy Giampa with an injury to his left foot.

Giampa has been out for six months and is suspected of illegally working another job. He's "cute," says McKenna; he's made two other private detectives who were following him, and one day last week, when McKenna was driving his other car, he lost Giampa's blue Subaru pickup on Wollaston Beach. Stuck at a light, McKenna was surprised to see the Subaru coming the other way and as they passed each other, Giampa flipped him the bird.

McKenna laughs. "Fuck him," he says. "I know he's working somewhere."

Houghs Neck is a pretty small place and I marvel at the number of people cheating on workmen's comp, all employees of the same company. "It's an epidemic," I say.

"They're all patients of Dr. Sommerov," says McKenna, noting that the transportation company loses more than a dozen people a month to workplace injuries, and nearly 60 percent of them try to defraud their employer. "If they spend five grand per case on a P.I. but settle four out of ten, they're saving money," he says.

I ask McKenna if Dr. Sommerov is some crazy Russian they all go to, and he laughs. "Yeah, there's two doctors, actually," he says. "Dr. Summer-off and Dr. Winter-off."

Perusing Giampa's file, I learn that he's thirty years old, five foot nine and 195 pounds, muscular, with a large red lion tattooed on his left arm. McKenna thinks he's working at the gas station right down the hill from us, and just as I take the binoculars for a look-see, a blue Subaru pickup arrives in front and Giampa gets out and strolls into the office.

"His foot must be getting better," says McKenna, zooming in with the video camera.

The street is arrayed in sunlight, making it dark inside the gas station. Through the binoculars I can just make out Giampa lurking in the office, while McKenna explains that if we can videotape the subject driving his truck, et cetera, his employer will present the evidence to Giampa's doctor and he'll either return to work or be fired. "He's stealing from the honest people at that company," says McKenna. "Same as any thief."

Giampa emerges from the gas station, climbs into his truck, and we zoom off down the hill and attempt to follow him. Cutting in and out of traffic like a rally driver, Giampa beats us through a light near the YMCA, and we loop around an athletic field, driving past a squad of lacrosse players sweating through a workout. The blue Subaru is gone.

"Time for lunch," says McKenna.

Down on Wollaston Beach, we're halfway through an order of steamed clams when the client phones and tells us to drop Giampa for today and pick up surveillance on a woman in Dorchester. Her name is Lila Ogletree and she's been out of work only three days, but her background check revealed that Lila has filed six insurance claims in her last four jobs. This time it's a bad back, and McKenna says that Lila must be a regular patient of both Dr. Winterov and Dr. Sommerov.

A short time later we're on Columbia Road in "Poor-chester." Going through a notoriously rough neighborhood known as Uphams Corner, McKenna gropes along his pant leg and says, "This is not a good area to be without a gun."

He's left his at home, thinking that we were going to be in Quincy and Burlington all day. In eighteen years as a police officer, Kevin McKenna has been shot at, bitten, spit upon, and threatened by crack dealers and junkies. He's lost two partners to suicide. As a lowly housing cop, McKenna's had his best investigative work commandeered by state troopers and the Boston P.D., and as union president, he's been ostracized by his superiors, suspended on trumped-up charges, and placed on administrative leave. His doctor, a legitimate medical school graduate, has diagnosed him with post-traumatic stress disorder. But he still loves the street.

On a hill a quarter mile from Uphams Corner we find a neat, grayish green two-story house with a steep gabled roof. Driving past, I can see four derelict Cadillacs in the yard and a row of well-kept flowering plants on the wraparound porch, which is dotted by wicker furniture and painted in dark green trim. Nobody is on the porch or in the yard, and McKenna drives around the block and parks on a stretch of roadway looking down upon the house. Then he fiddles with the radio and tunes in a country station, which he listens to for hours at a time.

As a journalist, I'm supposed to notice things, and it's more than a little humbling when McKenna trumps every one of my observations. But just as Mark Donahue likes going out alongside Detective George Baker, the best cop on his job in Salem, I enjoy doubling up with McKenna. While we're sitting on Lila's house, a kid about nineteen or twenty years old wearing a do-rag and a Red Sox jersey walks in front of the van and crosses the street. There's a group of kids waiting on the corner, and McKenna sighs and puts the van in gear, rolling away down the hill.

"Where we going?" I ask.

As we're passing the kid, McKenna nods in his direction and says, "I don't want to see what happens next."

Attached to the kid's hip is what looks like a cell phone holster, and the black nub of something is sticking out of his right front pocket. "He's got a knife on his hip and a gun in his pocket," says McKenna. "We want to catch a lady carrying groceries, not appear in court as witnesses to a shooting."

Going around the corner, McKenna spots a woman from another case unloading bags from the open hatch of an SUV. "Awesome," he says, parking the van a little ways up the street.

Hoisting the camcorder, he jumps over the backseat into the cargo space in the rear and tapes the subject's peregrinations to and from the house. She's a heavyset woman in a blue denim jacket and a white blouse, huffing and puffing with her groceries but more agile than a person claiming a back injury should be. Before she's finished with the groceries, McKenna is on the phone to the client. "I just got Nadia," he says. "Uh-huh. Academy Award material. Her sciatica has been miraculously cured."

McKenna is happy but realizes that Lila is a bigger prize. She's a professional fraud, much too smart to get caught lifting weights on her front porch. For a while we sit on Lila's house, but the SUV that McKenna thinks is her car still isn't here and he decides to move to another location near Grove Hall. A friend of Lila's has an apartment there, and on the way, McKenna sings along with some cowpoke on the radio while the deep, reverberating beat of hip-hop emanates from the sporty little cars around us.

"You're the only guy in Dorchester listening to the Grand Ole Opry," I tell him.

McKenna parks in front of a grocery store near the Roxbury-Dorchester line. At the corner a trim fellow in a straw boater and neat gray suit and bow tie is greeting passersby in front of Mohammed's Mosque No. 11. A portable sign by his elbow announces a lecture entitled "Death Stands at the Door" scheduled for Sunday afternoon at 1:30, and a banner fixed to the telephone pole bears the likenesses of Martin Luther King and Rosa Parks.

"This is Castlegate territory," says McKenna, pointing out the gang tags scribbled over nearby buildings. "Known for more murders and drugs than any other gang in Boston."

Tied to a pole nearby is a collection of dead flowers and little rigid balloons on sticks and a well-worn teddy bear, the sort of makeshift shrine you'll see on the highway where a fatal accident has occurred. But this one is located on a city sidewalk, in front of a fire station and the Grove Hall housing development.

"A kid was stabbed to death there about two months ago," says McKenna. "Over drugs, in broad daylight."

Before I can ask him about it, McKenna jumps out of the van and saunters across the road, where he enters conversation with a tall, large-limbed, young black woman. She says something in an animated way and McKenna laughs, patting her on the shoulder. After a couple of minutes, he returns to the van and starts it up.

"Who's that?" I ask.

"I locked her up for crack a few years ago. Once in a while she gives me something. I had a shooting down here once, and she told me who it was."

"Does she know Lila?"

McKenna shakes his head. "She knows Lila's friend, though. Says the woman we're looking for might have a white boyfriend, an older guy."

When I ask him why he was laughing, McKenna imitates the woman's high-pitched voice and laughs some more. "She said, 'Kevin, you got fat!'"

TWENTY

Let Us Now Praise Famous Men

The point is, I'm not in business to be loved, but I am in business.
—Jake Gittes, *Chinatown*

During his tenure at McCain Investigations, Kevin McKenna learned a great deal about cultivating sources from the company namesake. According to McKenna and several other cops, Joe McCain was the undisputed champion when it came to informants. In the late 1960s there was a group of teenagers who hung around Revere Beach, from broken homes mostly, kids who might've worked a few hours in the concession stands or over at Bob's Discount but who spent the majority of their time drinking beer, committing petty acts of vandalism, or stealing from the carnies, who were thieves themselves. At its very root, Joe McCain's career was based on his knack for engendering trust in the sorts of people who, as a rule, didn't trust anybody. And even after he made detective and was busy tracking the migration of the gangsters shuttling from the Ebb Tide to Hurley's Palm Gardens to the Driftwood and back to Sammy's Patio Lounge and the Tiger's Tail, big Joe had a soft spot for these troubled kids. He'd go walking through the aromatic summer crowds looking for them, meting out a few words of advice, a couple of bucks here and there, or a kick in the ass if need be.

Among this group of nascent criminals and con men, one lad in particular caught McCain's attention. His name, for the purposes of this story, was Tommy Flynn; he was the half brother of a state policeman and one of the toughest kids who roosted along Revere Beach Parkway. Joe used to laugh and call him Jack La Lanne, because Flynn, even at sixteen, was constantly working out: running up and down the beach, doing push-ups and chin-ups, riding his bike, and shadowboxing in the alleyways off Ocean Avenue.

Joe lost track of Flynn when he enlisted in the Army and went away to Ranger School. In the mid-seventies, when he was discharged, Tommy Flynn bumped into Joe McCain on Revere Beach, and the two old friends had a cup of coffee together. The Army had done Flynn a lot of good: he was tall, well-muscled, and after years of boxing and karate, lethal with hand and foot.

"Joe, you know, I'm gay," Flynn said.

"Good for you," said McCain, with a shrug. "What do I care? You're a grown man."

But Flynn, who had always kept McCain informed of what was happening on Revere Beach, explained that, as a twelve-year-old kid loose on the boulevard, he'd been exploited and abused by a group of prominent men who ran a house of prostitution stocked with little boys—a pedophile's dream—less than two miles from the coffee shop where they were sitting, at 242 Mountain Avenue in Revere.

The third-floor apartment was being rented by the thirty-seven-year-old novelties salesman Richard Peluso, who had outfitted the main rooms with pool and Ping-Pong tables, dart boards, pinball machines, and magazines from an organization called NAMBLA that depicted sex between men and boys, while stocking the kitchen with ample supplies of popcorn, peanuts, candy, and beer. Boys between the ages of eight and thirteen, most of them latchkey kids with no fathers and very little structure in their lives, were being lured to the house with promises of fun and games, only to be anally and orally raped by Peluso and a continuous line of doctors, businessmen, and other professionals who paid a fee to Peluso for their depraved adventures.

This had been going on for years and was still going on, said Tommy Flynn; in fact, he had first been taken to Mountain Ave. by a "respectable" businessman named Eddie Mede, part of the family that owned Mede's Log Cabin in East Boston, a nightclub that featured transvestites—some of whom Joe McCain had locked up when he was a rookie cop. Not known as a pedophile or a homosexual, Mede taught self-defense tactics to the Revere Police Department and had given Tommy Flynn karate lessons at his studio in Beachmont.

This was the most outrageous and disturbing thing Joe McCain had ever heard. And, it got worse; Peluso's house of horrors was frequented by one of Boston's best-known child psychiatrists, a wealthy investment broker from Wellesley and a licensed social worker from Cambridge, among many others from all over the country. All of them were successful, well-educated men, often with children of their own, and too frequently in professional positions where they were entrusted with the education and safety of young people. Veiled in respectability, these predators had ruined the lives of dozens of prepubescent boys from Revere, Malden, Chelsea, and their environs, by sodomizing them, sucking their penises, and performing other bizarre and unnatural acts. This abuse was so brazen and systematic that Peluso and his cronies were using a school bus and driver to transport unsupervised young boys the eight or nine miles from the North End of Boston to Mountain Ave.

As he sat in the coffee shop, big Joe's lower lip began to quiver, and his right leg trembled beneath the table. In his eighteen-plus years on the job, he had witnessed a great number of terrible things: as a police diver he had hauled corpses out of the Mystic River with their eyes, lips, ears, noses, and genitals eaten away by scavengers; he had been the first to respond to automobile accidents involving multiple fatalities; he had seen gangsters with their faces torn off by shotgun blasts; and he had attended dozens of autopsies with an unlit cigar in his mouth and Vicks VapoRub stuck up each nostril to kill the stench. But what Flynn was describing made Joe McCain sick to his stomach.

McCain knew Flynn and trusted his information, but what proof did he have? Flynn told Joe that if he went into a certain room on the third floor of 242 Mountain Avenue he would find a huge stack of Polaroids depicting naked boys in the midst of various sex acts. The photographs, which Flynn described as perverse trophies hoarded by Richard Peluso, had been stashed in a heating vent.

"Are you sure, Tommy?" asked McCain.

The ex-Ranger stared Joe McCain in the face. "They're in there," he said.

McCain was working in the SCIPP unit at the time, with the mandate to be aggressive and make cases. His partner was Jack Crowley, who had a knack for getting in beneath McCain's volcanic temper and dictatorial manner, prompting him to laugh in the midst of his rages by impersonating Boris Karloff or Bela Lugosi.

Oftentimes McCain would show up at the office in a shirt and tie pockmarked with tiny burn holes from his cigar, and Crowley once asked him if he knew a good tailor.

"Sure, why?" asked McCain.

"Because you should ask him to make you a suit out of fuckin' asbestos," Crowley said.

A hardworking guy who moonlighted several nights a week in a liquor store and had seven kids of his own, Crowley said he would work the case with McCain even though there was a regime change in the SCIPP unit and he was on the way out. The reigning district attorney, Garrett Byrne, who was eighty years old and had served the county since 1952, had been defeated by Newman Flanagan, and the incoming D.A. wanted to put his own people in there. Assistant D.A.s Joe Doyle and Roger Emanuelson were resigning, Crowley was going back to his old unit in District A-1, and a host of other good cops were transferring out. Detective McCain was sitting on what looked like a huge, messy case, and as he did over his entire career, Joe resisted office politics and his own selfish interests to go after Peluso and his sex ring.

Personally he wanted to keep a low profile in the early stages of the investigation, remaining unknown to the perps and perverts who frequented 242 Mountain Ave., so armed with Flynn's tip and his own reputation, McCain convinced the D.A. to get a search warrant and asked Jack Crowley to go over to Peluso's house and look for the incriminating photographs.

"Okay, Joe," said Crowley, who called his partner No Show for his propensity to skip golf outings and other social commitments. "Just remember that I work *with* you, not for you."

McCain warned Crowley that he would find some terrible things on Mountain Ave., that there might even be some kids in the house, but still Crowley was shocked when on a cold, rainy afternoon he and another detective rang the bell to serve the warrant and a twelve-year-old boy, naked to the waist, ran past them into the street.

The evidence was right where Tommy Flynn said it would be. Crowley returned to the SCIPP office with a large collection of Polaroids, featuring a diverse group of naked boys in an array of vulgar poses. Some of the photos depicted boys as young as nine years old engaging in sex acts with older men in the bedrooms of 242 Mountain Ave., or sitting on the laps of these men, smiling and drinking beer. Eventually, Richard Peluso was indicted for the rape of three boys under the age of sixteen.

Although people who came of age in the 1970s might look back on those days as the height of the so-called Sexual Revolution, as far as Boston's straitlaced middle class was concerned, the phenomena of child molestation and perversion didn't really exist. Certainly they didn't occur in a place like Revere, among men of respectable professions, and if they did, those subjects and those men were not suitable for polite conversation or public display. And as Joe McCain girded himself for the unrewarding and difficult labor of tracking down the boys in the Polaroid photographs—and their parents—he realized that his most formidable opponent was denial: the good people of Massachusetts were going to have a hard time believing that such things could, and did, occur in the city named for one of America's greatest patriots.

For several hours a day over a period of months, McCain drove alone through the streets of Revere and Chelsea and Boston's North End, searching for the abused boys. He had duplicates of the photos made that featured just the heads of the victims, and he would stop his car beside playgrounds and street corners and ice cream stands, beckon a few kids over, and ask them if they knew the boys in the pictures. His reputation preceded him, and the most reticent of neighborhood kids would give him a name or describe something they'd seen.

In some ways, Joe McCain and the other detectives in the SCIPP unit felt that child molestation was the most heinous crime of all. The taking of a life is an atrocity against all human beings; but when it's over, the victim's suffering ends. For the young victims of perversion and molestation, the suffering is open-ended; they often spend their lives plagued by memories of their own weakness, by guilt, by sexual deviancy, and by related substance abuse. And as McCain worked on, eventually identifying sixty-three juveniles who had been abused at Peluso's apartment, including the sons of local policemen and firemen and longshoremen and even the son of a Met cop he was friendly with, he began to realize that there would be a number of trials and that enduring the trials would be hell on these kids.

As the investigation bore fruit, thirty-year-old assistant district attorney Tom Peisch was assigned to prosecute. A native of Burlington, Vermont, and graduate of Dartmouth College and Boston College Law School, Peisch had earned a reputation as a thoughtful, meticulous litigator over his three years in the Suffolk County D.A.'s Office. An undersized but determined fellow who spent his weekends playing for the Mystic River Rugby Club, Peisch was about to get married and would soon join the exodus of lawyers and cops from 73 Tremont Street. Private practice beckoned, and at a much higher rate than the $833 per month he had started with under Garrett Byrne.

But Peisch loved Joe McCain and relished the thought of working with him on such a difficult case. Together they decided to choose someone with a high profile from among the pool of suspects, acquire a conviction, and force a good number of the remaining defendants to avoid jury trials and plead out. That way, they'd be able to cut down the number of victims who would have to appear as witnesses, minimizing the psychic damage of their testimonies.

They had Richard Peluso; they had Frank Damiano, the forty-nine-year-old school bus driver; and McCain was turning up a slew of other names as the investigation continued. But it had already begun to wear on him. As he met with the young victims and their parents in Peisch's office, McCain conducted his interviews in as gentle a manner as possible; he would show the parents the obscene photographs with tiny strips of electrical tape covering the children's genitals while explaining the rigors of a trial and what defense lawyers might counter with.

Occasionally one of the mothers would become adamant about seeing the entire photograph. She would argue that she'd brought this little boy into the world and felt it was her obligation to know exactly what her child had been subjected to. "Why do you want to do that?"

McCain would ask. But she would insist and Joe would peel off the strips of tape, and the mother would see her child's exposed genitalia, break down, and weep.

Joe McCain didn't think he had the background or wherewithal to counsel the victims or their families. In his regular conversations with Peisch, Joe made light of the "triple-decker education" he had received growing up on Marshall Street, and often prefaced his opinions with "I'm just a dumb cop, but this is what I think . . ." But the victims, many of them young men by this time, responded to big Joe's honesty and the natural warmth of his personality. In the end, thirteen victims and their families agreed to cooperate in prosecuting or making plea deals with the accused.

McCain's doggedness and tortuous spadework paid off when an eighteen-year-old who had been abused several years earlier produced two names that shocked McCain and Peisch. Arthur P. ("Preston") Clarridge was vice headmaster at the Fessenden School in West Newton, an exclusive all-male primary school that had graduated luminaries such as the billionaire Howard Hughes and U.S. Senator Edward Kennedy. A mathematics teacher, Clarridge, age forty-nine, was a meek-tempered little man who was known in certain circles to possess a small black valise stocked with marijuana, alcohol, and various "sex aids."

The other offender named was a fifty-year-old child psychiatrist, Dr. Donald M. Allen, former chief resident at Children's Hospital Medical Center in Boston. The eighteen-year-old victim described an episode with Dr. Allen that culminated in the much older man "jerking off" onto the boy's chest.

"If I ever get near him, I'll kill him," the youth said.

Peisch and McCain had their guinea pig in Donald Allen, who would be indicted on four counts of rape of a child under sixteen. But they still needed a key insider to make sure Allen went down, an adult who would help make their case. In a piece of investigative maneuvering that McCain later called "a work of art," he "flipped" Preston Clarridge, making him into a witness for the prosecution. Many nights were spent in Peisch's office, where McCain and this Harvard-educated child molester would hold long philosophical conversations on human sexuality.

Clarridge's viewpoint was that the social norms governing heterosexual behavior were merely what parents taught their children at an early age, not irrevocable truths inherent in nature. By lending a sympathetic ear to these arguments, however much it pained him to do so, McCain earned Clarridge's trust and gradually convinced him to turn against his fellow pervert and friend.

By testifying against Allen, Clarridge would save the greater embarrassment of his own trial, an event that McCain presented in such a way that the very prospect filled the balding schoolmaster with terror. And Preston Clarridge was a smart fellow: he sized up his chances early, deciding it was best to cast his lot with the government.

But making a case against Dr. Allen wouldn't be easy. He had retained an attorney named Larry O'Donnell, an ex-cop and formidable litigator known for his bold gambits in the courtroom. Just selecting the jury was an ordeal: the presiding judge, Joseph Ford, a balding, nondescript fellow with a dry manner, was saddled with a lengthy pretrial hearing merely to decide what would be included in the voir dire, the questioning used to identify or rule out prospective jurors. A lot of discussion was focused on the terminology that would be used at trial, with O'Donnell taking issue with the word "homosexual."

"Even Kinsey couldn't define it, Your Honor," he said, during a long, frustrating day filled with procedural questions. "If it's sucking a cock, let's call it sucking a cock."

Eventually Judge Ford settled on seventy-eight questions, with the defense using their allotment to try to get rid of individuals who were opposed to gay sex and sex between adults and children, and the prosecution trying to keep those people in. There were so many questions and the process was so exacting that Judge Ford took the unusual step of tape-recording all seventy-eight queries so he wouldn't have to repeat them, then bringing the prospective jurors up to the witness box one at a time to answer them all.

A lot of the jury pool came from Revere and Chelsea and Malden, working men and women who were horrified by many of the details in the case. At one point a rugged-looking teamster was asked how he felt about hearing assertions that grown men—and Dr. Allen in particular, who was sitting in the courtroom—may have inserted their penises into the rectums of nine- and ten-year-old boys.

The teamster screwed his head around and looked at Judge Ford. "Are you crazy?" he asked. "Who did that? Him? Why don't you just take him out and kill him?"

"You're excused, sir," said Judge Ford.

The teamster continued grumbling as he stepped down from the box. "I'll take him out back and strangle him right now," he said. "Save you the trouble."

The trial, which ran for two weeks leading up to Christmas 1978, became both a prurient spectacle and an ideological battlefield, as the Irish cops and the Ivy League lawyers clashed inside and outside the courtroom with each other and the lunatic fringe of the gay revolution. Although television cameras were banned from the actual trial in those days, the Superior Courthouse in Boston's Pemberton Square was besieged with TV crews from all three local stations and the network news programs, as well as print reporters from across the country, including from *The Village Voice* and a number of gay publications. Picketers from the North American Man-Boy Love Association, the infamous NAMBLA, lined the entrance to the courthouse each morning, and other protesters, some of them attired in outrageous garb, lay down in the corridors outside the courtroom. It was even rumored that the openly gay author Gore Vidal would make an appearance at the trial, in support of the defendants.

Tom Peisch, with Joe McCain by his side, presented the government's case with his usual clarity and precision. Through his parade of witnesses, Peisch outlined the nefarious methodology associated with Donald Allen's conquest of little boys. It wasn't a matter of "overborne will" but rather a slow and gradual culturing of these nine- and ten- and eleven-year-olds; an ingratiating into their confidences, and then a systematic and ruthless deflowering.

There was certainly no question of consent involved, since in Massachusetts children under the age of sixteen were legally incapable of giving their consent regarding these activities. And there was no doubt that the victims of Donald Allen's crimes had suffered great consequence;

the fourteen women and two men of the jury needed only to look into the faces of these young men, aged and troubled beyond their years, to understand what this middle-aged pederast had done to them and their hopes for the future.

The wild card in the trial was the question of Donald Allen's defense. Since Larry O'Donnell was required during pretrial hearings to reveal only if his client would plead insanity or claim an alibi, the District Attorney's Office could only guess about the defense's strategy. So Tom Peisch laughed to himself when O'Donnell stood up to claim that Dr. Allen had been conducting a grant-funded study for Tufts University on sexual behaviors and had not participated in any illegal activity. Peisch knew that Clarence Darrow himself couldn't sell that load of horseshit to the jury.

This declaration raised the inference that Donald Allen considered himself a lot smarter than Joe McCain, and that the self-professed "dumb cop" from Winter Hill would never be able to prove Dr. Allen wasn't acting in a medical capacity while frolicking at 242 Mountain Ave.

"He made a very big fucking mistake," McCain would say, as the trial was recessed and he and Jack Crowley descended upon the Tufts campus with an armload of subpoenas. In very short order, the two street cops were able to establish that there was no grant, no protocol, no research notes, and no study; that, in fact, O'Donnell's assertion was nothing more than a "recently contrived defense." After this bit of police work, it was clear to Peisch and all the other courtroom participants that Joe McCain had graduated summa cum laude from Marshall Street.

But the trial itself was far from over. Under Peisch's steady hand, Preston Clarridge was a reliable witness: he told the jurors that he and Donald Allen were both frequent visitors to 242 Mountain Ave., that they each had committed illegal acts with a significant number of young boys (two former victims testified in the trial, corroborating this), and that they had paid the boys small amounts of money, between five and twenty-five dollars, in exchange for their pleasure.

A short rotund man who wore black-rimmed glasses and had a timid, halting manner, Clarridge looked like someone cast to play a child molester in a movie. On the stand he had a tendency to speak softly while addressing his shoe tops, and all McCain's efforts to convince the vice headmaster of the Fessenden School to look the jurors in the eye and project his testimony to the rear of the courtroom were in vain. Sitting there as Clarridge described what had gone on at Richard Peluso's house in that quiet, effeminate voice, McCain was struck by how Clarridge was so respectful of everything and everyone—with the exception of little boys.

Donald Allen's trial was wearing on big Joe. He made it a point to walk and talk like a professional, maintaining his composure even while he chatted with Dr. Allen during recesses, trying to get inside his head and pick up bits of information that would prove useful to the D.A. in subsequent cases. But McCain would walk across Pemberton Square at the conclusion of the day's testimony like someone who had lost the grounding weight of everything he had ever believed in and was in danger of floating away. Sometimes on his way home, he would stop at the Venice Café near Teele Square, where he had courted his wife twenty-five years earlier. Joe would sit by himself, surrounded by what he called "real men," the teamsters and longshoremen and truck drivers he'd grown up with, throwing down a shot and a beer with one eye on the Bruins game playing above the bar.

All the Venice Café regulars were following the trial in the *Herald* or on TV. Gore Vidal did, in fact, visit Boston, hosting a fund-raiser for the Revere defendants. (In a surprise twist, Robert Bonin, the Chief Justice of the Massachusetts Superior Court, attended Vidal's event and later was censured and forced to resign.) Inevitably one of the teamsters hunkered over the Venice Café bar would send McCain a drink, calling out, "Hey, Joe, why don't you bring that fuckin' bum, that big witness of yours, Preston Clarridge, over here, and we'll chop him up and throw him in the Dumpster." And Joe McCain would join in their chorus of laughter, and for a while he'd feel human again.

The nights were the worst. In the later stages of the trial, anticipating Larry O'Donnell's cross-examination of his star witness, Joe would drop into a fitful sleep, only to be awakened by Helen at two or three o'clock in the morning. His entire body was trembling, Helen said, and the involuntary motion of the bed threatened to toss her onto the floor.

Joe would go sit in the kitchen and drink a glass of milk, reminding himself that Allen and Clarridge and Peluso were sick—in fact, they were out of their minds—and consequently, what they had done in that house in Revere felt unnatural to him but not to them. Joe McCain had made it this far as a cop by never taking things personally. It was his job to build a tryable case on the facts, as he always had done, and then let the jury decide.

When the big day arrived, Larry O'Donnell didn't disappoint. Every seat in the courtroom was taken, with the overflow standing against the back and along both sides, and as they had each day of the trial, Dr. Allen's estranged wife and three handsome children occupied the front row of the spectators' gallery. Preston Clarridge sat high in the witness box, perspiring onto his sensible gray suit and replying to O'Donnell's preliminary questions in a tiny voice. The defense attorney was making his way past the jurors as he spoke, and when he turned to face the witness, O'Donnell was standing forty feet away, at the end of the jury box.

"Mr. Clarridge, you've been speaking like you're a nice little man," said O'Donnell. "Isn't that right?"

"Yes," said Clarridge.

"You're an intelligent man, you're an intellectual, and you're a pedophile, isn't that right, Mr. Clarridge?"

The witness looked down at his feet. "Yes."

"Let's understand one thing, I'm way down here and I can't hear you," said O'Donnell. "Speak loudly, so all of us can hear." O'Donnell turned to face the jurors. "It's been established, Mr. Clarridge, that you carry what is often referred to as a doctor's bag. And in your little black bag, you had your handcuffs and your rope and your marijuana cigarettes, which you gave to these boys. Isn't that right, Mr. Clarridge?"

"Yes . . ."

O'Donnell raised his voice. "And isn't it a fact, Mr. Clarridge, that you turned these boys against their God-given inclination for the exquisite female form?"

The little man sank even lower in his chair. "I suppose so . . ."

Tom Peisch and Joe McCain shot a look at each other: Judge Ford was giving O'Donnell enormous latitude in tearing Arthur Preston Clarridge a new asshole. But given that neither man had a shred of affection or sympathy for this admitted pedophile, and since other testimony had incriminated Donald Allen to the point where all of Larry O'Donnell's gyrations might well become moot, Peisch and McCain settled in to watch the fireworks.

"You had all kinds of sexual aids in your little black bag, didn't you, Mr. Clarridge?" asked O'Donnell, trying to underscore Clarridge's perversion and, by extension, his unreliability.

"Yes."

"And I bet you've had all kinds of sex, haven't you, Mr. Clarridge?"

Off came Preston Clarridge's eyeglasses. "Well, I . . ."

O'Donnell turned back toward the bench, straightening his tie and the cuffs of his jacket before fixing his gaze on the witness. "Mr. Clarridge, have you ever had sex with a goat?" he asked.

McCain looked at Peisch: *Did he just say sex with a goat?* He looked over at the court artist; he looked at the ceiling; he looked for somewhere to put his head.

The question hung there in the packed courtroom. Peisch started to his feet in order to object, then shrugged as if to say What the hell? and sat back down.

Clarridge mumbled something like "Well, whoa—"

Before he could finish, Judge Ford looked over and said, "That question is irrelevant. Continue."

This sort of raucous testimony continued until just a few days shy of Christmas, when both sides made their final arguments. Judge Ford, while instructing the jury, said, "These are superb lawyers who have tried this case in front of you, ladies and gentlemen."

The jury deliberated for quite some time, returning to the courtroom on Christmas Eve. Judge Ford asked for the verdict, and as several jurors wept, one of the women stood up and in a clear voice announced that Donald Allen was guilty on all four counts.

In the end, twenty-four men were indicted on over one hundred felonies in the Revere Sex Ring, thanks to Joe McCain's nose for a big case. And although the investigation took its toll, hastening his exit from the SCIPP unit, big Joe had a tremendous ability to absorb a blow and keep chugging forward in good humor.

Late one night during the trial, Joe and Tom Peisch and Preston

Clarridge were in the office, going over their strategy for the next day. The men were exhausted, and as they sat at a desk strewn with court documents and fast food wrappers, McCain asked Clarridge about the Fessenden School and his duties in the mathematics department.

"I have a son, Joey, who's not too sharp in math," said McCain. "Do you think you could tutor him?"

Clarridge was amazed. "Would you really consider me as a tutor for your son?"

"Oh, sure," said McCain, enjoying his ruse. He glanced at Peisch, who was staring across the desk at him. "Is there a problem, Tom?" he asked.

"Oh no, Joe," said Peisch. But when Clarridge was otherwise occupied, Peisch shot a look at the big detective that said, *You fucking wise guy, McCain.*

Joe McCain often remained on good terms with the men he put in jail. It reflected his belief that anyone could be redeemed that sought redemption. But there's an exception to every rule. Several years after the Revere Sex Ring case, when even the vilest perpetrator had finished his sentence, a man recognized the old detective as he went into the Statler Building in downtown Boston.

"Hey, Joe McCain, how are you?" said the fellow, coming the other way.

But Joe sailed past without a word or sign of recognition, the other man's hand extended as he stood frozen in the doorway. It was Donald Allen.

TWENTY-ONE

All You Need to Know

B EFORE HOOKING UP WITH KEVIN MCKENNA on the
Wednesday following our first case together, I leave my car at
Wellington Circle and ride the T into the city. It's one of several trips
I've made into various quarters, digging for information on the past
conduct of Jimmy Hyde and his vendetta against the McCains. Just last
week, a federal judge refused to dismiss Timmy Doherty's whistle-
blower's lawsuit against Hyde and the P.D. Judge Nancy Gertner noted
that several of Doherty's peers have been tormenting him since the
night of the Henderson beating nearly a decade ago. In her opinion,
Judge Gertner wrote, "Doherty's allegations are sufficient to permit an
inference that all of the defendants conspired to retaliate against him."

Doherty's suit alleges that the city of Somerville and various individual police officers punished him for breaking the "code of silence" when
he testified at the federal civil trial of Jimmy Hyde and others who had
been involved in a bar fight and the beating of civilians. Judge Gertner
stated, "The temporal proximity between Doherty's testimony and the
onset of the harassment as well as the content of the harassment (e.g.,
calling him a 'rat') provide a basis to infer a 'nexus' between the testimony and the alleged retaliation."

The depositions in the whistle-blower's suit will take months, but the transcript from the 1999 civil trial, accusing Hyde and other Somerville cops of beating a suspect in their custody, is a matter of public record. If I can ferret it out, I'll have a better understanding of what Jimmy Hyde has been up to.

Sifting through trial testimony and quizzing guys like Leo Martini is the most "private" investigation I've undertaken thus far. Joe Jr. thinks I should lay off, as his situation has improved and he's content in the detectives' bureau. But now that I've gotten hold of it, I know I'm on to something and have to keep going forward. As I see it, understanding the root of Jimmy Hyde's seeming infallibility will help determine what he might do next. If his reputation indicates anything, it's that he'll press his luck, even while under scrutiny.

The catacombs of the Orange Line are filled with noxious fumes and on the train, a man with a sparse goatee is coughing up his lung and sneezing like a goat. The underside of the city is teeming with grimy characters and shadows, an apt metaphor, it seems, for what has been going on beneath the gold braid and shiny brass of the Somerville P.D. What I've learned thus far is that on the night of October 8, 1994, a group of Somerville cops, including Jimmy Hyde and John Aufiero, were boozing at a joint called Night Games at the Holiday Inn a short distance from the police station. At the bar, Detective Patrick Irving, who was drinking with Hyde, encountered the thirty-four-year-old Somerville native Michael Henderson.

Detective Irving knew Henderson from a previous arrest and the two men exchanged unpleasantries and began fighting. When the altercation spilled into the parking lot, a trio of bystanders, German Alfonso, twenty-eight, of Los Angeles; Christopher Mittell, twenty-five, of Cambridge; and twenty-four-year-old Joseph Spear of Somerville, not realizing that Irving and his cronies were police officers, got drawn into the brawl. Over the next few minutes, the civilians absorbed quite a beating, sometimes facing two or three cops at a time. Soon Alfonso, Mittell, Spear, and Henderson were on their way to jail in the back of a paddy wagon, which was being driven by Somerville patrolman Timmy Doherty.

In a civil trial four years later, Alfonso and Mittell claimed that they were struck, choked, threatened, referred to as "spics," and arrested, along with Michael Henderson, as a means of intimidating them into silence. Named in the suit were the Somerville Police Detectives James Hyde, Christopher Ward, and Patrick Irving; Sergeants John Aufiero and Michael Cabral; retired Lieutenant John Bossi; and Patrolmen Joseph Blair and Timothy Doherty.

Although Henderson would later recant his statements and refuse to join the lawsuit, a few months before the trial he told reporters from New England Cable News and *The Boston Globe* that Jimmy Hyde had beaten him while he was handcuffed and then bit him on the chest. While under oath Henderson denied any of that had occurred, but Timmy Doherty would contradict his testimony and give details of the beating, which by Doherty's estimation lasted for thirty minutes. The implication was that certain parties had convinced Henderson telling the truth was not in his best interest. Using tips garnered from Mark Donahue and a little "due diligence," I want to find out exactly what happened by reading the pertinent testimony for myself.

Emerging from the train into the welter of State Street, I'm accosted by plumes of steam, hooting taxis, the grinding and whirring of motors, and a maze of Jersey barriers that section off the latest boondoggle in downtown construction. A ruddy-faced hard hat directs me along Atlantic Avenue, and soon I'm tramping over the old Northern Avenue Bridge with the shimmering expanse of the harbor spread out before me. The five-year-old J. Joseph Moakley U.S. Courthouse stands on the north side of the pier, opposite the Barking Crab restaurant and overlooking one of the priciest stretches of waterfront real estate on the East Coast.

Inside the vast stone cavern of the Moakley, the architectural proportions are on a Brobdingnagian scale and everything from the height of the atrium ceiling to the width of the staircase has been designed and calculated to make the individual feel small. In here, no one person is larger than the ideal that's central to our system of jurisprudence: serve the truth.

I wend and wangle my way through a series of security guards and

metal detectors and checkpoints, up to the clerk's office and finally to
the fifth floor and a tiny office adjacent to Courtroom 17. Inside is a
petite, silver-haired woman named Antonia Larson, a court reporter
with thirty years of experience; she's bespectacled, wearing a floral print
dress and a pale green jacket, with her hair pinned up in a bun and the
demeanor of somebody's feisty aunt. Courtroom stenographer is a
semifreelance position, and I've been directed to Ms. Larson's office because she was the reporter for Civil Action No. 97-12252, *German Alfonso et al., v. John T. Aufiero, et al.*, which began in January 1999 before
the Honorable Patti B. Saris and a jury. I'm surprised to learn that trial
transcripts must be purchased from the reporters who made them, not
from the district court itself.

Searching through records can be hit or miss, as they are sometimes
affected by human error while being compiled or cataloged. And my
hopes are further deflated when Ms. Larson says that there might not
be a typewritten account of the Alfonso-Mittell trial after all. Complete
transcripts are produced from a stenographer's notes only if a verdict is
appealed, she says, and to the best of her recollection, neither side in the
case wished to challenge the decision. This is disappointing, but Larson
announces from the outer office that she'll try anyway, and see if there's
paper testimony from any of the witnesses.

Apologizing for the glacial speed of her computer, Larson boots up
and scrolls through the list of files. "Huh. That's strange," she says. "All
I have is one hundred twenty-seven pages of testimony from a witness
named Joseph Spear."

A high school dropout and petty criminal, Joe Spear was also arrested
in the fracas outside the Holiday Inn. He knew the Somerville cops and
they knew him; Officer Aufiero walked up to Spear when he was smoking a cigarette and asked if he had any warrants. By all accounts, Spear
was a friend of victim Michael Henderson and took a beating himself
that night. Larson skims through her book to see who originally asked
for a transcript of Spear's testimony, but she has no record of it.

I already know that the jury found in favor of German Alfonso and
Christopher Mittell, awarding them $129,903.38 in legal fees and dam-
ages of $36,757.67. In rendering their verdict, the jurors stated that De-

tective James Hyde had used "excessive force" against one of the plaintiffs. No criminal charges were ever filed against Hyde or the other police officers, however, nor was Hyde disciplined or sanctioned by the Somerville P.D. (Long after unearthing these documents and conducting my interviews, I sent an overnight letter to Jimmy Hyde, offering to hear his side of the story. He didn't reply.)

"It was an injustice," says Larson, who has served as court reporter for hundreds of trials. Alfonso and Mittell "won, but I remember thinking that the judgment was too small."

Spear's testimony is worth the $106.24 that I'm required to pay for it. Throughout his appearance, which was compelled by a subpoena, the twenty-four-year-old stock clerk is inarticulate and halting, speaking in a voice so low that Judge Saris has to tell him to talk louder on several occasions. But there's something elemental, almost childlike, in Spear's descriptions of what he saw outside the Holiday Inn that night and what he experienced.

> Q. The next thing you can remember is you were in the parking lot, is that correct?
> A. Yes.
> Q. What's happening in the parking lot?
> A. I was getting beat up.

Joseph Spear goes on to testify that he and Mittell and Alfonso and Michael Henderson were loaded into the paddy wagon and that James Hyde entered and began screaming at Henderson and grabbed him by the throat. He described Hyde and the other cops named in the suit—with the exception of Timmy Doherty—as drunk, violent, and out of control. Once inside a holding cell in the Somerville police station, Spear says, he and the other prisoners, bound in handcuffs, were offered a deal: if they could fight their way out, they were free to leave. Faced with an enraged posse of off-duty cops, they declined.

Later, at their arraignment on criminal charges, Henderson showed Spear what had occurred away from the others, when he was assaulted by James Hyde:

Q. He was lifting up his shirt and he had bite marks.

A. He had a bite mark?

Q. Yes.

A. Where?

Q. On his chest.

In a bizarre moment during the trial, the lawyers approached the bench for a conference and one of them told Judge Saris that Detective Hyde's partner, Mike McGrath, who was sitting in the gallery, had been "talking on the phone and laughing" during Spear's testimony. This behavior was in plain view of the jury, and the clear implication was that members of the Somerville P.D. were belittling the witness and his credibility. Reading on, I expect Judge Saris to lower the boom on McGrath. But after the lawyer's complaint, Saris replies, "I will ask [McGrath] to try to keep it down."

The most telling bit of evidence against Hyde and his friends will appear during Spear's cross-examination by the attorney Peter Brown, who represented two of the defendants, Lieutenant Bossi and Sergeant Aufiero. After going over a list of the witness's previous run-ins with the law, Brown attempts to impugn Spear by noting that he has contradicted some of the statements he made before trial in his depositions, which were also under oath.

Q. Well, you took an oath to tell the truth and are you saying that you didn't tell the truth?

A. On some things, yeah.

Q. On some things you didn't tell the truth?

A. I was scared, yeah. What would you do if you were in a room with people that tried to kill you?

Spear also says that he was never in fear of what Timmy Doherty might do to him, and that Officer Doherty treated him with respect and professionalism when placing him under arrest and escorting him into the paddy wagon. In the second of two depositions, however, Spear refers to the presence of Hyde and Bossi while he's answering questions and asks, "How is it intimidating? I'm sitting in the room with two cops who beat me half to death practically, it's kind of uncomfortable. You would probably feel the same way."

Other cases are beckoning, and after making arrangements with Antonia Larson for the transcript, I bolt down the stairs and into the street. My impressions of "the 1994 Holiday Inn Massacre," as Timmy Doherty calls it, are that judges are so worried about getting cases through the chute they are more like bus schedulers than Solomon, and that Hyde and the other pugilistic cops should've been arrested immediately. The fact that they weren't, but that Alfonso and Mittell won the civil trial, forms a huge indictment of the Somerville P.D. and the integrity of its leadership during that era.

Going to work is still like going to hell for Timmy Doherty; he has no use for many of his colleagues nor they for him. Two cops named in his lawsuit, Captain John O'Connor and Lieutenant Michael Cabral, serve in the department's internal affairs unit and are expected to watch out for such unfair treatment. In a further indignity, Jimmy Hyde, after being recalled from the DEA, has been named the Somerville P.D.'s gang investigator, a job Doherty says he created. Recently Chief George McLean has begun to rein in Jimmy Hyde and those of his ilk, making them more accountable to the command structure, but a travesty of this magnitude still casts a very long shadow over the department.

In the aftermath of the Henderson beating, Timmy Doherty, troubled by what he had seen, approached Joe McCain, Jr., about setting up an appointment with Joe Sr. The elder McCain had been through this sort of thing before, and although he and big Joe hardly knew each other, the twenty-six-year-old Doherty wanted to hear what the old Met cop had to say before he crossed the blue line and testified.

For his part, Joe McCain had survived a couple of bullet wounds and gone back into detective work, like some kind of Winter Hill Lazarus. But some cops believed that working for defense lawyers as an investigator was only a notch or two above rolling winos on the Common. If that wasn't bad enough, others were convinced that McCain was prodding the Alfonso-Mittell civil suit along just to embarrass his son's enemies in the department.

Big Joe's meeting with Officer Doherty took place in the McCain kitchen; the agenda was brief and the old cop's message was succinct. "No matter what, you can't lie," said McCain, training his gaze on the frazzled young cop. "That's what the public hired you for."

Outside the federal courthouse, Boston Harbor is dotted with pleasure boats and ferries shining in the sun. As I'm walking along, I'm thinking of that old British snoop John Keats, and what he said about the truth: "That is all ye know on earth, and all ye need to know."

Engraved on the giant lower stones of the courthouse are the opinions of various Supreme Court jurists and other prominent thinkers. A quotation from Frederick Douglass strikes me as appropriate to the Mittell-Alfonso case in general and Timmy Doherty's situation in particular:

> *Where Justice is denied, and any one class made to feel that*
> *society is an organized conspiracy to oppress, rob and degrade*
> *them, neither persons nor property will be safe.*

Amidst the tattooed bike messengers, law clerks, and a lady with a pet dog, I go pinging over the corrugated steel of the old Northern Avenue Bridge. It's ironic and disturbing that the people most oppressed and degraded are those beautiful souls, like Joe McCain and Timmy Doherty, who endeavor to tell the truth.

As soon as I reach the surveillance point above Lila Ogletree's house, Kevin McKenna slides open the rear door to the van. "Get in," he says. "There she is." A large woman in black tights and a lime green windbreaker comes down the stairs and heaves herself into a small gray hatchback that has pulled up in front, driven by a middle-aged white guy.

"There she goes," says McKenna, scrambling into the front seat as I jump into the van with my backpack and McKenna hands me the video camera.

The little gray car races down the hill, makes a quick left, and runs in traffic along Columbia Road. "Is that her?" I ask.

"She fits the description: fifty years old, heavyset, black," says McKenna. "But there's no picture in the file. I'm guessing."

At the light, we pull up alongside and McKenna says, "Shoot some video of her. She doesn't see us."

Before I can focus the camera, the light changes and the hatchback speeds away. We follow the car to Jerome Street, where it stops in front of a lavender Victorian with a steep staircase in front and the woman gets out. I hand the camcorder up, and McKenna tapes the woman hustling along the side of the car and up the stairs.

"Hey—she's running," I say, as the neon green of the woman's jacket sloshes and billows. "Her back looks fine to me."

McKenna continues taping the woman as she climbs the staircase and goes into the house. "It might not be her," he says, shutting off the camera.

We park on the hill and McKenna calls in the license plate of the hatchback and finds out we're on the cleaning lady, not the subject. "Fuck," he says. We race back to Ogletree's house, and the SUV is parked in the driveway. "Good, she's still here," McKenna says. "I think."

While we're sitting at the bottom of the street, watching the driveway and side entrance, McKenna shows me the little silver-plated .25 he's carrying for protection. He takes out the magazine, clears the chamber, and hands me the gun: it's small and heavy in my palm, no bigger than a toy, and the clip is the size of a Pez dispenser.

"Hollow points," says McKenna, holding up one of the bullets.

"You'd have to be pretty close with this thing," I say, marveling at how light the gun is. I pull the bolt back and straighten my arm, and there in the backseat of McKenna's van, I sight over the bone of my thumb and down the silver line of the barrel. For some people, shooting a man is just that easy.

McKenna takes the .25 back, clears the chamber once more, and reinserts the magazine. "Most shootings occur within ten feet of the target," he says, returning the gun to its position under the seat.

The first shooting McKenna ever witnessed occurred in the Orchard Park housing project in Roxbury, where he and his partner, who was black, did an undercover drug buy. Although they'd been trained to avoid hallways, where it was usually impossible for the backup officer to maintain surveillance, the dealers insisted on meeting there and

McKenna's partner went down with the money while McKenna waited in the stairwell.

The two dealers tried the double cross, putting a knife to his partner's breastbone. "Gimme the drugs and the rest of the money, or I'll cut your fucking throat," the dealer said. The black cop took out his gun and shot the dealer in the groin; the other kid rushed him, and the cop fired a second round, getting him in the stomach.

Both drug dealers were down on the floor, screaming and rolling around in their own blood. McKenna burst from the stairwell just as his partner ran out the back and doors opened on both sides and the residents crept into the hallway. There he was, a white guy holding a gun, with two black kids on the floor and the smell of gunpowder in the air. But a woman from one of the apartments handed McKenna a pair of disposable diapers, and he gave them to the drug dealers to staunch their wounds. "Use these," he said.

The man who had been shot in the groin uncrossed his legs, revealing a bloody mess. A young girl standing nearby saw the wound and pointed at McKenna, screaming, "They shot his shit off. They shot his shit off."

After another hour of surveillance, McKenna acquires Ogletree's telephone number from directory assistance and calls the house, pretending to be a real estate broker. An old woman answers the phone and says that Lila doesn't live there, and that she doesn't know her address or phone number.

"If I had it, I couldn't give it to you," the woman says and hangs up.

McKenna explains that people who make a career out of false injury claims often list a relative's address as their own to keep investigators from knowing where they live.

We're still trying to figure out if we've got the target when a beat-up old Honda arrives in front of the Ogletrees'. A woman in a yellow sweatshirt is driving, and she climbs out and goes inside the house. A skinny old white guy with mottled skin and greasy hair stays in the car, reading a newspaper. Then the woman comes back out with what looks like a stack of mail. She gets in the car and drives off.

McKenna follows them, staying back at least 150 feet whenever possible. He theorizes that the woman at the wheel is Lila Ogletree, the dude with the newspaper is her boyfriend, and the voice on the telephone was Lila's elderly mother.

"She looks younger than fifty," says McKenna, studying her through the binoculars whenever the traffic on Columbia Road slows down. "But you can't tell sometimes."

At a stop sign on Dudley Street, McKenna calls my attention to a little four-door pulled up at the corner with a group of white kids inside. A black teenager on a bicycle is pedaling away. "Did you see it?" asks McKenna.

"See what?"

"The drug deal. The one on the bike gave something to the passenger, and the passenger handed him the cash. Kids on bicycles are hard to track. They use 'em a lot around here."

When I ask why he doesn't use his phone to tip Boston P.D., McKenna laughs. "They won't get here until tomorrow, even if we called yesterday," he says.

Trying to keep at least one car between the grimy red Honda and us, McKenna follows the target to a strip mall that contains an Office Mart. I'm reminded of the surveillance tips I received from Mark Donahue. Mark's advice was to keep a good distance from the subject and to blend in with the scenery. When following a car, stay on the right side of the target's bumper, where you'll fall into the blind spot in his rearview mirror. Mark usually carries four or five hats and a couple of spare jackets in the backseat, changing outfits here and there during the surveillance. The number-one rule: don't let the target see you.

In the Office Mart parking lot, McKenna hops out and tails the woman into the store while I jump into the front seat with the camcorder. Through the zoom lens I keep an eye on the man in the passenger seat of the Honda. He's wearing glasses and doing a crossword puzzle. Two minutes later McKenna thrusts open the door to the van, startling me. "She's at the cash register," he says.

He picks up the video camera and tapes the subject returning to the car with an Office Mart bag in each hand as I watch through the binoculars. The woman is in plain sight, just seven or eight car lengths away.

"She could be fifty years old," I say to McKenna, who's still taping her.

He puts the camera aside and watches the Honda pull out, then allows a pickup truck to get between us and the subject, and follows the woman into traffic. "I got a feeling it's her," McKenna says.

At the Walgreens on Dudley Street the target makes another stop. She goes inside and the white guy stays in the car with his puzzle. While we're sitting there a six-foot black woman with blonde hair gets out of a Cadillac Escalade driven by a man in a baseball cap. The woman is wearing a miniskirt and has the long, sinewy legs of a dancer.

The tall chick sashays around the nose of the SUV and climbs into a paving truck driven by a hefty, Italian looking fellow. "Hooker," says McKenna.

The subject emerges from Walgreens toting more purchases and the white dude has his nose buried in the crossword puzzle and doesn't even open the door for her. "If it's Lila Ogletree, she's got the laziest boyfriend of all time," I tell McKenna.

He laughs. "I'll make a notation in the file," McKenna says, pulling out behind them.

We tail the Honda to Maynard Street, where both occupants get out of the car and enter a dilapidated tenement building. McKenna uses his phone to call the office, trying to find out who lives at 78–80 Maynard Street. One of the names he comes up with is Beaudet.

"Wait here," says McKenna, handing me the binoculars. He gets out of the van and walks over to the house, turns at the gate, and goes up the front stairs to the mailbox.

A few seconds later, the chunky detective returns to the van. "Apartment Three has a tag for Beaudet," he says. "Underneath in pencil it says, 'Ogletree.'"

With the tall blue rectangle of the Prudential Building shining in the distance, McKenna phones the client and says we've got something on the Lila Ogletree case. They want to view the tape as soon as possible and will send a driver to Houghs Neck to pick it up. We're heading back there to sit on Billy Giampa.

The blue Subaru pickup is not in Giampa's driveway, and after the courier grabs the Ogletree tape, we drive to the Quincy assessor's office to find out who owns the gas station that Giampa frequents. McKenna believes that it's a family member or close friend, and that Giampa is working under the table for them. He thinks the manager of the gas station has tipped Giampa to other detectives and doesn't trust him.

The gas station is listed under an R-T-S corporation in upstate New York, and we have to shuttle back and forth between town offices to unearth the names of the two men who are running the business. They are Middle Eastern, and by checking their names against other lists we discover that they also own a salvage company and a small construction outfit.

"Giampa's in there somewhere," says McKenna. "I feel it in my falafel."

We return to our spot above the gas station a little bit wiser. After just a couple of minutes McKenna and I blurt out "There he is" at the same time and watch as Billy Giampa takes a circuitous route back to his house. He turns right on Sea Street when he should've turned left, and we can hear his engine as he passes on the street behind us.

"This guy's paranoid," says McKenna. "He thinks he's being followed."

McKenna glides down from the hill and tucks the van beneath a giant shade tree near the bottom. A moment later the blue pickup rattles past. "Yeah, he's cleaning himself," says McKenna. "Making sure he doesn't have a tail."

When Giampa turns at the stop sign, McKenna takes a left and then another left, trying to beat the pickup across Sea Street. But the crazy bastard is driving the little side roads at forty-five miles an hour and shoots through a hole in the traffic. "Fuck," says McKenna, as we pick our way across the intersection. "He's gotta show up now."

We hide in a little grass alley and wait for Giampa to pass by. My heart is beating fast, and it occurs to me that this whole thing is a goof; like when we were kids and Bobby Corey and I would ditch our Stingrays behind the wall at Howard Park and wait for Mary Lou Endyke to ride by. Then we'd pull our caps down low and follow her to Lawlor's Drug Store.

At the last second I remember that there's no tape in the camcorder and we miss our shot as Giampa runs around the block and scoots into his driveway.

"Ehh, we'll sit on him another half hour and call it a day," says McKenna, tossing me the binoculars. "We get paid, no matter what happens."

TWENTY-TWO

Hats on the Bed

Old times only buy you one ticket, and you just cashed that in.
—JIM ROCKFORD, *THE ROCKFORD FILES*

IT'S A RAW, WET AFTERNOON IN MID-MARCH, the light failing, with a large, amorphous cloud of mist and vapors hanging over Union Square, shrouding the passersby. Joey McCain has summoned me to the Tir na nOg without explanation, and after parking some distance away, I turn up the collar of my old hiking jacket and stomp toward the pub, wondering what the mystery is. I asked Joey over the phone, but all he'd say was to meet him at four o'clock.

For the past month, I've been working a string of fraud cases with Kevin McKenna in Dorchester and Roxbury and out on Houghs Neck in Quincy. Several of the cases have turned out well, so more have come in and we've been busy. The woman in the battered Honda that we videotaped in the Office Mart parking lot did turn out to be Lila Ogletree, who had filed workmen's compensation claims six times over her last four jobs. She was supposed to be immobilized by a back injury, and the video of her carrying shopping bags and jumping in and out of the little Honda proved otherwise. Her employers looked at it and discontinued her benefits; Ogletree hired a lawyer and took them to court. The judge saw the evidence and ordered her straight back to work.

We weren't so lucky with Billy Giampa, the truck driver with the ankle injury. McKenna and I chased him up and down Wollaston Beach for two solid weeks without getting any good video on him. If I were a betting man, I would've set the odds at two to one he was defrauding that transportation company of his labor. Zooming around in his pickup, Giampa was doubling back on his routes, charging through stop signs, playing cute with right-hand signals and left-hand turns; he knew he was being followed and did everything he could to shake us, a pretty fair indicator of guilt. But after McKenna finally got him on tape, in the parking lot of a strip mall, we watched Giampa go into a podiatrist's office, where he remained for three hours. Inside, a doctor performed surgery on his left ankle, and the company later extended his benefits for another six months. I told McKenna that Giampa must have hurt his foot trying to get away from us.

Our best case was the mechanic with the bad back who lives a half mile from Giampa on Houghs Neck. We sat on his place a few times, but the guy never came out. I saw him only once: a tall, portly fellow with blue-black hair and thick sideburns. McKenna heard a persistent rumor that the guy was working at night and spotted him leaving the house after dark and tailed him up to Revere Beach. With rain falling on the strip, the mechanic with the supposedly bulging lumbar disk entered one of the nightclubs on Ocean Avenue, carrying a small brown valise.

McKenna waited outside for a couple of minutes, then paid the three-dollar cover charge and went in. The bar was dark and smoky, populated by a dozen or so ratty beachcombers and smelling of old cigars. McKenna bought a glass of beer just as a lone spotlight illuminated the stage and a recording of "Viva Las Vegas" boomed over the sound system.

Wearing a sequined cape and a pair of oversized mauve sunglasses, his mop of black hair slicked into a ducktail, the erstwhile mechanic skittered onstage, gyrating his hips and lip-synching to a medley of Elvis Presley tunes.

Case closed.

AFTER SUCH CHILLY WEATHER, the narrow confines of the Tir na nOg are warm and dimly lit, smelling of grilled onions. The dark-paneled bar, which runs three-quarters of the way down the left side of the room, is occupied by a pair of teamsters with their backs to me and a cheerful young barmaid, who is standing by the taps. Pudgy and round-faced, she smiles and gestures along the bar and tells me to sit anywhere I like.

On the right side of the pub are a half dozen wooden tables, bolted to the floor and accompanied by tall metal stools. Hanging above each table is a single hundred-watt bulb protected by a rounded piece of metal that looks like a crinkled pie plate.

As I pass beneath the old megaphones, banjos, and tricycles suspended from the ceiling, Joe McCain, Jr., calls out to me from a table down by the stage. He's wearing a black leather jacket with his police radio sticking out of the front pocket and a dark blue Hawaiian shirt, patterned with white flowers. Joey has unscrewed the lightbulb above his table, throwing shadows over the two men he is sitting with. I don't recognize either of them.

"What're you drinking?" asks Joey, taking me by the arm. They've also just arrived and haven't ordered anything yet. "I want you to meet somebody. Somebody who knew my father."

The older of the two men sitting with Joey rises to shake my hand. He looks vaguely Middle Eastern, five ten, slim build, wearing a gray fleece jacket and an orange sweatshirt with "Plymouth" across the front; dungarees, brogans, a heavy gold watch, and a pair of sunglasses, lightly tinted in rose, complete his ensemble.

"They call me Black Jimmy," the man says, as he grips my hand.

"No shit?" I ask.

"In the flesh," says Jimmy, and the others laugh.

Jimmy has short dark curly hair, tinged with gray, and a pencil mustache. He's sixty-four years old but looks at least a decade younger. When he smiles, his teeth are even and white, and there's a glint of shrewdness in his eyes. "How ya doing, kid?" he asks.

The barmaid approaches and I ask for a pint of Guinness and we all lean back to scrutinize today's menu, which is written on a chalkboard nearby.

"What's good here, Joey?" asks Black Jimmy, noting that he hasn't been in this part of Somerville for years. In fact, he hasn't been anywhere near Boston since the early nineties.

"Best steak tips in the city," says Joey. "Best fries, too. Awesome." He grins at me. "One hundred percent natural."

"You wouldn't know it, but Joey's cardiovascular system is a hundred fifty years old," I say. "He goes to the museum for checkups."

Black Jimmy laughs. "That's a good one," he says, before turning to the barmaid. "I'll have the steak tips. And bring us a basket of those fries." Jimmy orders a Canadian beer from another chalkboard over the bar and Joey orders a diet Coke; he's working and this is his lunch hour.

Black Jimmy's companion is a small, reedy fellow wearing an Air Force baseball cap. He's about forty years old, with a close-cropped black beard and a set of false teeth. "I'll have a Coke" are the first words he speaks.

"That's Mike," says Black Jimmy. "He used to work with us."

Mike has doll-sized hands and a doll's expressionless black eyes. "Good to know ya," he says, with the enthusiasm of someone meeting his new dentist.

"This is Billy Dennett's kind of place," says Black Jimmy, glancing around. "He woulda liked this."

Meanwhile, our food is delivered to the table: strips of broiled chicken and vinaigrette over mesclun greens for me, and steak tips for everybody else. The cherubic young barmaid, who has the sort of robust manner not typically associated with New England girls, hears Black Jimmy say that he's living in Colorado.

"Wow. I'm from Colorado, too," she says, delighted at the coincidence.

Jimmy smiles at her. "Whereabouts?"

"I grew up in Evergreen. Do you know where that is?"

"Sure, I do," says Black Jimmy. "It's a great little town."

As he banters with his new friend, it occurs to me that Black Jimmy has laughed at all my jokes, marveled at my wisdom, and shined the same sort of light on me that he's shining on the barmaid right now. Of course he has. What else would a con artist do?

After the barmaid clears our dishes away, Jimmy takes out his wallet and plunks down a shiny new credit card. "It's on me," he says.

"Whose name is on the card?" I ask, winking at Joey.

Everyone laughs, punctuated by Jimmy's low, raspy chuckle. "It's mine," he says.

I pick up the card, tilt it toward the light from the bar, and replace it on the table. "I'm pleased to meet you, Mr. DiMaggio," I say, and Joey spits out his diet Coke.

I notice that Black Jimmy has several rubber bands wrapped around his billfold. A pickpocket once told him that the elastics, catching on the inside of his pocket, would make it harder to steal his wallet. Right on cue, Mike and Joey take out their elastic-bound wallets and demonstrate that I am the only guy at the table who grew up in the suburbs. Then Jimmy whispers that he ought to shortchange the barmaid, "for old times' sake."

"No fucking way," says Joey.

"Aww. I'd give it back," Jimmy says. "I just thought Jay would like to see how it's done."

In the Tir na nOg, Black Jimmy settles our bill by adding a hefty tip and signing with a flourish. As we make our way toward the exit, an old Lynyrd Skynyrd song plays from over the bar and Jimmy pokes Mike in the shoulder. "Remember this?" he asks, and Mike laughs.

"This was our theme song in the slow walkin' days," Jimmy says.

When the Skynyrd tune reaches the chorus, Black Jimmy does a little rumba move over the scarred wooden floor of the pub.

> *Gimme three steps towards the door?*
> *And you'll never see me no more.*

In their heyday, Jimmy explains, even a bit player like Mike could earn $2,500 just for tying up a pay phone until he arrived to take a prearranged call. "We could do no wrong," says Jimmy.

Black Jimmy decides to pay a visit to Helen McCain, and since Joey's cruiser is back at the house and I'm parked near there, we're all going to ride over in Jimmy's rental car. Out on the street, Jimmy lights a cigarette and flings the match away. Waiting at the curb is a brand-new SUV with racing wheels and tinted glass.

"I got lucky," says Black Jimmy as he climbs in. "I started with a little shitbox Ford, and it died at the airport and they gave me this."

Jimmy's been on a hot streak lately. He hit for $3,600 at the track in Denver, which allowed him to buy a nice round-trip ticket to Boston. But his first trip to his old stomping grounds in ten years is not a social visit. Back in 1974, when the slow walk was booming, he took $1,800 cash and bought his wife, Hope, an odd-sized parcel of land deep in the Plymouth woods. Jimmy kept his own name off the deed because there were warrants out for him.

Black Jimmy and Hope were divorced in 1986, and she died last year. It turns out that silent Mike, who is Jimmy's nephew, tipped him off regarding the value of his ex-wife's estate. Development has encroached on that once rural plot of land, and the probate court has estimated its value at $500,000.

"I'm gonna get my piece," Black Jimmy says. "After all, I bought the fucking land in the first place."

A heavy fog has descended over Somerville and the streets are gleaming in the darkness. Mike is driving; Black Jimmy says that everything looks different and he doesn't know his way around town anymore. We cruise past a huge Stop & Shop, illuminated like a Vegas casino, and Jimmy says there used to be a joint called Pal Joey's on that lot. The Winter Hill gang made its headquarters there and he used to avoid going in.

"In them days, you hadda walk around on your tiptoes," Jimmy says. "I never used a gun but I carried one."

When I ask Black Jimmy if he's stayed away from Boston because of possible retribution for his testimony against Jimmy "the Bear" Flemmi and other gangsters, he cuts me off.

"They're history, them guys. Who's going to pick up their play? Nobody," says Jimmy. "Martorano's in jail. Stevie [Flemmi] is through. The state oughta give me a medal for what I done."

But he's puffing away at his cigarette and shifting back and forth against the upholstery. You never know with the mob.

The old days are on Jimmy's mind. His former partner Jimmy O'Grady works a legitimate job at Fenway Park, which is seasonal, and in the winter lives on his savings. Earlier today, Black Jimmy visited O'Grady at the veterans' housing project in Braintree. His old partner is trying to resurrect the slow walk, and Jimmy went down there to humor him. "He's crazy," says Jimmy.

Apparently, White Jimmy sits around all day, drinking his bank account dry. "Used to be a sharp dresser," says Black Jimmy, noting that O'Grady hardly eats anything and is down to about 110 pounds.

"He didn't look good," says Jimmy. "Reminded me of Billy Dennett that last time, down in Florida."

Suddenly, a tall, clapboard house appears in the mist, rising above the hedges that demarcate the tiny front lawn. At the curb Joey gets out and heads for his patrol car. "Go ahead in, Jimmy," he says. "My mother's downstairs. I'll catch you guys later."

"There he goes," I say. "Super cop."

Joey snorts at me. "Look who's talking," he says, rounding the hood of the cruiser. "Dick fuckin' Tracy."

Black Jimmy and I laugh and start up toward the house. Mike is standing by the rental car. "What're you doing?" asks Jimmy.

"I can wait out here," Mike says.

"Helen knows you. Come in and say hello," Black Jimmy says.

We wait for Mike to join us and go up and ring the bell. Helen Mc-Cain answers the door gripping the handles of an aluminum walker. Her light blond hair is damp from the shower, and she's wearing a beige fisherman's knit sweater and black wool pants with house slippers. Helen's arthritic hip has been bothering her lately, but she refuses to take the walker when she goes out, complaining that it makes her look "like an old broad."

"Jimmy," she says, clasping his hands for a moment. "Come in, fellas. It's cold out there."

We follow Helen into the dining room and take seats at the table. China cabinets loom all around, and Gaelic music is playing from a radio in the den. As Helen stumps out there to turn it down, she says, "I used to have it playing in every room and Joe would say, 'Jesus, I can't get away from it.' "

The dining room table is heaped over with photographs of big Joe and letters from the state and federal governments regarding his pension. There's an admiral's cap from the Charles River Country Club lying atop one of the piles, and Black Jimmy puts it on the floor.

"Bad luck," he says, with a shudder. "Hats on the bed. Birds in the house. We believed in that stuff."

Mrs. McCain offers to make a pot of tea, but we all decline. Jimmy introduces his nephew; after a little prompting Helen remembers Mike from big Joe's retirement party in 1989, when Joe was still recovering from his gunshot wounds. Black Jimmy was in Florida because of a slow walking beef and couldn't attend. "I heard it was quite a shindig," he says.

"So many *people*," says Helen, rolling her eyes in mock exasperation. "And so much food."

"There was food everywhere," admits Mike.

For several moments the room grows quiet, except for the fiddle music emanating from the den, as Jimmy sifts through a stack of photographs, Helen arranges a letter opener and paperweight, and Mike, in the corner, studies the nap of the carpet. Helen and Jimmy have known each other for twenty-five years, and he's been a guest in her home before, but with big Joe gone there's a hint of formality in their meeting, a slight unease. The circle of Joe McCain's life eclipsed many other spheres, but most of those barely touched one another. What he did with guys like Jimmy, big Joe kept out of the house, and who he was at home he kept away from people like Jimmy. Still, Joe McCain was the bond that connects Helen and Jimmy, and each is left with a separate parcel of memories.

There's a stack of duplicate photos from Joe's retirement party, the big, white-haired Met cop wearing a broad smile, his arm around Helen and a line of well-wishers to either side, including Joey and Maureen, the police commissioner, and a U.S. senator.

"Can I have one of these?" asks Jimmy.

"Sure, go ahead," Helen says. "Joe would want you to have it."

A short while later, we all stand up; Jimmy and I kiss Helen on the cheek, and she escorts us to the door.

"It's nice to see you again," says Jimmy, crossing the threshold.

"Nice to see you, Jimmy," Helen says. She watches him descend the staircase in the gloom. "Good-bye."

A dank, penetrating chill occupies the neighborhood. Mike hustles around the front of the rental car and climbs in the driver's side and starts the engine with a roar. Jimmy and I are alone in the street, the fog shrouding the hedgerow and seeping in tendrils across the pavement.

"Joe McCain," says a wistful Black Jimmy, raising the photograph and squinting at it. "When other cops would give him shit about using me as an informant—that I was a bad guy, you know, like Whitey and Stevie turned out to be—Joe would throw up his hands. 'Oh, c'mon,' he'd say. 'Jimmy never killed anybody. He never hurt anyone.' "

Jimmy looks at me, and I realize this isn't a con. "In them days, kid," he says, "Joe McCain was the best fuckin' cop in the city."

TWENTY-THREE

Eddie Miami

I love the wild not less than the good.
—HENRY DAVID THOREAU

I'M SUPPOSED TO MEET BLACK JIMMY for dinner a couple of nights later, but he skips town pretty fast, disappearing like smoke. It seems that whenever I'm not working with Kevin McKenna or Mark Donahue, I'm out chasing the ghosts of Joe McCain and the men who knew him. And after several months of poring over old files, old photographs, yellowed newspaper clippings, and batches of memoranda and personal correspondence, I'm a little closer to understanding the personality and character of big Joe than I was before. It's no easy task to reconstruct a life after it's over; in that sense, the jobs of the detective, the journalist, and the historian are not far apart. The advantage I have over someone investigating, say, the legacy of Paul Revere, is that I can still talk to folks who lived and worked alongside McCain. You can tell a lot about a man by the friends he keeps.

A native of White Plains, New York, where his father was chief of police, the thirty-two-year-old Secret Service agent Stewart J. Henry had ten years' experience helping to break up counterfeit rings and investigating threats against Presidents Nixon, Ford, and Carter when he was shifted to the outfit's Boston office in 1980. Just a few days after he arrived in the city, Stew Henry met Joe McCain, Sr., who he had been told was a "cop's cop" and a man he could trust. The two hit it off immediately.

A hulking ex-football player, who had built himself up through countless hours in Jack La Lanne's gym in Manhattan, Stew Henry had a flair for undercover work. As a twenty-four-year-old rookie, he posed as a hit man in New York "for some schmuck who wanted to kill Nixon." At first the Secret Service didn't think it was such a big deal, just some garden-variety nutcase spouting off about the Republicans. But while researching the suspect's background, they discovered that he was an intelligent, clean-cut twenty-seven-year-old University of Pennsylvania grad named Andrew B. Topping and that he was quite serious about his threats. To sting Topping, Stew Henry created one of his most memorable characters: a slow-thinking, gold-chain-wearing mobster from the Bronx named Joey DeVito.

Through an informant, a meeting between Topping and the "hit man" was arranged at the Harvard Club. The three men convened at the bar and by prior arrangement, the informant withdrew and Topping and Joey DeVito moved to a table to discuss the assassination in more detail.

"At first I made him think I was just a fucking nut, like him," said Henry. "The next day I called back and asked for money."

On a bright August afternoon in 1972, Stew Henry drove to New York's Central Park to meet Topping, who carried with him a thousand dollars meant as payment toward Joey DeVito's "expenses." At that time the Secret Service used two different signals to arrest a suspect while working undercover. If the agent was wearing a wire, he used the word "Acapulco" in conversation and the other agents moved in. This was standard practice for years. It became so common that one time, when Stew Henry and a colleague were working a guy on a separate case, the other agent mentioned that he was going on vacation soon.

"You better not be goin' to that fuckin' Acapulco," said the suspect, while Henry and his colleague tried not to laugh. "The fuckin' police all go to Acapulco."

The other signal was visual: the undercover agent would open the trunk of his car. That day in Central Park, Stew Henry took the envelope filled with cash from Andrew Topping and opened his trunk to stow it away and the other agents rushed in to arrest Nixon's would-be assassin. They threw Topping against the car and told him to spread his arms and legs. But the roof of the car was sizzling hot and Topping kept picking up his hands.

"They thought he was trying to resist, so they tuned him up pretty good," said Henry, with a laugh.

Stew Henry's talent for playing OC—organized crime—figures landed him in Boston, where the wiseguy network was so tight-knit that local cops had a great deal of trouble going undercover to penetrate it. Henry met Joe McCain, Sr., at the height of his reputation, when the two men attended a law enforcement Christmas party in 1980.

"Joe always had the rep that he was a guy you could trust, that you could talk to, and that you could work with," said Henry. "Joe McCain knew everybody, and everybody knew him."

Beginning in the early eighties, Stew Henry and Joe McCain worked several cases in a row, none more involved, more dangerous, or more amusing than the "Eddie Miami" case. Eddie's real name was Edward M. Maiani; a "little greaseball from Revere," said Henry. One of the former owners of the Ebb Tide Lounge on Revere Beach Boulevard, where Joe McCain had rumbled with mob hit man Joe "the Animal" Barboza in the sixties, Eddie Miami was a hard little nut that law enforcement had been trying to crack for years. At one point in the late seventies, the FBI stuck a phony bomb under Eddie's car and blamed it on his associates in an effort to get him to roll over on them.

"He never did," said Henry.

As a private investigator and while he was a cop, Joe McCain was known for handling several cases at once with the dexterity of a symphony conductor. He was particularly adept with informants, who acted as his eyes and ears on the street. By cultivating a throng of "rats" over a long period of years, McCain learned exactly when to reward, admonish, ignore, punish, or coddle them. He also learned, through steady practice, how to discern the useful bits from the nonstop gab coming in from sketchy individuals who had apparently been vaccinated with a phonograph needle. Over a forty-year period Joe McCain put a lot of bad guys in jail because he knew how to listen.

But the key to his success in managing this link to the world of drug lords, hit men, and gangsters sprang from a large and well-used region of Joe McCain's character. At the very core of his existence was a love of people, and a love for rubbing elbows with them, high- or lowborn it didn't matter, from professors at Tufts University to the most rock-bottom junkie in Wilson Square. Among the many hours of taped conversations between McCain and his various informants, there's only one instance of somebody trying to get tough with him. During the Eddie Miami case, an angry middle-aged snitch named Bobby persisted in his complaints that he was being underpaid for his services. McCain was patient for a while, and then Bobby received some valuable insight into the sort of life he had chosen to immerse himself.

> Bobby (talking rapidly): Look, I just had a long talk with Eddie. I told him to put his fucking cards on the table. What's the story with us, Joe, moneywise?
>
> Joe McCain: You got three hundred dollars Friday. What have you done since then?
>
> Bobby (his voice rising): I told you I was going to Florida.
>
> McCain (calmly): I know what you told me. I'm not dumb. I'm not by any means dumb, Bobby.
>
> Bobby: Look at the pressures I got on me, Joe. It's not fucking easy out here.
>
> McCain: Just because you say "gimme" doesn't mean they're gonna give it to me. You can put all the pressure on me. I got broad shoulders. But I gotta go back to them.
>
> Bobby: You've got everything you've asked for, Joe.
>
> McCain: Me, personally? I'm not pleased with it.

A convicted bank robber and professional informant, Bobby eventually told Joe McCain that Eddie Miami was dealing large amounts of cocaine. McCain had recently been assigned to the Special Investigations Unit at the Suffolk County District Attorney's Office, a dream team of detectives from various law enforcement agencies. Their immediate supervisor was MDC Sergeant Mark Cronin, who had served as a courier for Army Intelligence out of Long Binh during the Vietnam War, and who would later work with McCain on the Melvin Lee case.

"I was a pretty good cop because I was trained to be a cop," said Cronin, who retired from the Massachusetts State Police as a major. "Joe McCain was born to be one."

The Special Investigations Unit, which focused on drugs and organized crime, was a new and rather expensive idea in 1980, a six- or seven-man team composed of local law enforcement, the DEA, and temporary assignees like the Secret Service agent Stew Henry. Under Captain of Detectives Tommy Keough and Sergeant Mark Cronin, the unit needed some publicity and saw Eddie Miami as their big ticket. "Joe was a good reactive detective, but he was a great proactive detective," said Cronin. "He could *make* cases."

Joe McCain and Stew Henry decided to set Henry up as a New York wiseguy. Posing as "Joey DeVito from the Bronx," the way he had with Andrew Topping, Henry was to start buying cocaine from Eddie Miami and see if they could follow him up the food chain. A crucial element was the relationship between the informant and the drug dealer. If the criminal didn't trust the informant, it wouldn't work, according to Henry. "But if you had a good informant, you could show up in a police uniform and the dealer would just figure you were a bad cop," he said.

As an informant Bobby was a wheeler-dealer. "He would give you information that suited him," said Henry. "So you couldn't really trust him." A bald, forty-year-old man with a round, reddish face, Bobby had a refined sense of taste: nothing too fancy in cars or clothes, but everything just so.

In those days Eddie Miami hung out at a steak tips joint in Chelsea called the Clubhouse Café, and Bobby took Henry in there one night. Eddie was in his mid-fifties and right out of central casting: about five-six with a bulldog face and jet-black hair. He dressed in loud clothes, drank vodka, and enjoyed a Revere guy's version of the high life. When he was introduced to this connected guy from the Bronx, Eddie misheard the name, and from that moment on Stew Henry was "Vito."

First deals are always nerve-racking, that awkward, feeling-out period when each party is trying to see through the other. But the main thing you want to avoid in undercover work, according to Stew Henry, is going to the bad guy's house. He has total control of that environment, which is a huge advantage.

"I always used to say, 'public places for private things,' which doesn't really make sense," said Henry. That night, he and Bobby left the Clubhouse Café and drove to an agreed upon spot in East Boston, where "Vito" bought an ounce of coke from Eddie Miami.

Henry noted that lots of cops want to jump the deal too quickly and thus scare the mark away. "My philosophy was, negotiate, just like you would if you were a real dealer," he said.

Eddie Miami and Vito hit it off from the start, and for about six months the two were frequent companions. In a way, Henry liked Eddie. One night they entered a classy nightclub on Route 1 in Saugus, and the girl at the door said there was a ten-dollar cover charge. Eddie flung his arm toward the empty ballroom and said, "What are you, fucking crazy? I ain't paying ten bucks. There's nobody in there."

The manager appeared and restated that there was a cover charge. "Yeah, yeah, well there's nobody in the fucking place," said Eddie. The guy let them in for free.

"He was a little shit, but he had balls," said Henry.

Another time, Eddie had difficulty starting his car outside a nightclub on Revere Beach Boulevard, and he went back in and brought out another wiseguy, a bookie. Eddie misapplied the jumper cables to the bookie's brand-new car and blew its electrical system. Ignoring the guy, Eddie managed to start his own car after several tries but broke down again just a short ways along the boulevard. Traffic began piling up behind him. Immediately Eddie started waving again, trying to attract another Samaritan. He stopped the next car, which happened to contain Metropolitan police officer Chris Brighton, who was on the case and working undercover. Brighton helped Eddie Miami get his car going again and the gangster drove off, oblivious to the fact that he'd just met one of the detectives working his case.

Gradually Stew Henry worked his way into a partnership with Eddie Miami. To build credibility, Henry arranged for the Secret Service to purchase two hundred pairs of designer blue jeans, explaining to Eddie that they had been lifted from a shipment in New York. Schooled in cocaine trafficking, where the sale of a football-sized package meant a huge score, Eddie grew frustrated with the pile of jeans, which he had to sell one pair at a time. "This is pick and shovel work," he said. "We gotta sell 'em in bulk."

At one point, needing a break, Vito told Eddie that his sister had been in a car accident and he had to go to New York to visit her. Upon his return a week later, Eddie asked, "How's your sister?" and then "Sell any jeans?"

In July, Stew Henry attended a Saturday cookout at Eddie's house on Lincoln Street in Revere. It was a hot day and several detectives, including Chris Brighton, were assigned to the surveillance on adjacent streets while Henry lounged by Eddie's pool with the other gangsters and his date, an undercover cop named Linda. During the course of the afternoon, Eddie asked Henry to take him to a nearby garage, where he was going to pick up his car.

On the way they drove past Brighton in the parking lot of a nursing home. Wearing shorts and a Hawaiian shirt, Brighton was sprawled on a chaise lounge, drinking beers from a cooler and watching the Red Sox on a battery-operated TV. "I had too much stuff out there to be a cop," Brighton would say later.

Soon enough, McCain's patience and Brighton's unorthodox surveillance methods began to pay dividends. While Eddie and Vito were selling coke to other hustlers in Boston and down on the South Shore, McCain was taping their conversations, building a list of coconspirators, and trailing them in an unmarked van. Eddie was quite a bit older than Vito and fancied himself a mentor to the young wiseguy. "These cops, they follow you," he said. He advised his protégé to keep an eye on his rearview mirror at all times.

"But he never did," said Henry. "You could have attached the cop car to his rear bumper."

One day Eddie Miami passed word to Vito that a guy he knew wanted to start swapping large amounts of cocaine for methamphetamine. Driving along the Southeast Expressway on the way to the meeting, Eddie had trouble pronouncing "Scituate," confusing Henry, who was at the wheel, and McCain, following in the surveillance van. They were approaching the split, where Routes 3 and 93 diverge.

"Up here you want to turn at Sip-switch," said Eddie.

"What?" asked Henry, who was unfamiliar with the area.

"Sip-switch. Turn there."

They were in the far right lane, approaching the place where the highway divides. "Turn left. Sip-switch. Sip-switch," said Eddie.

The car veered across all six lanes, passing beneath the sign for Scituate. A short way behind, the van nearly capsized when Joe McCain went off the road and down into a ditch. Luckily, he came bouncing onto the highway again and made the turn. A half hour later, Stew Henry and Eddie Miami arrived at a used car lot where they met a dark-haired, mustachioed fellow named Joe. During the exchange, Joe produced the meth and called a husky kid named Bruce off the lot and had him sample it.

Bruce obliged and then lost speech and motor control almost instantly: his limbs began to shake and his head lolled and he made a series of grunting sounds. "He was out in never-never land," said Henry. "That was some nasty shit."

Later, when the Special Investigations Unit ran a background check on the meth dealer, they learned that thirty-five-year-old Joseph P. Civita of Scituate was a former policeman. Nothing sets a real cop's teeth on edge like a dirty cop.

Just a week after discovering the identity of Joe Civita, Stew Henry learned that Eddie was going to meet a new source for cocaine at the Clubhouse Café. Surveillance was arranged inside and outside the bar, and Henry watched from across the room as Eddie talked with a large, round-shouldered man with an oversized head. The new source, Ernie, didn't say much and avoided contact with Vito altogether—the hallmark of a smooth operator. If a criminal is well-organized and intelligent, there's never any reason for him to do business with someone new. "Why would Ernie want to meet me when he could sell the coke to Eddie and have him deal with me?" asked Henry.

But Eddie was excited about the connection. "Ernie's the guy," he said. "We can do a lot of business with him."

Eventually the unit learned that "Ernie" was Ernest K. Field. Joe McCain was acquainted with the fifty-four-year-old Field, a shambling wreck of a man with a diverse résumé as a professional crook. Four years earlier, McCain and his old buddy, DEA agent Billy Simpkins, had tracked a loan shark, narcotics dealer, and fence known as Ernest E. O'Connell, which they knew was an alias. A team of detectives kept tabs on O'Connell for thirteen months. There were indicators of organized crime activity but little hard evidence at first. O'Connell lived in an ordinary looking Colonial on Burnside Street in Medford, Mass., and drove an eight-year-old car. Unlike most wiseguys, he didn't drink or gamble and preferred to spend his evenings at home. Investigators tried to pick up O'Connell's fingerprints from objects that he had touched in order to learn his identity but never succeeded in obtaining more than a partial print.

Day after day McCain and his associates followed O'Connell as he collected loan shark payments and met with prospective customers. At the same time they heard rumors that he was about to become the fence for $10 million in stolen bearer bonds and was involved in a drug trafficking operation that stretched from Latin America to Canada. McCain also learned that O'Connell had done time at Walpole State Prison, but corrections officers there didn't recognize him when shown a recent photograph.

After a year of surveillance McCain finally caught a break when O'Connell visited the Norwood home of Ernest and Grace Field, who turned out to be his parents. Investigators learned that Ernest K. Field, aka Ernest E. O'Connell, was born in Norwood, had a tenth-grade education and a lengthy arrest record for assault, car theft, breaking and entering in the nighttime, and armed robbery. This information, coupled with the lengthy surveillance orchestrated by Joe McCain and Billy Simpkins, led to Field's arrest and the warrants to search his home. Even they were surprised by what they found.

Squirreled away in Field's residence was $180,000 worth of stolen American Express money orders; loot from a two-year-old $300,000 burglary at a private home in Beverly, Mass.; and seventy-two men's suits, jackets, and coats, as well as several industrial sewing machines stolen from the Boston docks. The raid also netted a dozen guns, a hand grenade, fireworks, rolls of detonator cord, hundreds of stolen credit cards, eight diamonds, and a special type of camera and accompanying stamp used by the Registry of Motor Vehicles to create driver's licenses. Miscellaneous items included a large bag of marijuana, loan shark slips in the amount of $50,000, a significant number of burglars' tools, furs, skis, typewriters, cameras, handcuffs, tumblers from various-sized safes, blank gun permits, and twenty-two watches. Ernest K. Field was a one-man wrecking crew.

Field was convicted and served thirty-three months of a ten-year sentence for operating a loan shark ring before he was paroled. When Stew Henry, posing as Vito, met him in the Clubhouse Café and reported the news to Joe McCain, the detectives concluded that Field had not been reformed during his most recent stay at Walpole. And he was just as closemouthed as he always had been. But the fact remained that Eddie had introduced Vito to Ernest K. Field, and that development ratcheted up the investigation. The boys were on to something big.

In determining whether to continue an investigation as complex and demanding as the Eddie Miami case, there are always two considerations: penetration of the criminal organization and budgetary constraints. As long as you're getting to new people and new criminal activity, you keep going—if the money holds out. At a certain point, you take down the suspects and tally up the results. As Vito, Henry played Eddie Miami like a fish, maneuvering to get him, Joe Civita, Bruce Ziskind, and Ernie Field all within reach of the net. Then, on a bright August morning in 1982, four takedown teams composed of Met detectives, Secret Service agents, and Boston police arranged surveillance on each of the suspects and waited for Joe McCain's call.

Chris Brighton was assigned to Bruce Ziskind. The muscular twenty-four-year old had served less than twelve months of an eighteen-year sentence for robbing a jewelry store and shooting at two police officers and was living at a prerelease center in Mattapan. That morning Brighton was parked in the driveway of the center and three other members of the team were spread around the building. Apparently none of his counselors or his probation officer had questioned the fact that Ziskind, who worked at a menial job in Cambridge, was driving a brand-new silver-and-black Thunderbird.

At quarter to eight, Ziskind walked out of the center and climbed into his T-bird, and started to pull out. Squealing his tires, Brighton jerked forward and cut him off.

At the same time, a Secret Service agent named John Orrizzi ran out from the side of the building and closed on the drug dealer. Realizing that he was being pinched, Ziskind gunned the T-bird and tried to run Orrizzi down. But the former Rutgers lineman sidestepped the onrushing Thunderbird, and when Ziskind was cut off by two more unmarked cars and had to pound on the brakes, Orrizzi reached in through the window and grabbed the suspect by the throat. Ziskind was a tough kid, ten years younger than Orrizzi and well-built, but the Secret Service agent lifted him out of the car and threw him on the ground like a toy. Ziskind was arrested with sixteen hundred dollars in cash on his person, and two pounds of marijuana and an ounce of cocaine in the trunk of his car.

Meanwhile, a separate team of detectives battered down the front door of Ernie Field's house in Medford, arrested him, and searched the premises for several hours. They discovered ten pounds of cocaine, worth an estimated $1 million on the street, as well as three DEA badges that Field would attach to leather cases when he was moving the coke. Police also found a book entitled *100 Ways to Disappear and Live Free*. Ernest K. Field, Joseph P. Civita, Bruce Ziskind, and Edward M. Maiani were charged with conspiracy to distribute drugs and held in lieu of $700,000 bail.

Eddie Miami was sentenced to five to eight years in prison on three counts of conspiring to violate narcotics laws. A couple of years after they busted him, Stew Henry and Joe McCain were in the Suffolk County Courthouse in Pemberton Square when they spotted the little mobster, talking on a pay phone.

"Hey, uh, Vito," said Eddie, trying to stretch the metal cord in order to hail the two cops. "C'mere, you guys."

McCain and Henry went over and shook Eddie's hand. "You two guys were the best goddamned—hey, no hard feelings," said Eddie. "You got me good."

Shortly after Eddie got out of jail, Stew Henry saw him driving through the parking lot at the North Shore Mall. He followed, and when Eddie parked his car, Henry got out and once again the two men shook hands and made small talk. It was like two guys from rival high schools meeting up years after the big game: "How you doing? Everything's all right?"

A few years later, Joe McCain called Henry to tell him that Eddie had been sick for a while and died. He was just a wiseguy, but with his passing, and Stew Henry's retirement after twenty-six years in the outfit, and something as unthinkable as Joe McCain getting shot on the job, there was a definite sense that an era had ended.

TWENTY-FOUR

The Three-Hundred-Dollar Clowns

B Y GETTING TO KNOW ALL THE METS from the old Special Investigations Unit, I'm beginning to figure out why Joe McCain would draw the ire of cops like Joseph Civita and Jimmy Hyde. When William "Battlin' Biff" McLean greets me at the Mass. State Police barracks in Danvers, his ready manner is a welcome change from the brusqueness of the other troopers in and around the lobby. Widowed ten years and the father of two young sons, Biff McLean is a tall, friendly man with the build of a middle-distance runner: some power, a little speed, and a wealth of endurance. He's coming off a nice effort in a local road race and while we're standing there, a young trooper with a military haircut stops by.

"The lieutenant is pissed at you," he says to McLean.

The lieutenant he's talking about, Biff's supervisor, is a dozen years younger than he is. "What's he mad at me for?" asks McLean.

"You beat him by about six minutes yesterday," the trooper says. "Don't you know you're supposed to let the lieutenant win?"

Biff laughs, and the young trooper goes out. McLean's wavy, brown hair is flecked with gray, and he's wearing a pressed denim shirt and dark slacks, with a nine-shot Beretta strapped to his hip and the small gold State Police badge right-center on his belt. The former Boston English High hockey player and Army infantryman and gravedigger has been a cop for twenty-five years and is assigned to plainclothes narcotics. McLean waves at a trooper behind the Plexiglas and we get buzzed inside and head upstairs to his office.

Like the other Met cops who were there the night Joe McCain got shot, Biff McLean has moved on to a new phase in his life. And although they don't work together anymore, McLean keeps tabs on his former partners. Known by his old radio call sign, "One-fifty Gen-o," Gene Kee is now a lieutenant, assigned to the FBI Bank Robbery Task Force in Boston. The unit's surveillance expert, "Fat Al" DiSalvo, is back in uniform, manning the State Police detail at Logan Airport, while Dennis Febles, recently graduated from the New England School of Law, is in Troop H. Chris Brighton, who has thus far proved an elusive interview, is also in uniform, working out of the Lower Basin. And the unit's thoughtful, cerebral commander, Major Mark Cronin, has retired with his wife, Debbie, to a comfortable oceanfront home in Hampton, New Hampshire.

Biff McLean was just shy of his thirtieth birthday when he started with the Mets in 1978. One afternoon shortly after he came on the job, McLean was in his cruiser and heard over the police radio that a drug suspect had stolen a car and was speeding through downtown Boston. The car was a brown 1978 Ford Gran Torino, and as McLean was sitting at the light going south on Park Drive, he looked across the four lanes and saw a vehicle that fit the description on the other side.

The driver was a kid in his twenties, and "I'm looking at him and he's looking at me," McLean says. When the light turned green, Biff pulled out, glanced at the kid's license plate and grabbed the radio: "I got that vehicle down near Fenway."

Tires smoking against the pavement, the kid gunned the engine of the Gran Torino, darting in and out of traffic as he raced north on Park Drive. Clearing the light, McLean ran his cruiser up on the island and over the grassy median, bumping down the curb on the far side. He pressed the accelerator to the floor, chasing the Ford over the bridge behind the Museum of Fine Arts. When the kid tried to go left on Huntington Avenue, he spun out, and McLean, gritting his teeth and locking his elbows, shot across the intersection and T-boned him, the vehicles smashing together with a loud, dissonant clang. Bits of glass and chrome rained onto the street and other motorists screeched past on either side, blasting their horns.

Quick as a squirrel, the thief popped out of the driver's side window and took off down the street "like he'd fucking practiced," says McLean.

The car thief was a lightweight kid, wearing jeans and sneakers and an old sweatshirt. McLean went straight after him on foot, watching as the kid jettisoned bags of heroin left and right. At that moment, McLean recalled the advice of his first partner, a cop with twenty years on the job: "When they run, take the gun out. Don't fuck around with the stick." Doing his best John Wayne, Biff pulled out his .38 and yelled at the kid to quit fucking around and stop—he was a police officer.

Zigzagging through parked cars and down an alley McLean began to close in, and the kid, ten years younger and forty pounds lighter, couldn't believe it. ("That's why I started running," says McLean, who has made foot chases his specialty, "because the little bastards were getting away from me.") He got close and shoved the kid high on the shoulder and the car thief lost his balance and went ass over teakettle onto the sidewalk. Leaping on him, McLean yelled that he was a fucking cop and the two of them went sprawling over the pavement in a fury of knees and elbows.

When McLean started to apply the handcuffs, the kid put up the fight of his life. At that point, the young Met cop had produced a high-speed chase, terrified motorists and pedestrians, a wrecked cruiser, and a totaled stolen car—he needed a live body. While the kid continued to scrap, McLean smacked him in the head with the gun butt, opening a cut above the kid's eye that produced large amounts of blood.

A middle-aged woman cried out from a window above them, "Hey. You can't do that."

"Shut the fuck up and get back in your house," said McLean, still struggling with the kid.

McLean subdued the heroin dealer and had him cinched up pretty tight when a Boston policeman came galloping up on a huge white horse and the two cops arrested the kid. A couple of days later, the drug dealer accused Metropolitan Police Officer William Joseph McLean of pistol-whipping him and filed charges of excessive force. McLean was placed on restricted duty, and while inside the Lower Basin waiting to be interviewed by Internal Affairs, he noticed a big, strapping, white-haired guy who turned out to be Joe McCain, the dean of all Met detectives and known throughout the ranks as a cop's cop.

McLean was sitting there by himself and McCain walked over and offered his hand. "That was a good pinch, kid," he said.

Then Officer McLean went into a room with the two I.A. detectives, and one of them asked if he had hit the drug dealer with his gun.

"Yeah, I did," said Biff.

Both detectives looked up from their paperwork. "Hey, you're not supposed to say that," one of them said.

"But I fucking did it," said McLean, explaining that the kid had resisted and that he'd been alone and needed to protect himself and get the heroin dealer off the street.

Nothing ever happened as a result of the interview; no official reprimand, not even a mention of the incident in his personnel file. "I always felt that Joe helped me out with the I.A. guys," says McLean.

He goes on to say that "Joe McCain was not universally loved by law enforcement types, but he was universally respected. Some of it was political, some of it was jealousy. Most of these guys, they couldn't have been a pimple on Joe's ass. Hey, he could be difficult to work with. He had a temper. But we always had fun."

And when Biff McLean was asked to join McCain and Mark Cronin in the Special Investigations Unit, the fun really got started. One of their most memorable cases involved the investigation and subsequent arrest of sixty-five-year-old Louis Colangelo, a crack-smoking, whore-chasing drug dealer from Swampscott. When they closed on the house, the Met detectives discovered that Colangelo had a half pound of 95 percent pure cocaine and more than $35,000 in cash hidden behind a picture in his basement.

"Aren't you a little old for this shit?" asked McLean, as they handcuffed Colangelo.

"Don't knock it unless you tried it, kid," said the white-haired drug dealer.

After the uniforms took Colangelo away, Cronin sat down in the living room to tally up the money and cocaine while Al DiSalvo, Chris Brighton, Gene Kee, and McLean searched every drawer and cabinet. The doorbell rang, and Fat Al, dressed in plainclothes but with his badge, handcuffs, and gun attached to his belt, answered the door. A stout, gruff-tempered man who's rarely in the mood for anyone's bullshit, DiSalvo asked, "Whattaya want?"

Two punks from East Boston were on the stoop, wearing their wife-beater T-shirts and gold chains. "We wanna buy an eightball," one of them said.

DiSalvo jerked his thumb toward the living room. "Go see Sarge," he said.

Hunched over a coffee table, Cronin was busy making thousand-dollar piles out of hundred-dollar bills when the two greaseballs entered the room. Several other detectives were coming in and out.

"Hey, Sarge, we want an eightball," one of the East Boston guys said. "But we only have half the money."

Cronin glanced up, regarding the two men with a disgusted look. "Leave me your driver's licenses and I'll give you the coke," he said. "But you have to come back with the rest of the money by six o'clock."

The two cokeheads looked at each other and shrugged. Then they gave Cronin their I.D.s, which he examined and put aside, and the punks handed over several twenty-dollar bills.

Cronin shook his head. "Look around," he said, gesturing at the other detectives. "Do you see what's going on here? Do you know who we are?"

"Hey, man, we just want an eightball," one of them said.

"Are you idiots?" asked Cronin. "We're police officers. You're under arrest."

DiSalvo was called back into the room to handcuff the two men and read them their Miranda rights. "You should be ashamed to call yourselves Italian," he said, leading the men out. "Dumb freakin' guineas."

On another case, Gene Kee and Biff McLean were asked to join Lieutenant "Shaky" Blaine in questioning a suspect, a fresh little Greek kid from Roslindale, who had been arrested with one-half pound of

98 percent pure cocaine. "Tell us who your supplier is and we'll talk to the D.A. for you," said Kee.

The young drug dealer smirked. "Fuck you, you three-hundred-dollar-a-week clowns," he said. "My lawyer'll have me out of here before you finish your reports."

Approaching swiftly, Kee knocked the kid's chair over backwards while Blaine averted his eyes and headed for the door. McLean pressed his thumb and forefinger to his lips, stifling a laugh. It was hard to feel sorry for the bad guys.

Two bad guys that Joe McCain never felt any sympathy toward, according to McLean, were the murderous Winter Hill gangsters James "Whitey" Bulger and Stephen "the Rifleman" Flemmi. Like other cops in the know, McCain always had a feeling that Whitey Bulger was some kind of rat and thus shielded from prosecution for his own crimes, including multiple homicides. Even with all his contacts in law enforcement, McCain was unable to get at the nature of that relationship: who, exactly, was complicit, and how pervasive was it? Long before it was public knowledge, McCain suspected that Bulger was being protected by the feds and that his protection extended to all manner of heinous deeds and cloaked his position as an FBI informant. It also created a firewall between Whitey and his "legitimate" older brother, the long-time president of the Massachusetts Senate, William Bulger. So McCain was delighted when Flemmi turned up on another surveillance, and he soon struck upon the notion of taking Stevie and Whitey down via a case that somehow circumvented Whitey's immunity.

Joe pulled Biff McLean out of uniform for good to work on what became known as the Davis brothers case. Stevie and Mickey Davis were cocaine dealers from Randolph, Mass., small-timers mostly, with a supply connection to a big-time heroin and coke dealer named Marchand, who was the son of a Boston cop. Although Marchand was the original target of the investigation, the real attraction for McCain was that the Davises' twenty-five-year-old sister, Debra, a good-looking blonde with a penchant for bad boys, had been dating forty-six-year-old Stephen Flemmi. (When Debby's father voiced his disapproval of their relationship, he drowned in Boston Harbor after "accidentally" falling off a boat.) Like a lot of wiseguys, the Rifleman had several girlfriends at once, providing them with cash and jewelry and squiring them around Boston in his shiny new Jaguar. By injecting a little capital and a lot of gangster charm into a number of households, Flemmi and Bulger had access to untapped phone lines and rent-free offices, an arrangement that made their operation very hard to pin down.

Joe McCain's informant, a grizzled, balding ex-con named Tank Gaffney, provided the news about Flemmi and the Davis girl. Gaffney also told McCain that the girl's mother, Olga Davis, was aware of her sons' drug dealing and taking money from Flemmi, and that the Rifleman had designs on Debby's sister, fourteen-year-old Michelle Davis, who was described as a "young Ava Gardner."

Outside the ken of Boston's FBI office, McCain secured a warrant for a wiretap on the Davises' telephone and rented an apartment a mile away with the intention of "putting the ears" on the Davis boys, as well as Flemmi and Bulger. Since Biff McLean had grown up in neighboring Mattapan and knew people who were buying coke from the Davises and acting as lookouts and couriers—including a kid named Danny Jacie, who had been seeing Debby Davis before Flemmi and was missing— Joe wanted Biff on his team.

The young Met was thrilled. "If you were gonna try to be a detective, Joe was the guy," says McLean.

It was going to be an expensive operation and the district attorney in Norfolk County, where the wiretap was located, told the Mets that his office couldn't afford to pay for it all. They were going to need help from an agency with deep pockets. In Boston, that meant the FBI.

There's a saying in law enforcement: The feds eat like elephants and shit like birds. Joe McCain was already wary of the supervisor in the Boston FBI office, a man named John Morris, and had heard rumors about the friendship between Agent John Connolly and the Bulgers, who had grown up in the same South Boston neighborhood. Because previous spats between local police, the Norfolk County D.A.'s Office, and the bureau had derailed efforts at targeting organized crime, Mc-Cain knew that creating a partnership in the Davis brothers case would be tricky. He called a meeting at a pancake house on Route 1 in Nor-wood, during which he convinced those in attendance to forget their old grudges and "do our master's business—which is the public's." Through some delicate maneuvering Joe was able to get FBI backing for the wiretap operation, as well as the assignment of two agents he trusted, Jimmy Crawford and Matt Cronin (no relation to Mark Cronin, McCain's friend, former supervisor, and an MDC cop).

But as part of the deal McCain received one thing he didn't want, a shapely young FBI agent named Tanya Roberts, formerly a sheriff's deputy in Georgia and known for leaving broken marriages and turmoil in her wake. More than anything, McCain respected hard work and those who enjoyed doing it; in Tanya Roberts, he encountered a do-nothing who couldn't be bothered to show up for meetings and surveillance assignments and who had already "fucked half the agents in Boston," according to Joe.

At the apartment complex in Randolph where the Davis surveillance was being maintained, as many as eight detectives were seen coming and going at irregular intervals. McCain instructed Biff McLean and Chris Brighton and the other members of the unit to tell the neighbors they were airline pilots, since they often traveled in pairs, arriving and departing in the wee hours of the morning. But he didn't have to worry about Tanya Roberts; she was too busy working out at the Boston Athletic Club to need a pretext.

There were long, tough days in Randolph, with McCain and Biff McLean and the other handpicked guys working their tails off but always moving closer to Bulger and Flemmi. Joe's early years on Revere Beach had led to an intense interest in the Winter Hill gang, which had come a long way since then. Whitey Bulger had taken over most of the North End mob's loan sharking, racketeering, extortion, contract violence, and drug dealing. His henchmen—Stephen Flemmi in particular—were rumored to be committing murders at an astonishing rate; a number of those killings had nothing to do with "business" and were carried out on personal, petty whims. It was believed that Stevie Flemmi had an inside guy at a West Roxbury crematorium and was eliminating his victims by placing second bodies in coffins before they turned on the furnace.

While the surveillance team was staying on the Davises, the relationship between Joe McCain and Tanya Roberts continued to sour.

Assigned to "handle" Tank Gaffney's live-in girlfriend, a woman named Maggie, who was also an informant on the case, Roberts told Maggie that she could do better than the fat, bald Gaffney. Of course, this upset Gaffney, causing him to lose his interest in the case. To wrestle things back on track, McCain stayed up half the night, convincing Gaffney that he was handsome in an unconventional way.

McCain was raised to have the utmost respect for women; he was a chivalrous man, in the old-fashioned sense. But he had no tolerance for dirty or incompetent police officers, regardless of gender or race. In the midst of the Davis brothers case, he turned to FBI agent Matt Cronin, and said, "This douche bag with her tight fucking blue jeans is gonna ruin this case."

Cronin smoothed things over at the bureau, but then things went from bad to worse. In her brief stay in Massachusetts, Roberts managed to insert herself among FBI power brokers, led by John Connolly, a well-groomed, fastidious man who shared Roberts's inclination to work out on bureau time. One very hot day, McCain was following Mickey Davis and lost him up on Beacon Hill. When he tried to hand the surveillance to Roberts, the sexy young red-head never answered his radio calls.

McCain drove straight to the Boston Athletic Club on Summer Street. With the sun beating down, he spent an hour searching the parking lot until he found Roberts's little blue Mustang. Taking out one of his business cards, he scribbed "Hope you had a nice workout" on the back and stuck the card on Roberts's windshield. Then he climbed back in his rattling old shitbox and returned to work.

Later that day Roberts stormed into the Norfolk D.A.'s office, where McCain was meeting with Matt Cronin and a few other detectives. "What the fuck is this?" she asked, throwing McCain's card onto the table.

Joe swept the card aside. "We're out there busting our asses in the hot sun and you're nowhere to be found," he said. "Who do you think you are? Miss America with an FBI badge, who can do whatever she wants?"

Work on the Davis brothers case went on, but the tension was palpable. Listening over the wire one day, McLean learned that Stevie

Flemmi had taken Debby Davis on a vacation to Mexico. Upon their return, the telephone chatter indicated that Debby had met the rich, handsome son of a Mexican chicken and oil millionaire, and the two had taken a liking to each other. Within a few weeks Flemmi was spending more time with fourteen-year-old Michelle Davis, and shortly thereafter Debby was among the missing, rumored to have returned to Mexico and the company of the young millionaire.

Stevie Flemmi liked to take little weekend trips to Montreal with his paramours. Determined to hook the Rifleman any way he could, for a while McCain became fixated on catching Stevie crossing the border with the underage Davis girl. "If we can't get him for anything else, we'll arrest the bastard for statutory rape," Joe told Biff McLean.

But the whole case unraveled before Flemmi embarked on his next junket. Suspected alongside the Davises and Whitey and Stevie was a friend of Mickey Davis's called Paul Petros, a florist and their partner in the cocaine business. On June 2, 1983, five detectives including Chris Brighton and Biff McLean followed Petros and Mickey Davis from the Mystic Valley Parkway to State Street in downtown Boston. Driving a brand-new silver Audi, Petros was believed to have two kilos of cocaine hidden in his trunk and was on his way to meet the buyer.

High above the city, Matt Cronin was quarterbacking the surveillance from the FBI plane. Having rerouted air traffic to allow the pilot to fly low, Cronin had a clear view of Petros's car and the movements of its passengers once they stepped out. A well-dressed, meticulous fellow, the forty-one-year-old Cronin was a law school graduate and native of Connecticut. He admired Joe McCain for his integrity and love of police work; in a profession where it's easy to become cynical, this plain-spoken guy from Winter Hill treated law enforcement as a vocation, coming to work every day brimming with passion for the job.

"Joe could walk into any place in the city in full uniform, and even the wiseguys would talk to him," recalled Cronin, who considered McCain his mentor even though he had fourteen years of experience himself.

The team of detectives settled near Petros when he parked the Audi on the corner of Washington and Avery Streets. Carrying a folded newspaper under his arm, Chris Brighton got out of his car and walked along the sidewalk with Petros coming toward him. The drug dealer crossed Washington Street to a fruit stand, where he bought a couple of peaches. Meanwhile, an unknown black male approached Davis with a shoe box in his hand, and Petros crossed back to his car. Davis took the shoe box in his left hand, and Petros got behind the wheel of the Audi.

McCain and Cronin's plan dictated that their guys would witness the exchange of drugs and money, then let Davis and Petros go, and arrest the buyer. Pressuring him to cooperate, law enforcement would have the buyer declare his satisfaction with the Davises' product and ask them to triple his order. Such a large buy would force the Davises to go back to Bulger and Flemmi for help. That was the transaction that Mc-Cain and Cronin wanted to jump on; if they could catch Bulger and Flemmi in the open with that much cocaine, no amount of federal protection would save them. And having the buyer as their key witness would move the original source, Tank Gaffney, "one back" from the arrest, shielding him from reprisals and allowing him to continue as an informant. It was win-win.

So far, things were progressing as McCain's team had hoped. But before Cronin could radio down from the airplane to follow Petros and arrest the buyer, a voice broke in from Metropolitan Police headquarters ordering that all three parties to the transaction be arrested on the spot.

"No, stay back," said Cronin. He was furious; this was the worst possible time for interagency rivalry to get in the way of a great pinch.

"I'm telling you to move in," said Met headquarters. "Take 'em all down."

It was a major screwup. The detectives on the ground had not actually witnessed a transaction, and the shoe box turned out to contain a pair of shoes. The arrests forced the team to expose their probable cause, which was the wiretap, and once that news got out, the chance of hooking Whitey Bulger and Stevie Flemmi became remote.

Things were about to get worse. The team of detectives assigned to the case was operating out of the Harbor Unit on Beverly Street in Boston, over behind North Station. Although this arrangement was kept quiet, when Paul Petros got back on the street, he managed to steal a file on the case from the front seat of one of the detectives' cars, which was parked outside the Harbor Unit. Obviously there was a leak, and it had to be someone on the inside. Nothing was ever proven, but Joe McCain had a short list of suspects, including an FBI agent who wore tight blue jeans.

As soon as they found out about the theft, McCain and McLean drove up to New Hampshire, where Tank Gaffney was working, to tell the informant that he might be in danger. Then McCain met with the judge, in camera, to inform him how the operation had been compromised, and the judge ordered the contents of the wiretap to be sealed, where it remains to this day. Contrary to popular belief, then, Bulger and Flemmi's cozy relationship with the Boston FBI office did not allow them to spike the Davis brothers case. But someone did, and that person's identity remains a mystery.

The FBI's misguided protection of Whitey Bulger and Stephen Flemmi is already part of Boston lore, up there with Harry Frazee selling Babe Ruth to the Yankees to underwrite his production of *No, No, Nanette*. But with all his street experience, Joe McCain rarely saw things in black and white, and if there was ever a case that included a lot of gray area, it's the case against Whitey Bulger. Which law enforcement officials were aware of Bulger's murderous dealings while the gangster was a protected government informant may never be known. Whitey Bulger has been a fugitive since 1995, and his sightings, both real and imagined, push every other topic out of the local news. Stevie Flemmi is in custody, trying to sell his backlog of criminal information to avoid the death penalty. According to Colonel Thomas J. Foley, the superintendent of the Mass. State Police and a key witness against Flemmi, the government "has got him solid on a group of murders."

Not long after Joe McCain died, Bulger's FBI contact John Connolly was convicted of obstruction of justice for abetting the criminal activities of Bulger and Flemmi, and sentenced to ten years in federal prison. Connolly's supervisor, John Morris, admitted taking bribes from the Winter Hill gang and was granted immunity from prosecution in exchange for his testimony against Connolly. ("Morris took seven grand in an envelope from Whitey and he's retired," said Mass. state trooper Al DiSalvo. "Is that fair?") Connolly bashing has been a popular Boston sport for years, with politicians, judges, district attorneys, law enforcement personnel, and media types all guilty of piling on. But Joe McCain never did, in spite of the fact that he expended a great deal of time and energy and put his own life and those of his colleagues and family in jeopardy trying to break up the Winter Hill gang and put Whitey and the Rifleman in jail.

One aspect of the case that aggravated McCain was the fact that the mob rats "Cadillac Frank" Salemme and John "the Basin Street Butcher" Martorano, each a suspect in twenty murders, were offered limited immunity in exchange for their testimony against Connolly, who has not been accused of killing anyone. Martorano was offered a deal amounting to roughly four months of jail time per murder to provide information about a man he'd never met. From Joe Barboza and William Geraway on down, this sort of questionable bargaining drove McCain nuts. "You've got the shooters," he said. "What can they possibly give you that's better than they are?"

On October 19, 2000, a Bulger strong arm named Kevin Weeks led Massachusetts authorities to a makeshift grave beside the Neponset River where they found the remains of Debra Davis. Weeks told police that on a September evening in 1981, Flemmi and Davis were taking a ride through South Boston when Davis attempted to break off their relationship. Flemmi proceeded to his mother's house on East Third Street and forced Davis inside, where he and Whitey Bulger strangled her.

Later that night, Flemmi and Bulger drove to an isolated spot beneath the MBTA tracks in Quincy and buried Davis's body. After Weeks helped the Mass State Police unearth several more bodies, there was increased speculation that the twenty-seven missing persons known to the authorities represent a small percentage of the actual number of killings Bulger and Flemmi committed.

Since Weeks came forward, Debby's mother Olga Davis has appeared on Boston television several times, crying over her lost child and accusing the government of complicity in her death. By protecting Whitey and Stevie, and ignoring her pleas for assistance when Debby first disappeared, the FBI and the state of Massachusetts share in the responsibility for Debby Davis's murder, if Olga Davis is to be believed. She has filed lawsuits against the FBI and the state of Massachusetts.

What Olga Davis omits during her tearful media appearances is the fact that Metropolitan Police Officers Joe McCain and Biff McLean and FBI Agent Matt Cronin did offer to help her. When Debby first went missing, Stevie Flemmi told her family that she had returned to Mexico and her wealthy young boyfriend. Olga knew enough about Flemmi and Bulger and their way of doing business to be skeptical, even frightened. Debby Davis had intimate knowledge of Flemmi's criminal activities; when she fell in love with the Mexican kid and Stevie began his affair with her fourteen-year-old sister, Debby became a loose end that had to be removed.

Olga Davis didn't have to be a rocket scientist to figure out how Flemmi and Bulger solved these kinds of problems, or how they made the bodies disappear. In fact, the two gangsters would often commit a murder and then go into a coffee shop the next day and break bread with the victim's family. At first Mrs. Davis may have believed that Debby had taken off for Mexico. But after not hearing from her daughter for several weeks, which was out of character, Olga became worried and approached McCain through Tank Gaffney's girlfriend, Maggie, and the three of them sat down for a meeting. Olga had been told that McCain was the only cop in Boston who could be trusted and by this time, she was desperate.

Although she had no physical evidence that her daughter had been murdered, Olga insisted that Flemmi was a violent man and had learned of Debby's fledgling love affair in Mexico. McCain listened to her story without Olga knowing that he had the whole operation under surveillance. When she was through, McCain said he would think about it and get back to her.

Technically, Olga Davis was talking about a Randolph missing persons case, over which McCain had no jurisdiction. Joe brought her tale to Matt Cronin, and the FBI agent suggested that Olga Davis wear a wire and accuse Stephen Flemmi of having something to do with the girl's disappearance. Matt Cronin and his colleague Jimmy Crawford had their own suspicions about a leak in the FBI "front office," so nearly all of what they were learning about Flemmi and Bulger and the Davises they left out of their reports—which were being read by Connolly and Morris. So although there's no written record of what actually occurred, it's a source of both amusement and irritation whenever these retired cops and agents see Olga Davis on television, claiming that she approached the FBI but they wouldn't help her. (Nor does she ever mention that she accepted money from Stevie Flemmi, or that he conducted a significant drug-selling operation under her roof.) The truth is, when Joe McCain brought Matt Cronin and Olga Davis together, the FBI agent asked her to wear a wire and she refused.

It is also a fact that McCain put Biff McLean on the Davis brothers case because Biff, as a Mattapan guy, knew a lot of the younger players: kids who were buying the coke, some of the mules and couriers and lesser dealers, and an informant who ran in those circles and often produced new, fresh angles on what they were hearing over the wire. (One day in June, McLean heard the Davises planning a big Fourth of July barbecue. They were making scads of money in their cocaine business but were discussing in gleeful voices how they had shoplifted all the hamburgers and sausages for the party, while McLean and the other detectives laughed about it on their end of the line.)

Danny Jacie, the small-time drug dealer and former boyfriend of Debby's, was one of the minor players in the Davis saga. Long before Debby Davis went missing, McLean heard from his own informant that Jacie was supposed to meet Stevie Flemmi at five o'clock one night in a remote location in the Blue Hills, a sprawling rural area just south and west of Boston. The two men knew each other because of Debby Davis.

That night uniformed Mets were patrolling a gravel road called the Pipeline on the Milton-Quincy border. At dusk, a car passed them at high speed going in the other direction. The police car made a quick U-turn and chased after the car, losing it in Quincy, whereupon they turned back and drove up to the Blue Hills as ordered. There, in a tiny lot off the Pipeline, they found the body of twenty-one-year-old Daniel Thomas Jacie. He had been shot several times.

It wasn't until several years later, while manning the Davis wiretap, that McLean learned Jacie had been dating Debby Davis at the same time Flemmi was seeing her. Known as a ruthless, jealous bastard, the Rifleman lured his rival to the Blue Hills and then killed him.

The fourteen autopsy photographs are contained in an old brown envelope. In them a good-looking, young man with brown hair and brown eyes and a wispy beard is lying on a table. He is wearing a pair of tan pants, a white shirt, and a short, brown leather jacket, and his eyes are open. At the beginning of the sequence, Jacie is depicted from the waist up, his shirt unbuttoned and jacket peeled back to reveal a bullet wound on the left side of his rib cage, just below the heart. Dried blood encircles the hole, which is approximately an inch in diameter, and there are large pink stains on the inner flap of the shirt.

In the other photographs the corpse is naked. In one of the most gruesome images, Jacie is facedown on the examining table. The white-gowned figure of an attendant is depicted over Jacie's left shoulder, wearing latex gloves and holding a scalpel in his right hand. Gobbets of blood are everywhere. The hair on the lower part of the victim's skull has been shorn away, leaving the sort of ugly, gaping wound made by a large-caliber handgun at close range. The path of the bullet widens as it enters the skull, exposing the gory mass of the victim's brain.

Although Biff McLean would love to press Stephen Flemmi on what occurred in the Blue Hills that evening, Danny Jacie's murder remains unsolved.

TWENTY-FIVE

One-fifty Gen-o

There are no second acts in American lives.
— F. Scott Fitzgerald

C OMING UP FROM THE T STATION at Government Center is like rising from the depths of a Stygian underworld. As I climb toward the daylight at the apex of the stairs, heavy pipes rattle against the wall and another train arrives below, disgorges its passengers, and shudders off into the darkness. Topside is the bright gray chill of mid-March, City Hall to my right, the JFK Building straight ahead, and off to the left, the curving stone edifice of Center Plaza. It's March 20, the first day of the war against Iraq, and City Hall Plaza is occupied by satellite trucks from the major networks and cable television stations, in anticipation of the protesters who are expected to flood the area.

There are a lot of cops around, and I ask a Boston police officer the way to One Center Plaza and he points along the sidewalk to Kinsale's Tavern and the entrance to the adjacent building. Six floors above Cambridge Street, inside FBI headquarters where I'm going to meet Gene Kee, no one will be protesting the war—they'll be too busy fighting it.

Off the elevator *FBI* is printed on the wall in giant blue letters and I proceed down the corridor, through a metal detector, and into the reception area. The FBI lobby is part Brahmin living room—floral sofa, easy chairs, and shiny end tables—and part observation room at San

268

Quentin—a large sheet of bulletproof glass divides the room and off to the right is a steel-reinforced door. Behind the glass a pretty blonde receptionist asks me to empty my pockets onto the counter, return through the metal detector, and hoist up my backpack and shuffle around the notebooks and pencils so she can look inside. Then the young woman trades a red visitor's badge for my driver's license and asks me to take a seat while she calls upstairs to former Joe McCain protégé Eugene Albert Kee, Jr.

Today, fifty-year-old Gene Kee is a Massachusetts State Police lieutenant assigned as a detective to the FBI Bank Robbery Task Force. (And with fifty-five bank robberies in metro Boston in January alone, he's a busy man.) Kee has agreed to take me out to Wood Avenue in Hyde Park, where big Joe was shot, with the understanding that he might have to answer calls and meet with informants over the course of the day. But all this was arranged before the war started, and with new threats of terrorism and heavy security throughout the building, there's some question whether any extraneous visitors will be allowed inside.

After a few minutes Kee comes through a side door into the lobby. He slaps me on the back and shakes my hand, calling me Doctor and Commander. I'm neither, but am smiling and shaking my head in spite of myself. Dressed in gray slacks, white oxford shirt, and a beige-and-blue paisley tie, Kee has the wide shoulders and thickly muscled back of the habitual weight lifter. His short, brown hair, ruddy complexion, and square jaw are a road map to his previous occupations: U.S. Army regular, beer drinker, and college hockey player.

Gene Kee and Joe McCain go back to the early eighties and the first incarnation of the Special Investigations Unit under Mark Cronin; Kee is an unabashed Joe McCain fan and goes out of his way to keep an eye on Joe Jr. while he schools a generation of other young cops in the McCain legacy.

"This is your lucky fuckin' day," says Kee as we're buzzed through the door into the plush hallway of the FBI offices.

It turns out that the special agent in charge of Boston's FBI operation hails from my town, and his seven-year-old and my son play hockey and soccer on the same teams. So in a happy coincidence that would've made Joe McCain proud, the FBI has approved my visit, and the boss man wants to have a word with Gene and me before we go out on the street.

Gene Kee sticks his head into an office with a sweeping view of City Hall Plaza just as Special Agent in Charge William Chase comes strolling along the hallway. Chase is a trim, compact man with a reddish brush cut and is wearing dress pants and shiny shoes with a dark blue FBI jersey and his badge, dangling on a chain around his neck. He shakes hands with Gene and me, explaining that he's busy in the command post down the hall and will get "suited up" in shirt and tie only if he's called to do any media interviews today.

As the Chief, which is what Kee calls him, Bill Chase is a recognizable figure, appearing often on television and radio and in the Boston newspapers to explain high-profile cases and provide a connection for the public. But with rumors of terrorism increasing by the hour, he must be facing some tough decisions, the only hints of which are a few more crow's-feet around his eyes as he smiles.

"Be careful out there, Jay," he says, before turning to Kee. "Don't do any jump-outs, Gene."

"Oh, wow, Chief. You know I won't."

"Should I give Jay my Kevlar?" asks Chase.

"Go 'head," says Kee, grinning at us.

Chase slaps him on the back and laughs. "Get out of here," he says.

Kee says, "Let's go, Commander," and leads us down the curving hallway past the FBI Wall of Martyrs—black-and-white photographs of agents slain in the line of duty—around the bend and alongside another gallery of photos; this time it's the FBI's Most Wanted list, and Kee raps on one of the mug shots with his knuckles as he goes by and I stop and look: it's James J. "Whitey" Bulger, from Winter Hill in Somerville, ruthless gangster and murderer. The longtime Joe McCain nemesis "is being sought for his role in numerous murders committed from the early 1970s through the mid-1980s in connection with his leadership of an organized crime group that allegedly controlled extortion, drug deals, and other illegal activities in the Boston, Massachusetts, area. He has a violent temper and is known to carry a knife at all times. Considered armed and extremely dangerous."

It's no small irony that Whitey Bulger's mug shot has such a prominent place in the FBI office, since under a different regime he was a prized "informant," free to plunder and kill under agency protection. But all that was long before guys like Bill Chase and Gene Kee reported to work here.

Kee is an old workout rat and stops to show me the FBI gymnasium, which offers a stunning panoramie view of the plaza and where, by contract, he's allowed to exercise for an hour each day. (Biff McLean took me into the gym at the Danvers State Police Barracks and it's interesting to note that the troopers' facility is heavy on free weights and things like squat racks and Smith machines, while the FBI room is filled with cardiovascular equipment: treadmills, stair machines, et cetera. In a way, the exercise slant reflects the mission of each agency: security and deterrence for the State Police, tracking and pursuit for the FBI.)

Punching numbers into a panel on each level, Kee leads us up one flight to the offices of the Bank Robbery Task Force. Security is pretty tight everywhere, but there's no significant uniformed presence and other employees in the corridor and outside the photo and fingerprint labs smile at us and say a polite word or two.

"You might not have picked the best day to be in this building," says Kee, laughing at the notion. "We're a big target."

Typically the FBI Bank Robbery Task Force pairs an agent with a State Police detective, but because of the war the FBI is concentrated elsewhere and Gene Kee is working alone today. The seventh floor is a maze of forest green carrels and cabinets with slate gray indoor-outdoor carpeting, and while Kee settles at a desk adorned with photographs of his teenage son and daughter, I can hear the detective in the next carrel talking on his phone: "He's got one foot in the grave and the other on a banana peel. . . . Three heart attacks. . . . Yeah, the skinny one."

Gene Kee usually spends half his morning dealing with informants, whom he goes out of his way to treat like human beings. "I learned that from Joe—the respect," he says. "In this business, a lot of guys get the info they want and then kick the informant to the curb. Joe never operated like that. A lot of his informants stayed with him for years."

Illustrating that same loyalty, Kee dedicates an inordinate amount of time to making a phone call on behalf of a woman in danger of getting "locked up" and losing her Section 8 housing certificate. He talks to someone at the district courthouse and makes a second call to another cop about the woman, noting that she's entered a substance abuse program. "Could I ask you for some consideration?" asks Kee. "Uh-huh. Well, please keep it in mind." He hangs up, muttering, "Ugh. That doesn't sound good."

Even though we're in a secure FBI office, Kee pulls his chair right up to mine and talks in a voice so low that I have to lean forward to hear him. His old buddies have told me that everything with Gene is "under the dome," a reference to the 1960s TV show *Get Smart* and the Plexiglas "cone of silence" that Agent 86, Maxwell Smart, would insist on during his conversations with the Chief. One day after Joe McCain got shot and Sergeant Kee was in charge of Special Investigations, Dennis Febles and Mark Lemieux rigged a garbage bag to the ceiling in the shape of a dome, and when Gene answered his phone they used a hidden wire to lower it over his desk and then ran like hell.

Kee explains that before we drive out to Hyde Park we have to meet a guy outside, near the door to Kinsale's. The woman he's trying to help is the original witness and informant in the Winter Hill mob case, a drug user who one day got fed up with the murderous double-dealing of Bulger's gang and broke the public silence on what they were doing. Kee says that the woman has left the witness protection program in San Diego, moved back to Boston, and is using heroin again. The man we're going to meet is her son.

Beneath One Center Plaza is an open arcade, where the wind sweeps down from Beacon Hill, stirring up cigarette butts and scraps of paper, and the men and women who work in the surrounding offices hurry along with their collars turned up. Wearing his camel-hair sport coat and clutching a manila envelope, Gene Kee stands on the edge of Cambridge Street, looking up and down. Then a husky young man in a dark blue jacket and New England Patriots cap approaches on the sidewalk and shakes Kee's hand.

"How's your mother?" Kee asks.

The young man takes the envelope. "She's doing all right," he says. "She's trying."

Kee reaches over, unclasps the envelope, and pulls what looks like an application partway out. "Sit and walk her through it," he says to the kid. "Get it back to me and we'll see if we can get her the housing."

"Okay."

Shaking hands again, Kee says, "Your mother's a hero. I'll do everything I can for her."

The kid looks out from under the brim of his cap. "Thanks. I'll tell her."

Kee's "company car" is a brand-new Dodge Intrepid with leather interior and hidden police lights. Driving down the Southeast Expressway, Gene and I look like a couple of appliance salesmen listening to the war on 'BZ. In fact, Kee is something of an entrepreneur despite his twenty-three-year career in law enforcement. Not long ago, after a Boston cop was shot and killed while swinging a sledgehammer at a locked door during a raid, Kee invented and eventually patented and later sold the rights to the "one-man battering ram." (The first time he used his invention, A1 DiSalvo, Chris Brighton, Mark Cronin, and Biff McLean were all cut by flying glass—something they never let their old buddy live down. "We've been through a few doors," Kee says. "Into some real shitholes.") Allowing the officer employing it to remain in side profile and thus a smaller target while bashing through a door, the innovation made Gene Kee and his family a few bucks but, more important, saved lives among his fellow police officers.

Joe McCain's life is very much on Kee's mind as we cruise down Gallivan Boulevard in Dorchester, hunting for the street that will take us into the appropriate section of Hyde Park. Though his office is only a few miles away, Kee has been here just once in the fifteen years since Joe was shot and then only because he was working nearby and a colleague wanted to see the house. As we turn onto River Street, moving alongside the scarred brick of an old paper mill, Kee's characteristic good cheer evaporates and his weathered face takes on a dark, ruminative aspect.

He's been sober for many years and has told me that, not long after the shooting, he and Chris Brighton visited Joe McCain in Brigham and Women's Hospital, finding their mentor pale and weak, hooked up to all sorts of monitoring devices and oxygen machines and IV lines.

Leaning up for a moment but unable to speak, Joe made a cup-to-the-lips gesture, in effect asking, "You're not drinking, are you?"

They shook their heads, and "Joe gave us this look, you know, 'all right.' He was always worried about us, even then," says Kee. He takes a left onto Wood Avenue. "Joe transcended ego and politics to work with people from all walks of life, at every level. What a gift he had."

Seen through the windshield of Kee's Intrepid, Wood Ave. is a dingy neighborhood of ranch houses and grimy little Colonials. Parked cars are crowded along both sides, but the street is empty of pedestrians beneath a low, overcast sky. Just before we reach Ellard Road, Gene finds space along the curb and pulls over.

"That's it," he says.

Melvin Lee's former residence is a small, two-story house covered in grayish green siding trimmed with burgundy. Surrounded by a chain-link fence with the gate open, the front yard has been paved over and contains a single denuded oak tree in a concrete well. No fewer than six unregistered cars occupy the driveway, and the side yard is filled with headless dolls, broken wading pools, cinder blocks, three-legged chairs, rusted lawn mowers, and heaps of other charred and nameless refuse.

A single, inscrutable piece of graffiti is scribbled on the siding in white paint: "Romans." Gene Kee and I get out of the car and, for a moment, gaze at the house. "What a fuckin' dive, though, huh?" he asks, shaking his head. "Forty-eight seconds, and it was all over."

It occurs to me that I should purchase a throwaway camera and take some pictures, so Kee and I climb back in the Intrepid and he drives down to the corner of Ellard Road and turns left, showing me where the "takedown team" was located during the initial surveillance. But Melvin Lee kept coming back to his porch to stare at them, and when the Special Investigations Unit returned that evening, everybody was moved back a couple of blocks; the van was nosed into a blind street alongside Ross Park, with Al DiSalvo three hundred yards away, on the far side of the baseball fields.

"Knowing Joe and his impatience, when Mark [Cronin] said, 'Everybody move in, Chris is in trouble,' Joe and Paul [Hutchinson] were driving by the front of the house," Kee says, with a note of regret in his voice. "And we were over here."

A few minutes later, we arrive back at the house with a camera and approach the gate. There's a brief walkway leading to three stairs up to the front porch. "It was a 'rip' from the get-go," says Kee. "[Vladimir] Lafontant was just a guy who showed up and said, 'Fuck him, let's rip the white dude off and we'll split the money.' A crime of opportunity."

When I ask why Joe McCain wasn't wearing a bulletproof vest, Kee reminds me that issuing vests wasn't the rule back then like it is now, and that big Joe wasn't a member of the takedown team and arrived first on the scene only through a fluke. "Besides, picture that vest on a three-hundred-pound guy," he says. "It would look like a bib."

This time Kee has parked in the street, right where he jumped out of the van that night. Standing between a telephone pole and a fire hydrant, he points at a spot in the chain-link fence. Lafontant ran outside with a gun in each hand, exchanged volleys with McCain and Hutchinson, leaped the fence and then "dropped like a sack of shit right here," says Kee, gesturing at the pavement. "He was already dead, that was obvious. Shot through the heart. He did it all on adrenaline."

The Special Investigations Unit was as tight as any of the military units Gene Kee served in, as close-knit as any of his old hockey teams. When Mark Cronin gave that order, foremost in everyone's mind was, "Kegs" Brighton was in trouble.

The unit's wisecracking and beloved undercover man, Brighton often got himself in and out of dangerous situations. On another case Brighton posed as a bad guy for a wannabe Mafioso named Anthony Pucci from Everett, Mass. The bad guy was a drug dealer and punk who thought he was King Shit because Brighton drove him around in a little cream-colored Mercedes.

"You're big," Pucci told Brighton. "You're my muscle."

Trying to impress some girls in a nightclub, Pucci slapped Brighton across the face. "You're my protection," he said. "I want you right here on my shoulder."

In private, Brighton said, "I'm gonna kill this fucking guy before it's over." But he remained in character while the little gangster walked around like he was Al Capone. The tough-talking drug dealer cried when they finally took him down. "Guess what?" asked Brighton, slapping Pucci in the face. "We're cops." Later Pucci skipped bail and ran away to join the Italian Navy, and Brighton and the other guys laughed about it.

But that night on Wood Avenue was different. Before the operation, while they were sitting around the office, a palpable tension filled the air and there was some talk of canceling the buy—like a group premonition. At the scene there were gunshots and shouts and chaos, Gene Kee moving toward the house in what seemed like slow motion as Biff McLean came racing through the side yard firing his weapon.

"I think one of Biff's rounds ended up in the house across the street," says Kee, poking fun at his old buddy's marksmanship.

Lafontant's path into the street placed members of the unit in a potential crossfire. Less than fifty feet away, Al DiSalvo was "drawing down on us," says Kee. "Thank God he never fired."

Joe McCain staggered down the front walk and sat on the pavement, leaning hard against the fence. McLean knelt beside him and opened up Joe's shirt, and there was a little red hole in the center of his abdomen. Into McLean's ear, Joe said, "Tell Helen that I love her."

Gene Kee stands on that spot while I lean on the fence with my camera, snapping pictures of the trash strewn over the yard. "You wanna get out back?" asks Kee, but it's not really a question. He's already striding toward the front porch, up the stairs, a purposeful look on his face.

He pulls out his State Police badge and rings the bell. A large, ebony-skinned man in a bath towel answers the door, and Kee identifies himself and asks the man, who's in his late forties and has a gold tooth, if we can go into the backyard and take a few photos.

The man speaks very little English and at first does not understand the request. "A crime occurred here . . . a long time ago . . . nothing now," says Kee, his voice growing louder. "*We just want to see.*"

After a flurry of gestures and head bobs and single-word descriptions, the man agrees, indicating that if we'll wait a few moments he'll join us. In just seconds he reappears, dressed in old khaki pants, a quilted jacket, and one black loafer and a green flip-flop sandal. He stammers in a musical voice that he's Haitian and has owned the house for seven years and means to improve it.

In the backyard I take a handful of photos, and Gene choreographs

Mark Cronin's and Biff McLean's and Chris Brighton's movements while the owner of the house follows us without saying a word. Old tires and broken metal cabinets and smashed televisions and microwave ovens are strewn over the weedy lawn.

The back door is locked tight, and Kee asks if we can go inside to see the kitchen. The man says he'll unfasten the door and passes around to the front of the house while Gene and I stand there looking at each other.

"He probably didn't understand a word and is back in bed," says Kee.

But we hear the creaking floorboards, and several bolts are shot back and the man opens the half-rotted door and beckons us inside. A thick, musky odor pervades the kitchen, where every flat surface is crowded with dirty dishes, empty food containers, and scorched pots and pans. Kee indicates where Chris Brighton was sitting, and then we duck our heads into the tiny, adjacent bathroom, where Lafontant attempted to cock the sawed-off shotgun. It's strange, but the layout of the house seems familiar to me, though I've never before set foot in Hyde Park.

The three of us head into a dim corridor along the staircase toward the front of the house. Near the exit I mention the front room that was unfurnished on January 29, 1988, where Detective Hutchinson got his first glimpse of the shooter. Kee gestures and the owner of the house unlocks a padlock on the door and allows us a glimpse inside: clean, white-upholstered furniture covered in sheets of plastic, an array of expensive stereo equipment, and a thick blue carpet figured with gold designs. There's a cabinet lined with gold-trimmed urns and other ceremonial-looking crockery, not a smudge or speck of dust anywhere.

"That's the shrine," says Kee.

We thank the man for his kindness and go onto the porch and down the front walk. "He probably thought we were from the city inspector's," says Kee. "He's on a green card and afraid to say no."

Shuffling along, my camera in my pocket now, I say that the city should erect a plaque to Joe McCain on the sidewalk. But Kee's thoughts are elsewhere and he pauses on the street for a moment, looking back at the house. "That bullet would've killed any one of us," he says. "Joe was getting close to retirement anyway, and they wouldn't've been able to take him off the job in a tow truck. Joe McCain's true pride was being a Metropolitan police officer."

At Simco's hot dog stand on Blue Hill Avenue, Kee treats me to a grilled hot dog, vanilla frappe with honey, and a free call to my cardiologist. As we're headed back toward downtown, his pager goes off and Kee says, "Got one," explaining that a bank has just been robbed. He's holding the pager, and I look at the text message as the description of the bank robber scrolls across: "tall, 6'2", thin build, dark hair, sunglasses."

Soon we are speeding through the Callahan Tunnel toward the bank, which is on the VFW Parkway in Revere. "You don't run the siren on something like this?" I ask.

Kee laughs. "Nah. He's already home in bed."

Out near Logan Airport we navigate a maze of broken up temporary streets as jets crisscross overhead. Two minutes later we arrive at the bank, which is little more than a kiosk on a paved, triangular lot, surrounded by police cars. A slender black woman in a maroon suit and braided yellow hair greets us at the front door, which is locked.

"Gene Kee, Bank Robbery Task Force," says my partner, holding up his badge.

Inside the entrance is a polished marble counter flanked by a couple of offices behind smoked glass panels. Four burly Revere cops are off to my left, watching the surveillance video. "We got a good shot of him," says a sturdy-looking detective in plainclothes. "But he took back the note."

"He did?" asks Kee.

The detective nods. "He said, 'Gimme back my note.' "

The Revere cops, the bank manager, half a dozen wide-eyed tellers, and Gene Kee and I are standing in the semicircular lobby with a stock ticker running across the wall that everyone is ignoring. A young Russian woman with bobbed hair is the teller who was robbed of $2,200, and immediately upon being introduced Kee takes her into the manager's office and half-closes the door. The videotape can wait; Kee wants to speak to his best witness while the experience is still fresh in her mind.

"Who is he?" asks the Revere detective, gesturing toward Kee. He's a short, broad-shouldered fellow named Goodwin, dressed in beige corduroys and a long-sleeved blue jersey. "Is he with the FBI?"

"He's a State Police lieutenant," I say, as the detective writes it down. "Gene Kee. K-e-e."

Inside the office I can hear Kee asking the Russian girl a series of questions in a patient, friendly voice. Where was the robber standing? Did he look at you? Where did he put his hands? What do you mean, tall? Kee gets up from his chair. I'm five ten. Taller than I am? By how much?

A moment later, the Russian girl comes out of the office with Kee, points to the second teller window, says, "Right there," and then the two of them turn around and go back inside.

Someone from the bank's security department enters the building, hands his card to the Revere detective, and points at me. "Who's he?"

"He's FBI," says Detective Goodwin.

"Actually, I'm a journalist," I tell them.

The security chief is a stout man wearing glasses and an expensive, olive-colored linen suit. He huddles for a moment with the bank's employees, and they all skitter away from me. "You're a journalist," he says. "Are you with a local paper?"

"No." I point toward Kee, in the office behind us. "I'm with him."

The security chief looks me in the eye and then walks away, his fancy loafers ringing on the tiles of the lobby. Suddenly the area surrounding me is deserted, like I'm contagious. After a few minutes the young woman in the maroon suit plops down in the chair beside me, and I ask her if she's nervous and she replies that all the girls are a little upset. I ask when the robbery occurred, and the security chief races over and steps between us and says, "Let's talk for a minute," to the young woman and I'm by myself again.

Mr. Bank Security is a real pain in the ass, and I feel like reminding him that the bank has already been robbed. Just then Kee comes out of the office and beckons to me and when I try to follow him into the back room, the security chief walks over and attempts to have a private word with him.

"He's with me," Kee says, waving me into the room. "It's all right."

Inside, the Revere detective is running the appropriate section of the video back and forth on a monitor. "Watch. The robber is gonna come out from behind the big bald guy," says Goodwin.

A husky, bald-headed man is looking straight at the camera. "Too bad it's not that guy," says Kee.

"No shit," says the detective. Forty-one-year-old Detective Sergeant John Goodwin has a relaxed, easygoing manner and looks like a stockier version of Al Pacino in *Serpico*. He takes out his cell phone, dials a number. "Hey, Johnny, you know that guy in line behind you with the sunglasses? He robbed the bank about ten seconds after you left. . . . I wish it was you. I would've solved the crime by now."

Sergeant Goodwin's phone call reminds me of what Al Seghezzi, an old friend of Joe McCain's and a retired deputy superintendent of the Mets, has told me: just like politics, all crime is local. By being on the street and getting to know a lot of people, a cop will meet a few criminals and can later identify them.

On the videotape, the bank robber emerges from behind the huge bald guy and Goodwin cuts his phone conversation short. "You're no good to me, then," he says, snapping his phone shut.

The bank robber is a lean-faced man with short hair dressed in a zipped black jacket and wraparound sunglasses. Standing between Kee and Goodwin, I'm wearing a black hiking jacket and a pair of gray-tinted Oakleys. "Shit, he looks like you," says Goodwin.

"Good thing I've got Gene as my alibi," I say. Kee pretends not to hear and walks away. "Right, Gene?"

Goodwin laughs, stopping to print a series of still photographs of the robber from a machine built into the TV. "These are good. Like his graduation picture," says the cop. A self-described "grinder," John Goodwin is one of three brothers and a cousin on the Revere Police Department.

On screen and in the photo, the bank robber looks twenty-three or twenty-four years old, but the Russian girl has placed his age closer to forty. Back in the lobby, Goodwin spreads out the pictures on a table by the door. "I think I know him. He's a little older, but we grew up together," says the Revere detective. "His friends, that's what they do. They hit banks."

Kee asks Goodwin how he got a handle on the guy's identity. "I saw something," the Revere cop says. "That smirk. It looked familiar."

This is just the sort of little detail that Joe McCain taught a much younger Gene Kee to take seriously. Goodwin goes on to say that the "kid" he's thinking of has just been released from the Middleton jail and is living in Revere with his mother.

"Only a junkie would hit the bank down the street from his house," says Kee.

Goodwin holds one of the photos between his fingers. "It shows he ain't thinkin' straight," he says.

While the uniformed cops file out, Kee comes over beside me and opens up a fingerprint kit and dons a pair of blue latex gloves.

"He's a sharp kid," I say, nodding toward Goodwin.

"I used to be like that, once," says Kee.

"You still got the juice, Gen-o," I tell him.

Kee grins. "You're being kind," he says.

Using a soft brush, Kee spreads a fine gray powder over a glass shelf where the robber stood before joining the line. "How do you isolate the prints?" I ask him.

"You don't," says Kee.

From his kit he removes a small white box marked "Crime Scene Products" and "BVDA Instant Lifter," and decorated with a stylized blue fingerprint. "There's a beauty right there," says Kee, indicating a pristine thumb print in the middle of the shelf. "Could be anybody's, but if it helps convict the guy . . ."

Kee's self-proclaimed technical expertise has long been an object of derision among his old Met buddies. On one occasion, his assignment was to take surveillance photos of some wiseguys on a street corner, and afterward Kee was telling everyone he had gotten some great pictures. When they were developed, "all he had was a roll of feet," said Biff McLean, recalling that the photos only showed the mobsters from the knees down. "Look at this, Gen-o, a pair of size ten-and-a-half loafers," Joe McCain told him, while Kee replied, "You guys put me behind that fuckin' pole. Whaddaya expect?"

After Kee completes the fingerprinting, he and Detective Goodwin make plans to get the bank robber's photo into the *Boston Herald* and *Re-*

vere Journal. Then Kee packs up the videotape and his fingerprint kit, shakes hands with the manager, and waits for a moment while she unlocks the door.

Passing through the glass cubicle that houses the automated teller machine, Kee notices a young kid with buzzed hair and a Police Academy jacket with a Burlington Police patch on his shoulder. The young police cadet has his face shoved up against the ATM and, like just about everyone under forty, has a cell phone attached to his ear.

Kee whispers to Sergeant Goodwin: "C'mon. I gotta bust 'em on this guy."

As soon as we get outside Kee reopens the door to the ATM, hangs his badge around his neck, and motions for Goodwin to take his badge out. "Excuse me," Kee says, but the kid ignores him. "Hey, *Burlington*," says Kee, in his command voice.

The cadet lowers his cell phone and turns around. "Huh—?"

Kee and Goodwin are leaning through the open door, thrusting out their badges. "The bank just got robbed, and the guy ran right past you," says Kee.

"I—I just got here," the kid says.

"You missed him," Kee says. "What the hell are they teaching you guys?"

"I *just*, just got here," says the cadet, turning red from his collar to his hairline.

The two older cops begin smiling and then laughing. "We're just pulling your leg," Kee says. "But the bank *was* robbed."

Embedded into the wall, the ATM is speaking in a mechanized voice, but the kid is paralyzed with embarrassment.

"What week you in?" asks Kee.

"Eleventh."

"Good luck, kid," says the old Met.

Detective Goodwin smiles at us and shakes his head, and we jump in Gene's car and take off down the VFW Parkway.

TWENTY-SIX

The Pride of the Mets

*Cops get very large and emphatic when an outsider tries to
hide anything, but they do the same thing themselves every other day,
to oblige their friends or anybody with a little pull.*
— RAYMOND CHANDLER

O N MAY 26, 1980, AS THE PIPE BANDS and Civil War re-
enactors and high school glee clubs in the Memorial Day parade
marched past, five men drilled and blasted through the wall of a neighboring storefront and robbed the Depositor's Trust Savings Bank in
Medford, Mass. Among the crooks were Metropolitan Police officers
Gerald W. Clemente and Joseph Bangs, as well as Lieutenant Tommy
Doherty of the Medford Police. (In a saga of irony and interconnected-
ness that no fiction writer could make up, Tommy Doherty, who is not
a blood relation to the Somerville cop Timmy Doherty, later became
the beleaguered patrolman's father-in-law.) Bangs and Clemente had
been friends for more than ten years when they dreamed up the bank
robbery. By that time, they had collaborated on other larcenous
schemes, including insurance fraud, drug trafficking, and the theft and
sale of civil service promotional examinations, a far-reaching, lucrative
caper that would eventually tie the dirty cops to the Depositor's Trust
robbery. Nicknamed Exam Scam, the illegal distribution and sale of the
stolen tests netted Clemente and Bangs three thousand dollars per exam
and resulted in unfair promotions for certain Mets, as well as other cops
and firemen from departments across the state.

Soon after the bank robbery, one of Clemente's pals in the Exam Scam, MDC Sergeant Frank "Indian" Thorpe, tried to sell a copy of the sergeants' test to a former Met turned Wilmington patrolman named David McCue. A large, broad-shouldered man, Thorpe claimed to be a descendant of the Olympic and professional athlete Jim Thorpe and was known more for smashing up cop cars than for the breadth of his intellect. McCue told his boss about the overture, and together they went to the Massachusetts Attorney General's Office. The A.G. had McCue wear a recording device and meet with Thorpe in the parking lot of a Dunkin' Donuts in Lawrence, Mass., where the parties hashed over the terms of the deal. The contents of the wire led to Thorpe's indictment on a misdemeanor charge of trying to corrupt a public official, and the extent of the Exam Scam began to emerge.

Meanwhile, a mob associate named Vernon "Gus" Gusmini approached Tommy Doherty to say that a large amount of money stolen from one of the safe deposit boxes at the Depositor's Trust belonged to the Winter Hill gang, and Whitey Bulger and Stevie Flemmi wanted it back. In fact, Gusmini went on to tell Gerry Clemente that the mob wanted a piece of all his action. Later, sources reported that Gusmini was upset because he had conceived the original plan to break into the bank, and Clemente had welshed by going ahead without him.

Hearing that Gus Gusmini was busy applying the screws to Clemente on behalf of the Winter Hill gang, the superintendent of the Mets, a former Marine and straight shooter named Laurence Carpenter, summoned Joe McCain from the Suffolk County D.A.'s Office and briefed him on Clemente, the Depositor's Trust burglary, and Gusmini's extortion plot. After big Joe recovered from the shock that Gerry Clemente was dirty, he suggested that, for the time being anyway, they treat Clemente like a legitimate police captain being harassed by a hoodlum, and Carpenter agreed. They'd get more out of him that way.

McCain conducted interviews with Clemente and members of his family, then returned to Superintendent Carpenter with the recommendation that Clemente be taken to East Cambridge District Court to swear out a complaint against Vernon Gusmini for extortion. That way, McCain reasoned, they'd be able to hook Clemente *and* Gusmini, since the warrant would contain a tacit admission that Clemente had taken part in the burglary. In the meantime, Gusmini fled the state. But within just a few days he was arrested on an unrelated drug charge in Florida.

Joe McCain, Jr., was in his second year at the University of Miami, living on the eleventh floor of a high-rise dormitory, when he heard a voice coming from the elevator that sounded a lot like his dad. "Gee, I must really be homesick, because I'd swear that's my father out there," he said to himself. Tossing aside his book, Joey ran into the hallway, and there was the old man, big as life, smiling and laughing as he hugged young Joe, explaining that he was in Miami to bring back a prisoner.

When Gusmini was busted on the cocaine charge, the Mets issued a warrant for him and sent big Joe to execute it. At the same time McCain heard a rumor that the Mass. State Police sensed an opportunity to undermine their old rivals, the Mets, and had dispatched their own man.

Young Joe took a ride with his father over to the Dade County Sheriff's Office, where they were holding Gusmini. In the sun-baked parking lot, the McCains encountered Tommy Spartachino, a former Met who was by this time a Mass. state trooper. Earlier in his career, Spartachino had served as the "third man" with Joe Sr. and Leo Papile when they all worked together on Revere Beach.

Joe Sr. sent his nineteen-year-old son back to the car and hailed Spartachino. "What are you doing here?" he asked.

"I got a warrant for Gusmini," said Spartachino. "He's going back with me."

"Fuck you he is," said McCain, showing Spartachino a Metropolitan Police warrant. "This is a Met case, not a State Police case."

Joe McCain and Superintendent Carpenter wanted to go after the dirty Mets themselves, to prove that only Clemente and Bangs and their henchmen were corrupt, not the entire system they worked under. Big Joe also wanted to avoid the embarrassment of having the Mass. State Police meddling in what he considered his business—the reputation of the Mets. In the end, McCain won the argument and processed Gusmini out of the Dade County jail into his custody.

After McCain returned home with Gusmini, he was summoned to appear in front of a special grand jury on obstruction of justice charges. The implication was that McCain, and by extension the Mets, had wrested Gusmini away from the State Police to protect a widespread conspiracy. No one really believed that Joe McCain had a shred of information about Clemente's gang or the heist, but certain elements in the Attorney General's Office and the State Police, including Spartachino, wanted to give him "a little tickle." By painting all the Mets with the same brush, these individuals hoped to consolidate their own power and, by weight of negative publicity, force Governor Michael Dukakis to dissolve the Metropolitan Police.

Other than funerals, McCain's grand jury appearance was the first time in twenty years he'd worn his Met uniform, and he was embarrassed, hurt, angry, and proud all at once. Most of the questions were horseshit, given the circumstances, and after an hour of testimony several participants were glancing at their watches. But near the end of the session, one of the grand jurors asked, "You think quite a bit of yourself, don't you, Detective McCain?"

"Yes, sir, I do," Joe said. "The only thing a policeman has is his honor and his integrity, and I value mine very highly."

Later, Joe McCain would say, "He asked me a question, and he got a fucking answer." Emerging from the courtroom, McCain saw his adversaries grouped together in the hallway, laughing and talking. He started in their direction and his attorney, Jim O'Donovan, grabbed him by the sleeve.

"Joe, please don't say anything," said O'Donovan.

McCain frowned. "Jim," he said. "Fuck him."

Big Joe twisted out of his lawyer's grip and crossed the hallway to where the district attorney was standing with his cronies. "You knew I had nothing to do with the Depositor's Trust and yet you let these fuckin' people torture me," said McCain. "Shame on you."

At the Exam Scam trial, Clemente admitted that he'd been cheating on police examinations since 1964, and that when he and Tommy Doherty broke into civil service headquarters for the first time, it was "like playing God." Another immunized witness, the former Met sergeant Frank Thorpe, was asked on the witness stand if he was known by any nicknames.

"Everything but Late for Lunch," said Thorpe, adding that he was also called Indian, Bear, Crazy, and Wahoo.

Thorpe's testimony provided some of the trial's lighter moments, including the admission that while a police officer he had crashed so many cruisers other Mets refused to ride with him. And he was asked about an incident in Roxbury where he shot a young man outside the district courthouse. "You and General Custer have something in common," Thorpe had told his victim.

"What's that?" the man asked.

"You've both been shot by the Indians," said Thorpe.

But it was the testimony of Joe Bangs that amazed some of the most hardened courtroom observers. A veteran cop and criminal, Bangs avoided prosecution on all charges and even wangled a tax-free disability pension of $1,950 per month from the Mets for a supposed heart condition. On the stand he admitted to knowledge of at least four gangland murders before they occurred, as well as having participated in a major drug trafficking business with a hoodlum named Bucky Barrett. The former Met boasted that he once sold fifteen tons of marijuana in two hours, over the telephone in a bar called the Little Rascals that he and Barrett had purchased with drug money.

Joe Bangs's most shocking revelation was that Gerry Clemente had asked him to murder his girlfriend Barbara Hickey and burn her house down because Clemente was afraid Hickey would testify against him in the Depositor's Trust case. Bangs refused, but only because Hickey wasn't aware of Bangs's own role in the burglary.

"If she had known about me, I don't know what I would have done," said Bangs.

While Joe Bangs was testifying in the Depositor's Trust trial, Tommy Doherty's attorney, Tom Troy, asked Bangs if he had received the cash that the State Police had found in his trunk from Metropolitan Police Captain Bill McKay. In his testimony Bangs used McKay's name a dozen times, and even took the trouble to spell it for the court reporter.

That same afternoon a *Boston Globe* reporter named Paul Langner, who didn't really know Joe McCain, saw a big, white-haired man in the hallway outside the courtroom and asked another cop who he was. McCain was visiting the Middlesex Courthouse to testify in a rape case, but since he was talking to Attorney Troy, Langner believed him to be a witness in the attempted murder case.

In an article that appeared in *The Boston Globe* the next day, Langner made a significant error.

> Q. (by Troy) Did Mr. McCain give you the $10,000 in Canadian currency? (Capt. Joseph McCain of the Metropolitan Police and Bangs had met in a bar earlier on the day of the alleged crime, according to testimony.)
> A. No he did not, sir.

Another cop directed Joe McCain to the article, and after he read it, he wanted to tear the paper—not to mention Paul Langner—into little pieces. McCain called the new superintendent of the Mets to complain and was told not to worry about it. But Joe filed a million-dollar libel suit against Paul Langner and *The Boston Globe*, stating that they had "negligently, intentionally or recklessly inflicted emotional distress upon the plaintiff."

In dismissing the charges, Superior Court Justice Thomas S. Connolly decided that Langner was just a harried beat reporter with no special animus toward McCain. Still, big Joe had made his point. And Langner's deposition in the suit contained an accurate description of the legendary Met detective:

> He's a man slightly, I believe slightly taller than I am, sort of a little bit heftier without being fat. He's a—seems like a muscularly built man, but my recollection is grayish or almost white hair. I don't believe he wears glasses. He has sort of a square, Viking-like face, neatly dressed, you know, a friendly kind of man.

Langner also revealed that he heard about his mistake the day after the story appeared, during a conversation with two lawyers in the courtroom hallway. In his deposition, Langner stated that, upon learning of the error, "I burdened myself of an indelicate expression, but it was too late."

Despite the fact that the *Boston Globe* article wrongly linked his name to an infamous chapter in the doomed history of the Metropolitan District Commission police force, Joe McCain's essential puckishness allowed him to savor Langner's pained exclamation of "Fuck!" and his later description of that as "an indelicate expression." For all Joe's street smarts and Winter Hill toughness, he admired refinement of speech and men in possession of great book learning. In fact, he laughed at the very idea; he was, after all, an Irishman.

Joe McCain avoided any official taint related to the Exam Scam by virtue of the fact that the only test he took in his professional life was to gain entrance to the Mets in 1958. He was more than content as a detective, supplementing his pay by working at a second job.

Bangs's and Clemente's testimony was like Nero's fiddling—it signaled the beginning of the end for the Mets. The department was rotten with graduates of their accelerated promotion program and over the next few years, good honest cops like Joe McCain's old friend, deputy superintendent Al Seghezzi, were demoted and transferred to the hinterlands while the bad guys flourished.

A few years later, as several dirty cops were being paroled from jail, the state legislature debated the future of the organization these men had ruined. In 1992, four years after Joe McCain had been shot on the job and forced to retire, the Metropolitan Police department was dismantled and active officers in good standing were absorbed into the Mass State Police. Although there were more than six hundred Metropolitan Police officers and the vast majority of them were honest, hardworking cops, Gerry Clemente's criminal activity was the linchpin that decided the fate of the MDC.

TWENTY-SEVEN

Flowers of Evil

Look, the dead years dressed in old clothes crowd the balconies of the sky.
— CHARLES BAUDELAIRE

RETIREMENT WAS NOT A QUIET PERIOD in Joe McCain's life. He loved to play golf, especially at that little piece of heaven known as the Charles River Country Club, but Joe never entirely traded his sidearm for a pitching wedge. He was always busy with the P.I. firm, and his passion for investigative work, his mortgage, and his conscience wouldn't allow him to take it easy with so much going on in Boston. Every time Joe picked up a newspaper, he was reminded of some case he'd worked on, as the pigeons from the old Somerville-Charlestown wars came home to roost, and none so dramatically as the ghost of Teddy Deegan.

When Joseph L. Salvati was released from Walpole State Prison in 1998 after serving thirty years of a life sentence for Deegan's murder—a crime that he didn't commit—he thanked his wife, Marie, and their four children; his lawyer, Victor Garo; the Boston TV reporter Dan Rea; and retired Met detectives Joe McCain and Leo Papile for his freedom. And although he couldn't bring himself to utter the name, the man Salvati had to blame for his conviction and grueling incarceration was none other than Joe "the Animal" Barboza.

In the winter of 1965, Edward "Teddy" Deegan ran afoul of local mobsters after he and two other small-time hoods broke into the home of a connected wiseguy. Not long afterward, the bodies of Deegan's associates turned up in Boston Harbor. Meanwhile, a gang of thugs led by Joe Barboza was hired to take care of Deegan, a onetime club fighter and B and E partner of Roy French. French, who worked as a bouncer at the Ebb Tide on Revere Beach, was a large, well-muscled fellow with a volatile temper and a penchant for burglary. When the subject of Deegan's murder was broached, Roy French's only concern was that "the office" had authorized the hit. Barboza assured French that he had the blessing of the Angiulo brothers in the North End but expressed his concern that French and Teddy Deegan were pals. To that French replied, "I steal with Deegan; I'm not his friend."

Just after midnight on March 12, 1965, the killers met in the Ebb Tide and proceeded to a rendezvous point in Chelsea, where French had lured Deegan with the promise of a burglary score. Assigned to organized crime, McCain and Papile were sitting on the Ebb Tide that night, maintaining surveillance on Barboza and his crew as well as the Rhode Island mobster Henry Tameleo. When a group of ne'er-do-wells left the bar, McCain and Papile noted the presence of Barboza, French, Richard "Romeo" Martin, a fat, sausage-lipped gangster named Ronald Cassesso, and James Vincent "the Bear" Flemmi. McCain and Papile visited a few other joints down on the beach, and when they walked through the Ebb Tide later that night, they saw the same five men.

Just before Joe and Leo's arrival at the Ebb Tide, bouncers had rousted the drugged-up kid brother of a North End bookie. Noticing blood on Roy French's sleeve and believing it to have resulted from that fight, McCain wagged his finger in the bouncer's face and said, "Keep your fucking hands off people. You have a problem with a patron here, you call us, the police, and we'll come down and evict them."

Behind McCain, Papile was speaking in a loud voice, and when McCain turned around, he saw his partner telling a husky, balding man in a leather jacket to take a few deep breaths and relax. It was James "the Bear" Flemmi. Papile knew Flemmi from the Continental Café, where the hardworking detective moonlighted as a bartender.

"You guys all right?" asked the Bear, making a friendly gesture toward McCain. Later, Joe and Leo would laugh at such a vicious thug offering to back them up.

What McCain and Papile didn't know was that, in the interim, French and another man had driven Teddy Deegan to an alley behind the Beneficial Finance Company on Fourth Street in Chelsea. Unarmed, and believing that a door had been left open at the finance company to allow their entry, Deegan walked into the alley with French close behind him. As Deegan reached for the door, French took out a pistol and shot him in the head.

At the same instant a heavyset man stepped through the door, another figure rushed out from behind a stack of wooden pallets, and there were more gunshots. Deegan collapsed to the ground, bleeding from multiple bullet wounds.

His arm splattered with Deegan's blood, Roy French emerged from the alley with his gun still drawn. As he approached his getaway car, one of voices behind him said, "Get him, too." The car sped off and French, with a look of awe and excitement on his face, hurried away in the other direction. After walking a few blocks he boarded a bus to Revere, disembarking at Wonderland station. He walked to the Ebb Tide from there, stashed his bloody coat and took up his customary position at the end of the bar.

Ballistics examination later proved that at least three weapons had been used to kill Teddy Deegan. Although the police had several leads and a grand jury was convened to examine the evidence, his murder went unsolved.

Two years later, not long after his dustup with Joe McCain in front of the Ebb Tide and the discovery of his unregistered firearm, Joe Barboza was arrested on gun charges for the second time, which meant he was looking at a five-year felony. Suffolk County District Attorney Garrett Byrne, calling Barboza "the worst killer in the Commonwealth," set his bail at $1 million. With so many of his enemies in jail, a stretch in Walpole would've been a death sentence for Barboza. So he sent two of his cronies around to various bookmakers, enforcers, loan sharks, and thugs in an attempt to round up his bail money. At a bar called the Nite Lite, which was the headquarters of the connected mobster Ralph

"Ralphie Chong" Lamattina, Barboza's henchmen got in a beef and slapped Lamattina around. A short time later, the bodies of the two men were found, shot up and bloody, in the trunk of a Cadillac.

With his two collectors in the morgue, Barboza fell short of the bail money and chose the only available route out of prison: he turned state's evidence and gave up the participants in the Deegan murder. In his new role as government songbird, Barboza also discovered a wonderful opportunity to get at people he didn't like, settling his old scores by way of the electric chair.

During his grand jury appearance, and later at trial, Barboza testified that the North End underboss Peter Limone had paid him $7,500 to kill Deegan with Henry Tameleo's approval, and that Joseph Salvati had driven the getaway car. In reality Barboza had substituted the names of two men he had grudges against, Salvati and Limone, for one of the real killers, his murderous drinking buddy James Flemmi.

Several witnesses had seen Flemmi leave the Ebb Tide with Barboza that night. To account for the fact that the thirty-two-year-old Salvati had a full head of hair, and that a police captain also stationed near the Ebb Tide reported that one of the men in the car with Roy French had a prominent bald spot—Flemmi was balding—Barboza claimed that Salvati had donned a phony mustache and a "wig" that made him look bald. Barboza went so far as to testify that he watched Salvati put on the wig through the rearview mirror and heard "the snapping of the elastic."

Joe Salvati was arrested on October 25, 1967. In tune with the zeitgeist of the late 1960s, Barboza appeared in court for Salvati's trial wearing dark sunglasses and an open shirt, his lank, black hair down over the collar and his sideburns nearly meeting at the point of his chin. Cloaked in immunity and sneering at the defense lawyers, the hired killer and loan shark mounted the stand, took an oath, and lied, trading Salvati and Limone for Jimmy Flemmi and treating the whole experience like a great cosmic joke. His broad, Portuguese face was the color of a bruised ham, and he laughed and chain-smoked cigarettes and gestured like some sort of cranked up Revere Beach celebrity.

McCain and Papile were not called as witnesses. The Chelsea Police, Revere Police, and FBI, not the Mets, had conducted the "investigation" into Teddy Deegan's murder. And Joe and Leo admitted that they'd maintained only an intermittent surveillance on the Ebb Tide on March 12, 1965, and could've missed the arrival and departure of Joe Salvati. His trial came nearly three years after the Deegan killing, and the fact that, if anyone had cared to look, no mention of Salvati appeared in McCain's and Papile's reports was not considered an alibi. More than five hundred people were crammed into the little seaside bar that night, and it was also possible, as McCain pointed out, that Barboza or French had driven to the North End and picked Salvati up. Additionally, it was a fact that between Deegan's murder and Salvati's trial, McCain and Papile had investigated hundreds of crimes and made dozens of arrests; Joe Amico, Connie Hughes, Romeo Martin, and Buddy McLean were all dead; the wiseguys were killing each other wholesale. McCain and Papile were busy.

The Deegan murder trial lasted forty-nine days. Peter Limone, Henry Tameleo, Ronald Cassesso, and a man named Louis Greco were sentenced to death, which was later reduced to life in prison. Joe Salvati was convicted on two counts of conspiracy to commit murder and one count of being an accessory before the fact. He and Roy French each received life terms. (James Flemmi avoided charges in the Deegan murder but would soon end up in Walpole for the attempted murder of Joe McCain's informant Black Jimmy.)

Granting immunity to a known killer like Joe Barboza never made any sense to McCain. If someone asked him about the case or Barboza's credibility, his favorite response was "Hey, would a murderer lie?" But the mood in law enforcement was to get Barboza off the street at any cost. (As a protected witness, he'd be moved to another part of the country, at the very least.) Joe Barboza was a drug-addicted megalomaniac long before drug addiction and megalomania were in fashion, and grown men, tough guys who had fought in World War II, headed for the exits wherever Barboza appeared. His eyes glittered and his breath stank of methamphetamines, and when he strolled along Revere Beach, his porkpie hat and shiny half boots were like harbingers of the Apocalypse.

Barboza was suspected in more than twenty murders, including those of ordinary citizens in the wrong place at the wrong time when gangland hits were carried out, like the five people he was rumored to have killed inside the Mickey Mouse Club on Revere Beach. Three of the victims were mobsters; the fourth was just a poor sap having a drink at the bar; and the last one, an amiable bartender who was a favorite among Revere Beach wiseguys. Reportedly, Barboza apologized to the bartender before shooting him dead.

Over time Joe McCain learned that Barboza may have inserted the names of Joe Salvati and Peter Limone into his account of the Deegan killing because the Animal believed they had participated in the murder of his two bail collectors. Another scenario depicted Barboza as a dissatisfied creditor: Salvati had borrowed four hundred dollars from him, and although he repaid over a thousand dollars in "vigorish," he still owed the principal. By all accounts Joe Salvati was a street guy, rugged enough to tell Barboza to go fuck himself. Some also speculated that Barboza implicated Limone, who was Jerry Angiulo's right-hand man, to get back at the North End for not contributing to his bail. Barboza also may have reasoned that if Salvati and Limone had whacked his two friends, he was probably next.

They were all known criminals, and nobody on the jury—and certainly no one in law enforcement—shed any tears when Salvati and Limone went to prison. However, the rumor persisted that Salvati wasn't involved in Teddy Deegan's murder, and that the testimony of a confidential informant in a Chelsea Police report contained that fact, although the report never appeared in evidence at the trial. As things turned out, it would take a guy with an expensive haircut and perfect teeth to bring that report to light.

One of the rising stars in Boston television, the forty-four-year-old newscaster Dan Rea began investigating the Salvati conviction at the suggestion of his friend, Ronald Cass, dean of the Boston University School of Law. Rea was a graduate of the law school, and so was Victor Garo, a chunky, balding Medford lawyer who had represented Salvati pro bono since 1976 and would eventually donate more than ten thousand hours of his time working on various appeals. In one of their early conversations, Garo asked a rhetorical question about Joe Barboza that struck Rea as interesting: "Why would a man try to get a death squad together when he has his own band of cutthroats?"

Rea, an enterprising reporter and a practicing attorney, agreed to look into the case. One of the first calls he made was to a cop he knew in Chelsea, asking him to look up the file on the Deegan murder. The records on a case that far back were in the attic, and the cop said he'd take a look around and call back in an hour or two. What Rea's contact discovered would surprise the TV reporter and delight Victor Garo. There was a file, all right, and the first document in that worn manila folder was a single-spaced, typed Chelsea Police report from March 12, 1965, that contained a statement from a confidential informant. The informant had called the station on the night Teddy Deegan was killed and described his murder. Roy French, Ronald Cassesso, and a man named Romeo Martin, who was killed before the others went to trial, were the shooters. Joe Barboza and James Flemmi were also present in the alley. There was no mention of Joseph Salvati.

Dan Rea broke that story during a WBZ-TV newscast on May 17, 1993. A wry-tempered Irishman with a pie face and a mop of coarse, sandy hair, Rea researched and appeared in more than thirty WBZ-TV news spots over the next nine years about who really killed Teddy Deegan. Apparently it hadn't dawned on anyone in law enforcement that you didn't need such a huge conspiracy to kill a drunken brawler like Deegan. Usually it meant a single phone call from Jerry Angiulo to his preferred hitter, Joseph "J. R." Russo, and the matter was taken care of, quickly and professionally. Not a single witness ever identified Salvati as a member of Barboza's crew, and as Joe McCain would say later, in that line of work, "You never go outside those circles."

Years after he and Joe had retired, Leo Papile was watching the evening news on TV when Rea's story on Joe Salvati's role in the Deegan murder appeared. Within minutes, Papile was on the phone with his old partner, rehashing the facts of the case. "Geesh, Leo, we don't want to get involved in that," said McCain.

But what had begun as a tiny nub in Joe McCain's conscience had grown into something larger. During the hundreds of hours he and Papile had spent watching the Ebb Tide and the other nightclubs down on the beach, in the thousands of surveillance reports they had written, and in all their profiles of Barboza and his gang of thugs, Joe Salvati's name did not appear once. McCain had also been told by another cop that, during renovations at the Chelsea Police Station, workmen who ripped out the floor in the chief's office discovered a memorandum that listed who had killed Deegan. Joe Salvati's name was not among them. Attempting to explain how the report had ended up beneath the chief's floor, another Chelsea police officer said, "It must've fallen through the cracks."

The day after the initial news report, Papile contacted Dan Rea and gave him Joe McCain's phone number, and Rea called McCain. In a meeting at Joe's P.I. office, Rea produced the Chelsea Police report that he had referred to during his broadcast, and McCain examined it. "The only way I'd stick my neck out is if you verify that this is what it appears to be," said Joe, explaining that the Secret Service had a lab where they could examine the weave of the paper and the typeface and determine whether it was legitimate.

What McCain didn't say in this initial meeting with Rea was that he'd also heard disturbing things about the FBI's complicity in Barboza's scheme. In those days FBI agents assigned to the Boston office, many of whom were graduates of Boston College or Holy Cross, frequented Ray's Sub Shop on the VFW Parkway, and McCain was familiar with most of them, including H. Paul Rico, a top organized crime investigator who favored the "Hoover look"—expensive three-piece suits, gold jewelry, and shiny black shoes. The word was that Rico had written a report that listed Barboza, Flemmi, Cassesso, Martin, and French as Deegan's killers and turned it in to his supervisor, James Handley. As the agent in charge, Handley sent his own report to J. Edgar Hoover's office in Washington. No one from the District Attorney's Office and certainly none of the defense lawyers at the trial ever saw those reports.

The reason for such a damaging omission may have been that, just before Teddy Deegan's murder, Paul Rico "turned" Stephen and James Flemmi, signing them up as FBI informants. The plan hatched by Rico and others and later carried to its ugly conclusion by Agent John Connolly was to use the Winter Hill gangsters to get at the Angiulo brothers, who were perceived to be the real strength in the New England Mafia. So when James Flemmi was implicated in Deegan's murder, the FBI agreed not to indict him as a way to curry favor with his brother Stevie—or so the story went. For their part, the Flemmis were delighted. They understood that their status as protected government informants was a license to kill, which they would do on numerous occasions without hint of remorse.

Dan Rea was able to prove the Chelsea Police report was for real, and Joe McCain and Leo Papile agreed to sign affidavits detailing what and whom they had seen in and around the Ebb Tide on March 12, 1965. In the course of his reporting, Rea had learned that Joseph Salvati had been arrested a few times in the 1950s for receiving stolen goods, larceny, and possession of burglarious tools. While admitting on the air that Salvati "is not Mother Teresa," Rea continued hammering the Suffolk County District Attorney's Office for their past actions in suppressing the newly discovered police report, which Victor Garo considered exculpatory. Garo believed that the district attorney knew about the report and violated the law and common decency by not exploring the informant's claims or revealing the existence of the report of defense attorneys before the trial.

In a case tried today, these occurrences would have led to an immediate reversal of the verdict or a mistrial at the very least. Unfortunately for Joe Salvati, he'd been tried in 1965, when the rules of evidence and discovery were pretty much the same but in a legal climate that encouraged attorneys on both sides to bend them every which way.

Despite Rea's dogged chain of news reports and Garo's passionate advocacy, there were some frustrating setbacks. *The Boston Globe* and other media outlets accused Rea of "irresponsible advocacy journalism," and two Massachusetts governors, Michael Dukakis and later, William Weld, denied applications to commute Salvati's sentence, although neither official showed a particular grasp of the facts and both refused to participate in a WBZ-TV news panel.

In 1993 Joe Salvati, Peter Limone, and Louis Greco filed motions for new trials, which the Massachusetts Supreme Judicial Court heard and dismissed. The motion judge ruled that the defendants were not entitled to a new trial because the information in the missing report was not provided by a legitimate informant but came via that anonymous call to the Chelsea Police on the night of the Deegan murder. The judge's opinion deemed the source of that phone call a "non-disclosable citizen tipster," a term and a distinction that Victor Garo claimed had no legal meaning and that he scoffed at during subsequent television appearances.

Dan Rea wasn't the only one taking heat from his colleagues. As far as most cops were concerned, Salvati and Limone were bad guys and deserved to be in jail, if not for Teddy Deegan's murder for something else. Certainly many cops believed that tainting one's fellow police officers in search of "the truth" was too high a price. By signing an affidavit, testifying at hearings, and appearing on television, Joe McCain and Leo Papile were implying that other law enforcement officials had lied on their reports, conspired against an innocent man, and perjured themselves. But when big Joe heard that FBI Agent Rico might have been tipped by an informant about Deegan's murder before it occurred and yet did nothing to prevent it, he didn't care what his old friends and colleagues said.

It wasn't the first time McCain had ignored the "blue wall" and done the right thing. As a private investigator, he often found himself working for the defense in criminal cases, a situation that made some of his cop buddies uncomfortable. A retired MDC deputy superintendent with an impeccable reputation, his old friend Al Seghezzi managed the P.I. office for several years and occasionally expressed his dismay at the sorts of clients they were representing. McCain would put his big mitt on Seghezzi's shoulder, look him in the eye, and say, "Al, we're looking for the truth. Same as always." And regardless of the fact that Joe "the Animal" Barboza had been dead for more than twenty years, Joe McCain was also rankled by the idea that his old nemesis had been allowed to put one over on the judicial system. After Barboza left the witness protection program and was convicted of murder in California, he once boasted to a cellmate that he had subjected Joe Salvati "to the long, dry death."

Louis Greco, Ronald Cassesso, and Henry Tameleo died in jail. In 1997, Governor William Weld finally commuted Joseph Salvati's sentence, and he was released from Walpole State Prison. Three years later, Middlesex Superior Court Judge Margaret Hinkle took the additional step of vacating Salvati's conviction. Eventually Paul Rico retired from the FBI and took a job as vice president and director of security with World Jai Alai in Florida, at a far greater salary than he had ever earned in law enforcement. It came as no surprise to Joe McCain that the Winter Hill gang leader, Whitey Bulger, had a controlling interest in the fronton where Rico was employed, a fact that became known after Bulger became a fugitive. In August 2003, Joe Salvati filed a $300 million suit in U.S. District Court, alleging that the FBI helped lay the blame on him for Teddy Deegan's murder and later fought against the effort to have his conviction overturned. Among those named in the suit was former FBI agent H. Paul Rico. (In the fall of 2003, two years after Joe McCain's death, Stephen "the Rifleman" Flemmi implicated Rico in a 1981 murder case, and the elderly ex-G-man was arrested in Florida and indicted. Rico died in January 2004, shortly before his trial was scheduled to begin.)

Joe McCain appeared before the Governor's Council at the commutation hearing for Joseph Salvati. Tall and gaunt, the old Met cop wore his gray suit with a red-and-blue tie and a white shirt, the collar loose around his neck and his face and hands covered in age spots. Before him on a raised dais were the eight members of the Governor's Council and the lieutenant governor, who serves ex officio. The council, which meets at noon on Wednesdays in the State House chamber beside the governor's office, acts on issues such as payments from the state treasury, criminal pardons and commutations, and approval of gubernatorial appointments.

Standing at the podium, McCain testified that over the years several informants had made it common knowledge among police officers that Joe Salvati wasn't present on the night of the murder. McCain went on to say that he believed Salvati was innocent, and that in his forty years as a detective this was the only time he'd ever appeared at a hearing on behalf of a convicted felon.

It came as a surprise to some people and certainly to members of the Governor's Council that Joe McCain didn't hate Joe Barboza. Rather, the notorious hit man fell into a category, along with Richard "the Pig" DeVincent, James "the Bear" and Stevie "the Rifleman" Flemmi, Nick and Jerry Angiulo, and Whitey Bulger, for whom he had no feeling whatsoever. During McCain's testimony, just prior to an 8 to 0 vote in favor of Salvati's commutation, one of the council members fumbled with her papers and misspoke, asking where Joe Barboza was now.

Before she could correct herself, Joe McCain looked at the councilor over the top of his spectacles. "In hell, I imagine," he said.

TWENTY-EIGHT

The Third Man

Four months? Baby, four seconds *in this whorehouse'll get you greased.*
— MICHAEL HERR

BEFORE HE BECAME A POLICE OFFICER, Chris Brighton served with the U.S. Marines in Vietnam. Even in December it was eighty degrees and humid enough to swim through the air, a meteorological combination that guys from New England could never quite get used to. A nineteen-year-old corporal with the First Marine Division, Brighton was just three weeks shy of his thirteen-month tour of duty in Quang Nam Province, a few miles south of the Demilitarized Zone, when he was assigned to regimental headquarters. After months in the bush, Brighton acted as squad leader for a mechanized unit that patrolled a section of dirt road connecting HQ to the battalion area.

Regiment was no safer than the jungle; in fact, a lot of people were killed or wounded on the dusk-to-dawn "rat patrol." But there were hot meals and cold beer and pickup basketball games at HQ, and Corporal Brighton was able to write his family to say that he'd be home in less than a month.

The middle of seven children, Christopher Robert Brighton was the son of a salesman and a secretary, and a 1968 graduate of Scituate High, where he played football and golf and ran track. An affable kid with dark hair and a loose grin, Brighton entertained the other jarheads with his deadpan wit, often ending conversations with "Cheer up. Things could get a lot worse." Mostly, he looked forward to going back to the South Shore and getting a job as a bartender, where he'd turn his charm on the ladies.

On the night of December 7, 1969, Chris Brighton rode in the first of three jeeps, sitting beside the driver trussed up in a flak jacket with his M-16 and a two-way radio. Four Marines occupied the second vehicle, which had a .50-caliber machine gun mounted on it. The third jeep contained three Marines and a 60 Mike-Mike, a portable cannon the size of a golf bag. The unit provided mine detection and security from the bridge near Hill 55, one and a quarter miles north to checkpoint Alpha, two miles west to battalion HQ, and two miles south to Route 1, the main artery for U.S. military traffic in that part of Vietnam.

The convoy left battalion shortly after 2:00 A.M., running without lights and keeping a ten-yard interval between the jeeps. Three quarters of a mile from checkpoint Bravo, they reached a tiny, nameless hamlet that occupied both sides of the road. The driver of the first jeep detected movement in the ville, and Corporal Brighton signaled the convoy to a halt. Using a tiny penlight, one of the Marines in the second vehicle identified a small figure dressed in ragged pajamas crouching by the shoulder of the road.

"I got something," said the Marine.

Twisting a knob on the penlight, the Marine widened the beam of light, illuminating the face of a ten-year-old boy who squatted in the weeds.

"It's all right," called a Marine in the third jeep. "I know the kid."

The Marine spoke to the child in Vietnamese, and he rose out of the tall grass and approached the convoy. When the boy reached the gap between the second and third jeeps, the abrupt noise of an explosion rent the air and Chris Brighton was thrown from the jeep onto the ground.

Dazed for a moment, Brighton reached up and grabbed the radio handset, calling in their position and asking for immediate air support. He felt something oozing from his head and realized that the back of his helmet was gone. Men were screaming, and the smell of cordite from the spent ordnance and the *whoop-whoop* of helicopter rotors filled the night sky.

Brighton looked at his hand; it was covered with blood. Then he passed out.

Marine investigators would learn that the ten-year-old had two claymore mines strapped to his torso, and when he reached the optimum killing zone, a member of the Vietcong hidden in the jungle detonated the mines, throwing hundreds of steel ball bearings in every direction. Two Marines were killed instantly; a third would die of his wounds at the battalion aid station, and all the rest were injured, some quite badly.

Chris Brighton's flak jacket absorbed most of the blast, saving his life. The child was obliterated.

Drifting in and out of consciousness, Brighton was patched up in the battalion area, then stabilized and sent on to Japan and later to Walter Reed Naval Hospital in Washington, D.C., and finally, the Chelsea Naval Hospital in Massachusetts. His convalescence lasted over a year. Brighton lost the upper portion of his left lung. His skull was fractured and a small plastic plate was inserted to cover the hole left by the missing bone fragments.

CHRIS BRIGHTON IS TELLING ME this story at the bar in the Fours Grille, a short walk from North Station in downtown Boston. "I still got shrapnel in there," he says, rotating his arm like a pitcher warming up.

The Fours is decorated in mahogany wainscoting, with frosted half windows separating the lounge from the dining area. Autographed jerseys from Boston sportsmen adorn the walls: Larry Bird's number 33 in Celtics green; quarterback Tom Brady of the New England Patriots; and, of course, hockey legend Bobby Orr's number 4, adorning the home whites of the Big Bad Bruins. On the menu is a veal cutlet sandwich named for Red Sox slugger Tony Conigliaro, a handsome kid who was born in Revere, got hit in the head with a pitched ball, and ended up dying young. While most people are struggling to get their tax returns done, the patrons at the bar are more concerned about the Sox-Orioles game on TV.

When the bartender, a squat, florid-faced gent with wavy hair, comes over, Brighton winks at him and says; "You look familiar. Ever been locked up?"

I'd been told that "Kegs" Brighton likes to tip 'em and has been dogging his favorite hangouts for a while now: the Burren in Somerville, Tavern on the Green, the Fours. Chris is a close friend of the McCains and played a significant role in the defining moments of big Joe's life. But instead of the bitter, introverted, perhaps even hostile man that I had imagined, state trooper Chris Brighton is friendly and charming. He apologizes for his busy schedule and keeps trying to buy me another drink.

Brighton looks more like a professional golfer than a cop. He's a shade over six feet but looks taller, and is dressed in a blue madras shirt, beige slacks, and tasseled loafers. Brighton has high-crowned dark hair, his face is tanned very dark from cruising on his boat, and his eyes are brown and lively, crinkling at the edges when he smiles, which is often.

But there's something about him that suggests a Johnny Mercer lyric: detached, world-weary, with a profound sadness lurking beneath the grin.

Quarter to three. There's no one in the place
Except you and me.

Brighton became a cop in 1978, choosing the Mets over the State Police because they allowed him to keep his monthly $681 disability pension from the Marine Corps. Several of Joe McCain's feats were mentioned at the Police Academy, and when the two met by chance a year later, recalls Brighton, "Just the way he said his own name set the tone for his personality. Joe was tough, he was honest, and he had a great knowledge of organized crime."

Shaking his head, Brighton says, "He could meet somebody once, just once, say, walking down State Street, and five or six years later he could tell you exactly where he met the guy and what he was doing at the time."

When our conversation turns to the night that big Joe got shot, Brighton borrows a pen from the bartender, squares up his place mat, and sketches a diagram of Melvin Lee's kitchen in Hyde Park. The drawing is meticulous and precise; it looks like a geometry equation.

"I was sitting at the table," says Brighton, making a little x on the place mat. He stares at it for a moment. "Right here."

The room was occupied by Brighton and the three drug suspects and filled with boisterous talk. Melvin Lee wanted Brighton to get him a bartending job up in North Conway, New Hampshire, and Brighton was kidding him about never having skied before. Then, in the space of a minute, Melvin Lee and Tommy Lofgren disappeared upstairs and Vladimir Lafontant retreated into the bathroom off the kitchen.

Where'd everybody go? Brighton asked himself.

It didn't take long to find out. Brighton heard a click from somewhere behind him and Lafontant rushed back into the room. The drug dealer circled the table, menacing Brighton with a sawed-off shotgun.

"Take off your fucking clothes," said Lafontant.

When the barrel of the shotgun reached eye level and Brighton could see right into it, he thought, This is it. I'm dead.

In one movement, Brighton says, he shoved the gun barrel aside and leaped up from the chair while reaching for the .38 tucked into his waistband. But Lafontant kicked him in the balls and snatched his gun away and ran out of the room, down the narrow hallway toward the front door.

I've been in that house and that hallway, and can picture everything Chris Brighton is saying: the cramped, filthy rooms, the dirty dishes and musky odor; even the sense of desperation oozing from the walls. Poorly lit and badly ventilated, 276 Wood Avenue is the sort of place where evil things are likely to occur—and they did.

Several gunshots echoed through the house. Brighton crawled over the grimy linoleum, staggered to his feet and jumped out the back door. There was a four-foot drop-off from the porch and he tumbled onto the ground.

His gun drawn, Mark Cronin ran through the yard and up the back stairs. On his way by, Cronin asked Brighton if he was all right.

"I'm okay," he said.

When Brighton ran around the house, Joe McCain was lying on the sidewalk bleeding, with Al DiSalvo and Biff McLean kneeling over him.

Backup was arriving from every direction and there were a lot of revolving lights and sirens.

"Did we get him?" McCain asked Brighton.

Brighton looked over toward Lafontant, who was lying dead in the street. "Yeah, Joe," he said. "We got him."

Then the paramedics pushed Brighton away and he walked over to the porch and buried his face in his hands.

Later, after the investigation was finished, one of the Boston cops who was on the scene gave Chris a memento: the sawed-off Continental shotgun that Lafontant was carrying. He keeps it at home, in the lockbox next to his service revolver.

AROUND THE CORNER FROM WHERE Chris Brighton and I are sitting is a giant concrete structure known as the Fleet Center, where the Celtics and Bruins play their home games. A few years ago, it replaced a much more beloved and significant architectural landmark, the Boston Garden, a dilapidated brick building that contained a dank ice rink and the famous parquet floor.

Atop the Garden was a huge billboard depicting a fifty-foot animated camel smoking a cigarette. To simulate a burning ember, the tip of the cigarette featured a red lightbulb. You could see it from miles away.

In that era, Joe McCain and Chris Brighton and Leo Papile and Sergeant Tommy White liked to drink at the 99 restaurant over on Friend Street. When they left the bar in the wee hours of the morning, the quartet would draw their revolvers and take potshots at the giant cigarette until one of them put it out. It was over 200 feet on the wing, in the dark, under the influence.

Brighton laughs as he tells me this, adding that the outdoor shooting range was all Joe McCain's idea. "He wasn't *that* bad of a shot," says Brighton. "He hit it once in a while."

Behind us, three college kids are hooting over a Red Sox home run, and the scent of broiling meat wafts out from the kitchen. Chris Brighton did his tour in Vietnam and worked undercover for years, got shot at, blown up, stabbed with a hypodermic needle, and threatened with knives, guns, and baseball bats, all with the insouciance of Dean Martin, a cocktail glass in his hand and a wisecrack on his lips. So what if he hasn't eaten a thing all day and puts away the beer like he expects Prohibition to be reinstated? He's entitled.

Saying there's a blonde waiting for him down the street, Brighton gets up from his barstool. As he puts on his coat, it occurs to me that I haven't asked him how he really feels about Joe McCain and what happened that night. Anyway, I don't have to. It's all right there, in his eyes.

TWENTY-NINE

Big Joe's Last Case

I've still got a few teeth in my head—and a few friends in town.
—NOAH CROSS, *CHINATOWN*

IN THE FALL OF 2000, McCAIN INVESTIGATIONS was churning along with a steady flow of business. Most of its employees were in the field and making out reports, permitting the agency to bill a fair number of hours, and more and more big Joe was staying in the office, working the phone in search of new contracts and directing his investigators from behind a desk. Although he downplayed their effects on his habits, the bullet wounds he had suffered nearly thirteen years earlier played a major role in limiting his activity. Compounded by years of physical strain and more than a few sips of hard liquor, brittle diabetes was taking a toll on Joe's legendary constitution. His blood sugar rose and fell precipitously and with little warning; Helen kept a testing kit handy and a notable supply of candy and other sweets.

Then one day the flamboyant defense attorney J. W. Carney, Jr., called McCain and said he needed him on a big case. In a lurid tale worthy of the supermarket tabloids, James Kartell, a fifty-nine-year-old plastic surgeon, had confronted his estranged wife's lover in her sickroom at Holy Family Hospital in Methuen, Mass., where Dr. Kartell frequently treated patients. The two men quarreled and during what began as a fistfight, Kartell felt himself being overpowered, drew a revolver from the waistband of his trousers and fired two shots at close range, killing his rival in front of his wife, psychotherapist Dr. Suzan Kamm.

The Kartell case had already drawn a lot of play in the Boston newspapers, and none of it was helping Jay Carney's client. Dr. Kartell, small, roly-poly, and less than photogenic, stretched the caricature of the arrogant physician to its absolute limit. In possession of Mensa-level intelligence and renowned for his prowess with a scalpel, Kartell had trouble uttering a syllable that did not advertise itself as condescending, and the notion of a fat, dumpy egomaniac shooting an unarmed man in a hospital room was not raising an iota of public sympathy.

Enter Joe McCain. In this case, McCain's sympathies would appear to lie with the prosecution: what sort of man fires a second shot into another man's skull when his first shot ended their fight, and why the heck is a doctor carrying a gun in the first place? But as McCain often said to Al Seghezzi, the one thing that he'd always been interested in was the truth. Seghezzi and McCain went back to the late fifties, when Al was a sergeant and Joe a patrolman in the Old Colony district and they both worked in the same building. And while Seghezzi was sometimes troubled by the notion that the P.I. firm was "helping the bad guys" by working on behalf of people like Kartell, the retired Met was comforted by McCain's belief that "sometimes we couldn't help the guy—you don't find stuff that isn't there."

The day that he was headed to a fact-finding on the Kartell case in Jay Carney's office, big Joe sought out Mark Donahue in his cubicle on Fulton Street. "C'mon. You're gonna work the Kartell case with me," said McCain.

Donahue was ecstatic but struggled to maintain the stone-faced professional demeanor he'd been taught. "It was kinda Joe's acknowledgment that I was an adult," said Donahue, who was thirty-seven at the time. "A real murder case."

McCain and Donahue arrived at the Statler Building in downtown Boston and were joined by a ballistics expert, a doctor, another lawyer from Carney's staff, and Carney himself. "This is like stepping up to the plate for your first major league at-bat," said Donahue.

The object of the meeting was to arrive at what actually occurred on February 23, 1999, in Room 440 at Holy Family Hospital. Carney explained that James Kartell, plastic surgeon, had been married to Suzan Kamm for thirty-two years and that they had no children, were quite wealthy, and had become estranged. During their separation Dr. Kamm, a moderately attractive woman, had been living with fifty-six-year-old Janos Vajda, a native Hungarian and divorced father of three daughters. The day of the shooting, Dr. Kamm had called her estranged husband to her room, ostensibly to consult with him on her medical condition, which was pneumonia. She had also invited Vajda, a tall, muscularly built man who had once been an Olympic swimmer and still competed at the Master's level.

Kartell told his wife to ask Vajda to leave the room, since he wanted to discuss her case in private. But Kamm replied that her other visitor was free to stay or leave as he wished. Kartell became agitated and took Vajda by the arm. The larger man resisted, and a fight ensued. Vajda quickly got the better of the doughy Kartell, looming over him, knocking him to the floor, smashing punches into his face at will. Afraid that he was about to lose consciousness, Attorney Carney said, Kartell reached around to his lower back, groping for the concealed .38-caliber revolver that he had a permit for and always carried. He fired two shots, dropping his assailant.

Next, the ballistics expert explained that such a weapon could not be accidentally discharged. In minute detail, he described the type of gun that Kartell used, its weight, the properties of the bullets, and the grain of the powder, as well as the exact amount of pressure required to pull back the hammer and depress the trigger. Illustrating his presentation with drawings and crime scene photographs that Mark Donahue called "absolutely gross," the ballistics man depicted the trajectory of the two bullets and estimated the time that elapsed between them.

"Someone deliberately pulled that trigger," said Donahue.

Although some media accounts claimed that the first shot disabled Vajda, and then Kartell, extricating himself, walked around the kneeling victim and delivered the fatal blow, execution-style, to the back of the head, Jay Carney's medical expert stated that "the first shot killed the guy," according to Donahue. The bullet's path through Vajda's shoulder and down into his chest severed a major artery, causing his heart to fail due to volumic incapacity. When that occurred, "the body's natural response was to drop to its knees," Donahue said.

Newspaper photos taken immediately after Vajda's death showed that Kartell had been absorbing a terrific beating when he drew his gun: both eyes were swollen shut, his nose and jaw broken. A substantial number of people believed—and a jury could perhaps be convinced—that Kartell's initial response was in self-defense. Vajda was banging Kartell's head against a very hard floor, and the first shot had put a stop to that unpleasant activity. What the majority couldn't stomach was that Kartell had fired a second round.

After the doctor finished giving his medical opinion on how Vajda had died, Jay Carney took over the discussion. A colorful, gifted lawyer and veteran of several high-profile defense cases, Carney first set out to establish a reason for Kartell to carry a gun into Holy Family Hospital, which was against their well-established policy. Carney stressed that James Kartell was a gun collector and enthusiast and had never been in trouble with the law. Kartell's father, a New York City judge, had once foiled his own abduction by producing a gun, and Dr. Kartell had lawfully carried one for twenty years. He often performed surgery at Lawrence General Hospital, in a rough inner-city neighborhood, appearing there at all hours to see his patients, and thus had a valid reason to carry a gun, Carney asserted. *Ergo*, the presence of Vajda in his wife's sickroom had no bearing on the presence of the .38 revolver in the waistband of Dr. Kartell's pants. The gun was always there.

What most people also didn't realize was that Dr. Kartell was almost legally blind. Early in the fight with his wife's lover, Kartell's glasses were knocked off his face. Just as he was losing consciousness, he reached for the gun and fired it "center mass" on his assailant, by that time an indistinct target. Although Vajda was mortally wounded, his adrenaline and superior fitness allowed him to continue fighting, even as he lurched downward, his weight pinning the much smaller man to the floor. Unable to see, Dr. Kartell remained in fear of his life and fired another round.

Jay Carney had a brilliant tactic planned for the courtroom. He was having twelve pairs of eyeglasses made up in Dr. Kartell's prescription so that jurors would understand just how poor his vision was, according to Mark Donahue. "The papers would have you believe that Dr. K said 'Now you're going to get it,' and then shot him deliberately in the back of the head," said Donahue. But Carney reminded his team that only two people knew what really happened in Room 440 at Holy Family Hospital: Dr. James Kartell and Suzan Kamm. The job of a good defense lawyer was to create reasonable doubt in the minds of the jurors regarding the scenario that the prosecution would describe.

Carney acknowledged that his hardest task would be getting the jurors to like Dr. Kartell. A markedly unattractive fellow, Dr. Kartell compounded his first impression on people by talking down his nose at them. His favorite topic was himself, and he went around town and through the hospitals where he operated as if ordinary folks weren't even there. He was wealthy and he was smug, never a good combination for eliciting sympathy. But in the course of their investigation, McCain and Donahue spent a lot of time with Kartell, often meeting him for lunch at Bishop's Restaurant in Lawrence, where the doctor would have at their Middle Eastern cuisine like "a man on his way to the gas chamber," said Donahue. "Which he was."

It certainly looked like the deep six for Dr. James Kartell. When Jay Carney was through talking that day, Joe McCain asked a lot of questions about the ballistics evidence, the exact cause of death, and so on. The D.A. wanted to portray the case as premeditated murder, and it would be up to Joe McCain to prove that Kartell may have despised Janos Vajda but he didn't plan on killing him. The list of witnesses included nurses, security guards, nurse's aides, and other patients who had responded to the tumult in Room 440.

"We have to take every name we have and work it," McCain said to Donahue.

The first name on everybody's list was Brian McGovern, twenty-seven-year-old nurse's aide who was purported to have been the first person on the scene, just seconds after the shots were fired. McGovern told police that he ran into the room, grabbed Kartell, shoved him against the wall, and asked, "What kind of man are you?"

Upon hearing McGovern's account of these events, McCain said, "It doesn't make sense that he ran into the room. Most people run away from a shooting."

McCain and Donahue convinced McGovern, after half a dozen attempts, to talk to them. In this instance, McCain was blunt. "Do you think you might have embellished a little?" he asked.

"Basically, he told us to go shit in our hats," said Donahue of McGovern.

McCain was ailing by this time and was often visited by dreams of Vladimir Lafontant, the man he had killed in a gun battle. One day it got to him pretty bad, and Joe walked over to St. Clement's Church, where he found Father Dever alone in the sacristy, laying out his vestments. "Father, I'd like to talk to you," he said.

Pastor Dennis A. Dever was roughly the same age as his troubled parishioner, a thin, white-haired man with a raspy voice. "What's bothering you, Joe?" he asked.

"Well, you see, Father, a few years ago I killed a man . . ."

The priest nodded his head. "I know, Joe."

"Yeah, everyone said he was no good, a Jamaican posse guy, and over the years, Father, I knew the good, the bad, and the ugly, believe me," said Joe. He wiped his face with a handkerchief and stared off toward the altar.

Father Dever regarded him with a calm look, and after a moment or two in the great silence of the church, Joe continued: "He shot me, and he shot Paul, and I returned fire, and after I was shot he went out in the street and he died right there, in the street." He rubbed his chin and worked his lips and then looked up at the priest. "It's just bothering the hell out of me, Father, and I want to confess that part of it, and get it over with."

Father Dever blessed him and absolved him and gave him Hail Marys to recite as penance. "I want to tell you something, Joe," said the priest. "I've had a bit of psychiatric training, and most people don't know what policemen go through. It's a very, very difficult job that you do."

"I've been through a lot, Father. Taking bodies out of rivers with a grappling hook, all the shootings, the autopsies," Joe said.

Father Dever continued to look into his parishioner's eyes. "You know, Joe, some people are put on this earth because they have a mission and they don't know it."

"I'm not overly religious, Father, in that I come into church and sit in the front row," said Joe. "I stand in the back; I put my money in the poor box. Whatever the church needs, I give. It's like I'm hedging my bets in case there is a heaven. I'll be the guy, when they tell me I'm dying, who'll be screaming, 'Where's my priest?' "

Father Dever chuckled. "Always remember, Joe, that you were put on this earth to accomplish certain things, and maybe if this guy gets by you, and the police are coming, he would've shot somebody else, maybe someone's mother. Maybe that's why you were put there on that particular day—to stop him from doing something like that. And because sometimes God's will is hard, you had to pay a price for that."

Joe McCain sat breathing in the scent of candle wax and incense, and then he reached across and gripped the priest's hand. "I can live with that, Father," he said.

Joe was getting tired. In a gesture that was more than symbolic, he instructed Mark Donahue to work the names on the Kartell case by himself, with an eye toward contradicting Brian McGovern's version of the story. The young nurse's aide's tale may have been adopted as gospel by the newspapers, but to McCain it still didn't add up. He knew from his own experience that everyone wants to be a hero, although few have the mettle for it. That role is not chosen but thrust upon you.

As a kid, Mark Donahue had spent the lion's share of his free time at the McCains', and Joe had been grooming him for such a job since he'd started as a detective. But working a murder case was a lot different from tailing some deadbeat who was cheating on workmen's comp.

After numerous interviews that went nowhere, Donahue was getting to the end of his list when, late one afternoon in December, he drove to Haverhill, Mass. and knocked on the door to Thomas Montecalvo's apartment. Montecalvo was one of several unarmed security guards working at Holy Family Hospital the day Vajda was killed. No longer employed at the hospital, Montecalvo had kept a low profile, eschewing media interviews and responding to anyone who asked him about Dr. Kartell that Holy Family management wanted all inquiries routed back to them. Thomas Montecalvo was just a name on a piece of paper.

He came to the door that afternoon in a Massachusetts Police Academy sweatshirt, his hair buzzed short. Cutting Donahue off in midsentence, Montecalvo said that he didn't want to talk. He hadn't really seen anything that day and was busy doing other things.

"You a cop?" asked Donahue.

Montecalvo said, with a measure of pride, that he had graduated from the academy a couple of months earlier and was on the job in Lawrence. Donahue noted that he was a cop, too, and just wanted to ask a few basic questions.

"Okay, I'll give you a minute," said Montecalvo, opening the storm door.

The two men went into Montecalvo's kitchen. Producing a little notebook, Donahue asked the former security guard where he was assigned and what he'd been doing when Dr. Kartell shot Vajda. He almost dropped his pencil when Montecalvo replied that he'd been the first security officer to respond and the only other person on the scene except for Suzan Kamm. As he approached the room, Dr. Kartell was coming out. He handed Montecalvo his weapon and allowed himself to be escorted to a small room off the nurses' station, where they both waited for police.

"Actually, I fucked up," said Montecalvo. "I had a radio. I should've just called for help and sat back and let the guy come out. I had no idea what his state of mind was."

Donahue asked if anyone else was there in the room or hallway with him; specifically, had Brian McGovern already disarmed Kartell and had conversations with anybody?

"No," said Montecalvo. "I was the only one there."

Thomas Montecalvo's account established two things: Brian McGovern was not telling the truth, and Dr. Kartell was no longer aggressive or pursuing the fight when help arrived. In fact, Montecalvo described Kartell as a "wet rat"; he was completely beaten up.

"And this kid had credibility, because he was a cop," said Donahue.

Donahue took notes and hustled out to his car. He made the thirty-minute drive back to the office in a state of rising excitement and told McCain the entire story. "Joe got right on the phone with Carney's office," said Donahue. "They were ecstatic."

With Montecalvo testifying in his police uniform, Jay Carney was able to debunk McGovern's account of Kartell's belligerence. Although facing charges of first-degree murder, Kartell was convicted of voluntary manslaughter and received only a five- to eight-year prison term, which he is currently serving at the Souza-Baranowski Correctional Center in Shirley, Mass.

"What I learned is, even if you think a witness has nothing to say, you have to be persistent," said Donahue. "A lot of people said they were told by the hospital not to talk to anyone, to go through their legal office. Joe used to say, 'This is America. You can talk to anyone you want, about anything you want.' "

THIRTY

The Erin Society

Life is made up of ever so many partings.
— CHARLES DICKENS

T HE PLOT IS LOCATED ON A PROMINENT CORNER in
Holy Cross Cemetery in Malden, surrounded by a low concrete
berm approximately ten feet square and marked by a granite stone engraved with Celtic crosses and an intaglio of the Virgin Mary holding
her grown, dead son. Late in April, the sky is heavy and gray, tinged
with the last cold front of a pretty bad winter. At Joe McCain's grave,
the toughest guy in Somerville shifts from one side of the berm to the
other, knotting and unknotting his thick, rough hands and finally looking away, his gaze skimming over the monuments and minarets that occupy the lot to the horizon.

"It's hard to come here," says Brian O'Donovan, exhaling a long,
slow breath.

Like Mark Donahue and countless other two-fisted kids who
haunted Foss Park and the MDC rink, O'Donovan, now thirty-nine
and a lieutenant on the Somerville Fire Department, came under Joe
McCain's influence at a young age. He grew up on Rogers Avenue off
Ball Square, in a large, rambling house overseen by his father, James, a
lawyer, and his mother, Pauline, who owned an answering service and
"took shit from no one." The middle son among five boys, Brian

learned to get his shots in at a tender age as he and his brothers Jim, Kevin, Mike, and Sean followed a pretty set schedule from the time he began to walk until he graduated from Somerville High.

"There was a battle royal every day after school, and then it would be street hockey time," says O'Donovan, laughing at the recollection.

The fights in the O'Donovan household were not the ordinary tussles associated with having five healthy boys under one roof: they were prolonged and sometimes bloody free-for-alls, like the old turf battles of the Irish chieftains. "We did some serious damage to that house," says Brian.

Standing by Joe's grave, Brian O'Donovan is wearing a long-sleeved Black Dog T-shirt, blue track pants, and sneakers. He has the heavy, muscled hands and shoulders of a stonemason and an Irish pug's face: wide, flat nose, stubby ears and close-cropped black hair under a sun-faded baseball cap. When he smiles, little crescents of scar tissue rise on his cheekbones and above his eyes, the remembrances of a habit that began at home and was raised to the level of a talent in the back alleys and ball fields around Rogers Avenue.

With his father at work, sometimes Brian and his siblings became so furious with one another that his mother would catch a punch on the jaw while trying to break them up. "A couple of times she went down," he says. And there was a period after high school when Brian drifted away from his warring brothers and began to find trouble on his own. "We thought as teenagers we'd never be close when we got older, because we fought so hard," he says.

Then Joe McCain came into the picture. O'Donovan had known the big man since he was twelve, when he and Joey and Mark Donahue played peewee hockey together. In those early days, Mr. McCain was just another dad at the rink, albeit a friendly one, with hands the size of baseball gloves and an easy way with his son's young friends.

"He'd tell you stories like you were one of the guys," says O'Donovan.

Joe McCain the cop and Jim O'Donovan the lawyer became good buddies in those chilly old rinks, and over time it just seemed natural when big Joe became another member of the family. Brian and Joe McCain, Sr., became friends and shared a passion for ice hockey and then golf. When Brian was eighteen, Joe gave him a little MDC police sticker that said "Erin Society" and instructed him to affix it to his car. And if he ever got into any trouble, he was to say that Joe McCain was his uncle.

Late one night, a few pints under his belt, Brian was weaving down Revere Beach Parkway more occupied with the bagful of roast beef sandwiches from Kelly's than he was with his driving, and a huge, bald-headed Met cop threw on his lights and siren and pulled O'Donovan over.

"Who do you know?" the cop asked, gesturing toward the Erin Society sticker.

O'Donovan replied that he was Joe McCain's nephew and was amazed at the cop's reaction. "Go home," the cop said. "And please tell your uncle that I was asking for him."

Brian O'Donovan was twenty-four years old when Joe got shot in 1988, and after the big fellow recovered from his injuries, the two friends often played golf together at the Charles River Country Club in Newton Centre. After years of duffing, big Joe was able to put a pretty solid game together, especially for a guy who had topped out at over three hundred pounds and spent more of his youth swinging a hammer than a nine-iron. O'Donovan, by contrast, was a six handicap and had once considered joining the pro tour. To throw the younger man off his game, Joe would stand by the tee and open up his shirt. "Gee, look at this," he would say, indicating the surgical staples that crisscrossed his massive torso. "I'm bleeding all over the place."

"Go to hell, Joe," O'Donovan would respond, and the two would laugh.

One day in the fall of 2001, Brian O'D's cell phone rang when he was driving his two boys to tae kwon do. It was Helen McCain, and she was worried about Joe; his diabetes was kicking up and he refused to go to the hospital.

Brian asked Helen to put her husband on the phone. "How you doin', Joe?" he asked.

McCain's voice was weak and hollow. "Not good, Brian," he said. "Not good."

Alarmed by this, O'Donovan left his two boys at karate, called his wife, Denise, to pick them up and sped over to the McCains'. When he jumped the stairs and burst into the foyer, there was Joe, sitting on the window bench, hands grasping his knees, as yellow as lemon peel with jaundice and struggling for breath.

Joe refused to go in an ambulance, so Brian slung his arm across the big man's shoulders and helped him down the stairs into the front seat of his car while the neighbors looked on. They drove straight to Mount Auburn Hospital in Cambridge, where Joe was admitted, and over the next few days O'Donovan spent every free minute by Joe's bedside. One evening he brought his five-year-old, Seamus Patrick, who drew a picture of Joe and sat in his lap watching the Eagles beat the Giants on *Monday Night Football.*

Joe was quiet and thoughtful that evening, but the force of his personality had returned, and when O'Donovan and his young son left the Mount Auburn at halftime, they joked and said good-bye like it was any one of a thousand other nights they had taken leave of each other.

Joe has been dead for a year and a half now. Hands at his sides, Brian O'D stands gazing at the headstone amidst the crowded expanse of Holy Cross Cemetery.

McCain
"Our love is forever"
Joseph E. 1929–2001   *Helen L. 1936–*

Little strips of muscle appear along O'Donovan's cheekbone as he works to keep his jaw together. "He was so concerned about his grand-kids—what they were going to do without him," he says.

He starts to say something else but clips his teeth together, for a moment gazing at the clouds overhead. At five-thirty in the morning after Brian and Seamus Patrick's visit to the Mount Auburn, Joe Jr. called the O'Donovans, waking them from a sound sleep.

"He said his father was gone," says O'Donovan. And then the toughest guy in Somerville begins to weep.

ON THE MORNING OF JOE MCCAIN'S FUNERAL, retired Met superintendent Al Seghezzi and his wife, Mary, left their modest home on Sealund Road in Quincy and drove to the foot of the Neponset Bridge to pick up Joe's old partner Leo Papile. Al, Leo, and Joe McCain went all the way back to the Old Colony district in the late fifties, when the three patrolmen worked out of the same building. Even then, McCain was impressive, a big, rangy fellow, very outgoing, already making a name for himself among the wiseguys on Revere Beach. Leo Papile was a colorful figure in his own right, with his slicked back hair, profane wit, and the kind of swagger that moved him out of patrol into the detective bureau in short order. Al was the quiet, steady one, staying up late to cram for the sergeant's exam, polishing his brass, looking after McCain and Papile like they were his wild younger brothers.

So it was that Al Seghezzi was dispatched to Leo's house before the funeral. Hearty, fit, and white-haired at seventy-seven, with his rough cement worker's hands and straight white teeth, Seghezzi looked like a grandfather in a magazine advertisement, the square, handsome face, pink-cheeked and freshly shaven, trousers pressed, shoes shined. But he had a wife to look after him and had always kept the cop job in perspective; Leo Papile was a widower, lived alone, and according to Joe McCain, Jr., had been struggling with the news of big Joe's death.

Al honked the horn in the driveway, and Leo came out dressed in a neat blue suit and climbed into the rear seat. Sitting beside Al, Mary Seghezzi wore a simple black dress and had her hair swept up in a new perm. There were a few pleasantries, but within minutes, the two old Mets were bickering like a couple of fishwives as Al drove up the Expressway toward Doherty Funeral Home in Somerville.

"Al, you're in the wrong lane," said Leo, hanging over the front seat.

"What do you mean, Leo?" asked Al. It was a cold Tuesday morning in October, with clouds scudding overhead, and commuter traffic was light heading toward the tunnel; they were making good time in the far-left lane.

"Al, you've got to get in the right lane," Leo said.

Al glanced over at his wife and then turned his head and looked Leo in the eye for a moment. "I like to ride in the left lane," he said.

"Great, but if something happens up there you'll never be able to get off."

"Leo, who's driving this thing?" Al asked.

Joe's old partner thrust himself back against the seat. "I *always* drive in the right lane," said Leo.

After their little debate, the Seghezzis and Leo rode north in silence. As they turned off, skirted Medford, and drove into Powder House Square, they were not prepared for the scene they encountered.

Doherty Funeral Home has been a fixture in Somerville since 1906, and the large white Colonial with the green awnings and immaculate lawn has buried such local notables as the mayors Dr. G. Edward Bradley and William Brennan, a firefighter killed in the Hotel Vendome fire in 1972, and a young Marine killed in Beirut in the 1982 bombing. On the day of Joe McCain's funeral, cars lined every street radiating from the traffic circle, and the sidewalks were roiling with cops, dignitaries from the state house, a host of Joe's old cronies and retired Mets, wiseguys from Winter Hill, and dozens of women, young and old, wearing black and sobbing into their handkerchiefs. By Doherty's front door, state trooper Mark Lemieux, a wiry, intense man who had worked undercover for Joe, paced up and down in his dress blue uniform and shiny boots, getting up the nerve to go inside.

"No tears in here," Leo said to Al. "Joe wouldn't go for any of that."

Clutching each other, Al and Mary Seghezzi mounted the front steps and followed Leo Papile into the funeral home. A dense crowd filled the hallway amidst the stench of too many flowers, and red-eyed men in ill-fitting sport jackets, staring down at their feet or gazing at the thin silver brocade of the wallpaper, occupied several rows of chairs.

Halfway along the main room, two large easels contained photographs of Joe's grandchildren, Joseph, Liam, and Lucas, posing on their beloved dirt bikes or grinning from beneath Somerville Little League caps. At the entrance to the odd-shaped chapel where Joe lay in state, wearing his double-breasted Met uniform and flanked by two state troopers, additional photographs of Joe McCain, Sr., at work occupied two more pinboards: Joe accepting yet another award from the police commissioner; Joe and Leo smiling at newspaper photographers as they led a manacled prisoner up the courthouse steps; Joe back in '45, tall and lean and straight in his Navy whites.

For three days Leo Papile had been telling anyone who would listen that there would be "no bullshit" at Joe's funeral; from his days growing up as "Little Hash" on Marshall Street in Winter Hill to the last, agonizing stay at Mount Auburn Hospital, big Joe had prized his own inner strength and stoicism as much as anything else. He wouldn't have wanted any crying or gnashing of teeth, Leo insisted, demanding of those closest to him what he demanded of himself. Certainly Helen was hanging tough, standing beside the coffin in a tailored black pantsuit, her blonde hair just so, greeting visitors with a dry eye and a steady hand.

Joe McCain's round, visored Met cap was on a little table beside the coffin, and as Leo approached the bier, he picked up the cap and put it on his own head. Kneeling beside the coffin with Al and Mary Seghezzi right behind him, Leo began mumbling to Joe like his old partner was listening to him. Then he reached over and smoothed Joe's lapel, patting his chest and weeping.

Al Seghezzi was stunned. He leaned to his wife's ear and whispered, "Let's go sit down."

While Al steered his wife through the crowd of mourners, Joey's wife, Maureen, came through the side entrance feeling like she was in a movie. A city kid who had grown up in a tiny clapboard house over the bridge in Charlestown, the former Maureen Taylor had endured somewhat of a love-dislike relationship with her old-school father-in-law, sharing an address but few of the same opinions with a man who had grown up during the Depression and served in the Great War. The two of them knew how to get under each other's skin, and the brash, outspoken kid from the 'town had eventually come to a détente with the tough old Irish cop for three reasons: Joseph, Liam, and Lucas, the tousle-haired, freckle-faced princes who wielded the most power in the McCain household.

One time, when the boys were very young, big Joe said he would buy a bicycle for Joseph. Despite never earning more than a patrolman's salary and what he could get from moonlighting, Joe had always been generous with a buck. That night, after a few constitutionals at the Fatted Calf on Beacon Hill, he returned home with brand-new full-sized bicycles for all the boys stowed in the backseat of his Caddy. While

Maureen protested that the bikes were too big, Joe watched shiny-eyed as the boys pedaled up and down the street.

Maureen had skipped the front entrance of Doherty's to avoid seeing her father-in-law in his present state. He wouldn't really be dead, and their arguments over the kids and the house and local politics would not be at an end (nor would their conciliatory cups of tea, shared in Maureen's second-floor kitchen) if she didn't have to see him there, too big for the largest-sized coffin Doherty had squeezed him into.

Thirty-six-year-old Maureen McCain had never seen so many grown men crying in all her life; especially given that most of them came from places where men never cried; the O'Donovans of Ball Square and Stew Henry from White Plains and Dennis Febles of the Spanish Harlem Febleses and Mark Lemieux and Mark Donahue and Gene Kee and Biff McLean and Al DiSalvo, weeping openly, like children, like nobody ever wept in Stoneham or Mattapan or up in Haverhill.

Finally Maureen angled through the shifting mass of people and knelt at Joe's side. In their battles over the years, she'd tried never to lose control of her emotions in front of him; her father-in-law wouldn't have respected that. But now she let it all go; looking at him with his tie knotted up to his neck and brass shining, she let out a long, low wail that cracked over into blubbering, and her knees gave out and she slumped against the bier.

Helen came straight over and placed a hand on Maureen's shoulder. "Stop crying," she said, in a quiet voice.

After forty-two years of marriage, Helen McCain knew that her husband would've been honored but embarrassed by a funeral more suited to a United States president than a tired old cop from Marshall Street. Somebody had told Helen that there were four sitting judges inside Doherty's, and all that kind of fuss was never Joe's style. A few hours before Joe died, when Helen was sitting with him at Mount Auburn, a resident came in and asked how he was feeling.

Joe McCain sat up in bed, crossed his arms over his chest, and glared at the young doctor. "How am I feeling? I can't breathe," he said in a strong voice. "The air in this room is just terrible. I should be out on the sidewalk, walking around."

That was the old Joe. And today, just like in 1988 when Joe got shot, Helen had rushed out to get her hair done and her clothes pressed and had spent a full day cleaning her house because that's what the old Joe would've wanted her to do. Then she had come down to Doherty's and thanked all these people for their sympathy, had actually comforted *them*, and would go over to St. Clement's and up to Holy Cross in possession of herself, in the midst of a deep and secret knowledge of what she and Joe had meant to each other, and keeping all that private, honoring it in that way.

Shortly before 10:00 A.M. Joe's coffin was rolled out to the hearse and the procession started at the bottom of the Powder House Square rotary, wound its way counterclockwise, and began emptying into Warner Street. St. Clement's Roman Catholic Church is less than half a mile from the funeral home, and even after the hearse arrived in front of the wooden doors, with an army of white-gloved policemen blocking all the side streets and the kilted members of the Boston Police Gaelic Column playing "Amazing Grace" on bagpipes and drums, cars with little magnetic "funeral" markers continued out from Doherty's for the next twenty minutes.

Onlookers stood on their porches, in driveways, and on street corners, mouths agape, watching in silence as eight rough-looking men accompanied the cherrywood coffin up the stairs and into the church.

Over a thousand mourners packed the nave of St. Clement's, a massive stone church in the style of the basilicas, with an ornate, hand-carved ceiling and a curved half cylinder of boxed glass forming the backdrop to the apse. Standing in front of the altar was Father John McLaughlin, a former collegiate wrestler and friend of the McCains who had returned to St. Clement's from his new parish in Foxboro to say Joe's funeral Mass.

Father John said, "Please rise," and the weight of all those people unburdened the pews in a great *harrumph* and the sound of their knees clicking was like a myriad of crickets.

In his adult life Joe McCain was never a churchgoing man, but the nuns of St. Ann's had made a lasting impression on him. After he got shot in '88, the former altar boy developed a habit that intrigued his daughter-in-law. Maureen noticed that every morning when Joe walked the dog, or climbed into his car for the drive to the P.I. office, he would stop at a neighbor's house several doors down and stare up the driveway. One day Maureen just couldn't take it anymore, and when Joe and the dog returned to the house she met them at the bottom of the stairs. "What do you do up there?" she asked.

A sly Irish grin appeared on Joe's face. "Go look," he said.

Maureen left the porch and walked up the street and looked into the neighbor's driveway. At the top of the pitch was a statue of the Virgin Mary encased in an upright bathtub and surrounded by little yellow flowers. Maureen turned and walked back to where her father-in-law had unleashed the dog and shooed him into the house.

"I sit and pray to Mary and give thanks that I'm still here, and for my grandchildren and Helen and all of you," Joe said. "I'm not even supposed to be alive. Every day since the shooting has been a 'gravy day.' "

Halfway through his father's funeral, Joey got up from the front pew, made the sign of the cross as he passed the tabernacle, and mounted the altar. Dressed in a kilt, high stockings, and his long-sleeved, blue Somerville P.D. uniform shirt, young Joe stood at the lectern and removed a piece of folded paper from his pocket. He read:

"This is a fitting tribute to my father, a packed church, considering that if today were any of your funerals and it was a beautiful day, he wouldn't have come or he would have been late because he would have been chasing the little white ball around. It's what he loved doing most.

"When Maureen and I renewed our wedding vows after ten years of marriage in this church with Father John, in front of my family and Maureen's family, there was one person who was not here that day. Can anyone guess who it was? He was playing at Charles River. He had told us a month before that he wouldn't be at the church because it was 'the most important tournament of the year.' We thought he was kidding; we should have known better."

The congregation laughed, their feet stirred, and then they settled down again. At the rostrum, Joey turned the wrinkled piece of paper over.

"I would like to read a poem by William Canton that I think describes my father best.

Heroes

For you who love heroic things
In summer dream or winter's tale
I tell of warriors, saints and kings
In scarlet, sackcloth, glittering mail
And helmets peaked with iron wings

They beat down wrong, they strove for right
In ringing fields, on grappled ships
Singing, they flung into the fight

They fell with triumph on their lips
And in their eyes a glorious light

That light still gleams from far away
Their brave song greets us like a cheer
We fight the same fight as they
Right against wrong, we, now and here
They, in their fashion yesterday.

Here Joey began to falter, and Brian O'Donovan, sitting right in front of him among the pallbearers, mouthed, "You're doing good. Stay strong." And Joey continued, his voice breaking over the church.

"I chose that poem because for many of us in this room, Joe McCain was our hero. I say our hero because although I was his only son, big Joe had many sons."

At this, Stew Henry dropped his face into his hands, Mark Lemieux rubbed his eye sockets, and the sound of men weeping came from several places among the congregation.

"Those men young and old who came to him in time of trouble or confusion or indecision. His door was never closed. The question that was asked most often was 'Joe, what should I do?' You always left with an answer, whether you liked it or not. In the end, it was usually right.

"My father was from the greatest generation to ever live. He understood what duty, honor, and courage meant. He was courageous, he had faith, he was, in the words of a close friend, 'the most honest man I ever met.' He was proud and unbending when he knew he was right. He taught many of us do what was right regardless of the consequences. He taught us to live every day as if it were our last and to be thankful for each day.

"In closing:

"When you tee up a ball and hit it straight up the fairway, remember the old man.

"When you walk down a fairway in the bright sunshine or as he would in the pouring rain, remember Joe McCain.

"When you scratch your dog's ears while watching television, remember Joe McCain.

"When you tee up a ball and hit it two fairways over, remember Joe McCain.

"When you have a one-foot putt and hit it six inches short, remember what the old man would have said: 'You gotta hit the ball, Mary.'

"When you sip a cold beer or a good Scotch with a close friend, think of 'the big guy.'

"When you are afraid because you have to do something you know in your heart is right, think of Joe McCain, he'll give you the strength.

"When you think all is lost and there is no answer to your problem, look to the heavens and think of my father, he may give you an answer.

"Live every day to the fullest, remember the love he had for all his friends, remember his inspiration, remember his integrity, but most of all, remember the love he had for life, the joy he brought to all of us, his infectious laugh and his smile."

Joey folded up his paper and left the altar to an encompassing silence. A short while later, Father John dismissed the congregation and then a friend of Joey's named Cheryl Arruda sang "Amazing Grace" from the choir loft and the pallbearers walked abreast of Joe's coffin as it rolled down the aisle. The doors to St. Clement's were thrust open on the first note of the second chorus and Arruda's sweet clear voice was joined by the piping of the Gaelic Column lined up on the sidewalk.

Content, as he always had been, to loiter on the sidelines, Joe's old partner Jack Crowley was surprised to see Mark Cronin standing in front of him when he and his wife, Ellen, rose from their pew. The taciturn old Met shook Crowley's hand and then struggled to compose himself, looking down at the tessellated floor of the church.

"The lion is dead," said Cronin.

Helen and Maureen and the three grandchildren followed the coffin outside, blinking in the sunlight, and waited in one of Doherty's gleaming black limousines as the congregation poured out of the church; Maureen McCain had never seen so many cops in her life, their grim, honest faces made that much more poignant by a single member of the Outlaws motorcycle gang, dressed in his colors, there to pay his respects.

Maureen watched the Seghezzis go by, then Leo Papile walked past the limo, clutching his brow. On an impulse Maureen got out of the car and embraced him. "How you doing, Leo?" she asked.

His forearms crossed over Maureen's upper back, the retired Met cop squeezed her tight. "I'm okay, kid," he said.

They separated, and Maureen turned to open the limousine door. But Leo had not yet followed Al and Mary Seghezzi back to their car. He stood leaning against the elongated rear quarter of the limo, his hands jammed into his trouser pockets, staring at his shoe tops. While the other mourners streamed past on all sides, Maureen felt like she and Leo were alone in some remote location despite the throng that crowded Harvard Street.

Leo turned to profile, his face strained but his voice calm and quiet. "My friend is gone," he said, and he leaned up and walked away.

With the hearse leading the procession, a line of cars a mile long began rolling toward the cemetery. They crossed beneath Route 93 along the tidal estuary in Medford, passed the Wellington T station and turned onto 16 East, alongside the Everett gasworks and the old Charleston Chew building hard by the railroad tracks.

When they reached Holy Cross Cemetery, the McCains disembarked from the limousine and watched as car after car drove through the gates. A wind had come up, and by the time the funeral director had arranged Joe's coffin on the canvas straps over the grave, and Father John stood opposite the headstone with his vestments flapping, a large group of mourners encircled the plot. Helen and Joey and Maureen and the children were off to one side, and Brian O'Donovan stood near them as three white-gloved state policemen fired a trio of synchronized volleys into the air.

Before the sharp, sudden noise had died away, Cheryl Arruda's brother Scott and a former Met cop and trumpeter named Jimmy Cullinane played "Taps" from one end of the cemetery to the other, the notes echoing back and forth in plaintive succession.

As the reality of Joe's death fixed itself in his heart, Brian O'Donovan felt his jaw convulsing, and then the tears came. It was uncomfortable for him to show such a depth of emotion, in part because his own father was just a few feet away and here he was crying over the death of a man that wasn't even a relation. But Jim O'Donovan walked over and wrapped his arms around his son and held him like he had when Brian was a child.

"It's all right," he said.

Just as Father John reached the lines "ashes to ashes, dust to dust," an armada of clouds passed overhead and the wind increased, stiffening the flags and making them crackle all at once across the cemetery.

Right at that moment Leo Papile, who had been crying and trembling, yelled out "Joe!" and several good-sized men rushed forward and caught him before he fell. In the midst of his own grief, Brian O'Donovan remembered thinking how sad and beautiful it was that someone could love a man that much, and how Leo wouldn't be around for long now that Joe McCain was dead.

THIRTY-ONE

The Punisher

*It was like I was a messenger, and someone was sending me messages
and I don't know why. Why was I, I want to say, lucky,
in a position to make the arrests that I did? Why me?*
—JOE McCAIN, SR., SHORTLY BEFORE HE DIED

M ARK DONAHUE IS WEARING HIS FULL DRESS police uniform as we walk along the plush main hallway of the Alexandria
Hilton, following Joey and Maureen McCain and their three kids and
Helen McCain and one of big Joe's old partners, retired Boston police
detective Jack Crowley and his wife, Ellen. Mark and I and one of his
friends from the Salem P.D., Officer Jonathan Hoellrich, have flown
down to Washington, D.C., to participate in the twenty-second annual
National Peace Officers Memorial Service, held on the lawn behind the
U.S. Capitol. Thanks to Joe Jr.'s tenacity and the work of their family
lawyer, Joe Doyle, fifteen years after he was shot in that crummy Hyde
Park tenement, big Joe's name will be inscribed on the National Law
Enforcement Officers Memorial in Judiciary Square, dedicated to peace
officers killed in the line of duty.

In the hotel ballroom two women from the Fraternal Order of Police
Auxiliary issue our security badges, and then we all queue up on the
walkway for the bus ride to the Capitol. We're surrounded by the survivors of those who were killed or, like Joe McCain, died of their
wounds in the past year: a tall, gaunt man from Tennessee wearing a
photo badge of a young police officer smiling in his motorcycle jacket; a

pretty young Hispanic woman clutching the hands of her five-year-old daughter and two-year-old son; and a whole squad of police officers from Sterling Heights, Michigan, including a guy big enough to play in the NFL wearing pants a couple of shades lighter than the rest—too large to fit. Seeing them all reminds me that there is indeed evil in the world and that the vast majority of cops shoulder a fair amount of risk every time they report to work.

On the bus I'm sitting next to eleven-year-old Joseph McCain. He and his brothers are attired in colorful Hawaiian shirts and pressed dungarees, each of them wearing a survivor's tag and one of their grandfather's detective badges on a beaded chain around his neck. The boys all love their "Papa," and eighteen months after his death are still struggling with the fact that the big man with the crinkled blue eyes and white hair is gone for good. But the McCain kids are also voracious pack rats and are hounding every peace officer in sight for a patch or a pin, competing to see who can accumulate the largest and most varied collection. They are far from shy, and not even the hard-eyed state troopers can deter them from asking; Liam's strategy with an Oklahoma highway patrolman who says he has nothing to trade is to ask the tall, well-built fellow if he'll pop one of his buttons off. The husky young Oklahoman smiles and declines and then gazes out the bus window, lost in his own thoughts.

The McCain children have been treated to a guided tour of the FBI Academy in Quantico, Virginia, and young Joseph tells me that he met plenty of other kids there. "One boy told me that his dad died when he was riding a police horse and tried to light a match and the horse went crazy and ran away and he hit his head on a barn," says Joseph, who wears his hair in a waxed crew cut and has those McCain blue eyes above a smattering of freckles. "Another kid's dad was moving equipment at the police station and there was gas and he blew up. Another man was writing a ticket for his friend and because he was a nice guy he let his friend sit next to him in the police car but the guy had been drinking and he grabbed the policeman's gun and shot him with it."

Joseph forms a pistol with his right hand, putting his index finger up to his head. "Right here," he says. "In the temple."

Our bus is being escorted by a police motorcade, and at every crossroad patrol cars block traffic and we go speeding along the Belt-way, unimpeded. There are thirty motorcycles paired in a long line be-hind us, and as Joseph and I crane our necks to watch them downshift into a turn, the eleven-year-old tells me of a dream he once had. "I was sleeping on the futon upstairs, and in the dream I was sleeping on the futon just like I really was and my papa walked into the room and I stood up and hugged him and then—*poof*—my eyes opened and the room was empty and I said 'Ohh.' "

The motorcade drives past the Washington Monument and along-side the Mall and pulls up at the Capitol with ten police cruisers and all those motorcycles streaming in behind. Out the window we can see po-lice officers and their families from jurisdictions around the country heading for the sea of chairs arranged on the Capitol lawn. There are tall cops, stubby, red-eared cops, muscle-bound cops, gray-haired cops, cops in ascots and leather jackets, brown uniforms and blue, tiger suits, jumpsuits, female troopers in knee-high glossy boots, and sheriffs from Alabama who haven't taken a fitness test since Jimmy Carter was president.

Getting off the bus, Maureen tells young Joseph to zip up his fly. "I said that to my father-in-law once and he said, 'Dead men don't fall out open windows,' " Maureen tells me, with a laugh.

A six-foot hurricane fence encircles the lawn, notched with three se-curity checkpoints and guarded by the Capitol Police and the U.S. Bor-der Patrol. High up on the Capitol roof I can make out half a dozen snipers, their binoculars glinting in the sunlight. President Bush is ex-pected and security is tight, although I can't help noticing that there are hundreds of cops and almost all of them have guns. It occurs to me that the government must have enormous faith in the police chiefs of this country. The chiefs supervise these cops and grant them their powers, including the right to carry a weapon in the vicinity of the president.

A heavy downpour was expected, but so far the wind has staved off the clouds and there's blue sky overhead, scented with flowering trees. It's the sort of May afternoon that, when the McCains were young, Helen, with her hair newly marcelled, and Joe, after putting on a neat-looking sport coat, would've taken the roof down on the Cadillac and gone for a drive up through Lynn and Salem.

In the shadow of the Rotunda, three sections of folding chairs are arranged in a crescent facing the gigantic temporary stage. Beside me Jack Crowley is wearing a rose-colored Palm Beach sport jacket and fiddling with the zoom lens on his camera. The former Boston detective, a broad, white-haired man with a cropped white beard, retired three years ago after thirty-eight years on the job. Big Joe called Crowley the best police photographer in the business and spent many evenings with him and Joe Doyle on the ground floor of their building at 73 Tremont Street in Boston, at the Fatted Calf.

The site of the old Waldorf restaurant, the Fatted Calf had a steer's head etched into the frosted glass of the windows facing Tremont, and walls paneled in the original gleaming mahogany of its former tenants. One night Jack Crowley and Joe McCain were having a few drinks after work, making little note of a diner at a table beside them as the man polished off several beers, a huge sirloin steak with all the trimmings, a fine dessert, and two or three glasses of liqueur. When his bill arrived, the man could be seen writing a lengthy message on the back of the slip.

The manager of the Fatted Calf was a diminutive fellow named Sy, with a few long strands of hair combed over his balding pate. When the waiter retrieved the solo diner's check and carried it over to Sy, the manager turned and stalked across the barroom. Hailing McCain and Crowley, who were regulars, he shoved the check under the detectives' noses, and they read the man's note:

> *Due to circumstances beyond my control, at this time I am unable to pay for the wonderful dinner that you have provided for me. I render my deepest apologies, and can only hope that you will forgive my transgression.*

"What the hell is that?" Sy asked.

"I think it's called a 'business loss,' " said Crowley, sending McCain into paroxysms of laughter.

The little bar manager began sputtering. "Aren't you going to arrest him?" asked Sy.

"We're not gonna lug a guy just because he can't pay for dinner," said McCain.

* * *

SUDDENLY A VOICE BREAKS OVER the loudspeaker, asking all uniformed police officers to form an honor cordon from the middle security checkpoint to the phalanx of chairs right in front of the stage, so the immediate families of the slain officers can be seated. Helen McCain is part of this group, escorted by Joe Jr. in his Somerville Police uniform.

The cordon of saluting officers divides the great lawn of the Capitol, with the survivors walking in silence between them, wives and mothers and husbands and sons, old men in wheelchairs pushed by New Jersey state troopers and babies in prams manned by deputy sheriffs from Ohio. After a while I see Helen and Joey walk past, but the survivors keep coming and coming, with the clean white spike of the Washington Monument looming in the distance. It's the magnitude of the silence and the sheer number of survivors that finally gets to me, as my sinuses fill up and a line from T. S. Eliot's "The Waste Land" pops into my head: "I had not thought death had undone so many."

When everyone is seated, the national chaplain of the Grand Lodge of the Fraternal Order of Police says the invocation, and a female police officer from Tucson, Arizona, sings the National Anthem. Then a recording of "Hail to the Chief" bursts over the sound system and every cop within a half mile snaps to attention. Wearing a dark blue suit, taller than he appears on television, President George W. Bush descends the stairs of the Capitol, past the color guards from various jurisdictions and a long line of Capitol Police frozen in salute.

We all stand up amidst the applause and whistles and cheers, beating our hands together until they're raw. Bush settles at the podium, grins for a moment, and gives that presidential wave: a swift half arc from the center of his chest downward to five o'clock as the music dies away.

President Bush is not a great public speaker, and his staff could use an upgrade in the speechwriting department. He tends to run words together and uses a peculiar halting cadence that has the unfortunate effect of making him appear to be trying to sound smarter than he is. But when he utters the words "The death of a peace officer is a reminder that peace can be fragile," it strikes me that George W. Bush is a man who lacks any doubt.

On the dais behind the president are Attorney General John Ashcroft, FBI Director Robert Mueller, the secretaries of Labor and the Interior, and several congressmen and congresswomen. "You can tell it's an election year," says Mark Donahue, sitting to my left.

Jonathan Hoellrich is on my right, wearing a pin-striped suit, sunglasses, and his police badge with a black mourning band around it. He's twenty-eight years old, an average-sized guy in a profession dominated by giant men. I have heard that Hoellrich survives—even flourishes—on the strength of his king-sized wit.

"I never voted for him, but I gotta admit, George W. has balls," I tell Hoellrich. "He's done all the things that Clinton should have done and didn't."

"Except for the one thing that Clinton shouldn't have done and did," Hoellrich says. "But this is fantastic. We're close enough to be in a scrum with Ashcroft."

Also onstage are private-sector boosters of the event, heavy-hitting law enforcement supporters, including the president of Miller Brewing Company, who gets a rousing ovation from the cops, record company mogul Tommy Mottola in what looks like a pair of Sam Giancana's sunglasses, and the pop singer Marc Anthony. In a bizarre piece of theater, the Latin heartthrob rises to sing a number after George Bush sits down. Marc Anthony is a little guy in black slacks and T-shirt, and when the prerecorded introduction to his hit "You Sang to Me" begins, he stands with the microphone, listening through his earpiece and tapping his foot. Behind him, Ashcroft and Bush and the rest of the suits are unsmiling and motionless, looking like members of the Soviet Politburo.

"This is kinda weird," says Hoellrich.

"It's like when JFK would have Sinatra show up," I tell him. "Bring the mob guys in, entertain, and get 'em out."

After Marc Anthony sits down amidst polite applause from George Bush's cabinet, there's a break in the action while each of the surviving parents and spouses is allowed to pose for a photograph with the president. Dozens of press corps members close in, their cameras whirring like locusts, and we're left to kill an hour in the sun.

"If I had a sausage cart I'd make a fortune," says Hoellrich.

After his photo op, Bush departs, and the P.A. announcer states that the Roll Call of Heroes will begin. Three hundred and seventy-seven officers from thirty-four states, several federal agencies, and Puerto Rico were killed on the job last year. Texas has suffered the loss of eighteen cops, while California, South Carolina, and New York have each lost ten. There were two in Massachusetts: Joe McCain and Lawrence Michael Jupin, a patrolman from the Westminster Police Department who was shot by a fleeing suspect in May 1999, lingered in a coma, and died on November 29, 2002.

As each name is called, the family approaches the podium where the surviving parent or spouse affixes a rose to a star-shaped wreath and is handed a medal commemorating the fallen officer. It's almost like a graduation ceremony, only more solemn; no caps thrown in the air, no cheers or applause, only the breeze ruffling the trees on the Mall and the distant growl of commercial airplanes.

Back in the last row, Donahue and Hoellrich and the Crowleys and Maureen and the kids and I stand up when Massachusetts is announced. With Joe Jr. on one arm and a large, blue-jacketed trooper from the Mass. State Police on the other, Helen McCain approaches the podium when her late husband's name is called. She's wearing a light green pantsuit and has had her hair done for the occasion. When the police officer hands her Joe's medal and Joe Jr. and the state trooper return his salute, Helen drops her gaze for a moment and is led away, wobbling on her bad knees.

Bagpipers from several police emerald societies are playing on the lawn adjacent to the stage, the keening of their music punctuated by the boom and rattle of the drummers. Derived from Near Eastern hornpipes and traced to fourteenth-century Scotland, the bagpipes have long been used to celebrate the bardic tradition of *brosnachadh*—the praise of warriors and chieftains and lament for their passing.

In a few minutes Joe Jr. and Helen rendezvous with our group by one of the checkpoints, and Joe Doyle and his daughter Jessica walk out from beneath a giant shade tree and join us. The curly-haired attorney settled a big case at the eleventh hour back in Boston and flew down just in time to make the ceremony. He kisses the women and shakes hands all around, pausing to admire Joe's medal. It's inscribed "Fraternal

Order of Police Supreme Sacrifice Medal of Honor," arranged with a blue-and-gold ribbon in a crushed velvet box. No doubt it will take its place on a shelf filled with Joe's decorations back in Helen's TV den in Somerville.

Joe Doyle has never seen the National Law Enforcement Officers Memorial, which is just a few blocks away, and we decide to walk over while Helen and the children and the Crowleys hail a cab to take them back to the hotel. Doyle has known Jack Crowley for over thirty years and calls out to him from the sidewalk when the taxi arrives.

"Be careful, Jack," says Doyle, resurrecting an old office joke. "Watch out for that guy."

"Who?" Crowley asks, laughing. "Arnold Sphincter?"

"Yeah," says Doyle. "Don't get rear-ended by Arnold Sphincter."

"Don't worry. I won't," Crowley says, laughing harder now. He waits until the ladies are seated and then makes an up-yours gesture toward Doyle, who roars as Crowley shuts himself inside and the taxi zooms off.

The National Law Enforcement Officers Memorial, dedicated by the first President Bush in 1991, is located on the 400 block of E Street NW. It's a grassy site dominated by two "pathways of remembrance" made from blue-gray marble engraved with the names of 14,000 officers killed on the job dating back to 1794. Contained inside the park is a second ring of marble with a smaller circumference, forming a kind of bench where visitors can sit and contemplate the many names. When we arrive, hundreds of people are moving in both directions inside the circle, past an inscription from Tacitus: IN VALOR THERE IS HOPE.

There are a large number of police officers, as well as senior citizens, young women, men in business suits, and kids of every size, race, and description. On this day every year the Capitol Police allow visitors to leave mementos on the site. Photographs and prayer cards and bunches of flowers are crowded against the berm. While we walk along searching for "Joseph E. McCain," a black girl about ten years old, thin and very tall for her age, stands in the open center of the memorial in a light blue dress, festooned with white ribbons. I can tell by the look on her face that the name of her older brother or her father has gone up on the wall today, and I want to go over and hug the kid.

Earlier today, Helen McCain and the Crowleys visited the memorial, and we find Joe's prayer card and a Met patch taped up beside his name. Everyone crowds around for a moment, and Joe Doyle squats on his heels, running his fingertips over the one-inch letters carved into the rock. "There he is," says Doyle, with the trace of a smile.

Two hulking state troopers from New Jersey stoop over me when I attempt to make a rubbing of Joe's name with a pen and a page from my notebook. They hand me a slip of paper imprinted with "National Law Enforcement Officers Memorial" in blue letters, along with the stub of a pencil. "Sir, try this," says one of the policemen, tipping his cap. "It works much better."

When I turn around, Joe Jr. and Donahue and Hoellrich are a little ways off, talking to some other cops. Joe Doyle is seated on the opposite bench, his suit jacket removed and thrown over his arm, ankles crossed. The afternoon has grown hot, and he pats his brow with his sleeve and gazes into the distance, a wistful look on his face. No doubt the gentleman from Milton is engaged in some reverie of Joe McCain, a mental motion picture of all the bad guys they investigated, indicted, and put away; all the Scotch they drank, all the practical jokes and the laughs, and all the indelible characters they knew in the dusty corridors of long ago. At that moment, looking at Doyle, I understand that no one who really knew Joseph Elmer McCain ever regretted a minute of it. That despite the bad times and the grief—and a life as big as Joe's brought as much sorrow as triumph—all of Joe's many friends considered themselves lucky.

Now that the serious part of the day is over, it's time to get down to the real tribute. A few blocks away, the Fraternal Order of Police has cordoned off the street in front of their building and is about to crank up the party. En route we pass through a bazaar of cop paraphernalia, and Mark Donahue and I pick up some trinkets for our kids. Hanging from one of the racks is a T-shirt that depicts a policeman holding a can that says "Whoop Ass" with the caption "Don't Make Me Open This."

Strolling past the booths, Donahue reminds me that we're in D.C. to party for Joe McCain, not to bury him. "That bullet saved his life," Donahue says. "He was fifty-eight years old and way up over three hundred pounds. His heart never would've lasted."

As a result of his wounds, big Joe changed his diet, quit drinking, and took up golf with a vengeance. He even hired a personal trainer to help him lose weight. "We had him for thirteen more years," says Donahue, as we turn into the block party. "So let's get some beers."

Beneath a giant white tent anchored by plastic barrels filled with concrete, four hundred cops are crowded around a makeshift bar constructed of sawhorses and planks. Although most are in plainclothes, nearly every one of them is wearing his badge and a gun, their voices rising in a great din.

"Smell it?" asks Donahue.

"What?" I ask.

"All the testosterone."

Many of the cops are white guys over six feet tall, and there are a lot of ex-military, especially jarheads. But there are a significant number of blacks, every shade of brown, Amerasian sheriffs from the desert, and Latinas in tight jeans packing .38s. Music is blaring from a stage at one end of the block, and the stench of motorcycle exhaust fills the air as more and more partygoers arrive by the moment.

Security is lax, almost nonexistent. Each of the dozen or so bartenders—all of them cops—is wearing a T-shirt that says "Staff" and carrying a sidearm. But there's no perimeter, and no metal detectors—not that they would do much good. With all that is going on these days, I have the strange feeling that this is both the safest and the most dangerous place in the entire country.

"It's like the wild, wild west," I say to Hoellrich.

He stands with his hands on his hips, surveying the crowd. "I'd rather finger-bang my own ass than hang around a convention with a bunch of cops," he says.

Hoellrich sure is a funny bastard, and Donahue pays his buddy from the Salem P.D. the ultimate compliment when he laughs into his beer and says, "Joe would've liked you."

Soon we are pouring the caramel-colored truth serum down our throats and making a passel of new best friends. Though it's early in the evening, the sky has darkened and the first drops of rain begin pattering against the tent. Everyone on the outside moves under the roof while an enormous Arkansas sheriff bellows from the midst of the throng. He's the size of a professional wrestler, barrel-chested and bald-headed, and has his arms around two lesser titans: a dreadlocked undercover cop with gigantic biceps and another large black dude wearing a "Detroit Police" T-shirt. The sheriff from Arkansas is wearing a pistol the size of my forearm and downing cans of Miller like it's nobody's business.

Jonathan Hoellrich, all five feet nine and 160 pounds of him, says, "Watch this," and hands me his drink. Approaching the three swaying giants, Hoellrich flings his arms out wide and proclaims in a loud voice, "I want to fight all three of you guys, right here, right now."

For a moment the big sheriff is stymied, his eyes bulging, a tiny upturned baseball cap riding the crown of his head like a yarmulke. Hoellrich snorts through one nostril and raises his hand in a bullshit kung fu pose. "I'll tear you apart," he says.

The sheriff roars with laughter, spraying the crowd around him with a mouthful of beer foam. He drops the Rastafarian cop and reaches out to grab Hoellrich by the neck, crushing him in a bear hug. "Aaaarggh," he says. "I like you."

Hoellrich comes sauntering back to us. "He's lucky I didn't kick his ass," he says.

The rain has increased, and brown water awash with flotsam is rushing along the sidewalk. Joe Jr. is nearby, talking with Dave Moseley, a Metropolitan cop from D.C. They're both members of the Renegade Pigs, a contingent of whom, including Joey, have ridden their Harleys down to the memorial from New York City. Stocky, bearded, and mustachioed, Joe Jr. and his buddy have shed their badges and guns and are drinking beer with one foot on the curbstone and the other in the gutter.

"It's like Calcutta," says Joey, watching the water stream by. He squats over the torrent and pantomimes taking a shit and then a drink. "Soup, anyone?"

McCain and Moseley share the opinion that real cops understand and recognize one another and don't have to advertise what they do for a living. Joey eyes the pretty boys in the crowd with the sleeves rolled up on their polo shirts and their badges hanging out and says, "I don't know if you guys realize it or not, but there's a shitload of cops around here."

Moseley and Hoellrich and Donahue snort into their beers while

Joey laughs and spits into the gutter. The weather has driven more par-tyers under the tent, and we get squeezed onto the sidewalk, bare-headed, no umbrellas, the rain diluting our drinks. In a moment of inspiration, Hoellrich unfastens the two bottom cords of a Miller Lite banner tied to the fence and lifts it up to form a shelter-half. Soon five more cops duck beneath Jonathan's invention, the water slanting off to each side.

"Now *that's* leadership," says Hoellrich, who's planning to take the sergeant's exam next month. "If I was in 'Nam, I woulda made a tent out of a matchstick." He peers out at the crowd. "Hey, where's all the hot prosecutors?"

Nearby is a short, stocky guy with a Jersey accent. "You look like a fed," he says to me.

Because I'm trim and have short hair and don't say much, everyone thinks I'm with the FBI. But really I'm just an old-time newsie, a pad and pen stuck away in my pocket, eavesdropping on all the conversa-tions swirling around me. Everybody's drunk and armed to the teeth, a scene right out of the 1850s, and there hasn't been a scoop like this since the lords of the inkwell chased Pinkerton and his men as they pur-sued the Wild Bunch across the Texas Panhandle. I should be wearing a bowler hat and carrying Apache charms.

The guy from Jersey is a forty-one-year-old detective with the Newark P.D. named Bobby Clark, and he's certain that I taught a course he took in New York City called "High Intensity Drug Trafficking," which is offered through the FBI Academy. "Your hair was darker, but it was you, all right," Bobby says. "The thin nose, the posture, every-thing."

I tell him that he's mistaken and he buys me a drink. He buys every-one a drink. His partner, Rueben Torres, is a muscular Puerto Rican kid with his hair combed straight back who proclaims himself "the best-looking cop in Jersey." The Newark guys are a couple of hot shits and they gain immediate acceptance in our corner; Rueben even tries to make time with Joe Doyle's daughter.

Donahue takes delight in pointing this out. "Lookit, Joe," he says.

"Gimme a fucking break," says Doyle, laughing.

The Newark guys are busy telling Donahue and Hoellrich that two cops ride in every patrol car in their jurisdiction, an example of largesse that amazes the New Hampshire cops but something the Jersey detectives insist is a necessity.

"Fucking killers out there," says Rueben. In the Vailsburg section of Newark, a small number of Russian mob types have managed to unseat a powerful chapter of the Bloods, a California-based gang made up of violent black kids.

"These guys are fucking *scared* of the Russians," says Rueben, noting that the Russians operate a string of chop shops in the South district, off Frelinghuysen. "They have no respect for anything."

Rueben and Bobby are also stuck on the notion of genuine cops versus fake cops. Bobby explains that real cops write letters to the chief asking for more typewriter ribbons, while the phony cops brag about gunfights they've been in.

"You wanna meet a real cop? I'll show you a real fuckin' cop," he says, jerking my elbow.

We hop across the narrow alley of rain and pass under the tent. Standing in a circle of other guys is a light-skinned black kid from Howard County, Maryland. He wears his hair in short, tight cornrows and shakes my hand and nods when Bobby introduces us.

In baggy jeans and an oversized windbreaker, Mark Taylor looks like a guy who hangs out on a corner somewhere, doing a little business, one of those urban account executives you'll find in every city in America. But he's an undercover narcotics cop, albeit a soft-spoken one, a humble man in a job that has often been filled by bigmouthed cowboys. Taylor explains that the marijuana and Ecstasy dealers in his neck of the woods are not particularly violent but are well-organized, and he and his partner, a tall, young, silent kid with darker skin, are making a ton of good pinches.

"You been in a drug raid yet?" Taylor asks me, flashing a smile. "It's a rush."

When Bobby the Newark cop and I return to our previous spot, he shakes his head, indicating a group of muscle-bound cops tricked out in their monogrammed golf shirts and nouveau high-and-tight haircuts. "I'd take that kid from Maryland over those guys anytime," he says, rounding out his vowels in a thick Jersey accent. "Don't ask me how I know, but he's a real cop. There are five hundred guys in here and about two dozen real cops and he's one of 'em."

Bobby says that a real cop goes to work every day realizing there's a possibility he may die on the job but doesn't sensationalize the danger of his profession or himself. He does the job for its own sake, and doesn't seek recognition or commendations. Sergeant Bobby Clark, who has made a thousand arrests in the past ten years, is describing someone he's never met: Joe McCain.

A few yards away, several guys from the Norfolk P.D. are affixing their departmental stickers on the proffered rear ends of some exotic dancers who have shown up at the party. A gang of cops has circled the bent-over strippers, hooting and whistling as each sticker is applied with greater flourish.

"They're getting Norfolk-ed," says Mark Donahue, his eyes turning sixes and sevens.

Jonathan Hoellrich runs over and juts out his butt and the other cops turn away in disgust. "Whattaya mean?" asks Hoellrich. "Look at me. I got a made-for-television ass."

It's getting late and we decide to head for a place called Harry's Bar. Mark Donahue, Hoellrich, Joe Doyle and Jessica, Joe McCain, Jr., Maureen, and I reach Harry's just as the waiters begin circulating for last call and we order a round of beers. The waiter comes back right away and slings the beers and several bowls of popcorn onto the table, and we raise our bottles to three kilted members of a police emerald society who are seated across the way. They are smoking cigarettes and a set of bagpipes is strewn over the table between them.

Doyle asks Joey how Helen is doing, and Maureen jumps in with a story about her feisty mother-in-law. On a recent Sunday morning, Helen McCain got dressed in her nicest outfit and headed out to church only to discover that a vandal had "keyed" the side of her car. Several deep gouges ran the length of the door panel, and Maureen raced outside when she heard the angry shouts of her mother-in-law.

"Look what this bastard did to my car," said Helen, shaking her cane at the damage.

Maureen patted Helen on the shoulder. "Maybe you should go pray for him, Ma," she said.

"Yeah, I'll pray for him," said Helen, climbing into the car. "Pray that his fucking arm falls off."

Doyle laughs so hard at this story that he shuts his eyes and his face turns a deep crimson while his eyelids go white. We're all laughing and pounding our beer bottles on the tabletop, and Donahue says to Doyle, "Hey, Joe. Tell us the quintessential Joe McCain story."

The laughter dies away, although an occasional titter erupts here and there. Wiping his eyes on his sleeve, Doyle pauses to straighten out his cuffs and then gazes at us with that jury box stare. "The quintessential Joe McCain story," he says. "All right. Let me think for a minute."

There are hundreds to pick from. But after swallowing a mouthful of beer, Doyle replaces the bottle on his coaster and raises a forefinger. "I've got it," he says.

It was after Joe had retired and was spending part of every year at the McCains' condo in Deerfield Beach, Florida. One January morning he had to catch a 7:00 A.M. flight out of Logan Airport and rose at five to let his dog, Jack, out of the house. At the same time that Joe Jr. ran downstairs to start his father's car, a series of high-pitched noises arose from the backyard, what sounded like a woman being attacked.

Rushing halfway up the driveway, Joey caught a glimpse of Jack, shaking his head to and fro with another, smaller animal caught between his jaws. It was a skunk and Joe Jr. sprinted in the other direction just as his father burst into the backyard shouting, "Jack, Jack, no," and the sharp, sudden stink of the skunk penetrated the morning air.

Jack dropped the skunk and bolted halfway around the house, leaped onto the front porch and shot into the foyer. Roused from sleep, Maureen was descending the stairs when she head big Joe say, "Let the dog in. He might be hurt. Let him in."

Just then the smell reached Maureen, and she slammed the door in Jack's face and locked it. No way was she letting Jack inside their apartment after he'd been doused with skunk spray.

Big Joe coaxed the dog out of the foyer and up the driveway and in the back door. The skunk had crawled off beneath the porch to die. After shooing Jack into the pantry, Joe glanced up at the clock—he had about twenty minutes to clean up and catch his flight. He called for a taxi, jumped in the shower, and had changed his clothes just as the cab pulled up in front of the house.

Grabbing his suitcase by the front door, Joe thundered down the stairs and climbed into the taxi, instructing the driver to head for Logan. "Can you smell anything?" asked Joe.

"No," the cabbie said.

Fifty feet down the road, the driver leaned over and opened both windows. "Now that you mention it . . ."

Joe arrived at his terminal in the frozen semidarkness and hailed a state trooper he knew. As they walked toward the gate, out of the corner of his eye Joe noticed the trooper sniffing the air. And some of the folks passing by were stopping short and asking each other, "What's that smell?"

Big Joe hurried on.

When he arrived at the gate, he learned the plane was full and ready to depart. Joe McCain was the last passenger onboard, and as he squeezed his bulk down the aisle and located his seat in the back of the plane, a flight attendant asked no one in particular "What is that *smell*?"

"It's me," said Joe.

The woman laughed, thinking that he was kidding, and went up the aisle looking for the source of her complaint. The plane was loaded with sunbirds, and Joe's assigned seat was next to a guy who must have weighed four hundred pounds, his fat spilling over the armrests. A large man himself, Joe wedged himself in beside the man and reached up to unscrew the little valve that controlled the overhead fan, thinking it might help dispel the odor.

But he only managed to spread the smell throughout the plane, and moments later passengers up both sides of the aisle were looking around and expressing their intense displeasure. Joe raised his eyebrows toward the fat man sitting beside him and shrugged his shoulders, as if to say, "Who knew?"

Our laughter rings out across Harry's Bar, and I'm so taken with Joe Doyle's story that I fall off my chair and Donahue bats me over the head with the popcorn bowl. "That was Joe," says Doyle. "The bull in the china shop."

The waiter tells us that it's time to go. As we rise from our chairs, the kilted bagpiper notices Joe Jr.'s survivor's tag and they start talking while the other revelers begin making for the exits. Joey tells the piper that he plays drums in the Boston Gaelic Column and that his father has been enshrined on the memorial today.

"Can I play something for you?" the piper asks.

Sure, says Joey.

The gray-haired cop stubs out his cigarette and takes up the bagpipes. He tucks the bag under his arm, moistens the tip of the blowstick and spreads the drone pipes across his left shoulder. As soon as the piper inflates his bag and utters the first note, cops who had been heading for the door pull an about-face, grope on tabletops for that last, abandoned beer, and then crowd around with their glasses raised.

The wail of the bagpipes fills the bar to the rafters as the piper hits the grace notes segueing from "The Wild Colonial Boy" to "Amazing Grace." His tone goes lower, the pipes somewhat quieter, and it occurs to me that a piece of Joe McCain has been left on the lawn of the U.S. Capitol, and a part of him will forever reside in Judiciary Square, but the lion's share of the man can be found here, in the late night stench of Harry's Bar. I glance around at the people who loved him—Joey and Maureen, Mark, Joe Doyle and his young daughter—all transfixed by the music, their expressions a mingling of amusement and regret as they praise the great warrior and lament his passing.

The saga of Joe McCain reminds me that, now more than ever, we need heroes. We're just looking for them in the wrong places. If you're searching for a man or a woman made from the stuff they used in World War II, or at the Chosin Reservoir in Korea, or out on the paddies of Vietnam—if it's the genuine article you're after—forget about Major League Baseball or the local cinema. Ballparks and movie theaters produce entertainers, not heroes. So if you're stuck for a name, pick up the Quincy phone book and give Joe Doyle a call. He'll give you the address of a little park in Washington, D.C., and you can take a walk through. If you really want heroes and you've got the time to go looking, you'll certainly find some in there.

ACKNOWLEDGMENTS

WHEN I BEGAN working on this project and was searching for a way to take hold of Joe McCain's saga, I received a letter from a woman named Marcy Richardson, who worked for my late father, Jim Atkinson, in the 1970s and 1980s. Her memories of my dad, who ran a small insurance agency here in our hometown, were vivid: "Every May first, your very distinguished father would arrive at the office in his perfectly groomed suit and tie (he reminded me of Mr. French on the original *Family Affair*) and announce, 'Hooray, hooray, the first of May, outdoor screwing starts today.' He loved children, loved life, and loved good food. I have many stories to share about your dad, but here's just one. It's 4:30 on a Friday and the office is winding down for the weekend. My husband, Mike, plans to pick me up at 5:00 so we can head into Boston for a wedding. I have brought my formal dress with me so I can dress at work and save time. I unzip the garment bag and remove the dress. As I give it the 'once-over' before putting it on, I am horrified. I never hemmed the dress. The bottom is jagged and crooked and I am freaking out. It's 4:40 P.M. and I am wearing the dress, standing on my desk, and your father is stapling the hem of the dress as I slowly turn. . . .

"Back then, the cast of characters included Mike the Italian cop, who stopped to flirt with Louise Carney; Gerry the Irish cop, who shared the local news with your dad; Dick—I can't remember his last name— owned a lot of commercial and residential real estate in the area. He never made a move without consulting your dad. Smith Williams was a retired attorney in his seventies who dressed like Mark Twain, was well read, and had traveled the world and enjoyed eating snake meat. He would tip his hat when he arrived and left. Your uncle John, who your father adored, visited often. Jim saw him as the 'swinging bachelor,' and your father's face would just beam when John stopped by. One of your father's clients, a man named Roger, was arrested for killing his girl-friend. He was hauled off to jail and allowed one phone call. He called your father and canceled his auto insurance. Shorty DeGaspe (who was a town worker with a few missing fingers and the shortest man I've ever seen) always checked in during rain and snow—I think he had some-thing to do with cleaning out the storm drains—and your father always treated him with great respect. From your dad, I learned a lot from this seemingly simple gesture. There is nobility in all work and always ac-knowledge a job well done. . . ."

When I was a kid, I knew people looked up to my dad, and when we walked down the street together, I felt like a king. Reading Marcy Richardson's letter, it occurred to me that by writing about big Joe Mc-Cain, I was also paying homage to my own father and my mother, Lois, as well as an entire generation, reared during the Depression, that per-ceived duty and sacrifice and integrity as facets of the human condition and lived up to those responsibilities with a sense of humor and per-sonal style. These Americans knew how to live, and we owe them all a great debt.

A lot of people cut from that same cloth helped get this story into print. My agent, Peter McGuigan of Sanford Greenburger, is patient, knowledgeable, and works tirelessly on my behalf. Pete Fornatale, who bought this book for Crown, continued to champion it even after going to work someplace else. My editor, Caroline Sincerbeaux, offered innu-merable keen-eyed suggestions. Helen McCain, Joe McCain, Jr., Mau-reen McCain, and their kids, Joseph, Liam, and Lucas, treated me like a member of their family and provided heaps of great information and insight. Mark Donahue and his wife, Maureen, and their children, Connor and Julia, helped shape this book from start to finish. I could not have done it without them.

All of big Joe's friends came through in the clutch, as they always have: Metropolitan District Police assistant superintendent Al Seghezzi (ret.) and his wife, Mary; Mass. State Police Lieutenant Gene Kee and his wife, Ellen; Mass. State Police Major Mark Cronin (ret.); Secret Service Agent Stew Henry (ret.) and his wife, Diane; Attorney Joe Doyle and family; Brian and Michael O'Donovan and their families; Mike Kettenbach and family; Mass. State Trooper Bill "Battlin' Biff" McLean; Mass. State Trooper Al DiSalvo (ret.); Mass. State Trooper Dennis Febles; Mass. State Trooper Chris Brighton; Mass. State Trooper Mark Lemieux; FBI Special Agent Matt Cronin (ret.); Attorney Tom Peisch; William Simpkins of the Drug Enforcement Agency; and Boston Police Detective Jack Crowley (ret.) and his wife, Ellen.

Many individuals in law enforcement contributed to this project, including Mass. State Police superintendent Colonel Thomas J. Foley (ret.); Mass. State Police Detective Lieutenant John Tutungian (ret.); Mass. State Police Detective Lieutenant Paul Stone (ret.); Mass. State Police Sergeant Bob Beckwith; Detective Sergeant John Goodwin of the Revere Police and his family; FBI Supervisory Special Agent Patrick Gibbons; Chief Paul Donovan, Sergeant Sean Patton, Officer Jonathan Hoellrich, Sergeant Bill Teuber, Canine Officer Mike Robbins, Lieutenant Bill Ganley and Detective George Baker of the Salem, N.H., Police; Boston Police Detective Gerard McHale; Sergeant Mike Ewing, Detective Gus Flanagan, and Officer Rob Prindle of the Methuen Police; Sergeant Bob Clark and Detective Rueben Torres (ret.) of the Newark, N.J., Police; FBI Assistant Special Agent in Charge William Chase and family; Chelsea Police E-911 operator Andrea Doherty; as well as Captain Dan Murphy (ret.), Officer Leo Martini, Officer Mike Kennelly, Officer Timmy Doherty, and E-911 operators Scott Lennon and Terry Medeiros of the Somerville Police.

Special thanks to Darrell M. Agnew of S.O.S. Services, Inc. in Kingston, MA, and investigator Kevin McKenna; you guys taught me a lot. I also want to thank attorneys Stephen Hrones and Jessica D. Hedges, who provided court documents and facts pertaining to *Timothy*

Doherty v. Det. James Hyde, et al. Salem State College reference librarian Eleanor Reynolds, the staff of the Nevins Memorial Library in Methuen, Mass., and the West Roxbury Public Library helped me dig up a large number of elusive facts. Paul Marion, Keith Bowden, Frank Baker, Steve Whipple, J. D. Scrimgeour, and Joe "Dutch" Kurmaskie offered many useful suggestions and paced me through the early drafts. "Surfer" John Hearin, Bill Fitzgerald, the late Jeff Ness, Glenn Gallant, Bob Sheehan, Frank Posluszny, Norm Litwack, Jason Massa, Jim and Maryanne Connolly, and Tim Croteau encouraged the project and bought most of my drinks. For putting up with this book and all my quixotic endeavors, I'd like to thank John and Jackie Atkinson and family; Paul and Shirley Crane and family; Arthur and Natalie Wermers; Lawrence Berry and Peg Burr; John, Jodie, Matthew, and Katelyn Berry; Patrick, Deanna, and Owen Bower; Jill Atkinson; James Atkinson Jr.; Patricia Foxx, Eric Shaw, and my son, Liam.

One last Joe McCain story: It has been well established that Joe was a little clumsy at times. One morning, riding to play golf in Michael O'Donovan's brand-new Chevy Tahoe, big Joe asked his friend to stop at Dunkin' Donuts in Arlington. Returning with two cups of coffee and a blueberry muffin, Joe proceeded to scatter bits of the muffin over his shirtfront and onto the floor of O'Donovan's immaculate new truck.

In a calm voice, O'Donovan said, "Next time, Joe, you should get two muffins."

McCain arched his eyebrows "Why's that?" he asked.

"One to eat, and one to crumble all over my fucking truck."

Jay Atkinson is the author of *Ice Time* and *Caveman Politics*. His work has appeared in *The New York Times*, *The Boston Globe*, *Newsday*, *Men's Health*, *The Boston Herald*, *The New York Post*, and many other publications. He lives in Massachusetts.